INTERACTION IN POETIC IMAGERY

WITH SPECIAL REFERENCE TO
EARLY GREEK POETRY

INTERACTION
IN POETIC IMAGERY

with special reference to
early Greek poetry

M.S.SILK

Lecturer in Classics, King's College
London

CAMBRIDGE UNIVERSITY PRESS

Published by the Syndics of the Cambridge University Press
Bentley House, 200 Euston Road, London NW1 2DB
American Branch: 32 East 57th Street, New York, N.Y.10022

© Cambridge University Press 1974

Library of Congress Catalogue Card Number: 73–90813

ISBN: 0 521 20417 8

First published 1974

Printed in Great Britain
at the University Printing House, Cambridge
(Brooke Crutchley, University Printer)

CONTENTS

APPENDICES

BIBLIOGRAPHY

INDEXES

PROLEGOMENON

This book is not an attempt to apply to classical literature the habits of modern literary criticism, but as it might be supposed to be just that, I may as well forestall the supposition at the outset. Despite intermittent efforts in recent times, it is still comparatively rare for practising classicists to attempt such 'applications' and, if anything, especially rare for Hellenists. But the present work represents something much less fashionable altogether: an attempt by a practising classicist to extend the 'theory' of an aspect of literature in general in the practical context of the literature of antiquity. But in case the claim should seem unduly immodest, it can be said at once that the 'aspect of literature' in question is, in itself, a small aspect, although not a trivial one. And by way of glossing the claim, let it be said also that the 'habits of modern literary criticism' and the theoretical apparatus (if any) that accompanies them are not simply separable from their 'traditional' counterparts. There is rather, as anyone familiar with the ancestry of modern criticism will know, a developing tradition, complex and many-sided, but continuous, which, in its development, sometimes modifies, sometimes innovates entirely and sometimes reconstitutes, in effect, earlier modes. The present study is not a matter of taking over (as from the outside) a tradition at a given point in its development, whether a more 'traditional' point or a more 'modern' one; but, as I hope, a matter of taking that development a little further, irrespective of which of the above-mentioned possibilities – modification, innovation or reconstitution – are incidentally involved. And this is to be attempted with regard to poetic imagery and, specifically, an aspect of imagery that I shall be calling 'interaction'.

So much has been written about poetic imagery, in connection with particular literatures and in general, that some account of interaction was almost bound to have been taken. And in practice, some, at least, of the various forms and features of interaction have not been entirely unnoticed. Witness, for example, the commentators on Aeschylus, *Agamemnon* 966ff., an image in which the king, returning home and by his return bringing security to the royal household, is compared to a vine:*

---

* *Vine*, as ὄμφακος (970) retrospectively suggests. The Greek text quoted follows Fraenkel (σημαίνεις, 969); the English paraphrase ('sun' for 'dogstar' etc.) is my own.

vii

ῥίζης γὰρ οὔσης φυλλὰς ἵκετ' ἐς δόμους
σκιὰν ὑπερτείνασα σειρίου κυνός·
καὶ σοῦ μολόντος δωματῖτιν ἑστίαν
θάλπος μὲν ἐν χειμῶνι σημαίνεις μολόν.

If the root lives, the leaves reach home, stretching
Their shade upwards against the sun. And you,
Home with the family, betoken warmth
Coming in winter.

On ἵκετ' ἐς δόμους ('reach home') Fraenkel says: 'Vahlen...puts the passage into its proper setting; he points out that...the image which serves as a comparison and the thing compared are not always...kept strictly apart, that, on the contrary, the image frequently assimilates elements of the thing compared...' – and he goes on to cite other eminent Hellenists including Verrall, Hermann Fränkel and Wilamowitz.

In English studies, Mrs Nowottny supplies an instance: 'a further advantage of metaphor to the poet (simile shares this) is its power to play in with the faded metaphors of ordinary language and to draw special effects from the interplay'.* She exemplifies this power with

When to the sessions of sweet silent thought
I summon up remembrance of things past,

'where the metaphor of *the sessions of...thought* plays in with the faded metaphor in *summon up*' and 'the familiarity of the phrase *summon up* acts as a guarantee of the propriety of the metaphor of the sessions of thought; the old metaphor ratifies the new metaphor, supports it... The reanimation of dead metaphor may become a means of contriving effects of great subtlety and power...'

And on a Shakespearian passage again, Wolfgang Clemen, apropos the 'associative rise of the image':

You are too shallow, Hastings, much too shallow,
To sound the bottom of the after-times.

'*Shallow*, meaning here superficial in character, assumes a concrete significance in Shakespeare's mind and thus leads to the (unuttered) image of the ocean...'†

These three discussions are representative of ordinary adequacy: they haven't been chosen as containing any gross errors. But for my purposes they all evidence a simple but basic inadequacy. Compare a fourth discussion, this

* Nowottny 70.   † Clemen 74f.

time from an ancient theorist. For one can in fact point to examples of Greco-Roman 'criticism' (so-called) which show the critic as having occasion to discuss an interaction, but – and here the same inadequacy presents itself conveniently conspicuously – lacking the conceptual apparatus needed to make his discussion articulate. The critic may have a perception about it, may have an inkling of something which prompted him to discuss the interaction in the first place, but can't interpret his perception with any particularity. Quintilian 5.11.24:

admonendum est rarius esse in oratione illud genus, quod εἰκόνα Graeci vocant...quam id, quo probabilius fit quod intendimus: ut si animum dicas *excolendum*, similitudine utaris terrae, quae neglecta spinas ac dumos, culta fructus creat...

it is to be noted that the kind of comparison that the Greeks call εἰκών is less common in oratory than the kind that helps us enforce a point. If, for instance, your point is that the mind should be *cultivated*, you might use a comparison drawn from the soil: in a state of neglect, the soil produces thorns and brambles, whereas under cultivation it yields fruit...

It isn't entirely clear that this *is* an interaction. That would depend on the precise form that the recommended comparison took: with *excolendum animum* ('the mind should be cultivated') as an actual part of the image, we would appear to have another example of Mrs Nowottny's broadly characterized 'playing in with the faded metaphors of ordinary language'. But in any case, 'broadly characterized' brings us back to the main point. Quintilian, like Mrs Nowottny, deals in broad terms, too broad. The most he can give us to indicate the nature of his prescription is the vague phrase 'the kind that helps us enforce a point', a phrase that doesn't, in itself, imply interaction at all. His problem is that he doesn't know what interaction is – and the same goes for our modern critics. None of them, by way of enlightening themselves **or** their readers, can appeal to 'interaction', for the simple reason that the name is lacking and the concept lying behind the name. None of them can do what I did, blandly, just now – relate their varied instances as instances of one thing. The boundaries aren't drawn. Fraenkel's slightly opaque expression, 'the image assimilates elements of the thing compared', is in fact a reference to one particular category of interaction; Mrs Nowottny's 'plays in with the faded metaphors of ordinary language' is a phrase, a rather unfortunate phrase, that would cover many instances of several different categories, but not all the instances of those categories and probably very few of the instances of any other category; and

Clemen's 'associative rise of the image' is a formula both too narrow and too wide for interaction, a formula that would exclude many of its categories and include many instances that are not to be thought of as instances of interaction at all.

This brings us to a related consequence of conceptual inadequacy. The critic isn't able to differentiate, when occasion arises, between instances of interaction and instances of some other thing, some different aspect of imagery. Or worse, he can't see when the occasion *might* arise, can only press on regardless. So Clemen, thinking in terms of his 'associative rise of the image', is unable to allow for, let alone do anything with, the difference between the interactive imagery of 'You are too shallow, Hastings...' and the imagery of the non-interactive passage that he cites immediately before it:

> And shall our quick blood, spirited with wine,
> Seem frosty? O, for honour of our land,
> Let us not hang like roping icicles
> Upon our houses' thatch...

Clemen's gloss is, '*frosty* was here the occasion for the associative image of the icicles', and he then passes on to 'You are too shallow...' without further comment. His reflections, though not devoid of interest, could hardly be said to evince true discrimination or to encourage it in his readers. My conclusion is that discussions of this kind – and that means any discussion of imagery – will stand to profit from a comprehension of interaction and the conceptual framework that the word will imply.

A little while ago, I made mention – blandly, once again – of *categories* of interaction, and before that I noted that Quintilian, representatively, isn't able to define the nature or effect of the interaction he cites. My suggestion now is that the comprehension of imagery could profit from not only the concept of interaction, but also – for the purpose of defining natures and effects – a framework of categories within it. Look at our instances. 'Enforcing a point' is apparently a function of Quintilian's interactive (?) soilimage, but it isn't clear whether it's a function of its interactive aspect or of some other aspect; nor is it clear whether the interactive aspect is to be credited with any other function. Clemen's 'shallow...leads to the... image of the ocean' might be essentially a statement about the poet's mind, rather than (or as well as) about the effect of his words, but taking it as a statement about the effect, there's certainly room for doubt as to whether 'leads to' covers the *whole* effect. If nothing else, it might be said that 'shallow' serves to add a concrete detail to the image of the ocean represented by 'sound the bottom' and probably to make it more decisively 'of the ocean' than it would otherwise seem to be. Fraenkel's generalized statement, 'the image... assimilates elements of the thing compared', certainly purports to concern itself with a poet's words and represents a recognizable description of the category to which his present instance would actually belong, but signally fails to indicate the consequent effect: it isn't even clear that any distinctive or recognizable *effect* is in question at all. Mrs Nowottny's discussion is different in kind, concentrating on effect; but despite certain suggestive formulations ('the familiarity of the phrase... ratifies the new metaphor, supports it'), she does not in fact define with any precision the character of the interaction before her. This can be shown simply by noting that her description of the 'sessions' passage could stand, as far as it goes, as a description of Clemen's

> You are too shallow, Hastings, much too shallow,
> To sound the bottom of the after-times.

This piece, like Mrs Nowottny's, would seem to have a familiar phrase and a new metaphor in the appropriate configuration; and her remarks about the one 'ratifying' the other (and so on) might be applied without any obviously gross injustice to the Hastings passage. But the availability of Clemen's piece for comparison and contrast makes it possible to see some of what Mrs Nowottny might have said but hasn't, for want of such comparison and contrast, seen any occasion to say. For a start, she hasn't noted the humble fact that 'summon' comes after 'sessions' (whereas 'shallow... leads to the image...'), nor the comparative unobtrusiveness of the 'sessions'/'summon' relation (whereas 'shallow'/'sound the bottom' has an almost punning assertiveness). And by adducing other comparable or contrasting passages, one could say more. Take, for instance, Macbeth's

> My way of life
> Is fall'n into the sear, the yellow leaf.

The relation between 'fall'n', a familiar element, and 'the sear, the yellow leaf', a new metaphor, might once again seem more or less suited to Mrs Nowottny's phraseology. Yet this time there is a new and quite radical difference in respect of, let us say, internal coherence. By itself, 'to the sessions... I summon' is acceptable English, whereas 'is fall'n into... the leaf' is inconsequentially odd.

It's clear, then, that these instances differ. What isn't so clear is how much, and what kind of, significance the various points of difference have. And for this to become clear we need more comparisons, appropriate comparisons. The *fact* of a difference can only be established by an appropriate comparison; and likewise the *significance* (or otherwise) of the difference only begins to emerge after whole sets of appropriate comparisons: the critical comparisons of particular instances that are summed up by the system of categories. It's the categories that make the apt comparison – or contrast – available: the categories and the detailed comparisons and contrasts that they represent make it possible to interpret and define an instance, an old instance or a new instance, more fully and more precisely. With such a system of categories to appeal to, and if necessary to correct, one might hope for a more satisfactory scrutiny of the 'effects of great subtlety and power' that Mrs Nowottny speaks of.*

This, therefore, is the rationale of the present study: to establish the concept of interaction and to relate and differentiate between particular instances in terms of various suggested categories, provisional categories.

Interaction has not hitherto been favoured with a sustained or rigorous discussion in connection with English poetry or Greek poetry – or, apparently, any poetry.† Such a discussion, it seems to me, can best be conducted in a formal treatise, unfashionable though formal treatises as a medium of criticism now are: a theory of interaction, in fact. As regards the 'particular instances' to work from, the discussion could take various forms. It must presumably be based on a large number of instances in any event, but these might, perhaps, be drawn impartially from different languages and periods, or drawn exclusively from one language and one period. The procedure I have chosen is not of these kinds. I shall be studying interaction chiefly as manifested in the imagery of early Greek lyric and dramatic poetry, offering, in fact, a comprehensive treatment of the interactions here; at the same time, I shall adduce other instances from English poetry – for their illustrative value, rather than for any strictly 'comparative' purpose. The chosen period of Greek poetry is a coherent one and unusually rich in imagery. Concentration here naturally adds a certain literary-historical interest as well as providing a convenient working limit. At the same time, this is, of course, poetry written in a dead language and, as such, presents special problems, the general character of which can be indicated by transposing Mrs Nowottny's words, 'the familiarity of the phrase', into a Greek context. Without your own experience or even some other first-hand experience to rely on, how do you identify a 'familiar phrase', or rather, as it usually will be, a familiar use

---

* Her sentence reads in full: 'The reanimation of dead metaphor may become a means of contriving effects of great subtlety and power, as I hope to show in Chapter VIII.' The promise is hardly fulfilled, except for an analysis of Blake's *Poison Tree* (pp. 180–3), which provides a single, though remarkable, instance (see p. 91 below).

† See further Appendix 1.

of a given phrase? This problem and related problems need to be dealt with, in the first instance, theoretically, especially as this area of scholarship (call it 'literary lexicography') has, like interaction itself, received as yet no 'sustained or rigorous discussion'. The necessity to deal with such problems is another reason for the limitation of period ('familiar, but familiar *when?*' suggests why), while the necessity to do it on the theoretical level makes the treatise form the more desirable; and a treatise will also provide the opportunity to treat various other 'matters arising' with the formal respect they deserve in this context. A few of these have already been foreshadowed, as when I characterized 'faded metaphors of ordinary language' as an unfortunate expression; and when I put a not wholly self-explanatory emphasis on '*provisional* categories'. Similarly in need of formal discussion are a number of matters ranging from technical terms to word order and sound effects; and, more generally, the nature of the aesthetic presupposed by or inferential from the given mode of interpretation. Such questions will be dealt with, as and where relevant, chiefly in Part I, along with the concept of interaction itself. Part II will contain a systematic treatment of the proposed categories and the instances subsumed under them.

ACKNOWLEDGEMENTS

My thanks to the following for comments, suggestions, help or advice: Professor W. S. Allen, Professor J. P. Barron, Mr M. H. Black, Dr P. Boyde, Dr A. W. Bulloch, Mr R. G. G. Coleman, Mr J. A. Crook, Mrs P. E. Easterling, Mr A. G. Lee, Dr G. E. R. Lloyd, Mr D. W. Lucas, Dr R. J. Mynott, Professor A. E. Raubitschek, Mr K. C. Sidwell, Mrs P. A. Singleton, Mr L. P. Wilkinson, Professor R. P. Winnington-Ingram.

ABBREVIATIONS

Abbreviations for Greek authors (and their works) are customarily those in LSJ. The most important for the purposes of this book are as follows:

A.	Aeschylus	Pi.	Pindar
Alc.	Alcaeus	Sapph.	Sappho
Alcm.	Alcman	Semon.	Semonides
Anacr.	Anacreon	Simon.	Simonides
Arch.	Archilochus	Sol.	Solon
B.	Bacchylides	Stesich.	Stesichorus
Epich.	Epicharmus	Thgn.	Theognis
Hippon.	Hipponax	Tyrt.	Tyrtaeus
Ibyc.	Ibycus	Xenoph.	Xenophanes
Mimn.	Mimnermus		

Other abbreviations (those of modern works) will be found in the Bibliography (pp.245ff.), along with a list of the editions of Greek authors used for reference and citation.

NOTE

The main part of this book is divided into short sections. The 'footnotes' in this part are to be found at the ends of the sections.

PART I
INTRODUCTION

1 Interaction

§ 1

'All the critical twiddle-twaddle about style and form, all this pseudo-scientific classifying and analysing of books in an imitation-botanical fashion, is mere impertinence and mostly dull jargon.'[1]

The first thing to say is that Lawrence's protest deserves honest respect. If one had to make an exclusive choice between that version of 'criticism' which confines itself to the technical and the typical, and a kind that sees as its task assessment of particulars unfettered by reference, even, to types and to any sort of technical consideration: if one must choose, one must choose the latter. Comparative inarticulacy is preferable to a decreative sophistication.

And the second thing to say is that we need not make such a choice. Our ability to confront literature fruitfully – to be creative – requires articulacy; and true articulacy requires the direction of the recreative mind. But must articulacy imply classification and analysis? It must, whether overtly or not, since language, without which there is no articulacy, is itself a classificatory and analytical system, although in any articulate use of language the classification and analysis need not be in any real sense overt, but may be pre-supposed. The question now becomes one of emphasis and tact. When, if at all, should the classifying and analysing be more rather than less overt? And, in particular, are there situations or causes for which such activities should be actively pursued? There surely are; and the chief is progress towards a finer articulacy.

The critical mode that Lawrence is attacking could reasonably be called the classical or neo-classical: here belong Demetrius' *On Style*, Puttenham's *The Arte of English Poesie* and Empson's *Seven Types of Ambiguity*. Any literary judgement, any intelligent comment about literature, is ultimately based on an appeal, implicit or explicit, to particular relations or effects: this relates to that in a certain way; this has this effect, that has that. And the rationale of 'classical' criticism is to make the appeal explicit in order to illuminate such relations and effects and, thereby, make the judgement itself more substantial and more deserving to be called articulate.

'Dull jargon' is not inevitable: even Lawrence only said 'mostly'. In this respect a mode of criticism is as good as its practitioners make it. As for

3

1-2

'mere impertinence', my conviction is that if the classical mode is to have much chance of going beyond that, it should involve not merely making the implicit appeal explicit, but a genuinely active pursuit of the explication in an evolutionary or, if need be, revolutionary spirit. That is, its categories should be constantly open to refinement or redefinition in such a way that each work of 'classification and analysis' might in some degree aspire to be a contribution to theory. And by 'theory' is meant the organization and apparatus of the available, provisional answers to the questions, *what sorts of thing can literature do or be? how does it operate to do or be them?* But the sorts of thing literature does or is, and the way it operates, these mean only what it has done, has been, how it has operated in specific instances. Therefore, a contribution to theory is only conceivable through the study of actual instances, that is of practice, the theory being the summary product of such study.

1 D. H. Lawrence, *Phoenix* (ed. E. D. McDonald), London, 1936, p. 539.

§2

In accordance with such an aspiration, which need not seem pretentious, this study is a sketch of a 'classical' literary theory, albeit one of modest scope, based on particular literary practice. The general subject is imagery: imagery as a matter of words; imagery in its 'micro-contextual' aspect, to use the possibly dull and certainly scientific jargon of the linguists. My attention, therefore, is not directed essentially towards the rôle of the image within the complete work; not towards its broad, perhaps thematic, significance; but towards its local significance, or rather, those aspects of its local significance that concern interaction. And the 'practice' is that of the early Greek lyric and dramatic poets up to, and including, Aeschylus, Pindar, and Bacchylides.

Interaction is not the whole of imagery, and in concentrating exclusively on it I am not suggesting that it is necessarily, or even often, the most important feature of imagery; for a start, many images do not involve interaction in my sense. Concentration on anything inevitably distorts its importance; but when a general possibility has been consistently undermentioned or partially misunderstood, or when reference to its particular manifestations has been inadequate for want of the corrective or stimulus of a systematic discussion, then distortion of this sort is legitimate and even necessary.

§3

By imagery I mean primarily metaphor, simile and the various forms of *comparatio*; the tropes and schemes, that is, based on analogy or similarity. 'Based', of course, refers to the logical basis: πάντες γὰρ οἱ μεταφέροντες κατά τινα ὁμοιότητα μεταφέρουσιν (Arist.*Top*.140a.10f.). It does not imply that the logical basis, or pretext, for a literary image is necessarily to be equated with the interest or 'point' of the image. As has been repeatedly demonstrated,[1] this interest characteristically derives from the unlikeness as much as from the likeness; and indeed without a sufficient unlikeness, all 'point' in the true sense tends to disappear: as Johnson remarked of a passage in Dryden's *Eleonora*, 'there is so much likeness in the initial comparison that there is no illustration'.[2] Contrast the positive relevance of the unlikeness in *Il*.8.306ff., where Gorgythion in his death is compared to a 'droop-headed' poppy – drooping under the weight of its seed and the spring rain:

μήκων δ' ὡς ἑτέρωσε κάρη βάλεν, ἥ τ' ἐνὶ κήπῳ,
καρπῷ βριθομένη νοτίῃσί τε εἰαρινῇσιν.

Plainly, the point of similarity (the tilt of the man's head and the poppy's head) makes possible a fine sensory effect. But equally plainly, that single point is outweighed in interest by the points of dissimilarity, the contrast. The poppy is alive and flourishing in a peaceful garden; Gorgythion is dead on the battlefield. Life and maturity, evoked by the specific circumstantial detail of seed and rain – the poignancy of the contrast needs no labouring. Nonetheless, the likeness remains logically prior: the force of the unlikeness depends on it. Without any substantial likeness, an 'image' tends to be gratuitous and idle: Edith Sitwell's 'the light is braying like an ass'. But the principle of 'relevant unlikeness' is not affected by this caveat; and, as will appear in due course, such unlikeness has a special relevance for one of my categories.[3]

Under the heading 'imagery' I shall also include, on occasion, certain other stylistic modes, notably the omen, which, in the form widely used in ancient poetry, has obvious affinities with imagery proper:

Full of his god, the reverend Chalcas cried,
'Ye Grecian warriors! lay your fears aside.
This wondrous signal Jove himself displays
Of long, long labours, but eternal praise.
As many birds as by the snake were slain,
So many years the toils of Greece remain.'

(*Iliad* 2.322ff., trans. Pope)

5

I shall not be concerned either with symbolism, where this means something other than imagery as interpreted above, or with metonymy; and my use of the words 'metonymy' and 'metonymic', I should add, follows the precedent of the eighteenth-century rhetorician George Campbell. By metonymy I mean any of the tropes based on contiguity:[4] notably the kinds traditionally distinguished as synecdoche,[5] enallage (transferred epithet) and metonymy proper.[6] Hence none of the following count as instances of imagery:

> And *drowsy* tinklings lull the distant folds
>
> I am *gall*, I am *heartburn*
>
> O for a beaker full of the *warm south*
>
> I will speak to my Lord, whereas I am *dust and ashes*

Other considerations relating to my practical definition of imagery will be discussed later. For the moment, the discussion will centre on metaphor and the aspect of metaphor that concerns interaction.

1 Explicity by e.g. Richards 127, Leavis *IM* 232f., Nowottny 53, Waldron 176f., Ricks 127ff. Not so often by Hellenists, though Fränkel *HG* moved somewhat along these lines apropos the Homeric simile (most obviously in the case of the explicit 'contrast function', as exemplified in *Il*.11.86ff. – Fränkel 106); and Ed. Fraenkel pointed excellently to the 'contrast that intensifies the horror' in some Aeschylean imagery (on *Ag*.437ff., similarly on *Ag*.65); cf. also Stanford *AS* 109 on A.*Eu*.253.
2 Johnson 1.441. Cf. his remarks on Cowley, 1.20.
3 Link.
4 On this term see Wellek–Warren 194f., Ullmann *LS* 177f.
5 *Nec procul ab hoc genere* [sc. synecdoche] *discedit metonymia*, Quintil.8.6.23.
6 I had hoped to add that, as a rule, I would not be dealing with catachresis (*abusio*) either, but eventually decided that I can neither define the trope in question, nor confidently identify examples of it, nor, in particular, distinguish it from metaphor. (See further Appendix II.) Presumably, then, I shall be including as instances of imagery what some would regard as catachresis.

§4

Aristotle's celebrated definition of metaphor has, as Mrs Nowottny notes,[1] a certain emphasis on what might be called its terminological aspect: 'applying to a thing a word that belongs to something else'.[2] The emphasis is more explicit in her own paraphrase: 'speaking of X in terminology proper to Y'. Where poetic metaphor is concerned, this is not, one might comment, an especially popular emphasis; or at least it has not been so since the

Romantic revolution. More typical of modern attitudes is the non-verbal, even anti-verbal, emphasis apparent in, for instance, Lorca's somewhat extreme manifesto, 'la métaphore unit deux mondes antagonistes dans le saut équestre de l'imagination',[3] or in I. A. Richards' more restrained comment, 'fundamentally it is a borrowing between and intercourse of thoughts'.[4] That 'fundamentally' is provocative and symptomatic of a reaction. The shift to 'mondes' and 'l'imagination' and 'thoughts' is certainly not in itself illegitimate or unwelcome. The tone of post-Romanticism is less prosaic and its formulations are, in an obvious sense, more impressive than Aristotle's – but in what sense can its definitions claim to be more 'fundamental'? Poetry, like all language, is made of words, and nothing can be more fundamental than that.

Here are two Hellenists at work: 'Das Epitheton ἐρεμνός befremdet für Eros, denn das ist ja bei Homer die αἰγίς und die λαῖλαψ: Eros ist nicht finster.'[5] And: 'A second, archetypal image is that of the road or way, ὁδός or κέλευθος. It is used of behaviour by Hesiod.'[6] The value of these particular specimens depends, of course, on where the discussions go from there. But so far there can be little doubt that the emphasis of the first (Wilamowitz) is terminological or verbal, that of the second (Bowra) conceptual;[7] and that the former is closer to 'fundamentals'. One notes that, for a conceptualist, not only is the word not primary; it may not even matter *which* word ('ὁδός or κέλευθος'). The 'it' that is used by Hesiod is a notional relation, at a remove from any specific and concrete sequence of words. 'The image' is thoughts or, as might have been said, ideas or areas of experience, irrespective of the particular words used.

Now plainly, if one is ever to pursue or invoke or even merely presuppose any of such obviously important matters as the propriety or suggestiveness or originality of an image-relationship, one must have this conceptual emphasis behind one. There are certainly occasions when one reasonably wants to say that 'the image' κακῶν πέλαγος (A.*Pe.*433) 'recurs' in the form κλύδων κακῶν (599), despite only a partial verbal resemblance; or that Shakespeare's 'sea of troubles' and Aeschylus' κακῶν πέλαγος are 'the same' image, in that they bring into metaphoric relation the same areas of experience. But if one's purpose required the more fundamental, verbal conception of imagery, one would, at the very least, feel obliged to say 'corresponding', not 'same', in such a case. And if one's purpose did require it, as mine does, one would resent the appropriation of 'fundamentals' by the conceptualist.

At all events, it is clear that 'thoughts' and 'words' represent two possible and different emphases. To vary the example, it is important to be able to say

7

that ἀνάγκης ἐς ζυγὸν καθέσταμεν (E.*Or*.1330) has something in common with ἀνάγκας ἔδυ λέπαδνον (A.*Ag*.218), but it is at least as important to make the distinction that whereas the one phrase is trite,[8] the other is novel and striking.[9] It is true that the areas of experience, the conceptual relations, involved are hardly distinguishable. It is also true that for effect the verbal sequences are to be contrasted rather than compared. The phraseology that encourages us to equate the two as 'the same image' or 'the image of...' can be seriously misleading.

Note, therefore, the convenience of the expression 'the image' for anything that may be called a conceptual approach to metaphor. By contrast, any verbal orientation, and especially any that involves an active interest in the question of 'terminology', has not been well served. Terms that promote, or at least suit, such an emphasis have not, until fairly recently, been forthcoming. As is well known,[10] technical (or non-technical) terms for the two basic constituents of metaphor have generally been unfortunate expedients and hardly conducive to any serious purpose. The chief problem has been to avoid terms that invite confusion between the figurative element and the image as a whole. Such well-established terms for the former as 'figure', 'comparison' and 'image' itself create just such a confusion. (Besides which, 'figure' and 'image' – not to mention 'picture' – are in any case tainted with visual associations: tainted, because the largely eighteenth-century assumption that there is something in the nature of poetic imagery to create a demand for a specifically visual or pictorial effect is not defensible.[11]) Another problem has been to find terms to make clear that the non-figurative element is not the same thing as the total meaning that arises from the two elements in combination; hence the inconvenience of such terms as 'meaning' and 'referent'. Ironically enough, the pair of terms most amenable to my purpose was invented with thoughts and ideas, *not* words, in mind. 'A first step', wrote I. A. Richards in 1936,[12] 'is to introduce two technical terms to assist us in distinguishing from one another what Dr Johnson called the two ideas that any metaphor, at its simplest, gives us. Let me call them the tenor and the vehicle.'[13]

1 Nowottny 49. Let me acknowledge here that it was through Mrs Nowottny's discussion of metaphor (pp.49ff.) that I first perceived the potential utility of the word 'terminology' for the study of imagery.
2 Arist.*Po*.1457b.7.
3 Quoted by Ullmann *LS* 174.
4 Richards 94.
5 Wilamowitz *SS* 124, on Ibyc.1.11 Bergk (= 5.11 Page).
6 Bowra, *Pindar* 252.

7 The term 'conceptual' is convenient, although the antithesis could be misleading. Concepts and words are not opposites nor happily separable.
8 See below, p. 67.
9 And presumably Aeschylus' invention.
10 See in particular Richards 96ff., and cf. Johansen *GR* 20 (with n.18). The problem is not peculiar to modern criticism: cf. McCall 217 and 221f. on Quintil.
8.3.77.
11 Cf. e.g. Richards 16f. and 98.
12 Since which time his terms have been widely used by English-speaking students
of imagery, though rarely by British Isles Hellenists.
13 Richards 96.

§ 5¹

As used by Richards, the tenor is 'the underlying idea', and the vehicle the
other idea, the one brought in from outside, so to speak, the one to which the
tenor is, in logical terms, compared.² The same writer suggested in addition
the term 'ground' to denote the likeness, the feature or features held in
common between tenor and vehicle. This 'ground' might seem to be
inherently a conceptual, not a verbal, matter.³ On the other hand, tenor and
vehicle can be reinterpreted as matters of words. Thus, taking Aeschylus'
κλύδων κακῶν, one might say that the vehicle is 'rough sea', conceptually
understood, or that the vehicle is the actual word κλύδων. Similarly, one
might say that the tenor is 'impending series of disasters' (or whatever), or,
if the tenor is conceived as words, – but here a difficulty presents itself,
beginning with a problem of formulation. The verbal tenor must evidently
contain, in the first place, the word κακῶν and, secondly, the word or words
that could have been used instead of κλύδων had there been no metaphor: the
literal equivalent, if any, which has, in a sense, been suppressed under, or
presupposed by, κλύδων. Or rather, 'in the first place' should apply not to
κακῶν but to this literal equivalent which is the nominal object of 'comparison'. One might in fact wish to confine 'tenor' strictly to this suppressed
equivalent or (if a conceptualist) to the concept in question, 'impending
series'. The importance of the alternative – 'κακῶν plus' or merely 'plus'? –
will emerge shortly.⁴ As for the question, 'what is the ground?', this seems
to demand, as I say, an answer in conceptual terms. 'The ground is whatever
is held in common between the impending series of disasters and a rough
sea'; or '...between impending series and a rough sea'. In any event,
however we chose to formulate the tenor and the ground, it would be
necessary to insist that the tenor is distinct from the product of tenor and
vehicle combined, the total meaning; and that the ground is similarly distinct.⁵
Likeness, to repeat, is not the be-all and end-all of imagery.

9

Mrs Nowottny's discussion of metaphor may be invoked at this point, making as it does a clear and relevant distinction between ideas or concepts and words. 'Metaphor directs us to the *sense*, not to the exact term. The directions lead us not to. . . [any one of the available literal formulations]. . . but to that which. . .is the common target of all these verbal shots. . . Metaphor indicates how to find or to construct the target, but it does not contaminate the mental image of the target by using any one of the literal terms available in ordinary language for referring to such a target.'[6] Evidently this 'target' has something to do with 'the product of tenor and vehicle combined'. It is not the same as any of the literal equivalents,[7] i.e. the 'suppressed tenor'. And, without any question, it is inherently and necessarily non-verbal.

We have, then, adequately defined for present purposes tenor, vehicle, ground and target. As may have been divined, I intend to make use of Richards' main terms, tenor and vehicle, and to use them not as their maker meant them, but as referring to words. Henceforth, the ground and, in particular, the target will not, on the whole, concern me directly.

1 The mode and direction of the analysis in this section are indebted to Nowottny 55ff., though I would not subscribe to every detail in her discussion.

2 My paraphrase. Richards gives no formal definition.

3 It is certainly true that other names for the ground tend to be used of the concept – e.g. the German *Vergleichungspunkt* and the scholastic *tertium comparationis*, an unwieldy expression mercifully out of fashion (and so bizarrely misunderstood by Taillardat 24, with n.6, and 473ff., who thinks it means the vehicle).

4 It does not appear that the distinction between these alternatives has occupied much attention. Richards does not give enough detailed analysis to make it clear what his own answer would be.

5 See Richards 110 and cf. Stanford's discussion of Hermogenes' definition of metaphor, *GM* 14f. and 20f.

6 Nowottny 59.

7 If it is, the vehicle must be mere surface ornament (cf. Richards 100); or else mere subterfuge, as sometimes in Delphic utterances.

§6

I shall now return to κλύδων κακῶν to continue the exposition and thereby, *inter alia*, explain my intermittent bandying about of the cumbrous words 'terminology' and 'terminological'. Cumbrous, but valuable, if, as I hope, they evoke the difference between my tenor and vehicle and Richards' and, incipiently perhaps, hint at the perceptual significance of the difference. His dualism, with its orientation towards abstractions, is *logical*. In logical terms, metaphor, as Hermogenes noted[1] in the second century A.D., involves a 'subject at issue' (Richards' tenor) and an 'extraneous object of reference' (Richards' vehicle). But, as Hermogenes also noted, metaphor involves them not simply as such, but as elements of what I have already casually alluded to in speaking of 'the total meaning', which he called a 'composite concept' and which, as 'composite' suggests, must represent a new *unity*, and, surely, a unity *felt* or feelable as a unity by its audience; but a unity which Richards' logical bias is likely to undermine. A Richards-based mode of analysis, therefore, would tend to go against the hearer's perception, the *feel* of the thing. My dualism and analysis, not logical but *terminological*, and so dealing with the immediate words we hear, aspire to explicate and, modestly, enhance perception, rather than replace it.

In κλύδων κακῶν, the two words belong to different terminological contexts. One is in marine or nautical terminology, the other is in the terminology of human affairs in general. As far as the quotation goes, κλύδων is the representative, the sole representative, of the vehicle. κλύδων, and only κλύδων, is in the marine terminology of the vehicle; or, as I have indicated I would say, *is* the vehicle. (The terminological emphasis is thus implicit.) And the tenor here, as already stated, consists first of a suppressed literal 'equivalent' to κλύδων, say, for the sake of argument, πλῆθος,[2] and secondly of κακῶν. κακῶν and the suppressed element, πλῆθος, cohere terminologically; both are also 'predictable' in a sense and a direction that κλύδων is not; and it is κακῶν, in its significance as the predictably literal context, that determines our awareness that there is a 'suppression', something presupposed, and our awareness of the implicit coherence. By itself, taken as a single word *in vacuo*, κλύδων does not presuppose anything, does not imply any suppression. In the light of κακῶν, κλύδων does presuppose. But note: if we say that κλύδων presupposes something in the 'human affairs' terminology, e.g. πλῆθος, we find no corresponding necessity to say that κακῶν presupposes anything in the marine terminology of the vehicle, λάβρος for instance. The feasibility of saying this does not arise, because κακῶν is there by right, as it were, there being nothing in the context to make us take it at other than its face value. The tenor, in short, is the norm; the vehicle is a departure from the norm; and under normal circumstances we follow the dictates of the norm. And the norm is 'there' all the time.

It would, therefore, appear undesirable to think of tenor and vehicle as exact opposites, if the tenor is liable to be 'there' all the time, sometimes in verbal embodiment, sometimes presupposed, whereas the vehicle is 'there' only part of the time.[3] Exact opposition, one might add, is not suggested by the names 'tenor' and 'vehicle', whereas it is implicit in such alternatives as *le comparé/le comparant* and *illustrans/illustrandum*.[4]

This appearance of disparity is readily confirmed if we look at the context preceding κλύδων κακῶν in the same analytical way:

> φίλοι, κακῶν μὲν ὅστις ἔμπειρος κυρεῖ
> ἐπίσταται βροτοῖσιν ὡς, ὅταν κλύδων
> κακῶν...

If we are to say that the second κακῶν is 'in the terminology of the tenor' or, perhaps, is 'part of' the tenor, we may find it impossible to deny such titles to the first κακῶν or, indeed, to the sequence κακῶν...βροτοῖσιν as a whole. For clearly this sequence coheres terminologically with the second κακῶν as against κλύδων. And on similar though somewhat less cogent grounds, one could extend the use of 'tenor' to φίλοι and probably to whatever precedes φίλοι, depending, naturally, on what it is.

It emerges, then, that the tenor may be conceived of as a sequence which the vehicle interrupts and presupposes in part. The word 'tenor' is certainly well suited to such a conception; we speak, for instance, of 'the whole tenor' of a work. And a vehicle, terminologically abnormal and unpredictable, represents the interruption of such a sequence and the suppression of part of it in favour of 'extraneous' material, material not 'at issue'. Once again, although less obviously, we are only pressing a non-technical use of a current term: one speaks of something as a 'vehicle for' something else; and Dr Johnson, for instance, found occasion to criticize those unable 'to separate propositions or images from the vehicles by which they are conveyed to the understanding'.[5]

It is, of course, true that φίλοι does not relate to, or cohere with, the tenor terminology as closely as the first κακῶν does; nor does this κακῶν cohere as closely as the second κακῶν, which has a greater immediacy of relation; and the second κακῶν is itself not on a par with the 'suppressed equivalent'. There are, if one needs to say so, degrees of tenor-ness, and we might wish to distinguish between (1) the suppressed tenor, πλῆθος, (2) the immediate tenor, the second κακῶν, (3) the wider tenor, which in this instance is the rest of the passage, although one would probably ignore the 'empty' words, ὡς and ὅταν, as being effectively in no terminology at all. If and when such distinctions seem to be useful, one can use them. For the moment we need say no more than that 'tenor', *pace* Richards, not only refers to 'words' not 'ideas', but also to words which would often not be reckoned as having much to do with 'the image' at all.

1 Hermogenes II.254 Spengel, as translated by Stanford *GM* 14.
2 'For the sake of argument' and to minimize obscurity at this stage in the discussion. I regret the need to spell out what should not, indeed cannot, be spelt out in this way, and have deliberately chosen an obviously inadequate 'equivalent', lest any virtue be made of this necessity.
3 Any context in which the vehicle might be said similarly to be 'always there' would represent abnormal circumstances, such as sustained allegory; or a passage in which it was clear thet there was an image, but not clear what was tenor and what vehicle, so that both would be constantly in the interpreter's mind.
4 The former pair is used by some French linguists. The latter was coined by Johansen (*GR* 20) and approved by Kamerbeek (*Mnemos.* 1961, p.43) and Ole Smith (p.12). It was, to be fair, coined with reference to analogy, not to metaphor.
5 In *The Rambler* no.168, apropos *Macbeth*.

§7

But why pervert the word 'tenor' in this way? Why not rather use 'literal', for instance, perhaps in antithesis with 'figurative'? I have apparently been stating the obvious at some length – 'in a metaphor there are figurative words and also words used literally' – but without using the obvious terms. But there are statements and there are restatements. It would be adequate simply to answer that it is impossible to speak of 'immediate' and 'wider' literal elements; that 'literal' does not imply an image orientation in the way that 'tenor' does – 'literal' might contrast with 'hyperbolic', for instance; and again that some, though not I, would be reluctant to use 'literal' for a tenor element which happened to be a 'dead metaphor'. Nor are any other existing alternatives much more satisfactory in these respects; nor in fact do they have the various other advantages of 'tenor' and 'vehicle' which have already been mentioned: 'tenor' does not suggest that tenor and target might be the same thing, but actively suggests the relationship with a wider sequence that the vehicle does not have; 'vehicle' avoids confusion with the image as a whole, the total product of vehicle and tenor, and has no irrelevant pictorial associations; both 'tenor' and 'vehicle' are words in general use in comparable, non-technical ways, but, as a pair, they are not inherently antithetical, hence do not suggest that the two constituents of the image are on an equal footing.

I. A. Richards' two terms, then, have important advantages for the study of metaphor. But I am not dealing with metaphor only, but with imagery as a whole; and for my purpose it is an overriding advantage that these terms can be employed with equal ease in the analysis of the formally distinct types of 'explicit imagery',[1] whether epic simile, short simile, comparison, or what

13

Dornseiff[2] called *Vergleich ohne wie*, the paratactic analogy. 'Literal' and 'figurative', of course, cannot be used in such a connection at all. As Mrs Nowottny puts it: 'metaphor, unlike simile,...conveys a relation...by using a word (or words) figuratively instead of literally'.[3] This characteristic of literal phraseology is precisely what distinguishes simile and all the schemes of explicit imagery from the trope metaphor. But the distinction is not necessarily of central importance.[4] Like metaphor, explicit imagery brings in something 'extraneous' and brings it in 'for comparison'. And this is merely to say that explicit imagery involves a vehicle which, as is, or will be, immediately apparent, is formally and also terminologically distinct. And if it involves a vehicle, it involves also a tenor; this is what the vehicle is distinct from.

1 On this expression and its implications, see Ullmann (*LS* 179ff.), who, like others, does indeed use 'tenor' and 'vehicle' of imagery in general (184ff.).
2 Dornseiff 97f.
3 Nowottny 52.
4 Depending on one's purpose, naturally. For some purposes the distinction is crucial: cf. the complaints voiced by Brooke-Rose 13ff. and Stanford *GM* 28ff., and in general see Nowottny 51 and 66, Leavis *EU* 78, Tuve 100f., Ullmann *LS* 179ff.

§8

Consider first an epic simile, *Il.*16.364ff.:[1]

ὡς δ' ὅτ' ἀπ' Οὐλύμπου νέφος ἔρχεται οὐρανὸν εἴσω
αἰθέρος ἐκ δίης ὅτε τε Ζεὺς λαίλαπα τείνῃ,
ὡς τῶν ἐκ νηῶν γένετο ἰαχή τε φόβος τε.

No difficulties present themselves. Evidently, the νέφος and the λαίλαπα, though set out 'literally', have as much and as little to do with the terminology of the ἰαχὴ ἐκ νηῶν as Aeschylus' κλύδων had with κακῶν. Here, then, the same justification exists for speaking of tenor and vehicle, terminologically understood. The vehicle is ὡς..., and the tenor – or the visible part of it – is ὡς.... It is also evident that here there is, in an important sense, no actual suppressed element,[2] although there is still a lacuna in the sequence of the tenor for the duration of ὡς...τείνῃ, and indeed that lacuna may be thought to contain something relating to the tenor which is not explicit in the ὡς clause. We might wish to think of ὡς... as the 'immediate tenor' leaving it open whether there is also a 'suppressed tenor'. Hermann Fränkel dubbed the epic simile's immediate tenor *Sostück* and its vehicle *Wiestück*,[3] a prosaic but useful pair of terms, as suggesting that remaining distinctive feature of such a simile, the formal frame that marks off the terminologies. ὡς and ὥς, the parallel markers that demarcate *Wiestück* and *Sostück*, are themselves, it may be remarked, 'empty' and colourless as far as terminological colour is concerned.

I may at this point be suspected of an attempt at deception. It may be felt that the epic simile just discussed is in some relevant way not typical of its kind. Before I confront suspicion openly by demonstrating the validity of the feeling, let me turn from simile to analogy. Take E.*fr*.1047:

$$\text{ἅπας μὲν ἀὴρ αἰετῷ περάσιμος,}$$
$$\text{ἅπασα δὲ χθὼν ἀνδρὶ γενναίῳ πατρίς.}$$

Up to a point, analysis presents us with nothing new. ἅπας μὲν... is the vehicle, ἅπασα δὲ... its immediate tenor. There is, of course, no formal marker of the ὡς/ὥς type ('Vergleich *ohne* wie'), although the 'empty' and terminologically colourless μέν and δέ incline towards that function. More important, there is a very obvious parallelism between ἅπας, nominally a term of the vehicle, and ἅπασα, nominally a tenor term. I say 'nominally', because while the two words are not wholly of the order of the epic ὡς and ὥς, they are hardly less 'empty', hardly more *of* their terminology. None the less, they differ from the epic pair inasmuch as their collective presence is not predictable; this parallelism is not obligatory. And though it might not be easy off the cuff to say with any precision what this parallelism does for the image, it is clear that it brings tenor and vehicle, formally separate, together.

It appears, then, that the possibility exists of modifying the outward separateness of tenor and vehicle. The forms that such 'modifying' can take in this and in other types of imagery, the effects it can produce in creative hands, make up the subject of the present investigation.

1 A remarkable 'impressionistic' image (blindly done down by D. J. N. Lee 7ff.), whose ground seemingly takes the form of what Richards (117f.) called 'a common attitude' on our part towards tenor and vehicle.
2 Cf. Nowottny 55f.
3 Fränkel *HG* 4. In scholastic circles, the sombre names 'protasis' (vehicle) and 'apodosis' (tenor) are also used.

§9

To continue the examination of explicit imagery, consider another epic simile, *Il*.16.428ff. The extent of my 'deception' can now be laid bare.

οἱ δ' ὥς τ' αἰγυπιοὶ γαμψώνυχες ἀγκυλοχεῖλαι
πέτρῃ ἐφ' ὑψηλῇ μεγάλα κλάζοντε μάχωνται,
ὣς οἱ κεκλήγοντες ἐπ' ἀλλήλοισιν ὄρουσαν.

The basic pattern is a familiar one – this is the point.[1] What was absent from the simile discussed above was the kind of parallelism represented here by κλάζοντε/κεκλήγοντες, a parallelism one recognizes immediately as characteristic of the simile in its epic form. And in this instance the parallel elements are in no sense 'empty'. Unlike ἅπας/ἅπασα, and quite unlike ὡς/ὥς, they have a full terminological coloration. Each is an important part of its *Stück*, and the reference of each varies properly in accordance with the particular 'area of experience' evoked; the κλάζειν of αἰγυπιοί and the κλάζειν of οἱ are not the same kind of κλάζειν. The passage is organized in such a way as to exploit the verb's potential dual reference.[2]

It can be said without hesitation that such a repetition of elements identical, or virtually identical, in form, but different in precise meaning, is a simple means of enforcing the tenor–vehicle relation. The repeated element is a distinctive one, distinctive by virtue of a terminological status that can be called *neutral*,[3] and it carries with it a distinctive effect.

And what of the 'short' similes? – those less stylized forms whose outward distinguishing mark has not, in fact, much to do with length but with the absence of a *so* from the *Sostück*. It is possible to produce examples containing a parallelism corresponding exactly to the epic type, as *Il*.13.389:[4]

ἤριπε δ' ὡς ὅτε τις δρῦς ἤριπεν...

But one might again suspect that such parallelism is not particularly common and, more important, that these similes characteristically have something not identical with epic parallelism but analogous to it, *mutatis mutandis*. One would be right. Take A.*Ag*.48ff. (the Atridae):

μέγαν ἐκ θυμοῦ κλάζοντες Ἄρη
τρόπον αἰγυπιῶν, οἵτε...

τρόπον 'empty' marker; αἰγυπιῶν οἵτε... the vehicle; everything else, no doubt, tenor terminology – except for κλάζοντες. One cannot fail to recall the phraseology and the structure of Homer's ὥς τ' αἰγυπιοί...κλάζοντε...,

Decrepit age that has been tied to me
As to a dog's tail   (Yeats, *The Tower*)

I have already indicated that my coming concern is with 'modifyings' of the separateness of tenor and vehicle, and these shifts might be thought to embody just such. That would be misleading. Without any disparagement, one should rather say that the shifts involve not any modifying of the separation, but a recapitulating of it: from vehicle back to vehicle ($V-V$), with or without a tenor intervention (strictly, $V-T-V$) as well.

One more simile to consider, a new one, A.*Pe.*424ff., from the Persian messenger's account of the disaster at Salamis:

τοὶ δ' ὥστε θύννους ἤ τιν' ἰχθύων βόλον
ἀγαῖσι κωπῶν θραύμασίν τ' ἐρειπίων
ἔπαιον, ἐρράχιζον.

The vehicle is θύννους...βόλον, the tenor τοί and ἀγαῖσι...ἐρειπίων; and ἔπαιον, ἐρράχιζον is neutral,[2] like οἴχεται – but not like οἴχεται. The effect is a new one – an altogether more decisive effect, let us say, than any other yet produced – and the formal structure is also new: $V-T-N$, in formulary terms, not $N-V$. Such a difference is perceptible and analysable – as also is the fundamental relatedness: these instances, and the others of their type, are all interactive, albeit, in some cases, at a pretty rudimentary level. Equally perceptible is the disparity between the interactive images collectively and the $V-V$ group whose mode of effective operation is surely different in kind.

1 The movement is indeed so familiar that commentators 'expect' it, as Dodds on E.*Ba.*778f.
2 In common with men and other animals, fish have a ῥάχις (e.g. Arist.*PA* 655a.37); and one can ῥαχίζειν (a very rare verb) a human victim (e.g. S.*Aj.*56) as well as an animal (e.g. S.*Aj.*299, cf. Eub.15.4).

§11

Finally, comparisons. In some ways, one might well have started with comparisons. As it is, one can say that their formal nucleus tends very clearly to resemble that of the short similes, except for being more highly stereotyped – often to the point of triviality: in Greek, a comparative adjective and a noun in the genitive case is the commonest pattern. And the simple, relevant truth is that in this guise, as in other guises, the comparison has a built-in interactive basis. It has a neutral element – the comparative adjective is, of course, the neutral element – as a predictable norm. Thus:

Alc.372 (subject, presumably, 'warriors') Ἄρευος στροτιωτέροις
Sapph.31.14 (subject 'I') χλωροτέρα ποίας
Thgn.715 (subject 'you') ὠκύτερος...Ἁρπυιῶν

Warriors are warlike, Ares is warlike; I am pale, grass is pale; and so on. Another common form, equally interactive and, if anything, still more trivial, is exemplified by Theognis in the verse preceding the last instance,

γλῶσσαν ἔχων ἀγαθὴν Νέστορος,

the neutral element here being γλῶσσαν ἀγαθήν, corresponding to the comparative adjective of the first three instances.

Stereotyped form is not to be thought of as a Greek peculiarity. English comparisons, including, symptomatically, a large number of proverbial expressions, most commonly take the form '(as) N as V'. 'White as snow', predicable of a good many things, is typical and in its pristine, stereotyped simplicity could claim, as plausibly as any of its Greek counterparts, to represent interaction at its most rudimentary. But even rudiments may permit some variation. One notable variety of the English 'N as V' comparison, especially in proverbs, has the relation of the neutral term to the 'vehicle' pointed by alliteration (if one may speak, licentiously, of vehicles in respect of what are, being proverbial, barely images): 'good as gold', 'plain as a pikestaff', 'bold as brass', 'dead as a doornail', 'cool as a cucumber', 'pleased as Punch', 'blind as a bat', 'fit as a fiddle', 'proud as a peacock', 'brown as a berry', 'pretty as a picture', 'dull as ditch-water', 'right as rain', 'dead as the dodo', 'thick as thieves', 'large as life', 'dry as dust'.[1] A more fundamental variation emerges from these examples: a few of them are not actually 'N as V' at all. Take 'good as gold' and with it contrast a particularly clear instance, 'dead as a doornail'. Babies (or whatever) may be *good* and likewise gold may be; so 'N as V'. But whereas people (T) may be *dead*, doornails can't be;[2] so, in fact, only 'T as V'. And another, less disturbing, variation: looking at the instances where the adjective *does* work both ways, one finds some with the adjective used, as we would casually say, 'in the same sense'; e.g. 'her face was as brown as a berry' (to give an instance a plausible context), where 'brown face' and 'brown berry' seem to involve the 'same sense' of *brown*. Whereas in other cases, one might want to speak of a *pun*, the adjective being used in 'different senses': e.g. 'he's as dry as dust', where *dry* means impassively pedantic (of 'he') and moistureless (of 'dust'). The place that such differentiations have in the comprehension of less rudimentary and more creative interactions will appear later.

To return to the Greek forms and the main line of the exposition: the pattern 'more *N* than *V*' (or 'the *N* of *V*') is stable, as is an intimate relationship between the neutral term and the ground of each image. In χλωροτέρα ποίας, that which 'I' and ποίας have in common is indicated by the neutral term, χλωροτέρα, and, as one expects, by no other term. We can call χλωροτέρα, simply, the *ground-term*, and the same tag can be attached to γλῶσσαν ἀγαθήν in γλῶσσαν ἔχων ἀγαθὴν Νέστορος, to 'whiter' in 'whiter than snow' and to the corresponding items in any of the '*N* as *V*' or 'more *N* than *V*' comparisons cited. Looking back to the instances of neutral terminology discussed earlier, we can see in some cases an almost identical relationship with the ground. Thus, in the οἴχεται νεβροῦ δίκην instance, οἴχεται is ground-term to νεβροῦ, although here at least it is apposite to add that while the reference of οἴχεται is to the ground, it obviously isn't to the *whole* of the ground.[3] The idea of 'pursuit', for instance, is part of the ground, but is hardly embodied in its entirety in οἴχεται.

1 Svartengren (p.465) suggests that about a fifth of all the similes in his massive collection are alliterative in some way and about four-fifths of these in the 'good as gold' way. This means that there may be about a thousand recorded instances of this type in English, though many of these are not proverbial but creative coinages and many others are dialectal or defunct. (On the other hand, his catalogue is incomplete: one or two of my instances are not, in fact, there.)

2 This is the case *now*, irrespective of the earlier history of the phrase. Various theories about its origin, plausible and implausible, are considered by Svartengren 143ff., Hulme 52f.

3 This point about the ground-term in simile is taken by Aristides Quintilianus ii.9 in his discussion of *Od.*10.304 (on the herb moly):

ῥίζῃ μὲν μέλαν ἔσκε, γάλακτι δὲ εἴκελον ἄνθος.

Superficially, there is no ground-term here, but in context εἴκελον obviously = 'white'. Whiteness, however, is not the whole of the ground, as Aristides notes: πολλῶν γὰρ χἀτέρων λευκῶν ὄντων τὸ καὶ γλυκύτητος ἔμφασιν ποιησόμενον ἐπελέξατο.

§12

So much, for the moment, for explicit imagery. It will be remembered that in my analysis of the metaphor in *Persae* 598ff., I stopped short at κακῶν. The passage continues as follows:[1]

φίλοι, κακῶν μὲν ὅστις ἔμπειρος κυρεῖ
ἐπίσταται βροτοῖσιν ὡς, ὅταν κλύδων
κακῶν ἐπέλθῃ, πάντα δειμαίνειν φίλον,
ὅταν δ' ὁ δαίμων εὐροῇ...

There is not much to note about the status (terminological status) of πάντα...εὑροῇ. Some words are colourless, as ὅταν. Some belong to the tenor, as δαίμων. And εὑροῇ is a term of the vehicle that coheres with κλύδων and carries through certain of its implications. πάντα δειμαίνειν φίλον might be characterized as neutral, but to all intents and purposes is relatively colourless tenor terminology; tenor, because the κακῶν terminology, not the κλύδων, is as yet dominant. Colourless terms, one perceives, follow the terminology of the moment, chameleon-like.[2]

What is left is ἐπέλθῃ, the point of present interest. The word has a relevant dual reference, is neutral: characteristically tenor (τῶν ἐπιόντων κακῶν, Hdt.7.120.1),[3] characteristically vehicle (ἐπῆλθε πλημυρὶς τῆς θαλάσσης, Hdt.8.129.2).[4] It thus has some affinity with any of the neutral terms discussed above, but most with the ἔπαιον, ἐρράχιζον of *Pe.*426. The structures are schematically very close, over and above the simile/metaphor distinction:

τοὶ δ' (*T*) ὥστε...βόλον (*V*) ἀγαῖσι...ἐρειπίων (*T*) ἔπαιον, ἐρράχιζον (*N*)
ὅταν (*T*)   κλύδων   (*V*)   κακῶν   (*T*)   ἐπέλθῃ   (*N*)

And in particular, in both passages the neutral terminology is, we might say, *articulated* by its position at the end of the syntactic unit before a following pause. The effect produced by ἐπέλθῃ is recognizably distinct from that of, say, οἴχεται in οἴχεται νεβροῦ δίκην. Apart from anything else, ἐπέλθῃ is not *the* ground term (metaphor does not entail one), although it is still *a* ground term. All neutral terminology, one would presume, will have some relation to the ground.

That the character of neutral terms may be expected to vary in context has been provisionally shown. I hope it is clear also that the neutral compressions exemplified in these Aeschylean passages *and* those in the comparisons and similes *and* the parallelisms noted earlier all have one thing in common: a breakdown of the rigid terminological barrier that stood between tenor and vehicle in Homer's

ὡς δ' ὅτ' ἀπ' Οὐλύμπου νέφος ἔρχεται...
ὡς τῶν ἐκ νηῶν γένετο ἰαχή τε φόβος τε.

We have just as much of a barrier, let it be said, in

Decrepit age that has been tied to me
As to a dog's tail

for all the 'movement' between 'tied' and 'dog's tail' (*V–V*); and we have it likewise in the *V–V* group in general. And it will be useful to give an equal emphasis here to the fact that, unlike simile and comparison, metaphor more often than not has the barrier intact – and good metaphor as much as any:

Men must endure
Their going hence, even as their coming hither:
Ripeness is all. (*King Lear* v.2)

ὡς Διωνύσοι' ἄνακτος καλὸν ἐξάρξαι μέλος
οἶδα διθύραμβον οἴνῳ συγκεραυνωθεὶς φρένας.
(Arch.77)

I am not concerned with the barriers, but only with ways of breaking them down. Any such breakdown I shall call 'interaction';[5] and 'such', as is already apparent, conceals a good deal of diversity. I shall now suggest how much more diversity can be subsumed under the same heading.

1 I stop this time at εὐροῇ, because the textual uncertainty that follows would complicate the discussion irrelevantly.
2 This suggests, if it was not already evident, that *neutral* and *colourless* are not rigidly distinct; that there is a spectrum with imperceptible gradations. At the opposite end to colourless *N* terms come punning *N* terms, like the 'dry' of 'dry as dust', which is 'two-toned', in current commercial jargon.
3 Of κακά similarly: *h.Cer.*257, Phoc.16.2, E.*fr.*135.2, Hdt.7.139.2, Hp.*Epid.*7.14, Demad.*fr.*15.
4 Of flowing water similarly: Pi.*fr.*140c, A.*Supp.*559ff., Hdt.2.14.2, Th.3.89.2, Hellanic.28 Jac., Hp.*Vict.*1.27, Thphr.*HP* 4.7.4. The verb is used as *N* likewise at A.*Supp.*469 and *Prom.*1016.
5 *Faute de mieux*, but to the further sorrow of Dr Richards, did he but know, who used the word of the tenor–vehicle relation itself. It is not wholly satisfactory for my purposes, because it implies a two-way relation; whereas the relation involved in my interactions will often be one-way. I am, however, gratified to note that the word has already been used in my sense, and by a distinguished classic at that. 'The interaction of comparison and thing compared', writes Fraenkel (II.39), the reference being to 'intrusion', as I shall be calling it.

§13

Almost all the instances of interaction cited so far have involved neutral terminology,[1] but in discussing comparison I noted an instance of a different kind; a trivial image, hardly an image, more a fossil; but still embodying a different kind of interaction: the English proverbial comparison, 'dead as a doornail'. To recapitulate: the predictable structure of an English comparison is '*N* as *V*'; but 'dead as a doornail' (of an animate being) is, in fact '*T* as *V*'; in sum, the tenor term has *displaced* something else – a term belonging to both tenor and vehicle. Compare an Aeschylean passage that I discussed in the Prolegomenon,[2] the home-coming king and the vine, *Ag.*966ff.:

ῥίζης γὰρ οὔσης φυλλὰς ἵκετ’ ἐς δόμους,
σκιὰν ὑπερτείνασα σειρίου κυνός.
καὶ σοῦ μολόντος δωματῖτιν ἑστίαν. . . .

‘The image’, says Fraenkel (after Vahlen), ‘. . . assimilates elements of the thing compared.’ That is, ἵκετ’ ἐς δόμους, applicable to the king but not to the vine, and therefore in tenor terminology, stands as part of – or instead of part of – the vehicle: a displacement once again, notwithstanding the extreme dissimilarity in other ways between the Aeschylus and the English proverb. Such displacements I shall call *intrusions* and intrusion is another main kind of interaction.

Now a new instance, Stesichorus 8.2f. (the subject is ᾿Αέλιος, the Sun):

ὄφρα δι’ ὠκεανοῖο περάσας
ἀφίκοιθ’ ἱαρᾶς ποτὶ βένθεα νυκτὸς ἐρεμνᾶς.

There is clearly a relation of some sort between ὠκεανοῖο and the vehicle, βένθεα. The two words belong to the same ‘watery’ semantic field (θαλάσσης πάσης βένθεα, *Od.*1.52f.);[3] structurally, one could say, a passage like *Odyssey* 12.1f. is evoked: λίπεν ῥόον ὠκεανοῖο / νηῦς ἀπὸ δ’ ἵκετο κῦμα θαλάσσης. It is equally clear that the relation is of a new kind. In the first place, there is obviously no question of any displacement; and secondly, ὠκεανοῖο is not neutral but in tenor terminology. Yet by virtue of the relation, the familiar barrier is broken – interactively. The difference between this interaction and those involving neutral terms is important: this one, let us say, is *extra-grammatical*; it operates not through but outside the grammatical structure.[4] And unlike those, again, it has nothing to do with the ground of the image: ὠκεανοῖο has no bearing on the likeness, whatever it may be, between the *x* of night and depths of water. All of which goes equally for the *Macbeth* image cited in the Prolegomenon:[5]

My way of life
Is fall’n into the sear, the yellow leaf.

As ὠκεανοῖο is to βένθεα, so ‘fall’n’ – more or less – is to ‘leaf’. And that ‘more or less’ predictably implies significant variation within this third main type of interaction.

Persae 599f. again:

ὡς, ὅταν κλύδων
κακῶν. . .

The last major type of interaction differs fundamentally from all the others. These others are overtly and directly *semantic* interactions. Between κλύδων and κακῶν there is a perceptible *aural* relation, an alliterative relation. Since the two words are vehicle and tenor terms respectively, this simple relating is *ipso facto* interactive; it represents another way by which the 'natural' terminological barrier may be overcome – irrespective of the specific effect of the alliteration in this particular case. So: we have, apparently, a separate class of aural interactions, and to this may be referred the patterns briefly remarked above as characteristic of the English '*N as V*' comparisons: 'good as gold', 'dry as dust'.[6] In the latter case, one might point out, the alliteration is – more or less predictably – between vehicle and neutral ground term; in the Aeschylus, between vehicle (κλύδων) and its immediate tenor (κακῶν); not that alliteration is to be thought of as the only possible source of aural interactive effects.

These, then, are the four main types of interaction: neutral-based, intrusive, extra-grammatical, aural. Each of these seems to justify in its own way the common general name, interaction: they all involve an *active* relationship *between* the terminologies. That should be clear enough, even before any closer examination into the varieties of relationship – the particular categories within the four main types.

1 I.e. discounting the Prolegomenon, where the passages discussed were more mixed.
2 Prolegom. pp. viif. For full discussion, see below, pp. 140f.
3 βένθεα is largely confined to epic (to which the Stesich. is rhythmically akin), where it is almost invariably used of waters: λίμνης *Il.*13.21, Hes.*Th.*365; θαλάσσης *Od.*1.53; ἁλός *Il.*1.358; πόντου *h.Cer.*38. It seems not to be attested in specific connection with ὠκεανός itself, though cf. *Il.*7.422, *Od.*10.511.
4 For the tag, cf. Trypho *Trop.*III p. 198 Spengel, where tropes of one particular kind (in fact, trope proper, including metaphor etc.) are described as τῆς γραμματικῆς τὴν κοινὴν συνήθειαν παραβαίνοντες. Extra-grammatical signification in my sense was also recognized in antiquity, even perversely, as by Aristid. Quint.*de Mus.*2.9, who claims that in *Il.*7.421–3 the epithets ἀκαλαρρείταο and βαθυρρόου add a feeling of βραδυτής to the sun's rising (!).
5 Prolegom. p. xi.
6 See above, p. 20.

§14

Now that it is apparent what I mean by 'interaction', it may be wondered why I have approached the subject in this oblique way, via what are presumably not its most striking manifestations. I hope it is sufficient to answer that it is no less important to be able to say, 'In this instance such and such features are perceptible, though not remarkable', than 'In that instance there is a remarkable effect ascribable to such and such'. Each, of course, presupposes the other: one cannot understand 'major' if one does not understand 'minor', and *vice versa*. But in practice it is usually the minor that is presupposed, and presupposed too much.

In addition, it is something if the preceding pages have sufficiently shown that bigger and better interactions are liable not to be freaks, but, as G. M. Hopkins said poetry should be, 'the current language heightened'. A comparatively unremarkable interaction like, say, Aeschylus' ἐπέλθῃ may itself be seen as a heightening of a lower form, one which at its lowest is virtually a built-in feature of the language, the neutral ground term in comparisons. It is valuable to demonstrate how interaction relates to fundamentals, and, to do this, one may as well begin with fundamentals; particularly so, in view of the fact that fundamentals have been largely ignored in the sporadic attention given to this whole field hitherto.

I hope also that the oblique approach has served to make it clear that interaction cannot be accounted a universal 'key' to the appreciation of imagery. Many images do not harbour any interaction and in few of those that do is it the main feature; interaction's tenuous relation to the conceptual aspects of imagery is one very relevant factor here and ultimately, as with any partial emphasis, a limiting one. On the other hand, interaction is a notable feature of many – surprisingly many? – of the most celebrated images in Greek poetry and English poetry too.

2 Dead Metaphor and Normal Usage

§15[1]

Inasmuch as all imagery embodies the temporary displacement of the terminology 'at issue' in favour of 'extraneous' terminology, all imagery embodies a deviation from the terminological norm, albeit a familiar kind of deviation. Metaphor alone[2] has the distinction of achieving this deviation through a simultaneous departure from the normal usage of the language as a whole. This, as is well known, is precisely what the so-called 'dead' or 'faded' or 'linguistic' metaphor does not do. *Tree* in *a family tree*, for instance, is a 'dead metaphor' and involves no departure from normal usage.

To speak of 'dead metaphor' is to imply two statements about a word. (1) A historical statement: if this word, used thus, had been so used x years ago, there would have been a metaphor (where 'metaphor' means a departure of the analogy/similarity kind from normal usage). (2) An aesthetic statement: this word, used thus, feels and therefore is normal usage (where 'normal' includes slang, jargon, archaism, high-falutin and so on). To call a word a metaphor, meaning live metaphor, is to imply only an aesthetic statement: this word, used thus, is not normal usage but a departure of the appropriate kind.

In linguistic terms, the historical statement implied by 'dead metaphor' involves a diachronic fact, a fact that can be labelled 'semantic change', a fact that concerns historical linguistics. The aesthetic statements implied by 'dead metaphor' and by metaphor proper involve synchronic facts. In literature, as in all other functions of language, the synchronic–aesthetic and the diachronic–historical are distinguishable and distinct.[3] In particular, 'dead metaphor', diachronically operative, and metaphor, operative synchronically, are not directly comparable: 'dead metaphor' is not of immediate relevance, *qua* metaphor. Which is not to say that 'dead metaphors' are *de facto* of no aesthetic interest, as if any word or class of word ever could be. On the contrary, they have characteristic and important powers of multiple reference through the simultaneous possession of a primary and an analogically related secondary sense, unless of course the former has been entirely superseded. And this multiple reference makes them specially important to

27

the present study, in that they provide ideal material for neutral terms in interactions.[4]

But this does not mean that there is any point in trying to make separate categories of 'dead metaphor' neutral terms and neutral terms with a different origin. The origin is irrelevant to the status, here at least.[5] This being so, the expression 'dead metaphor' is an unfortunate distraction. I give notice, therefore, that whenever I speak of 'metaphor' without qualification, I mean live metaphor and only that; that, except where lucidity demands it, I shall not use the expression 'dead metaphor', or any equivalent, at all;[6] and that whenever I speak of 'normal' or 'standard' or even 'literal'[7] usage, these may refer to what is demonstrably 'dead metaphor'. That is, I shall treat 'dead metaphoric' usages as any other normal usages, 'dead metaphors' as any other terms of potential multiple reference. And 'multiple reference' here means what it says. It seems sometimes to be supposed that to speak of 'dead metaphor' is to imply that the word, when used in its secondary sense, has lost effective connection with its primary sense,[8] whereas, it is suggested, the difference with live metaphor is here one of degree, not kind. It is obviously true that there is no black-and-white contrast as regards the mere number of senses available; both metaphor and 'dead metaphor' can give you 'two ideas for one'. But the latter has the primary sense available only as a connotation,[9] whereas metaphor compels reference to the denotative sense in question. *In fine*, the contrast between normal and abnormal usage remains black and white.

One proviso: there are not only metaphors and 'dead metaphors'. There are also metaphorical clichés,[10] a class occupying an intermediate position, in which the garment is 'worn' but not yet worn to death. All one can say in general about cliché is that it more or less approximates to the status of 'dead metaphor',[11] i.e. normal usage. *The kingdom of heaven*, for instance, is as normal as *a family tree*.

---

1 Not much in this section is strikingly new. Cf., among others, Nowottny 52f., Wellek–Warren 195f., Stanford *GM* 84f.

2 Other tropes likewise depart from normal usage (unless 'dead' tropes), but of the tropes only metaphor comes within my definition of imagery.

3 The importance of the distinction between synchrony and diachrony is axiomatic in linguistics. (See e.g. Ullmann *LS* 50–62, 117.) In some circumstances the 'data' relevant to aesthetic and to historical considerations may coincide. This is the case, to take an easy and obvious instance, with poetic 'etymologies'. But such coincidence is not itself an aesthetic datum. Aesthetically it is of little importance whether the 'etymology' is historically correct.

4 Cf. Nowottny 70. Some of the neutral terms already noted may be presumed to

owe their status to just such a semantic history, although what looks like 'dead metaphor' can be produced by 'linguistic drift' (see Waldron 170–4) as well as by 'the institutionalizing of an *ad hoc* metaphor' (*ibid.* 178).

5 The great Romantic insight, 'origins show the nature of a thing' (Herder), is, like many insights, sometimes profoundly true, sometimes partly true, sometimes irritatingly irrelevant.

6 Similarly, I shall avoid expressions like 'reviving a dead metaphor', whatever their applications.

7 Cf. Nowottny in Knights–Cottle 61.

8 So, apparently, Richards 100f. I might again invoke my remark above, 'unless ...the primary sense has been entirely superseded'.

9 Cf. Empson *SCW* 331, and see below, §27.

10 Like 'dead metaphor', the word 'cliché' is not in itself to be regarded as pejorative.

11 Hence clichés can be neutral terms. Thus 'slippery' in 'a slippery customer' is cliché, though not, one might think, quite 'dead'. But if one calls such a customer 'slippery as an eel', the effect is that of a punning '*N* as *V*' comparison. Puns presuppose the existence of two recognized and recognizable senses. (In practice, I should mention, I shall tend to restrict 'cliché' to usages with a largely poetic, or equivalently heightened, currency: 'kingdom of heaven', rather than 'slippery customer'.)

§ 16

So far, so good. The problem, of course, is that Greek, archaic and classical Greek, is not now spoken. How is one from such a distance to distinguish metaphor and 'dead metaphor'?[1] Some of the relevant considerations and some important principles can be illustrated from English usage.

In modern English, crowds literally 'stream' out of a sports ground or on to the playing area; or 'pour' over a barrier. But 'flowed' in Eliot's

A crowd flowed over London Bridge, so many

is live metaphor. Conversely, modern electric currents 'flow' as a matter of normal propriety. If they ever 'stream', they do this metaphorically, and the perceptible difference is considerable, even in such a trivial instance. Implication: given two partial synonyms $Xa\ldots$ and $Ya\ldots$, the knowledge that $Xa\ldots$ is in fact $Xab\ldots$ does not provide any ground for thinking that $Ya\ldots$ is in fact $Yab\ldots$. Hence, the knowledge, or presumption, that ὀξύς, 'sharp', is normal of both sound[2] and touch[3] does not make Alcman's καρχάραισι φωναῖς normal: 'with jagged voices' (Alcm.138). It *may* be normal, although I greatly doubt it, but the evidence of ὀξύς is worth nothing, for or against. Again, the volcanic ῥύαξ πυρός of Th.3.116.1 is presumably

29

a literal ῥύαξ,[4] but that likelihood is irrelevant to the status of Aeschylus' similarly volcanic ποταμοὶ πυρός (*Prom*.368). Again, ὄζος Ἄρηος is venerable epic cliché. That does not make κλάδον Ἐνυαλίου (Ibyc.38) a cliché.[5] And again, the knowledge that πέλαγος κακῶν in the fifth century is a fairly common poetic metaphor, though hardly a cliché, does not make κακῶν θάλασσα common: only A.*Th*.758.[6] Yet these are precisely the references one expects – and finds – in the commentators, preoccupied as so many of them are with 'same images', and heedless of whether the 'image' is a poetic, aesthetic datum or a fact of the language and the language's history.

Contemporary English tears literally 'stream' down cheeks. But if one wrote 'a stream of tears', the effect, surely, would be that of live metaphor. Similarly, birds 'build' nests, but their nests are not 'buildings'. Implication: given two cognates, knowledge of the status of one is not evidence in favour of a like status for the other. I suspect the existence of comparable pairs in Greek. Thus ζευγνύναι seems to be normal fifth- and fourth-century Greek for 'constructing a bridge over' something – so Aeschylus, Herodotus and others, repeatedly.[7] But the cognate ζυγόν for 'bridge', not so: only Aeschylus once and an oracle once.[8] In these two passages I take ζυγόν to be live metaphor. Again, ποιμένα λαῶν is epic cliché, whereas the verb ποιμαίνειν thus is neither epic nor any other cliché. In the isolated ποιμαίνεις πολιήτας (Anacr.3.8), I take the verb to be live metaphor.

In English, one event 'foreshadows' another as a matter of normal usage. If it merely 'shadowed' another, it would have to do so metaphorically. Implication: the usage of derivatives is not necessarily a reliable guide to the usage of the simple form. Hence the status of ῥεῖν in Aeschylus' ῥεῖ πολὺς ὅδε λεώς (*Th*.80) cannot be established merely in the light of the fact that ἐπιρρεῖν is normal Greek for the advance of bodies of men – ἐπέρρεον ἔθνεα πεζῶν[9] – and συρρεῖν similarly.[10] The simple verb does *not* appear to be normal in this sense.[11]

---

1 I do not find that previous discussions have come to grips with the problems. In fact, the problems have rarely even been discussed. Hence, as elsewhere, I am obliged to go back to fundamentals. Contemporary linguistics has little to offer, if Ullmann's chapter on 'The reconstruction of stylistic values' (*LS* 154–73) is representative. Contemporary 'English' scholarship, similarly, has done little more than its classical counterpart to establish principles in these matters, as is shown e.g. by the elementary character of various points which Hulme (herself a trained linguist, incidentally) judges it necessary to make in the course of her investigations into the language of Shakespeare's time (Hulme, *Explorations, passim*).

2 *Il.*15.313, Hes.*Sc.*348, Thgn.1197, Pi.*N.*9.35, Ar.*Ach.*804, Hp.*Prorrh.*1.45, Aeschin.2.157 etc.

3 *Il.*12.64, Pi.*N.*4.63, Hdt.2.29.5 etc.

4 Cf. Hanno *Peripl.*15 πυρώδεις ῥύακες (*torrentes ignei*, so *ibid.*17) and LSJ *s.v.*

5 Cf. only κλάδος Μελιταῖος, the pretentious sepulchral inscription dreamed up by the μικροφιλότιμος for his Meletean dog (Thphr.*Char.*21.9). Regarding the ὄζος of ὄζος Ἄρηος: note that it is not relevant to invoke the probability that this ὄζος, unlike κλάδος, had in the first instance nothing to do with twigs and branches. For the archaic Greek language, it has no other meaning.

6 This image, along with other Aeschylean 'sea' images, is invoked by Ole Smith (p.22) in a similar way, though a certain confusion appears in his appeal to the dichotomy between 'topos' and 'vivid and deeply felt'. The former term refers wholly to the typicality of *ideas*, the latter, ultimately, to the novelty of *words*.

7 E.g. A.*Pe.*722, Hdt.7.24, Lys.2.29, Isoc.4.89, X.*An.*2.4.13, Pl.*Lg.*699a.

8 A.*Pe.*72, Orac.*ap.*Hdt.8.20.2 (neither noted in LSJ *s.v.*). Compare the case of usages restricted to what we casually regard as particular forms of a given word, e.g. the specialized uses of the perfective forms of βαίνειν (see LSJ *s.v.* A.1.2): βαίνω and βέβηκα might be better regarded as cognates. (For a new instance of such restriction, see below, pp. 115f. with n.1.)

9 *Il.*11.724; so Hdt.9.38.2 (twice), Pl.*Phdr.*229d, Aen.Tact.10.24.

10 Hdt.5.101.2, 8.42.1; X.*HG* 2.3.18, *An.*4.2.19, 5.2.3, 6.3.6; Isoc.8.44; Pl.*Lg.*708d.

11 Only E.*Rh.*290 and *fr.*146 (in addition to the Aeschylean passage). (The usage is found in other compounds of the verb as well – *vid.* Taillardat 386.) The elementary points made in this section have been implicitly ignored by the many who confuse a relating of two areas of experience, which may be stock and traditional, and the placing of a particular word in a particular context where the *iunctura* may be entirely novel. So (e.g.) Gildersleeve on Pi.*P.*1.30 ὄρος,... γαίας μέτωπον: 'the transfer of the designation of parts of the body to objects in nature is so common as not to need illustration'. True enough, but (adds Gildersleeve) 'whatever original personifying power this transfer may have had seems to have faded out in Greek poetry'. Yet μέτωπον thus is not normal usage (except in one isolated and ungeneralizable context: Scyl.68 Κριοῦ Μέτωπον, ἀκρωτήριον τῆς Ταυρικῆς). Again, note Taillardat's use of the word 'cliché'. At times it apparently refers to words and expressions ('tout cliché fut une métaphore neuve', p.19); at other times to ideas, so that of the relationships 'poète: architecte' and 'poème: édifice' Taillardat writes (p.27): 'cette image étant un cliché'.

§17

How, then, are we to characterize the relationship between, for instance, ὀξύς and κάρχαρος, assuming that the former is normal, the latter not? However we do it, we would be well advised to avoid any vague phraseology like 'κάρχαρος has the normal language behind it', which might suggest something quite different. For instance, one could plausibly characterize in this way the image κλάζοντες Ἄρη τρόπον αἰγυπιῶν with reference to the interaction: κλάζοντες is 'the normal language behind' αἰγυπιῶν. Headlam's solution[1] had a certain merit; metaphors may be 'heightened synonyms' of normal phraseology. But 'synonym' is limited and hardly covers the relation between ζευγνύναι and ζυγόν, for instance, although the formula does prevent any possible confusion with interaction based on neutral terms, which Headlam himself called 'development from the equivocal meaning of a word'.[2]

I have not found an adequate answer. 'Extension' is the likeliest possibility, but this label is more appropriate for a quite different linguistic phenomenon which is, indeed, relevant to the general issues under consideration and poses another problem. The *callidae iuncturae* created by metaphor are novel collocations, analogically based. But not all novel collocations, analogically based, are metaphorical. There was a time when 'sputnik' was not a word in the English language. Next there was a time when it was. Soon after that, doubtless, some epithet was for the first time tacked on to form a phrase like 'big sputnik' or 'noisy. . .'. Now any such collocation was novel: 'noisy', or whatever, was used in unfamiliar collocation by analogy with its more usual contexts. Rockets (etc.) are noisy; sputniks are like rockets (etc.); therefore. . . . But patently this is not metaphor; this is analogical 'extension'; and, unlike metaphor, it does not involve *perceptible* deviation from normal usage. As such, it does not, in effect, involve deviation at all. Though novel, it is normal.[3]

What now is one to say of the following example from Pindar? In the Sixth *Paean* (*fr.*52f.137–8), that poet uses the phrase χρύσεαι ἀέρος. . .κόμαι, with κόμαι metaphorical – there is no problem here. The problem concerns χρύσεαι. The word obviously coheres with κόμαι, 'golden hair', but what is its relation to ἀέρος? It is used of νέφος in early Greek,[4] but not, as it seems, of ἀήρ. Would χρύσεος ἀήρ be extension[5] and therefore effectively indistinguishable from normal usage, or is it recognizably distinct from normality?

I suspect that there is no way of answering the question, or at least no way of demonstrating the truth of an answer. But we can console ourselves with the thought that if Pindar's use and other imponderable uses of this sort are not extensions, but live imagery, they are almost certainly instances of imagery so subdued and altogether marginal – perhaps catachrestic – as hardly to deserve the name at all. This being so, our inability to recognize extension need not have the serious consequences of a failure to distinguish 'dead metaphor' from metaphor, possible implication from compulsively evocative reference. Such a failure may distort the whole balance of a passage. At least we may be spared that.[6]

1 Headlam 436.

2 Headlam *loc. cit.* This formula is not in fact satisfactory either: 'development' suits only a minority of neutral-based interactions. It should be added that Headlam devised the expression for metaphor, not for imagery as a whole.

3 Cf. the semanticists' concept of 'drift' (see e.g. Waldron 142–61).

4 *Il.*13.523, 14.344, 18.206; *h.Ap.*98; Pi.*fr.*52f.92 (the same poem).

5 If this is extension, I do not mean to imply that it is exactly parallel to the English 'sputnik' example, where a neologism is involved.

6 A final word on extension. The fact that the student of Greek must make due allowance for it does not entitle him to postulate it as the fancy takes him or for the sake of tidy exposition. A major heading of LSJ on κύκλος (*s.v.* II) is 'any circular body'. *Any?* How can one know that?

§18

But I have not yet answered my own question. What are the criteria for distinguishing metaphor and 'dead metaphor'? – or rather, since the latter represents but one kind of normal usage, for distinguishing metaphorical usage and normal usage. Whatever they are, they must involve reconstruction. There is no inspired short cut via (e.g.) the principle that live metaphors, and only these, are consciously intended. Even if this 'principle' were inherently plausible, it would merely push the problem back a stage, for we have no sure means of identifying such an intention; and since we cannot in any case guarantee the accuracy of the intention,[1] the 'principle' would create additional and totally irrelevant problems of its own. It is not intention of any sort but perceptible abnormality that must be established.

'The fact that a phenomenon is without a parallel is of course *per se* no proof of something being wrong.'[2] A constant preoccupation of commentators, however, is to find parallels, especially lexical parallels. The reasons vary, though usually no reason is given. The exercise has become a habit, and the nature of the habit has been determined by an age-old textual orientation. 'The gist is..., and, by the way, the text is sound: the same poet (*vel sim.*) uses the same words (*vel sim.*) with the same gist in...' – a sequence of thought along such lines is characteristically implicit. One regrettable product of this understandable procedure has been the virtual canonization of the kind of parallel that textual considerations prescribe, *viz* like to like. To parallel Aeschylus one adduces Aeschylus or, failing that, another tragedian or, failing that, whoever is adjudged next in the scale. For textual criticism such a procedure is correct. A poet's text must be established first in the light of his own usual practice, second in the light of the practice of his genre, and so on. But if one's concern is different, these habits of mind may have to be discarded. If, in particular, one wishes to distinguish normal from metaphorical usage, the 'like to like' principle will lead one in the wrong direction altogether.

What are the criteria? In most cases there is only one available: distribution. Distribution, that is, of the given usage of the word in question; not, in the first instance, the usage of its derivatives, nor of its cognates; and not the usage of its synonyms at all; but the word itself. Under 'distribution' are to be subsumed: (1) the quality of usage. In which authors and in which portions of their work is the word used thus? (2) The quantity of usage. How commonly is the word used thus? (3) The period of usage. *When* else is the word used thus?

If one is to make inferences from distributional data, one must have general assumptions about one's aims, about the relative value of these three considerations, and about the various implications of different sorts of distribution. My assumptions, some of them implicit in the preceding discussions, can now be considered in detail.

1 The intention need not correspond to the truth, the whole truth, etc. In any case, 'it is doubtful whether any general distinction between the literal and the metaphorical use of a term was consciously and explicitly drawn before the fourth century' (Lloyd 228). If this is true, there may not even have been a formulatable intention for us to identify, quite apart from its dubious evidential value if it did exist. But the habit of trying to distinguish metaphor and dead metaphor on the intentional criterion is almost automatic for many. Typical are Waldron's comments, p.178, 'to the *user* there is no metaphorical *awareness*...', 'living metaphors which are *intended* as such by the *user*...', 'not associated by the average *speaker*...'; or Earp's, p.94, 'it would be waste of time to include all common and *unconscious* metaphors....I have endeavoured to include only those which seem to be *conscious* and would be felt [oh, by whom?] as metaphors. Even so, it was not always easy to draw the line...' (my italics throughout). The unexamined dual faith in the reliability of intentions and a reader's capacity to recognize them is particularly common in this connection. On 'intention', more in §25.

2 Leif Bergson, *Eranos* LXV, 1967, 18.

§19

Assumption 1: in trying to reconstruct normal usage, one is trying to reconstruct the state of the language[1] presupposed by the work containing the usage in question. In general, this is the contemporary language, with minor modifications according to genre and dialect.

Assumption 2: the language to be reconstructed is the literate language.[2] We cannot hope to get beyond this.[3]

Assumption 3: one is trying to reconstruct a language, not an idiolect, the 'individual language'. 'The linguist is not primarily interested in idiolects... his ultimate target is the common norm.'[4] The student of literature *is* interested in authors' idiolects, but not in such a way that he would, or should, assess the effects of the author's linguistic usages against a background of the author's linguistic norms. For example, the association apparently formed by Pindar between Heracles and the word ἔσχατος is wholly personal and therefore of some interest to Pindar's biographer.[5] It is not a datum of the language, and cannot be made one by a presumption that to Pindar it was a datum. Again, κορυφή, with the reference 'excellence',[6] seems to be Pindaric and only Pindaric. It is a *prima facie* idiolectal peculiarity, and, as such, cannot be 'dead metaphor' or even cliché by virtue of its Pindaric usage alone. The possibility that to Pindar himself it felt very 'worn' is immaterial.[7]

Assumption 4: presumptive normality can be established positively, by the citation of adequate evidence. Presumptive abnormality can be established only negatively, *ex silentio*. Therefore, the emphasis must be put on establishing normal usage. Any usage not demonstrably normal is *prima facie* abnormal, i.e. live metaphor, provided that the abnormality is of the analogy/similarity kind.

Assumption 5: any usage found in all or virtually all Greek of the period in question and earlier periods is bound to be normal; any usage approximating to this character likewise. The problem is to define the limits of this 'approximation'.

Assumption 6: quality. The principles relating to the qualitative criterion must be established *a priori* but can be supported by explicit ancient testimony where this is available. Normal usage, meaning specifically non-metaphorical usage, is much more likely to occur in some kinds of writing than in other kinds, *a priori*. It is most likely to occur in those authors whose language is in other comparable respects least heightened. This means that, with certain qualifications, prose evidence is a better guide to normal usage than poetic evidence.[8] Prose usage is, in a relevant sense, generally nearer the norm. These axioms are supported by, e.g.: (*a*) Aristotle (*Mete.*357a.27), ἡ γὰρ μεταφορὰ ποιητικόν, (*b*) Aristotle (*Rh.*1404a.28f.), ἑτέρα λόγου καὶ ποιήσεως λέξις ἐστίν, (*c*) Isocrates (9.8ff.), τοῖς μὲν γὰρ ποιηταῖς πολλοὶ δέδονται κόσμοι· καὶ γάρ...οἷόν τ' αὐτοῖς...μεταφοραῖς...διαποικῖλαι τὴν ποίησιν· τοῖς δὲ περὶ τοὺς λόγους οὐδὲν ἔξεστι τῶν τοιούτων.[9]

Assumption 7: the influence on normal locutions of specifically poetic ones is in general marginal.[10] Hence in any case of coincidence between later usage which is presumed normal and earlier poetic usage, it is not likely that the poetic usage engendered the norm, and most likely that the pattern reflects poetic employment of what was already normal usage.

Assumption 8: notwithstanding the previous assumption, certain poetic authors whose works are subsequently felt to have a classic or definitive significance can represent for later poetry almost a second norm. For all the poetry in my corpus, early epic usage, especially Homeric usage, has a status different in kind from any other poetic usage.

Assumption 9: quantity. The greater the frequency of a usage and, in particular, the larger the number of different authors represented in the evidence, and the larger the number of different genres they represent, the more likely that the usage is normal.

Assumption 10: period. Contemporary or earlier evidence is more reliable than later evidence, but, within reason, period is less important than quality (see Assumption 7). In addition, the criteria of quality and period in combination carry more weight than the criteria of quantity and period in combination. Suppose the problematic usage to be Pindaric. If the evidence, the sum of directly comparable usages, consists of six passages, comprising two elsewhere in Pindar, two in Aeschylus, one in Anacreon and one in Euripides, such evidence is far less conclusive of normality than evidence consisting of only three passages, one in Anacreon, one in Herodotus, one in Theophrastus.

1 I am aware of problems involved in defining, on a theoretical level, such a 'language state'. But we all effectively recognize a current state of our own language; that is, we all feel ourselves equipped to recognize deviations from it, including metaphorical deviations. And the existence of language states depends on the ability of the users of language to recognize them, not on the ability of current theory to define them. The phrase 'normal usage', again, is problematic. 'Normal' must be interpreted to mean 'relevantly and availably normal'. I do not mean: 'there is only one sort of normal usage'. I mean: 'there are as many sorts of normal usage as there are – but metaphor, qua metaphor, cannot be referred to any one of them. If it can, it is not what I would call metaphor.' If Yeats uses a 'dead metaphor' which happens to be in its secondary sense an esoteric astrological expression, this is 'normal' in at least one relevant sense, as belonging to the normal linguistic apparatus of astrology, an apparatus presupposed and available to readers of the poem in question. Again, a locution abnormal in poetry may be normal in prose, or vice versa; or normal in one dialect or social level or profession, abnormal in others. All these are 'availably normal'.

2 Consuetudinem sermonis vocabo consensum eruditorum, Quintil.1.6.45.

3 Wittingly at least (cf. Hulme 40). But in any event, is the literate norm likely to differ much from the colloquial in relevant ways? As Wyld wrote (pp.16f.): 'the characteristic features of the colloquial vocabulary of received standard at any given time consist rather in what is omitted than in what actually occurs'.

4 Ullmann *LS* 118.

5 The evidence:Pi.*O*.3.43f., *N*.3.22f., *N*.10.32f., *I*.3/4.29f. For all the scholarly interest in Pindaric biography, I have not seen any such association specifically remarked.

6 LSJ *s.v.* 11.2.

7 But suggests only that poets can miscalculate the effects of their poetry, can lose in part their sense of the social aspect of language which is its central aspect. '"But glory doesn't mean 'a nice knock-down argument'," Alice objected. "When I use a word," Humpty Dumpty said in rather a scornful tone, "it means what I choose it to mean – neither more nor less."' Alice stands correctly with Varro, *LL* 9.6: *ego populi consuetudinis non sum ut dominus, at ille meae est.* And with Wordsworth, *Preface* 268: '. . . those arbitrary connections of feelings and ideas with particular words from which no man can altogether protect him-self. . . . in some instances feelings even of the ludicrous may be given to my readers by expressions which appeared to me tender and pathetic. Such faulty expressions. . .'. Cf. further Horace *AP* 71f., Sextus Empiricus *Adv.Math.*1.178 and see §25 below.

8 Cf. Goheen 126. The point is astonishingly rarely made, despite its importance.

9 Isocrates may be exaggerating here, but the principle is unassailable: cf. the parallel evidence collected below, p. 211. The kind of prose Isocrates has most in mind is naturally oratory, which is closer than most kinds to poetry; and if such a point could be plausibly made of oratorical prose, how much more plausibly of prose in general.

10 Not a new assumption and one that receives its due support from contemporary linguists: cf. e.g. Hockett 563f. I grant that poetry might be expected to exercise more influence on the 'literate standard' than on the ultimate, 'casual' norm; and I am not suggesting that poetry (in eras like the Hellenic) has no influence on the sensibility of the times, an influence necessarily mediated through language. But such influence would tend to be indirect and formal (for a possible example see below, p. 227). Any direct influence would more likely resemble the minor kind mentioned by Varro *LL* 9.17. Even in the case of those poets sometimes regarded as 'makers of their language' (Dante, Chaucer, Shakespeare), direct influence of any relevant kind will still have been marginal. As Wyld says (p.101), 'the makers of Elizabethan English as we know it in the imperishable literature of the period were the men, *illustrious and obscure*, who were also making English history' (my italics), i.e. the *whole* linguistic com-munity. (The rôle played by a Chaucer in helping to establish a *pre-existing* dialect as the standard is another matter; it does not constitute 'influence of any relevant kind'.) Finally, let it not be forgotten that even in fifth-century Athens, with all its unique attentiveness to high culture, the tragedian who was a pre-eminent object of that attention had only one day in the year on which to make

his linguistic innovations publicly, if momentarily, available – let alone accept-able – to his 100,000-odd fellow citizens.

§ 20

Such are my main assumptions. Refinements and implications must now be considered.

'With minor modifications according to genre and dialect' (Assumption 1). In many cases the two sorts were not distinguishable, and in many cases they were entirely superficial; one thinks of the trivial 'dorizing' of epic forms in choral lyric. But in general one would, naturally, wish to parallel usage in one dialect with usage from the same dialect.[1] Fortunately, the bulk of my poetry is overtly or effectively or largely Attic–Ionic and for this one has to hand Homer at one end and a wealth of classical prose, Attic and Ionic, at the other. 'Attic–Ionic', I should emphasize, is more than a formula of convenience here: the lexical divergences between Attic and Ionic must have been highly marginal at all times.[2] Which means that while Ionic verse usages may be documented with particular propriety from Herodotus or Hippo-crates[3] and Aeschylean usages from Thucydides or Lysias, the distinction is not ultimately decisive. Homer, of course, will have equal relevance in either case. Where Lesbian poetry is concerned, the situation may look less favour-able: Lesbian Aeolic seems in many ways to keep itself to itself.[4] However, this isolation largely concerns the phonetic and grammatical aspects of the language, rather than the lexical aspect. In sum, dialect variation is not to be thought of as a major consideration.

The mention of genre usage prompts a note on cliché. To establish cliché status, it may be enough to show that a genre habitually shows the usage. It would often be impossible to produce evidence that would establish 'dead metaphor' in Homer, but one can often establish epic cliché, which amounts to the same thing. Of course, the instance in question need not necessarily come from a poem belonging to that genre in which the usage is a cliché; epic cliché is 'normal usage' for (e.g.) Aeschylus.[5]

'Greek of the period in question' (Assumption 5). The poetry in my corpus and the usages whose status must be reconstructed extend from the seventh to the mid fifth centuries. If it were possible, one would always confine oneself to earlier and contemporary evidence. But it is not possible, there being far more literature extant, and therefore far more evidence available, from the fourth and later fifth centuries, and, in particular, hardly any prose extant before this period. It is, however, prudent to go no later than the fourth; not only because the usage involved would be dangerously further in time from the literature under consideration; also because after the death of Alexander the literary language was artificial in a sense it never had been before. 'Greek ambitions, Greek patriotism and the natural wish not to lose touch with a unique and glorious past led to the breaking of the links which had existed until then between the language of artistic composition and the spoken idiom.'[6] Such an artificial language might sound, indeed, a good guide to past usage. Not so; a metaphor used by a canonical classical author might, in the eyes of his later admirers, have the same classical respectability as a normal usage of the classical period.[7] These factors make the close of the fourth century a natural limit, though in stressing this, I do not mean to suggest that the pre-Hellenistic language was all uniformity, that it was in 400 what it had been in 600. Obviously not, for *consuetudo loquendi est in motu*;[8] but this is no reason for making matters worse by the desperate expedient of appealing to *any* evidence, however late and deceptive.[9]

'Prose evidence... a better guide... than poetic evidence' (Assumption 6). This requires a good deal of qualification. Much classical prose is decidedly poetic itself, earlier prose no less than later. A writer as early as Anaximander is credited with poeticisms by Simplicius,[10] perhaps relevantly, perhaps not; there are ways and ways of being poetic. Heraclitus, as the *Suda* notes, 'often wrote poetically' and that poeticality, one would think, is certainly relevant, as is the kind that Plato developed, employing, as Aristotle said, a kind of language midway between prose and verse;[11] and likewise the almost proverbially poetic mode of expression favoured by, notably among his sophistic contemporaries, Gorgias, which was never altogether rejected in rhetorical circles – and so helped to establish the permanent tendency of Attic oratory to leave room for poetic features or techniques.[12] This last instance is of particular importance. Oratory in general had a heightened flavour and, probably in conformity with this, much direct speech in other literary forms showed a similar tendency, Plato being the most spectacular instance. Some prose evidence, then, is more reliable than other prose evidence: Plato is less reliable than Herodotus before him or Aristotle after him. And similarly, one could add, some poetic evidence is somewhat more symptomatic of normality than other poetic evidence. No one would be likely to dissent from a suggestion that Theognis is, in general, less heightened than Pindar or that tragic iambic is nearer the norm than tragic lyric.

It may happen that only poetic evidence is available. If this is because the word in question is a purely poetic word in any case, certainty is simply less attainable; one will usually have to be content with postulating, at most, poetic cliché. If, however, the limited distribution applies not to the word itself, but only to a particular employment of it, we may have a *prima facie* metaphor, depending, naturally, on the further quality of the distribution.

'Coincidence between later (normal) usage and earlier poetic usage' (Assumption 7). Once again, I do not mean that usage remained unchanged from each century to the next, that what was eventually normal usage always had been normal usage. Nonetheless, closer consideration of this problem serves to suggest that even this extreme position is, for operational purposes, a proper one. Consider the status of a usage first extant in Sappho (*fr.*31.10): χρῷ πῦρ ὑπαδεδρόμηκεν. To my knowledge, the substantial evidence for its normality, admirable in quality, consists of only one passage: Hp.*Fract.* 27, ἔρευθος...ὑποτρέχει.[13] Assuming that this is all the evidence, there are three possibilities:

(1) Both authors are using live metaphor. This is implausible for the Hippocratic usage, coming as it does from a highly prosaic treatise.

(2) The usage is metaphor in Sappho, 'dead metaphor' in the περὶ ἀγμῶν: there was an intervening semantic change affecting the Greek language. If so, (a) the coincidence may be coincidence in the sense of accident: Sappho has fortuitously anticipated a later development of the language. This possibility can be dismissed as marginal. Or (b) the coincidence may mean direct influence: Sappho[14] coined a metaphor which was disseminated by later poets, became poetic cliché, and ended up in Hippocrates. This too must be a marginal possibility (Assumption 7). Or (c) Sappho used a newish and still live metaphor, one recently coined in the colloquial language, which was only subsequently disseminated, anonymously, by the whole speech community and, again, became current parlance. This is a possibility worth consideration; the situation must occasionally arise. But it still cannot be thought likely in any particular case. One has only to think of the rapidity with which a coined metaphor like the currently fashionable 'escalation' passes into the general stock of normal usage to see why. The time taken for poetic metaphor to become poetic cliché may well be a matter of decades, even centuries: the poetic 'community' is loosely knit; there is no necessary pressure to conform to any new fashion. In the spoken language, the dissemination is effected with ease and the transitional period may be measurable in months, rather than years – whatever allowance one makes for the difference between the massive modern rapidity of communications and the ancient situation.[15] How likely can it be that Sappho's usage dates from such a transitional period, a period of unpredictable duration, but liable to be very brief?[16]

(3) There remains only one possibility: the usage is normal in Sappho's period and in Hippocrates' period – and in the intervening period. The absence of corroborative evidence for this intervening period is taken to be

an accident, ascribable to the scantiness of extant archaic literature. Even in such an extreme case, then, when the direct evidence consists only of one considerably later parallel, I would feel more justified in assuming that Hippocrates, being wholly prosaic, testifies to the normality of Sappho's usage than that Sappho's usage, despite Hippocrates, is live metaphor,[17] although in practice I shall not be allowing anything like so large a margin of error.

'Especially Homeric usage' (Assumption 8). For all later poetry, Homeric usage is effectively a standard in its own right, almost irrespective of its relation to the later norm. Hence, while reusage of a Homeric live metaphor, if any, may have the contemporary flavour of an archaism or, specifically, an epicism, it can rarely have the status of live metaphor.[18] Homeric usage can therefore be used with great confidence for the reconstruction of the poetic norm, expecially as even on the most generous interpretation Homer uses live metaphor (as opposed to cliché) very infrequently.[19]

'The larger the number of different authors...genres' (Assumption 9). A 'spread' of evidence like Archilochus, Solon, Aeschylus would be better evidence for the normality of a usage in (e.g.) Ibycus than one consisting of three (or more) passages in Archilochus alone. And a spread such as Homer, Herodotus, Aeschylus would be wholly adequate to establish normality for any poet in my corpus.

---

1 On the other hand, coincident usage between authors in different dialects would be better evidence for the normality of the usage in Greek as a whole than the same coincidence between authors in a single dialect.

2 One could in any case argue, with these and with other dialectal oppositions, that such variations as are not simply trivial anyway may *all* be 'availably normal' (above, p. 36, n.1) in their own right. 'Och aye', though usually heard only on the lips of Scotsmen, is normal usage, not just for Scottish, but for English too: it belongs to the passive vocabulary of modern English.

3 Also inscriptions, but the extant remains are relatively scanty and, in any case, rarely deal with the relevant kind of topic.

4 Cf. Page *SA* 327 (with references).

5 'Availably normal.' Epic cliché would in any case carry a special weight (Assumption 8). Lyric cliché, if really well established, might also pass as normal for a lyricist or, indeed, for Aeschylus – though this pattern rarely arises. Tragic cliché, however, would in itself mean nothing for earlier lyric and little for Aeschylus; one can seldom, if ever, demonstrate that purely tragic cliché is cliché for Aeschylus when his usages are the earliest in the series. Cf. n.16 below.

6 Bolgar 20.

7 The point is not that use of a given expression by, say, Lucian indicates nothing

about classical Attic usage, but that we have no means of knowing precisely what it indicates beyond the presumed 'Atticness' of the expression, where 'Atticness' refers primarily to choice of words or to choice of forms of words, rather than to use of words. As regards use of words, the situation might in fact be that the expression was commonly so used in classical Attic; or that the usage was so used occasionally *by creative writers*, but not regularly, and was actually metaphorical in classical Attic. Thus with Lucian *Bis.Acc.*33 ἀναβαίνοντα ὑπὲρ τὰ νῶτα τοῦ οὐρανοῦ. The phrase is impeccable Attic. Plato has it (*Phdr.*247c ἐπὶ τῷ τοῦ οὐρανοῦ νώτῳ) and who could be more Attic than Plato? But the usage was, and doubtless still is in Lucian's time, live metaphor. We can only know that a Lucianic usage had been normal in the classical period by independent evidence from that period; and if we have this, we have no need for evidence from Lucian.

8 Varro *LL* 9.17.

9 Cf. Fraenkel 1.59 on Headlam's method. Hulme 271, speaking up for later evidence, wrongly equates its status with that of earlier evidence. She ignores the fact that, whereas a usage has no existence in any sense until its birth, it may exist almost indefinitely, once it *is* born, being available at least as an archaism. Hence (e.g.) Archilochus is a much more relevant source of evidence for establishing the status of a usage in Theognis than *vice versa*.

10 Simp.*in Ph.*24.13.

11 Suid. *s.v.* Ἡράκλειτος and Arist.*fr.*73.

12 Cf. D.H.*Lys.*3.

13 There is also some evidence from cognates: Hp.*Prorrh.*2.40 ἐπὶ τοῦ προσώπου ἐπιτρέχει τι αὐτοῖσι χρῶμα...ὑπέρυθρον, Hp.*Epid.*7.110 τὸ γαγγραινῶδες ἀνέδραμεν ἄχρι πρὸς γόνυ, *Il.*23.717 σμώδιγγες...ἀνέδραμον. Throughout this discussion of ὑπαδεδρόμηκεν, I have left the dialect factor aside; cf. the argument set out above, n.1 and 2, and p. 38.

14 Or a contemporary or earlier poet coined the usage which was used by Sappho while still novel.

15 Although the practical difference can be exaggerated: witness the speed with which sophistic innovations were accepted in Athens towards the end of the fifth century (especially, new formations like those in -ικός, ridiculed by Aristophanes, *Eq.*1375ff.).

16 The above argumentation is basically my own, but on specific points I have followed through the implications of remarks by such linguists as Guiraud 51, Stern 163, Ullmann *PS* 186f. and *Semantics* 195. Note that a retrospective inference about normality (from Hp. I infer retrospectively that Sappho's usage is normal) must, in the light of my argument, be less reliable if the later normality is merely that of cliché, the product of poetic (*vel sim.*) dissemination, rather than the normality resulting from colloquial semantic change. Retrospective inferences are not unprecedented in discussions of this kind: cf. e.g. Hulme 26.

17 See §22(5) (besides n.13 above) for a further reason for the assumption in this instance. It can well be imagined how unsatisfactory I find the kind of discussion represented by Bowra *GLP* 335 on ὑγιής, 'morally sound', in Simonides 37.36.

'This ethical use...is common enough in the second half of the fifth century, but S. is a pioneer in it.' Bowra then cites passages from tragedy (including Aeschylus), Herodotus and Thucydides. In any case the scope of the later distribution is wider than Bowra implies (cf. the Aristophanic references in LSJ *s.v.* II.3), while *Il.*8.524 μῦθος...ὑγιής is hardly irrelevant. And the word itself is not common before Simonides: Sol.1.38 and 1.62, Semon.29.9, *Il. loc. cit.* (Derivative forms, however, occur also at *Lesb.Adesp.*18.1, Anacr.59, Simon.99, the roughly contemporary Heraclit.111 and Thgn.255, the presumably undatable *Carm.Pop.*36 and *Carm.Conv.*7.) Note finally that λόγον...ὑγιᾶ in Hdt.1.8 is evidently taken as normal usage by Dion.Hal. (see below, p. 54, n. 6).

18 Similarly, Stanford *AS* 23.
19 Cf. Milman Parry, *Class.Phil.*28, 1933, 30ff., Stanford *GM* 118ff. See further below, pp. 211f.

§21

It will be gathered, then, that there are certain authors whom, if necessary, I am prepared to 'trust'; authors whose usage I would take as operationally adequate evidence of 'normal' Greek: more-rather-than-less-reliable authors – *reliable*, for short. Such authors are predominantly prose authors and often very prosaic prose authors. They are all classical or pre-classical authors, fourth-century at the latest. And their inclusion in the provisional canon is decided in each case by the application of the principles discussed and, not least, one particular consideration mentioned during the discussion, but not yet treated at any length: explicit ancient testimony to the characteristics of an author's style. Let me say at once that fully relevant testimony of this kind is not overabundant and that where it does exist, it is often problematic in one way or another, although there is hardly ever any conflict between such evidence and *a priori* principles. I shall be discussing the bulk of the material in detail later,[1] but having broached the subject, let me give a single, clear-cut example, Dionysius of Halicarnassus on Lysias. For reasons already given, one would be predisposed against including Attic oratory on one's short list; and Dionysius himself says a good deal to confirm the predisposition in general. On Lysias, however, he is explicit: in extreme contrast to the poeticizing of Gorgias, Lysias adopted a style involving straightforward and ordinary locutions; he is the least likely of writers to use tropical and, specifically, metaphorical expressions.[2] Lysias, then, is an author one can expect, in any given case, not to use metaphor – live metaphor. And by way of indicating the force of that now familiar gloss in the particular context of 'ancient testimony', let me say that as well as being a formidable and formidably well-read scholar and theorist, Dionysius is one who, unlike some of his predecessors (notably Aristotle), is alive to the difference between metaphor and dead metaphor.[3] In other words, this is informed testimony and Lysias, accordingly, is in the canon.

An operational list of 'reliable' authors can therefore be drawn up. The following scheme, with its three main headings, is designed to show the general shape of such a list; it does not purport to be complete.

(1) Fully 'prosaic' prose, i.e. technical or non-literary prose: e.g. prose inscriptions, the Hippocratic corpus, Aristotle, Theophrastus, Aeneas Tacticus.

(2) Homer.

(3) 'Literary' but generally reliable prose: e.g. the bulk of Herodotus, Thucydides, Xenophon, and certain orators, particularly Lysias and Isaeus.

The less trustworthy sources, those excluded from the list, are (a) most verse and (b) most heightened prose – oratory, Presocratic and sophistic prose, Plato. Their rejection is decided on the same criteria, including, as before, the ancient testimony.

There are, needless to say, further qualifications to be made regarding the approved authors. For instance, certain Hippocratic treatises have a pronounced sophistic flavour;[4] as such, they are necessarily less 'reliable'. There are, again, practical queries about the authenticity of particular works: such a query has recently been put against many of the works ascribed to Lysias.[5] But this kind of case presents no material problem, unless the query about authenticity carries with it a serious doubt about dating: one merely has to speak of the Lysias-*corpus* as one does of the Hippocratic corpus.[6] Another point: technical writers, particularly those working at a 'growth-point' of a developing subject, are liable to coin new usages, which may be metaphorical, to express new findings or new concepts. 'Electric *current*', first coined as a live metaphor in such a situation, is a convenient English instance; and though such usages rapidly became normal, the fact remains that a scientific, or other technical, work may contain them on a pre-normal basis. But in practice, once again, no real problem arises: quite apart from the fact that such cases represent, presumably, a tiny fraction of their authors' usages, they are most unlikely to concern us, simply because the areas of experience in question are hardly of a kind that the poets in my corpus deal with.[7]

A more substantial qualification is called for vis-à-vis the approved instances of literary prose. Returning for a moment to a topic already discussed, one must make it clear that the inclusion of, for instance, Herodotus in this category is irrespective of the degree to which Herodotus is, in other *separable* ways, poetic. I would not wish to suggest that Herodotus is never in any sense poetic, but that the question of Herodotean poeticisms presents no material problems.[8] It is coincident usage between Herodotus and Homer that is most often invoked in this connection: but from any such coincidence, when the usage is not extant in Attic comedy or prose, it is not necessary to infer that Herodotus is poeticizing à la Homer; one might well infer that, if Herodotus uses it, the Homeric expression itself is not 'poetical' as such but standard Ionic.[9] But even if Herodotus could be shown to be borrowing specifically Homeric usage, this would serve only to indicate a preference for one kind of standard usage, the Homeric, over another. It would not indicate, and I doubt if there is any evidence to indicate, that Herodotus' poeticisms are those of a Pindaric or Aeschylean kind. It at once suggests a proviso to any assumption that Herodotean usage is in no sense heightened usage,[10] but it does not suggest that Herodotus uses live metaphor as poets do.

In any case, in practice I shall place my trust, not in individual authors, but in particular combinations, particular kinds of 'spread'. Most of the kinds in question can be illustrated from examples already discussed. Thus, the spread Herodotus – Hippocrates – early epic – Phocylides – Euripides – Demades is an eminently trustworthy basis for taking κακά ἐπέρχεται to be normal usage for the time of Aeschylus:[11] his own genre shows the usage, as does (more importantly) good, near-contemporary prose (both literary and technical) and likewise, for good measure, epic, archaic lyric and oratory. The same applies to the various spreads supporting ἐπέρχεσθαι of flowing water (inter alia, Herodotus, Hippocrates, Pindar, tragedy);[12] βένθεα of waters in Stesichorus (Homer, Hesiod, other early epic);[13] ὀξύς of sharp sounds (e.g. Homer, lyric, comedy, Hippocrates);[14] and ἐπιρρεῖν of advancing bodies of men (e.g. Homer, Herodotus).[15] One other kind, not yet exemplified, involves a suspect verse spread 'redeemed' by Homer. An example due to arise in Part II concerns the word or element ἄμπυξ of horses' trappings, so used only by Pindar, Aeschylus and Euripides, except for the author of the Iliad, four times.[16] Whatever the particular tone or flavour of these usages, they are all clearly normal usages according to my principles, and the patterns of distribution that they represent are those to which I shall repeatedly be appealing; the presence of Homeric epic and/or reliable prose is always the chief consideration.

The chronological criterion must be taken into account in each case. The fact that it is a fifth-century distribution that supports the intrinsic normality of Aeschylus' collocation κλύδων...ἐπέλθῃ presents no problems. Had it been Archilochus, for instance, whose usage was being considered, such a spread would be less cogent, although I would still have little doubt, for reasons already given. I shall not in practice rely on a 'spread' like that consisting of a single Hippocratic usage to infer the normality of an expression – and a significantly earlier expression – in Sappho, even though the balance of probability would still be on my side.[17] I am not claiming an ideally perfect solution, but one that is operationally adequate and adequately rigorous.[18] The available alternatives would seem to be total silence or else the naïve procedures familiar to anyone who has worked closely with commentaries or treatises on imagery, whereby 'dead' and live metaphor and cliché are simply lumped together as 'imagery', or else distinguished by *ad hoc* divination without discussion of implicit assumptions and without serious attention to what would constitute evidence for normality or abnormality.

As to live metaphor, the suggestive distribution patterns will be those altogether lacking in any 'trustworthy' element: no reliable prose, no Homer, sporadic or very selective spread. Hence, θάλασσα of adversity, occurring only once and that once in Aeschylus,[19] is live metaphor. So is ζυγόν ('bridge'), once in Aeschylus, once in an oracle;[20] and similarly ῥεῖν of 'men advancing' (only Aeschylus and Euripides),[21] and κορυφή ('excellence'), which is frequent but only in Pindar.[22] Or, to take a more complex pattern, κυμαίνειν of 'human passion' has the spread Pindar – tragedy (Aeschylus) – Plato.[23] Such a distribution, a pretty common one, I take to involve live metaphor, probably for Plato, certainly for Pindar and Aeschylus.[24] If the spread had closed with, say, Aeneas the Tactician, it would at once align itself with my Sappho – Hippocrates paradigm. As it is, it opens and closes with poetry (*sic*), and in a purely poetic spread of this type the assumption must be that the earliest recorded instances are, if not the actual origin of the sequence, at least close enough to the origin to avoid any suspicion of cliché. And cliché is the lowest status on the scale one could conceivably credit to κυμαίνειν, even for Plato. Purely poetic usages will never be fully 'dead', unless the word in question is itself purely poetic and the cliché of immemorial age.

1 See Appendix III.
2 D.H. *Vett.Cens.*ix U.-R. See p. 212 below.
3 See below, pp. 51f., 229.
4 See below, p. 84, n.2.
5 By Dover (see below, p. 212).
6 The question of the Hippocratic corpus (and likewise that of the Aristotelian corpus) is dealt with below, p. 84. A separate question from the authenticity of a treatise is the authenticity of its text in the form known to us; and this question is also relevant to the Hippocratic corpus. On the evidence, for instance, of a

papyrus fragment of Hp. *Just.* (*P.Ox.*2547), there is good reason to speak, as the editors of the fragment do, of 'the fluidity of the Hippocratic text in ancient times'. Nonetheless, variations from the *textus receptus* of Hp. known – or unknown – to us pose no real problem, *provided that* the variant features are of roughly equivalent antiquity – which is unfortunately something not likely to be susceptible of proof or disproof in any given case. The fluid text of the Homeric poems provides a parallel instance, although here one could say more confidently that variant forms tend to be equally authentic: i.e. if not 'Homeric', then at least equally 'early epic'.

7 Unlike, say, Empedocles. Cf. below, p. 220.

8 For recent discussion and further references, see Hoffmann–Debrunner 138, Schmid–Stählin 1.2.553, n.3 and 656f., Lesky 328, Leumann 307ff.

9 The idea of Herodotean poeticizing goes back to antiquity (e.g. Demetr. *Eloc.* 112f., cf. Russell on Longin.13.3), but it is not easy to give much weight to it on that account when one realizes that an ancient tradition taught that *all* Ionic was poetic anyway. See e.g. Hermog. *Id.*ii.421 Sp. Ἡρόδοτος...τῇ λέξει ποιητικῇ κέχρηται διόλου and ii.362 ἡ Ἰὰς οὖσα ποιητικὴ φύσει. The Homerisms alleged by modern scholars tend comparably to involve not usage (i.e. *how* words are used), but diction (*which* words are used): so e.g. with Leumann (*loc. cit.* n.8 above). See further below, p. 222.

10 Cf. Dover 10f. The case of Xenophon is similar to that of Herodotus. Whereas Hoffmann–Debrunner (p.145) ascribe poeticisms to him, Gautier (p.85) suggests that 'la grande majorité des expressions poétiques qui se trouvent dans X. sont aussi dialectales'.

11 See above, p. 22 with n.3. Here and elsewhere the evidence given is not necessarily the whole of the evidence available. In this instance one could mention also (e.g.) Sol.1.30, Thgn.445, A.*Prom.*98.

12 Above, p. 22 with n.4.

13 Above, p. 24 with n.3. This usage, one presumes, has nothing to do with 'dead metaphor', but it is not only that kind of normal usage that needs to be reconstructed. All kinds must be.

14 Above, p. 29 with n.2.

15 Above, p. 30 with n.9.

16 Below, p. 49 with n.11.

17 In such an extreme case Hp. would play the part of Housman's 'best manuscript': 'in thus committing ourselves to the guidance of the best MS we cherish no hope that it will always lead us right...but we know that any other MS would lead us wrong still oftener'. (Housman, 1905 preface, xv.)

18 I am not suggesting that Greek can be restored as a living language. Still, with caution and selectivity in reconstruction and after a decent interval for the assimilation of the knowledge so obtained, one can get surprisingly close to the impression of the living language. But 'living and partly living': one can feel the pulse, but only like the doctor; not, like the patient, from the inside.

19 Above, p. 30.

20 Above, p. 30 with n.8.

21 Above, p. 30 with n.11.
22 Above, p. 35 with n.6.
23 See LSJ *s.v.* 1.2.
24 The frequency with which Plato is associated with such 'unreliable' poets in these spreads, combined with a lack of any consistent and analogous association of other single prose authors with such poets, suggests that Plato uses live metaphor on a quite untypical scale. (For a few other examples see LSJ *s.vv.* κῦμα 1.2.b, λάμπω 1.3, ὀρφανός 11.3, πατήρ IV, πηγή 1.2, τρέφω A.11.6, ὑφαίνω III.1, φλέγω A.1.3 and cf. δρέπω, discussed below, p. 199, n.13.) It also, reversely, confirms one's faith in the indicative value of spreads, as does the notable *in*frequency of instances on the Sappho/Hippocrates model (i.e. isolated reliable prose plus isolated unreliable verse).

§22

Some further points concerning distributional evidence may conveniently be summarized here:

(1) Evidence from derivatives (e.g. ἀμπυκτήριον for ἄμπυξ) is better than evidence from cognates (e.g. ζευγνύναι for ζυγόν), especially if the derivative is uncommon and hence less likely to have developed significantly independent senses.[1]

(2) Compounds may legitimately allude to the senses of their elements but not, on the whole, *vice versa*. ἐπιρρεῖν might allude to any normal use of ῥεῖν, although lacking in the use itself, but not ῥεῖν to ἐπιρρεῖν.[2] The principle is that of 'etymological' reinterpretation.

(3) Within the range of compounds, some types are less untrustworthy than others. Preposition–verb compounds are perhaps the worst, being most likely to develop differently from the original verbal element. But a compound like χρυσάμπυξ may be plausibly enough evoked for ἄμπυξ; and ἀνάμπυξ, if it occurred in Classical Greek, still more plausibly.[3]

(4) In Homer the prepositional prefix is comparatively separable from its verb. Hence Homer's κατεπᾶλτο, of a goddess as bird of prey, is better evidence for the normality of πάλλοντ' αἰετοί in Pindar[4] than any identical but non-Homeric employment[5] of the compound verb would be, quite apart from the special status of Homeric usage in itself.

(5) When considering the criterion of quantity, one may have to note the relative frequency of the usage to that of the word in any sense. If the word is itself uncommon, one would more confidently infer the normality of a particular use of that word which rests on comparatively few items of evidence.[6]

(6) Some topics figure more frequently in Greek literature than do others.

It may be important to note that the *res* behind a particular *signum* is rarely alluded to, not merely through this *signum* but through any *signum*. Plato Comicus and Aeschines Socraticus might not by themselves be able to provide compelling evidence for the normality of a usage even of their own century, but when the usage happens to be γλῶσσα, in the sense 'shoe-latchet',[7] one may reasonably pronounce this evidence adequate. Similarly with Sappho's ὑπαδεδρόμηκεν: descriptions of what flushes do are not so common in earlier literature.[8]

(7) Dialect variants like ἰθύς/εὐθύς may in general be counted not as cognates but as 'the same' word.

(8) Neutral terms are evidence for the normality of their two senses. Thus ἐπέλθῃ in ὅταν κλύδων κακῶν ἐπέλθῃ is evidence for κλύδων ἐπέρχεται and for κακὰ ἐπέρχεται,[9] and may be used to support other instances of either use.

(9) With usages which are found in Homer, but only once, and have a subsequent distribution both limited and inherently suspect, the probability is that the usage was and remained live metaphor. Thus σπέρμα, of a spark, occurs only once in Homer (in the celebrated phrase σπέρμα πυρός) and the later spread consists of but two passages in Pindar.[10] These Pindaric passages I take to embody live metaphor. Such a case is to be distinguished from any that involves a word only used in verse anyway. The kind of spread suggestive of normal usage here has already been exemplified by ἄμπυξ (as a word or word-element) of a horse's headband: Homer (*Iliad*, four instances), Pindar, Aeschylus, Euripides.[11] In the latter kind of case a Homeric presence is almost essential.

(10) Longevity. The old are more resistant to linguistic innovation than the young;[12] their mode of expression is already formed; their usage, accordingly, tends to be that of the previous generation. Hence a usage employed by an author in 350 B.C. is more likely to have been current in 450 if the author was born in 420 than if he was born in 380. The same consideration serves to give greater value than would otherwise be the case to, for instance, Theophrastus' usage. Thus, his *Characters* is thought to have been written in or around 319,[13] a late date for present purposes; but as he was then in his fifties, this, like other works of his, can plausibly claim to reflect the usage of a pre-Hellenistic generation.

(11) Hesiodic usage in general may not be far behind Homeric for reliability; but isolated Hesiodisms, especially if from the *Scutum*, are certainly less trustworthy than isolated Homerisms, as lacking the special authority of Homeric usage. The earliest Homeric hymns rank roughly with Hesiod. Although for a long time after their composition they counted as Homeric

without qualification, they are later than 'Homer' and their prestige was certainly less.[14]

(12) It is difficult to pronounce generally on the value of Aristophanic and other comic usage. Aristophanic lyrics are presumably no better and no worse as evidence for normality than any other samples of fifth-century lyric poetry. But usage in the less heightened parts of comedy, if fairly frequent, may by itself indicate the 'ordinary' Attic norm,[15] in certain special circumstances, as with vulgarisms or proverbs ((14) below).

(13) Evidence for normality from fourth-century prose is more compelling when the word in question is not found before the fifth century.

(14) Normal usage may consist of proverbial expression, and apparent proverbs may not need the usual qualitative spread. They may well figure less in the more reliable sources, and more in such sources as comedy, Plato, and, of course, the late proverbial compilations.[16]

(15) Distributional criteria can establish the 'deadness' not only of 'dead metaphors' but of stock similes and comparisons. One thinks at once of the English 'good as gold' and 'plain as a pikestaff'. Similarly, Pindar's πυκνό-τατον παλάμαις ὡς θεόν is pure cliché and not to be accounted an image.[17] Again, the Homeric 'simile' πατὴρ ὡς ἤπιος ἦεν is part of the evidence for the normality of the 'metaphor' in Pindar's ξείνοις δὲ θαυμαστὸς πατήρ.[18] It would be wrong to think that ὡς (vel sim.) necessarily testifies to liveness, and wrong to separate in any rigid way stock similes and comparisons from other kinds of normal usage.

1 Not a new principle. 'Zipf was no doubt on the right track when he discerned a correlation between word frequency and diversity of meanings.' (Ullmann LS 6f.) The references are to n.11 below and p. 30.

2 See above, p. 30. It is, however, true that under certain very restricted conditions (viz repetition) the simple verb can stand for a compound, as at Pl.R.370e one has the sequence προσδεήσει...δεήσει, with the latter equivalent to the former. For a discussion of this apparently very ancient phenomenon and further examples, see Kühner–Gerth II.2.568; C. Watkins HSCP 71, 1966, 115ff.; R. Renehan, Greek Textual Criticism, Harvard, 1969, 77ff. Contrast the supposed 'tendency of poetical language to use simple verbs in place of compounds' (Fraenkel on Ag.1055f.) without any restriction. Such a tendency cannot deprive a particular novel usage (of a simple verb) of its novelty; it only makes it a familiar kind of novelty. Even here, though, one would grant that in a few cases of apparent and regular semantic equivalence between simple and compound verb (cases where, characteristically, the compounded verb is little used in verse – or indeed, for metrical reasons, is hardly usable in verse), the prosaic compound may be fairly adduced to support its poetic equivalent. Thus with ἐπικαθῆσθαι/ἐφῆσθαι and ἀπόλλυσθαι/ὄλλυσθαι below, pp. 89f., 92f.

3 See below, p. 202, n.9.

4 *Il.*19.351 and Pi.*N.*5.21.

5 Such as the similar κατεπᾶλτο at Stesich.32.1.4 (cf. also S.*fr.*581.4 and E.*Or.*
322); the reference is missing from Fatouros and the *index verborum* to Page's
PMG, but is duly noted in the new LSJ *Supplement.*

6 Cf. above, p. 43, n.17.

7 See LSJ *s.v.* III.2.

8 See above, §20. Note that Hippocratic flushes, if the subject of their sentence,
often have no verb (e.g. *Epid.*7.84 γνάθων ἀμφοτέρων ἔρευθος, a complete
sentence) or else the least specific (e.g. *Coac.*605 ἐπὶ προσώπου γενόμενα
ἐρυθήματα, *Epid.*5.50 ἔρευθος ἀμφὶ τὸ πρόσωπον ἦν).

9 See above, §12.

10 *Od.*5.490; Pi.*O.*7.48 and *P.*3.37. In Pl.*Tim.*56b πυρὸς στοιχεῖον καὶ σπέρμα, the
sense is different. Even from cognates and derivatives, only *Trag.Adesp.*85
σπείρων θεοκτίσταν φλόγα is at all comparable.

11 *Il.*5.358, 363, 720 and 8.382; Pi.*O.*5.7 and 13.65; A.*Supp.*431; E.*Alc.*428 and
*Supp.*586, 680; cf. also A.*Th.*461 (ἀμπυκτήρ) and S.*OC* 1069 (ἀμπυκτήριον).

12 Cf. e.g. Varro *LL* 6.59 and Ar.*Eq.*1375ff.

13 See Regenbogen, *RE Supp.*7, 1510.

14 On these points see e.g. Allen–Halliday lxiv–lxxi, cix, lxxviii ff. As regards the
prestige, 'extant literature shows little or no trace of imitation of the hymn'
(*ibid.*109 on *h.Cer.*) is a typical verdict.

15 Cf. Taillardat 11ff.

16 And how does one identify a proverb? The main characteristic to look for is
abnormally stereotyped phraseology, in the way that πρὸς κέντρον/κέντρα
λακτίζειν is a stereotyped phrase.

17 Pi.*O.*13.52. Cf. θεόφιν μήστωρ ἀτάλαντος *Il.*7.366, 14.318, 17.477, *Od.*3.110,
409; θεομήστωρ A.*Pe.*654; θεοῖς ἐναλίγκια μήδε' ἔχοντα *Od.*13.89; νόεσκε γὰρ
ἶσα θεῇσι Hes.*fr.*43a.72; οἶσθα καὶ αὐτὸς ὁμῶς μακάρεσσι θεοῖσιν Hes.(?)*P.Ox.*
2509.5; θεῶν δὲ προμηθείην αἰὲν ἔχειν Xenoph.1.24; αὐτὸν ὥσπερ θεὸν ἐθαυμά-
ζομεν ἐπὶ σοφίᾳ Pl.*Tht.*161c. The phraseology of the whole is not stereotyped,
one notes. This is a cliché but not a proverb; cf. n.16 above.

18 Pi.*P.*3.71; *Od.*2.47, 234, 5.12, 15.152; *Il.*24.770. Among the rest of the evidence
is Hdt.1.155.2 Λυδῶν...πλέον τι ἢ πατέρα ἐόντα σέ and 5.923.1; X.*Cyr.*8.1.44
πατέρα ἐκάλουν ὅτι ἐπεμέλετο αὐτῶν and 8.2.9, *An.*7.6.38; A.*Ch.*240; E.*fr.*72.2.

§23

Finally mention must be made of certain other possible means of distinguishing normal and abnormal usage. The first is explicit ancient comment on
the status of a particular expression. For my period such comment is not often
available. When it is, its usefulness may be considerable, not merely for
establishing the status of the given usage, but for confirming general
assumptions about distribution and the trustworthiness of given authors.

A good example is provided by Aristotle's discussion of Aeschylus' words: φαγέδαινα...σάρκας ἐσθίει ποδός.[1] Aristotle describes the verb ἐσθίει as κύριον and εἰωθός, i.e. standard usage,[2] thus corroborating the inference one would have made in any case from such passages as this, from the Hippocratic corpus: ὅπη ἂν φαγέδαινα ἐνέη ἰσχυρότατά τε...ἐσθίη...[3] On the other hand, theorists and rhetoricians from Aristotle onwards were sadly liable to invoke the word μεταφορά without due qualification when faced with 'dead metaphor'[4] or cliché. So we find the same Aristotle illustrating metaphor with such well-worn expressions as ῥοδοδάκτυλος ἠώς and a later expert doing the same with ὄρεος κορυφή.[5] This tendency creates problems. The wisest policy under the circumstances is, perhaps, to look the other way when antiquity speaks of or cites particular 'metaphors'; but when usage is cited as normal,[6] one can take this as important evidence in its own right.

A much more problematic method of establishing status would involve scrutiny of the precise way the given poet and other authors who employ his given usage do so: without explanation? glossed? qualified with an 'apology'? Any such evidence is intractable, to say the least. Metaphor may be glossed or not. There may be good reasons for offering its novelty and immediacy without qualification, or there may not. One must lodge a particular protest against the belief that an apparently 'unemphatic' employment implies the normality of a usage.[7] Equally serious, expressions other than metaphor may be explained or glossed or 'apologized' for: perhaps because ambiguous; because rare; because of colloquial or pretentious or neologistic or hackneyed or technical or prosaic or poetic tone, or tone alien in some other way; because overstated or misstated; or simply as a mannerism.[8] Such qualifying elements as ὥσπερ and τις are among the formulae sometimes brought up in this connection, the presumption being that these are 'apologizing for' live metaphor.[9] But with these, as with others, one cannot interpret their significance on any *ad hoc* basis without already knowing the status of the usage so qualified. For the range of τις, for instance, includes at least some of the wide diversity summarized above;[10] and likewise ὥσπερ, which may seem less devious, until one recalls merely a single use such as: καὶ ὁ Κυαξάρης...ὅτι ἐκεῖνοι ἦρχον τοῦ λόγου ὥσπερ ὑπεφθόνει.[11] The potentially diverse subtlety of these formulae indicates that evidence based on apparently apologetic or unapologetic tone is of no immediate value.[12]

Last, two ingenious but virtually unusable suggestions made recently by Taillardat.[13] The first involves the Headlam principle of live metaphors as heightened synonyms of normal usage.[14] Each normally used expression and its heightened synonyms are seen as forming a series and if, argues Taillardat, we can reconstruct a given 'série métaphorique', we can take one of its members to be 'la clef de la série' and thus identify it as 'banale'. But such a reconstruction, as Taillardat admits, in itself gives us no means of knowing *which* member of the series is 'banale'; nor – as he omits to mention – can we know *a priori* whether only one member of a series will be 'banale' or more than one. Another objection, which he overlooks likewise, is that the 'key' member need not be in active use, but may be obsolete in the given sense, or indeed may be an extinct word or expression in any sense: the beginning of the 'series' may antedate all records of the language. Again, neither Headlam nor Taillardat – nor anyone? – has explained whether the principle is universal or only common. Does every metaphor belong to a 'series'? If not, how can we know when to look and when to stop looking for the 'key'? And finally, the limits of a 'series' are not susceptible to any kind of precise formulation. To speak of a metaphor belonging to a series is to say that the areas of experience it relates are already related in at least one pre-existing phrase or expression. But how is one to decide what constitutes an area of experience? As far as the reconstruction of normal and abnormal usage is concerned, this approach has nothing to offer.

Taillardat's other suggestion[15] is that clichés used by Aristophanes can sometimes be identified by their use in what might superficially look like mixed metaphor, his assumption being that comedy, or at least comic dialogue, avoids such mixture. This may be an observable tendency, but would need detailed proof (by distributional criteria?), which Taillardat does not attempt to provide;[16] and it does not, on his own admission, apply to more heightened poetry in Aristophanes or elsewhere.[17] For present purposes, then, one would be able to apply the principle only to those cases where a word of dubious status in, say, Pindar occurred also in what could be taken to be a comic poet's mixed metaphor. But these cases must be few enough to make the principle of minor utility, at most; and, even in these few, inferences based on it would seem to be radically unreliable unless supported by adequate distributional evidence. (In particular, how is one to know whether the Aristophanic passages embody cliché and cliché or cliché and metaphor, and, if the latter, which is which?) But if so supported, the inferences would be themselves redundant.

One is forced to the tidy but sombre conclusion that in the present state of knowledge the one kind of evidence consistently reliable and available is distributional evidence.[18] The only other kind currently worth invoking, and the only other kind I shall invoke, is explicit ancient testimony to the normality of a given usage.

1 Arist.*Po.*1458b: A.*fr.*397.

2 Arist.*Po.*1457b.3 λέγω δὲ κύριον. . .ᾧ χρῶνται ἕκαστοι. (κυρίως is opposed to μεταφορᾷ or κατὰ μεταφοράν Id.*Top.*123a.33–6 and elsewhere.) On the philosopher's reasons for using both κύριον and εἰωθός here, see Bywater *ad loc.*

3 Hp.*Ulc.*10. ἐσθίειν thus also at Hp.*Aff.*4, *Aph.*5.22, *Epid.*4.19, *Gland.*12, *Liqu.*6, *Mul.*2.122; Thphr.*Char.*19.3.

4 πάντες γὰρ μεταφοραῖς διαλέγονται, Arist.*Rh.*1404b.22 (cf. *Po.*1459a.13f.).

5 Arist.*Rh.*1405b.19 and Anon.*Trop.*III.228 Spengel. ῥοδ. ἠώς has twenty-seven citations in Ebeling alone. For κορυφή thus, see LSJ *s.v.* I.2 and add e.g. *Od.* 12.74, *h.Cer.*38, Hes.*Th.*62, Thgn.879, Thphr.*Sign.*43. More examples of the theorists' 'metaphors' in Appendix v.

6 One also finds classical authors occasionally, and very helpfully, indicating the normality of their own usage, e.g. Thphr.*HP* 5.2.3 ἐν τοῖς λίθοις. . .τὰ καλούμενα κέντρα ('the so-called *centres* which occur in marbles', Hort), such being (as a rule) specialized or otherwise restricted kinds of 'normal' usage. Examples more directly comparable with Aristotle's ἐσθίει can be found in D.H.*Comp.*3 (where a piece of Herodotus, expressly cited for its literalness – τοῖς κυριωτάτοις ὀνόμασιν – contains such usages as λόγον ὑγιᾶ, cf. p. 43, n.17 above) and Demetr.*Eloc.*86f. The familiar problem of period arises here, inevitably. A rhetorician later than Aristotle might describe as normal a usage not normal in 500, let alone 600. (But recall the implications of my Sappho/Hippocrates paradigm, § 20.) Distinguish also the authority of an Aristotle from the speculations of later lexicographers and the scholiasts. The extraordinary incompetence of much scholiastic activity, product of the ancient grammatical tradition, is too well known to need documentation. Reference may be had to Rutherford, *passim.* 'Not a little in Herodian. . .and his compeers would seem to be guesswork' (Rutherford 76, cf. 392). (And as Taillardat notes, p.16, the grammatical tradition was concerned primarily with interpretation of usage, less with its tone, and hardly at all with its originality.) A good instance of the lexicographers' comparably unhelpful methods is noted by Denniston–Page on *Ag.*692.

7 Even so experienced a scholar as Fraenkel seems at times to make this assumption. So on *Ag.*786 we find that a Platonic usage, supposedly 'dead metaphor' (which Fraenkel, as elsewhere, calls simply 'metaphor', while metaphor itself he calls 'imagery'), is identified as such by some instant and unexplained criterion presumably of this sort. The more general principle which is often hard to dissociate from this assumption, *viz* that one can divine from a passage the 'meaning' of a problematic constituent of it, is dangerously equivocal. The most one can do by this means is indicate the present reference of the constituent. One cannot thereby know whether it *normally* has this reference (cf. Dornseiff 45f.). These remarks are not to be thought of as antagonistic to the stress rightly laid by e.g. J. H. Kells, *BICS* x, 1963, 47–9, on context as a determinant of the exact sense of otherwise indeterminate phraseology. Linguists tend to blur the issue with their ill-formulated 'datum that we can know the meaning of a word only after we have understood the sentence in which it is contained' (Hulme 289f.).

8 On the almost limitless uses of 'apologies', cf. Quintil.8.3.36f.

9 Ultimately, no doubt, on the strength of the peculiar emphasis in remarks like those Longinus makes, 32.3, on the provenance of which see Schenkeveld 93f.

10 τις no doubt qualifies live metaphor sometimes. But how is one to know when? Consider the problems raised by a passage such as A.*Prom.*567, where Io cries out,

χρίει τις αὖ με τὰν τάλαιναν οἶστρος.

Rose comments: 'as τις shows, Io is not tormented by a literal gadfly, but rather by recurrent fits of madness'. But οἶστρος of 'madness' is at the very least a cliché – witness the distribution in LSJ *s.v.* II.1, 2, where I see no particular reason to separate off the closely related sense of 'mad passion' as represented by Simon.36.10 (absent from LSJ but in the new *Supplement*) and Hdt.2.93.1. If the implication is that τις may 'apologize for' cliché, this sort of evidence is worse than useless. Murray, one notes, evades the problem by reading not τις but τίς (with interrogation). Instances of τις 'softening', but softening expressions that have obviously nothing to do with metaphor, are perfectly familiar. See e.g. the variety of items in Pearson's index, III.269; and N.B. *inter alia*, the kind of use represented by Hdt.3.14.11, αὐτῷ τε Καμβύσῃ ἐσελθεῖν οἰκτόν τινα. (Cf. the parallel discussion of ὥσπερ, Appendix VI.)

11 X.*Cyr.*4.1.13. See Appendix VI.

12 It would, however, be wrong to discount such evidence absolutely. Possibly a sufficiently rigorous methodology could be developed, leading to the formulation of general principles on the basis of instances whose status was already clear from distributional evidence; then to the critical application of these principles to instances whose status was not clear thus. But as things stand, I have thought it best to ignore any such evidence and its possible implications. Note in passing that these markers are related to, or in fact the same as, the markers that formally announce a simile. (Cf. Russell on Longin.32.3. It is sometimes very hard to distinguish the two kinds; see A.*Th.*758 and Ole Smith's comments thereon, p.22.) It might have been supposed that usage in simile form implies that the contents of the vehicle would be live metaphor if used outside that form. In that event, usages of uncertain status might be shown to be live metaphor by a like usage, especially a later one, in simile form. Hopes based on such a supposition are speedily dissipated when one recalls a point already made: simile may itself consist of cliché. Further, a simile vehicle may include neutral terms, i.e. words which would be normal usage, not metaphor, if used outside a simile; or indeed it may include 'intrusive' tenor terms.

13 Taillardat, one of the few to discuss these matters in any detail (pp.8, 15–24), has little to say on distributional criteria, and the little is wholly inadequate. An 'image usuelle' is one frequently used in ancient texts (p.16). But *how* frequent and *which* texts are questions he does not attempt to answer. The qualitative criterion is ignored entirely in this connection, although there is a parallel discussion (p.14) of the quality of evidence needed to establish the tone or social register of Aristophanic usage. Many of his discussions are marred by his

55

consequent lack of any reliable means of distinguishing the normal from the live metaphorical; for he, unlike most, does try to distinguish.

14 Taillardat 16f. See above, p. 32, for the principle.

15 Taillardat 19f. The remainder of his discussion produces nothing requiring further consideration here.

16 I cannot see why it is inherently plausible that comic dialogue should never contain 'unemphatic' mixed metaphor, despite Taillardat's remarks about comic sensitivity to the 'force évocatrice des images'. Cf. Dover's review-comment (on Taillardat 20, n.1), *CR* 82, 1968, 157.

17 Taillardat 19 with n.2.

18 For one last conceivably relevant line of thought, aiming to identify metaphor rather than normal usage, see Appendix VII.

3 Aesthetics

§ 24

What is the aesthetic status of these interactions? I am tempted to answer: that *is* it, aesthetic. The answer to a further question, '*whose* aesthetic?', is implicit in my opening argument. The aesthetic must be dynamic, representing 'not a having and a resting, but a growing and a becoming', as Matthew Arnold phrased the human ideal. It must accord with newly recognized possibilities of literature – of any literature – and equally with those long recognized. Above all, if it hopes to illuminate the particular literature in hand, it must be supported by that literature, must not supplant it.

Hence the dilemma posed by one eminent scholar seems to me a false one: 'do we rightly continue to read ancient poetry . . . on the basis of the ancient literary tradition? If we do, can we hope to respond to ancient poetry with personal vigour and subtlety? But if we do not, and approach ancient poetry with our, that is, modern, assumptions, do we not introduce a strange and unrelated note into the Graeco-Roman poetic world?'[1] False, because it is not the distinction between ancient and modern 'assumptions' that matters, but that between better and worse; and the better 'assumptions' are those that better suit the literature in hand, those that can provide a fuller and finer account both of its uniqueness and of its typicality. 'Assumptions' is, therefore, clearly the wrong word. It suggests a procedure of some inflexibility whereby, at most, the best available preconceived ideas are conscientiously imported from outside. But the goal cannot be reached by preconception and importation, although these must be to an extent unavoidable *en route*, but by the formation or reformation of ideas on the basis of any literature, or all literature, and, in particular, those works of literature of which the ideas purport to be taking immediate account.[2] The ancestry of the particular coloration that informs these ideas is by the way. We must start from somewhere: nothing can come of nothing. The 'fuller and finer account' which I have invoked is presumably what the original, ancient stylistic apparatus did, in the first instance, aspire to. The subsequent fossilization of the apparatus is not to later antiquity's credit and is certainly not a mark of the perfection of the apparatus.

But, in any case, for my period there are virtually no contemporary 'ancient assumptions' extant. And if, from misguided modesty, we were to import the 'best available' assumptions or preconceptions, why should we choose, say, Aristotle's, or Quintilian's? – unless we think these *are* the best, which would need a good deal of demonstrating. Naturally we must take account of any relevant *information* which an Aristotle or a Quintilian would have, or could have, possessed: conventions, allusions and so on. But our obligation here is independent of any reasons there might be for choosing an ancient theorist as a dogmatic guide. In practice, of course, most classicists of recent generations have not chosen thus: their Aristotle and their Quintilian have been cross-bred with various strains of modern Romanticism.[3] Although they may still not have chosen the available best, they have been, within the terms of this limited approach, justifiably eclectic: the ancients had no monopoly of plausible assumptions.

But over and above all this, there are not simply 'modern' assumptions. Croce, for instance, and some of the American New Critics – a tag itself concealing a diversity of individual orientations – are worlds apart; and one might well judge the Americans, in general, closer to Aristotle than to Croce.[4] And the ancient apparatus, along with all the attitudes and preconceptions it embodies, is itself far from monolithic; even Aristotle and Quintilian are not identical twins. Once we start to take the factor of choice at all seriously, even if we merely say, '*which* modern or *which* ancient assumptions shall we have?', a simple dichotomy between 'theirs' and 'ours' is seen as the untenable oversimplification that it is.[5]

---

1 Brink 3. It is only fair to add that his dilemma is more a starting-point for discussion than a bleak conclusion; and that his actual conclusion (involving 'questioning our assumptions as well as theirs', p.19) is not so far from what I would have wanted to say, if I *had* to adopt that starting-point. But it is also fair to say that in other hands than Professor Brink's the same starting-point can and does provide the basis for far less acceptable positions, especially defeatist pseudo-traditionalism ('well, at least we're not introducing a strange and unrelated note into the Greco-Roman poetic world'). Such positions can only be properly challenged by undermining their terms of reference.

2 In particular, one should never succumb to such argumentation as: 'your interpretation must be suspect. That sort of thing is uncharacteristic of this work/author/period/genre/literature.' The general tendency may be so; the interpretation may indeed be a misinterpretation; and an appeal to the typical may well serve, conveniently, to prompt reconsideration. But no 'argument from consistency' can *demonstrate* misinterpretation or, equally, justify a better interpretation. The *locus* is the datum; it is whatever it is, which is not necessarily the same as whatever one might suppose it ought to be; and it is not general tendencies, but the context within which the *locus* operates and the language as a

whole through which it operates, the *aesthetic* determinants, that must be the basis for any such demonstration or justification.

3 Cf. Quinn's comments, pp.5–7.

4 Cf. Abrams 26ff.

5 The situation is certainly more complicated if one is dealing, as Brink is, with the poetry of a poet-critic: in his case, Horace. One might then keep the Horatian terms of reference in mind throughout – but critically and without ever *assuming* that these terms can account for Horatian poetry, wholly or partly.

§ 25

Prescience can have no influence on the object foreknown,
inasmuch as it is only an intransitive action.

(John Milton, *Christian Doctrine*)

Closely related to these issues is the question of the author's intention and its relevance to the study and criticism of literature. The 'intentionalist' position is, to speak generally, that unless one knows or reconstructs the intention, one may misread the effect; or, in more extreme form, that the intention itself, and not the effect, is what one should really be concerned with. The latter proposition seems arbitrary and Platonically grotesque; above communication with and through the literary work is elevated quasi-mystical communion with an 'Idea'. At all events, legitimately or not, I *am* here concerned with effects, and it is the less peremptory proposition, referring to possible misreading, that needs closer consideration. The radical and inescapable weakness of this proposition relates, in fact, to a possible implication of the other: the effect and the intention may not correspond; and this is simply because the effect is not dependent on the intention in the sense that 'misreading' implies, the aesthetic sense.

It does not, however, follow that the intention, if known or knowable, is beneath consideration. It is not worth disputing that all poets at all times have had intentions; that most poets at most times were tolerably well aware of what they were doing at least in some sense, at least some of the time; that we know it is possible to feel what we think of as the creative personality in and through the creative work; that, felt or not, this personality, however 'impersonal', must always be there. And clearly there is some relation between this 'personality' and the 'intention'. If critical theory wished to expel intention as a consideration entirely, it would probably be obliged to expel personality with it; and if it did that, it must be prepared possibly to deny the reader's experience, certainly to ignore an entire aspect of literature.

But to grant this does not answer the crucial question of propriety: when is it in order to invoke the intention? The general answer is that there is no general answer. If, to take a clear-cut instance, one were to study the relation between Horatian canons of criticism and Horatian poetry, something would be seriously wrong if one did not comply at any point, formally or informally, with the injunction of Goethe's definitive statement of intentionalist procedure: 'Productive criticism...asks: what did the author set out to do? Is this plan reasonable and sensible? And how far did he succeed in carrying it out?'[1] But for an enterprise of the present kind it is not at all an obvious course, since it is not apparent or plausible that intended stylistic effects, supposing we can identify them, have any greater interest or 'validity' than others, unless one expressly wishes to contrast the two for some ulterior purpose. Further, the present enquiry deals with a period of literary history for which such a contrast would be most unilluminating. Although it might be right in any given case to ascribe to a poet of my period an awareness of the stylistic effect he was producing, it would never be plausible to credit him with even the ability, let alone the interest, to analyse his effects, before, during, or after composition, in any articulate way. The analytic habit of the relevant kind simply did not exist: *ante enim carmen ortum quam observatio carminis.*[2] To say this is not to depreciate the poetic activity. *Pace* Plato, it is not the poet's business to be articulate *about* his poetry;[3] his articulacy *is* his poetry.

In short, it is of no concern to me whether, or in what sense, or to what degree, an interaction is the product of intention or accident (unless 'accidental' means 'imperceptible' or 'contrary to the rules of the language') or, as it doubtless often will be, instinct. 'Even where the artist acts instinctively,' notes Grube (truistically, one would have hoped), 'the critic must still explain the nature of his success.'[4] To return to the prime objection to intentionalism, aesthetic effects are not determined by the intention (etc.) except in a historical sense; and unless one wishes or needs to take the history of the compositional process into account, there is no pressing reason to invoke this determinant at all, unless merely as a metonymic *façon de parler.* The aesthetic and presently relevant determinants are, as already remarked, the immediate context and the language as a whole: the relation of the words in question to the words that give them their local significance and their relation to the language-system presupposed[5] that gives them a signification of a more general kind. One is not, in so rejecting the omnipurpose relevance of the intention, committed to the dogma that a literary work is 'self-contained' in such a way that no historical knowledge is required for its interpretation; historical knowledge is always required, if only of the language.[6] Nor to the notion that anachronistic interpretation is acceptable;

any interpretation that goes against the language presupposed is automatically a misreading.

Inasmuch as classical scholarship has edged closer and closer to espousal of formal intentionalism, to acceptance of the universal relevance of the intention, it has submitted more and more to the modern, Romantic, emphasis noted in the previous section. To Galen, in the second century, exegesis is the elucidation of difficulties in the *text*: ἔστι...ἡ ἐξήγησις, ὡς πού τις τῶν παλαιῶν εἶπεν, ἀσαφοῦς ἑρμηνείας ἐξάπλωσις.[7] To Hermann in 1834, exegesis exists to ensure that the reader 'verba *mentemque scriptoris* intelligat'; it must consist 'in aperiendo *consilio scriptoris*'.[8] The shift, though not wholly without precedent, is considerable, representative, and symptomatic. Intentionalism, scholarly or otherwise, cannot claim, 'At any rate, students of literature have always done thus.' Such a claim would in any case be irrelevant to the merits of the case, but it would not even be true. In defining or interpreting or assessing without compulsive reference to the intention, one is, as it happens, doing what critics in most epochs have habitually done. As representative of antiquity, take Demetrius' wholly typical analysis of a famous verse from the *Odyssey*: 'In the elevated style the appropriate hiatus is of long vowels, as in λᾶαν ἄνω ὤθεσκε. The verse has gained length through the hiatus and has enacted (μεμίμηται) the powerful heaving-up of the stone.' So much and no more: not a word about intention.[9] Or consider Aristotle's procedure in discussing Homeric 'unity of action'. He states and assesses Homer's practice, noting: 'this is Homer's achievement, ἤτοι διὰ τέχνην ἢ διὰ φύσιν'. The τέχνη/φύσις allusion is dropped in mechanically, as the peripheral matter that in this connection it is;[10] but even such a mere condescension is perhaps less characteristic of antiquity as a whole than Demetrius' outright silence. When a purposeful contrast between intention and its opposite is made, especially in connection with style, it is commonly still with emphasis on the effect, not on the intention, and an implicit recognition that the former is what matters: *semper haec quae Graeci* ἀντίθετα *nominant...numerum oratorium necessitate ipsa efficiunt, etiam sine industria*.[11] 'This is the effect, even if unintentional', not, as a latter-day intentionalist might say: 'Even if this is the effect, it is unintentional – and hence of secondary interest.'

Critical procedure was not relevantly different by the time of the Renaissance. Rosemond Tuve wrote: 'it is characteristic of the Renaissance that most comments are in terms of what poetry achieves in a reader's mind rather than in terms of what poets feel or do'.[12] As late as the mid eighteenth century, when the new planet περὶ ὕψους swam into the learned Gibbon's ken, a specifically intentionalist procedure was still unknown, we gather:

'Till now, I was acquainted only with two ways of criticizing a beautiful passage: the one, to show, by an exact anatomy of it, the distinct beauties of it, and from whence they sprung; the other, an idle exclamation, or a general encomium, which leaves nothing behind it. Longinus has shown me that there is a third. He tells me his own feelings upon reading it; and tells them with such energy that he communicates them.'[13]

By the beginning of the nineteenth century an alternative way was available. It was without doubt the Romantic orientation towards 'literature as a revelation of personality',[14] in itself an entirely legitimate orientation, that engendered the distinctive, modern, and less appealing overemphasis on the intention.[15]

1 Goethe, *Werke* 37.180, from a review of Manzoni's *Conte di Carmagnola* (1820). The key terms in the German are 'die produktive Kritik', 'sich vorsetzen', and 'Vorsatz'. A virtually identical statement of procedure is to be found in Manzoni's own preface to the play.

2 Quintil.9.4.115.

3 On Plato, see below, p. 234.

4 Grube 222. Or, of course, his failure, as the case may be.

5 And here 'language' is to be interpreted broadly to include, for instance, the 'grammar' of certain kinds of genre convention.

6 Thus we cannot possibly comprehend the effect of e.g. a fifth-century 'Zeus' invocation, unless we know what 'Zeus' means. And this meaning, in the full sense of the word, is only accessible through an understanding of fifth-century religious attitudes.

7 Galen 7.825 (Kühn).

8 Hermann, *De Officio Interpretis*, Opusc.7.100.

9 Demetr.*Eloc*.72 on *Od*.11.596. We may note that Dionysius (*Comp*.20) speculates on historical origins (τέχνη or φύσις) after an analysis of the same passage. But we should note also that he is at pains to emphasize that the 'expressive' effect is 'there' and undeniable: οὐδεὶς ἂν ἄλλως εἴποι. There is no suggestion or implication that any misreading may be in question, nor that the effect would somehow lose status if shown to be unintended. It is simply that Dionysius happens to be concerned with the historical origin as well as the nature of the effect, for his own good reasons. (Whatever is not the product of τέχνη cannot, the rhetoricians assumed, be taught to a prospective orator or writer; and the rhetoricians' function was primarily to teach. Hence it must be decided what can and what cannot be ascribed to τέχνη.)

10 Arist.*Po*.1451a. This respectable procedure is common enough at all times. Modern commentators follow it often, e.g. Dodds on E.*Ba*.792f., Denniston–Page on A.*Ag*.834-7. I am not, however, suggesting that 'intention' and τέχνη are exactly synonymous: see below, p. 233.

11 Cic.*Orat*.166.

12 Tuve 399, cf. *ibid*.231 on Puttenham: 'like all men of this century he is aware

that though "the election is the writers, the judgement is the worlds, as theirs to whom the reading apperteineth"'.

13 Gibbon, *Journal*, 3 October 1762.

14 See the chapter of that name in Abrams 226ff.

15 The explicit reaction against intentionalism has come primarily from the American New Critics. The fullest statement, or rather overstatement, of their position is to be found in Wimsatt 3–18, a remarkable polemic to which, to a certain degree, I am naturally indebted. The connection between intentionalism and Romanticism is assertively indicated *ibid.* 6, but Wimsatt is wrong to bring Longinus in here. Longinus is no more and no less intentionalist than antiquity in general, for all his anticipation of other Romantic attitudes. (Wimsatt seems at times to regard intentionalism as inescapably entailed by Romanticism, rather than merely associated with it and fostered by it.) For some further notes on the curious history of the 'Intentional Fallacy', see Appendix VIII.

§26

To reject intentionalism as a criterion of effective status is not to espouse arbitrariness; there is no necessary link. Arbitrary interpretation of any kind is *ipso facto* at fault, but it is overstatement that the scholar finds particularly objectionable,[1] a kind that may often involve insensitivity to the difference between patent and latent effects.[2] By 'patent', I mean effects whose existence is not in doubt, though their character may be disputed; by 'latent', those whose effective significance is so tenuous or marginal that one resents the impression of solidity that even the mentioning of them produces. Such insensitivity is more common than it should be among American classicists, many of whom have also been influenced by the 'New Criticism' and its well-known hostility to intentionalism. They, perhaps, have given plausibility to the erroneous equation, 'non-intentionalist = arbitrary'.

The kind of overstatement I have in mind can be exemplified by Whitman's 'fires'.[3] Whitman's interpretation of the organic unity of the *Iliad* includes, *inter alia*, an attempt to trace thematic relations among the 'fire' similes and between these and the fires that come in the 'wider tenor', such as the pyres near the beginning and end of the poem. The effectiveness of some connections of this sort is not to be denied out of hand, and certainly not 'on principle', and it may at least be granted that some sort of pervasive intensification arises simply from the collective force of the fire motifs. But Whitman is prepared to see specific connections, equally specific connections, between individual passages irrespective of their individual prominence, or lack of prominence, and even, sometimes, of their distance from one another. The result is that some connections 'work' in context, some only in wholly artificial juxtaposition and isolation.[4]

Since I am not concerned with thematic relations, Whitman's particular kind of overstatement is not available to me. If I have managed to avoid the more general kind of confusion he represents, it is chiefly, perhaps, thanks to a particular characteristic of images in their contexts: *prominence*.

1 I suppose that the modern scholarly preference for intentionalism is due specifically to the belief that the reconstruction of intentions is history (which it is), and that history offers the promise of greater 'certainty'. If this is so, which may be doubted, it still leaves the questions of relevance and propriety unanswered.

2 The distinction is related to that between 'realized' and 'unrealized'. But whereas 'patent' and 'latent' are often reducible to formal terms, the other pair cannot be; see the fine statement by Leavis *EU* 76–8. And 'realization' is inevitably evaluative.

3 Whitman 128–54.

4 If and when such a theme is aesthetically established in its own right, individually faint echoes of it might derive perceptibility therefrom. But Whitman does not adequately show how and where his theme *is* established. And, of course, these connections are ascribed to a poem constructed in formulae, whose own repetition dulls the force of prospective 'significant' repetitions, and ensures that only very arresting possibilities of this sort really stand out.

§27

πολὺ δὲ μέγιστον τὸ μεταφορικόν, wrote Aristotle.[1] Most subsequent critics would agree with him on the special status of metaphor, and of imagery in general,[2] a status which justifies, if anything can, the isolated treatment that imagery so often receives. And most would in one way or another refer this status to the unparalleled creative possibilities which imagery embodies. But there is another characteristic, somewhat prosaic-sounding, without which the special status would be more debatable and an isolated treatment even more exposed to legitimate complaint: prominence. Whitman's fires, we recall, were of very unequal prominence in themselves and the supposedly active interrelations of some were hardly perceptible out of context. In contrast, the vehicle of an image in its immediate context has characteristically a quite abnormal prominence derived from its extraneousness and consequent unpredictability, a prominence which rubs off on to any stylistic elements actively, or interactively, associated with it. It is not 'at issue', not 'in question'; it stands out as terminologically alien. This is what distinguishes it from the contents of a comparison like 'I am better than you' or the ultimately kindred comparison in Pindar's Eighth Isthmian,[3]

γόνον. . .ὃς κεραυνοῦ τε κρέσσον ἄλλο βέλος
διώξει χερὶ τριόδοντός τ᾽ ἀμαιμακέτου,

where the 'vehicle' is in fact the topic of the moment. Thetis, if married to Zeus or Poseidon, would bear a son mightier than, precisely, Zeus (metonymically called 'thunder') or Poseidon (metonymically 'trident').

Metonymy, it may be useful to note, is similarly distinct. Metonymic deviation from the norm, metonymic extraneousness, metonymic prominence are of a lower order altogether. This is not to disparage the possibilities of such transferences; neither extraneousness nor prominence is a virtue in itself.[4] It is merely to note that their status is not that of imagery proper. It involves no depreciation of the force of Pindar's

κλέψεν τε Μήδειαν σὺν αὐτᾷ, τὰν Πελίαο φόνον[5]

to say that 'murder' for 'murderess' brings in nothing 'from outside' in the way that, say, these Aeschylean anvils do:

στεῦται δ' ἱεροῦ Τμώλου πελάτης
ζυγὸν ἀμφιβαλεῖν δούλιον Ἑλλάδι,
Μάρδων, Θάρυβις, λόγχης ἄκμονες,
καὶ ἀκοντισταὶ Μυσοί.[6]

The same goes for those usually more muted instances embodying the metonymic transferred epithet, like the classic

And *drowsy* tinklings lull the distant folds,

where Gray's elegiac sheep are 'really' the drowsy ones. It is pertinent to note that the transferred epithet shows the lack of extraneousness characteristic of all the contiguity tropes in its most extreme form. All the elements are in question; only reorganization is involved. But even an instance like Pindar's 'thunder' and 'trident', representing metonymy's other extreme, does not bring in anything much more extraneous.

The vehicle of an image, then, represents a 'peak of prominence', to borrow a phrase from linguistics; or a point of light in a dark sky (*quasi stellae quaedam, tralata verba*), as the spokesman for an earlier age put it.[7] Here is the reason for my exclusion of metonymy from present consideration; and here is a further reason for the exclusion of 'dead metaphor' and cliché. To restate a point already elaborated, these elements can give us something extraneous, but only as an implication, and the implication must be positively brought out if it is to be effective. We do not, cannot and should not try to call up every implication of every word in a poem: we call up those which present themselves. When Aeschylus in his 'anvil' passage uses the cliché δούλιον ζυγόν for 'slavery',[8] we have no more than an *option* of turning our minds to yokes and anything and everything to do with yokes. But when he writes λόγχης ἄκμονες, we are *compelled* to think of, and through, the 'area' that ἄκμονες calls up; we are given no alternative way of reaching the meaning (anvils stand up to the hammer), even in the crudest sense. Cliché and dead metaphor do not compel an evocation and, correlatively, have no such compulsive prominence.

It is obviously true that even within imagery proper some vehicles have a greater intrinsic prominence than others. Novelty (a live metaphor need not be entirely novel), length, boldness and particularity are among the simple features determining such prominence, and these may vary. But even the short and comparatively subdued stand out: 'ripeness is all'. The very subdued, lacking any real particularity, may not, and, if so, simply forfeit the claim to the title 'image'.[9] It is also true that the prominence of a word is relative; it varies inversely to the prominence of the words that make up its immediate context. But although vehicle terms may occasionally not be the most prominent in the context, their supra-normality in this respect remains characteristic. It is, indeed, partly this characteristic product of extraneousness that justifies the isolating, not of imagery itself, but of the interactions associated with imagery.[10] Some interactions, for instance, embody particular creative possibilities of alliteration, and it will be apparent that these same possibilities may be operative outside any association with imagery; they do not represent a separate kind of alliteration. But alliteration and stylistic elements in general are worth systematic scrutiny only when their usual perceptibility is more than a mere supposition; prominence is perceptibility *par excellence*; and the natural prominence of the vehicle makes effective, in the primary sense of that word, the interactions associated with it.

1 Arist.*Po.*1459a.6.
2 Arist.*Rh.*1406b.20; ἔστι δὲ καὶ ἡ εἰκὼν μεταφορά.
3 Pi.*I*.8.33ff. Cf. A.*Prom.*922ff. and, in general, Svartengren xxii.
4 Nor is prominence in itself a vice. It is not the same as the obtrusiveness that Clemen (p.45) sees as characteristic of Shakespeare's early imagery, whereas 'in later plays it often escapes our attention that images are being employed at all'. This contrast is quite another matter. Such obtrusiveness is the product of artifice, in the bad sense, and mechanical application; whereas the mature imagery is the sort that prompts expressions like 'organic propriety' and 'thinking *through* the image'. Such imagery that is not blatantly imagery is imagery so good, or so finely used, that it seems to have, or to have earned, its prominence by natural right. It has not ceased to be prominent.
5 Pi.*P*.4.250 (where LSJ and others weakly invent a feminine agent noun φονός; see Farnell). Cf. Headlam's well-conceived justification of metonymy, pp.435f.
6 A.*Pe.*49ff.
7 Cic.*Orat.*92. Cf. e.g. Quintil.8.6.4 and Arist.*Rh.*1405a.9f.

8 ζυγόν of slavery: Hdt.7.8γ.3, Thgn.1023, A.*Th*.471, *Com.Adesp*.524 (apparently), Pl.*Lg*.770e, Epigr.*ap*.D.18.289. The equally stock ζυγόν of necessity is obviously very closely related: *h.Cer*.217 (ζυγός), Thgn.1357, Pi.*P*.2.93, A.*Ag*.1071, E.*Or*.1330, X.*Cyr*.3.1.27; cf. the Pythagorean principle ζυγὸν μὴ ὑπερβαίνειν (see Diels–Kranz 1.465, §6) and (?) Arch.54.5 West. In at least one instance (S.*fr*.591.5) the two are in fact combined.

9 Nor again could one ascribe much prominence to 'images' with too much likeness. An example would be φωνήσαις ἅτε μάντις ἀνήρ (Pi.*I*.6.51), where it would be absurd to call μάντις 'brought in from outside'; it is virtually 'true'. Cf. Ullmann *LS* 178f. and see above, p. 5.

10 As extraneousness produces prominence, so it produces other distinctive characteristics of particular relevance to interaction. These include chiefly the need to *seem* 'in question' and not extraneous at all, and the power to allude to what is not 'in question' at the time, but was or will be.

§ 28

The natural prominence just considered is not the only kind of prominence, and it is convenient to discuss at this point a technical matter of wider stylistic relevance but with an important bearing here: *articulation*.

By 'articulation' I mean particular kinds of verbal organization and, in the first instance, certain kinds that produce what one might think of as *secondary* prominence. In particular, there are two of these kinds which need to be distinguished, but tend to be confused.

Secondary prominence can arise from abnormal word order or from prominent word-positioning without such abnormality; and the two may, but need not, coincide. The first kind presents many practical, but no theoretical, problems. That is, the soundness of the dictum 'prominence can arise from abnormal word order' should be distinguished from the practical difficulties involved in deciding what constitutes normal and abnormal word order in a language like Greek, where words have a considerable freedom of mobility in any case. As regards these problems, it can at least be said that the essential status and effect of what we usually think of as the extremer forms of hyperbaton are beyond dispute and, for the purposes of the present study, this is enough. A pair of simple and not particularly extreme examples from G. M. Hopkins:

> Hope had grown grey hairs,
> Hope had mourning on,
> Trenched with tears, carved with cares,
> Hope was twelve hours gone;
> And *frightful* a nightfall folded *rueful* a day...

3-2

The prominence resulting from abnormal word order has a special character, *emphasis*:[1] 'frightful' and 'rueful' are accordingly emphatic. The natural expressive correlate of emphasis is audible stress in reading aloud, at least in a language like English; and 'frightful' and 'rueful' would get such a stress.

Prominent word-positioning, without abnormal word order, involves no emphasis. It consists in the positioning of words in typically prominent stations within the larger unit, especially the syntactic unit, but also, on occasion, the metrical unit: in Dionysius' words,[2] ἐρείδεσθαι...τὰ ὀνόματα ἀσφαλῶς καὶ στάσεις λαμβάνειν ἰσχυράς. Such 'stations' are any that are preceded or followed by a pause,[3] this pause giving time for words so stationed to have a fuller impact, to sink in. And the operative pauses, inevitably, will come at the beginning and end of the unit. As Demetrius says of the κῶλον: 'Anyhow, we all remember in a special degree, and are stirred by, the words that come first and the words that come last, whereas those that come between them have less effect on us, as though they were obscured or hidden among the others.'[4] The principle applies in varying degrees to all units, though one thinks primarily of sentence and clause.[5]

It is such unemphatic prominence that I shall chiefly refer to when speaking of prominence articulation. It was on the strength of its final position that I characterized ἐπέλθη as articulated[6] in ὅταν κλύδων κακῶν ἐπέλθη – the clause ends there. In this sequence the vehicle, κλύδων, has natural prominence, the interactive term, ἐπέλθη, slighter, positional prominence, almost negligible, but not entirely.

Consider A.*Supp*.592ff.:

> αὐτὸς ὁ πατὴρ φυτουργὸς αὐτόχειρ ἄναξ,
> γένους παλαιόφρων μέγας τέκτων,
> τὸ πᾶν μῆχαρ οὔριος Ζεύς.[7]

Here ἄναξ, τέκτων and, above all, Ζεύς are prominently stationed; Ζεύς more so than the other two as being proximate to a weightier pause, sentence final rather than phrase final.[8] In contrast, αὐτός and τὸ πᾶν may have some prominence of this sort, but γένους, despite a similar articulation, has decidedly less. The implication is not, however, that initial articulation is inherently less weighty than final,[9] but that positional articulation does not *necessarily* produce effective prominence – why should it?[10] – and that the deciding factor is the absence or presence of something to attract or justify such prominence. In short, if there is some natural prominence already there, articulation of this kind will tend to enforce it.

The distinction between prominence and emphasis can bear elaboration.

All emphatic words are prominent, but not *vice versa*. The sequence ἄνδρα μοι ἔννεπε, μοῦσα, πολύτροπον is prominent, has a headline status as the opening of the *Odyssey*, but it is not emphatic.[11] We do not think of it as in italics or underlined. I do not suggest that final or initial position, even when a cause of prominence, is a necessary cause of emphasis. There may be emphasis on words so positioned, if hyperbaton, for instance, is involved; or there may not. This distinction, in conjunction with the observation that articulation does not necessarily produce prominence, has equal relevance to the topic of enjambement.[12] In A.*Ag*.13f.,

> εὐνὴν ὀνείροις οὐκ ἐπισκοπουμένην
> ἐμήν,

the word ἐμήν is fully enjambed. That is, it is articulated between two pauses, the syntactic pause that follows and the unmeasurable, but inevitably slighter, metrical pause that precedes. As such, it certainly has the option, so to speak, of prominence, but still no emphasis thereby. Whatever emphasis there may be stems from the hyperbaton, the abnormal separation of ἐμήν from εὐνήν.

The case of ἄξῃ in A.*Ag*.1629ff. is even clearer:

> Ὀρφεῖ δὲ γλῶσσαν τὴν ἐναντίαν ἔχεις.
> ὁ μὲν γὰρ ἧγε πάντα που φθογγῆς χαρᾷ,
> σὺ δ᾿ ἐξορίνας νηπίοις ὑλάγμασιν
> ἄξῃ.

This ἄξῃ represents the point of a joke (an interactive joke, as it happens).[13] It is enjambed and the enjambement, as usual, gives it the spotlight. But there is no hyberbaton and, unless an actor supplies it, no emphasis.

The relevance of this discussion of positional articulation may not yet be apparent. It is not that articulation has any inherent connection with inter-action in general; but that, as will appear, it is an important consideration in connection with some categories, as I conceive of them. Positional articulation is a source of secondary prominence, which in turn is often a factor in the effective functioning of the interaction. And in the main this does not mean the prominence of the vehicle, which is prominent enough by nature, but that of the tenor or neutral term with which the vehicle interacts. In ὅταν κλύδων / κακῶν ἐπέλθῃ, the neutral ἐπέλθῃ is articulated, albeit only slightly; it has its 'option' of prominence.

Before leaving this topic, let me note that neither hyperbaton nor enjambement will figure much in what follows,[14] except where either is incidentally associated with syntactic pause articulation. This is why 'articulation', when referring to sources of prominence, will in my usage customarily mean unemphatic positioning, initial or final, within the syntactic unit. Where enjambement comes up for mention, this will usually concern iambic trimeter and trochaic tetrameter.[15]

1 Emphasis in Greek can obviously be produced or at least supported by quite different means than order, e.g. by particles (cf. Denniston *GP* 33off., 537, 547, for instance). For discussion of emphasis by word order, see notably Dover 33ff.

2 D.H.*Comp*.22.

3 Whether the pause is actually heard or allowed for in silent reading is immaterial.

4 Demetr.*Eloc*.39 in Rhys Roberts' translation. Quintilian, among others, makes similar remarks about final position (9.4.29–30). The adducing of a Roman prompts a further comment. Here and elsewhere, I take it that certain 'principles' of style may hold in comparable measure for languages other than Greek, but I am not asserting their universality. I illustrate from outside Greek simply when a good parallel seems to present itself.

5 Its most extreme manifestation is the one word sentence (e.g. Pi.*O*.1.52), which is 'all pause'. The pragmatic definition of 'sentence' (etc.) must include the fact of such pauses.

6 Above, p. 22.

7 I have transferred τέκτων from the start of v.594 to the end of v.593 to avoid any impression that perceptible enjambement may be involved. Enjambement, presumably, cannot as a rule effectively exist in any lyrical scheme in which the metre breaks up into unpredictable notional units rather than predictable ones (in the sense that the iambic trimeter is 'predictable'). Hence one could hardly see effective enjambement in, for instance, most Pindaric metres, unless in an overlap into another stanza.

8 One might think that τέκτων and Ζεύς have a certain extra weight by virtue of unpredictable postposition.

9 Prominence from initial position in Greek is often perceived and commented on: 'graviter hoc verbo...hanc sententiam incipit...' (Hermann on A.*Ag*. 1438, followed by Fraenkel) is a common kind of appeal to the principle. But it is almost regularly characterized as 'emphasis' (so Fraenkel, *loc. cit.*). Much the same goes for final prominence: 'emphatically placed at the end of the clause' (Fraenkel on *Ag*.1436) – the prominence is recognized but misrepresented. Hence it comes about that some scholars (see Fraenkel III.677, n.1 – on *Ag*. 1436 – and Thomson, *Oresteia* II.253ff.), rightly denying the emphasis, but wrongly confusing emphasis with prominence, have refused to see any distinctive effect in such cases ('The final position as such is never emphatic', Thomson *op. cit.* 253). The reason why only final 'emphasis' (i.e. prominence) has been the object of scepticism, and not initial 'emphasis' as well, is perhaps that the latter is more commonly operative (so Fraenkel III.677, n.1; Denniston *GPS* 44).

10 It seems often to be assumed that if one says, 'it sometimes does', one is committed to thinking it always must. Cf. the sensible discussion by Wilkinson (p.52) on an analogous principle concerning euphony; see also the remarks made by Dover 33f. ('These three defects...').

11 One might wish to invoke emphasis with regard to the postponement of πολύτροπον, which is another matter.

12 With enjambement, as with unemphatic articulation in general (n.9 above), failure to make the prominence/emphasis distinction has confused the issues about its significance in Greek poetry. See principally Headlam *EA* 5ff. The dispute still goes on; compare and contrast Fraenkel and Denniston–Page on *Ag*.13f.

13 See below, p. 108.

14 I am not sure why. I have not been consciously selective here.

15 Cf. n.7 above.

§29

A second kind of articulation of present relevance is quite different: *parallel structure*. I use this expression as a cover term for such traditional figures as isocolon, antithesis and others of that family and, more generally, for any structures involving two or more matching clauses, phrases or smaller units.

Examples:

Friends, Romans, countrymen, lend me your ears;
I come *to bury* Caesar, *not to praise* him.

Some foreign writers, *some our own* despise;
The ancients only, *or the moderns* prize.

War and Peace.

April is the cruellest month, *breeding*
Lilacs out of the dead land, *mixing*
Memory and desire, *stirring*
Dull roots with spring rain.

and, once again, A.*Supp*.592ff.,

. . . αὐτόχειρ ἄναξ,

. . . μέγας τέκτων,

. . . οὔριος Ζεύς.

The effect of such structures is frequently climactic, with the crescendo on the final member:

Friends, Romans, countrymen . . .[1]

However, it is important to recognize that the climactic force devolves primarily upon the *whole* of the final member, not any single constituent element of it. That is, parallel structures do not in themselves give prominence to *particular* terms. And many such structures are not climactic in any case, as

I come to bury Caesar, not to praise him

71

where there is no question of a climax on the second phrase. If there is a climax, and if it does reach a peak on a particular term, this will characteristically be the final term of the final member, as with Ζεύς in *Supp.*594, where the prominence derives from word position not from parallelism. In a tricolon like *veni, vidi, vici*, with three one-word members, the effects on *vici* of parallelism and of final position are, naturally, difficult to dissociate; but the principle is unaffected.

Confirmation for the principle may be found in the tendency for a medial term in the final member of a climactic parallel structure to get no prominence from its position. (If it has prominence, this comes from some other source.) Thus, the medial οὔριος in *Supp.*594 is parallel to αὐτόχειρ and to μέγας, but gets no prominence therefrom. Similarly, the final Ζεύς gets no more prominence from its parallelism with ἄναξ and τέκτων than 'to praise' does from 'to bury'.

What Ζεύς does derive from its parallelism is something quite different. Where prominence would make it stand out from its context, parallelism assimilates it to the context. Although the whole structuring may itself be unexpected, parallelism, as it impinges, represents a *fulfilment* of expectation, albeit the expectation is only retrospective. And 'as it impinges' means: as the second, or later, element becomes perceptibly parallel. The later, in other words, is *cushioned* by the earlier,[2] and the contents of the later with it – but not cushioned by the contents of the earlier, but merely by the fact of there being an earlier. This cushioning is an important source of enforcement for certain kinds of interaction, particularly the kinds I shall be calling 'preparation'. In a sense, indeed, this cushioning has itself a preparatory character, irrespective of any connection with imagery or interaction. In *Supp.*592ff., Ζεύς is 'prepared' by ἄναξ and τέκτων; similarly 'to praise' by 'to bury'.

Both Ζεύς, which is part of a climactic member, and 'to praise', which is not, are articulated, then, to preparatory effect. But the preparatory force is not the whole of the effect in these or in any such cases. It is worth noting here that parallel structures have a second characteristic effect, fully compatible with the first and no less relevant to interaction, and this is to *link* the corresponding items. By setting them out in corresponding terms, the structure sets up an association between them. Fresh examples are not necessary. This general tendency applies, more or less, to all the instances quoted in the present section.

---

1 Cf. Demetr.*Eloc.*50 and 139; Quintil.9.4.23. 'Friends, Romans, countrymen' illustrates the 'law of increasing members' (see e.g. Stanford *SG* 82, Wilkinson 175f.).

2 I am not sure to what extent this principle is generally recognized. More attention is usually paid to the overall effect of parallel structures than to the effect of their earlier members on their later ones.

§30

I am now in a position to restate the rationale of this book. My primary aim is to establish the concept of interaction and, in particular, the categories; and my hope is that they make it possible to see and say things that were less possible before. They are not offered as permanent. They are offered for provisional use, and 'their use is justified in so far as it is shown to favour sensitive perception'.[1] It is not implied that theoretical knowledge is in itself a *sine qua non* of an informed response to literature, nor, specifically, that the whole substructure of my system has to be invoked on every available occasion by anyone persuaded of the value of one or more of the categories: there is a difference between putting up a building and using it (or admiring it in passing). But *mihi cane et populo* – as Cicero put it – *ut qui audient quid efficiatur, ego autem cur id efficiatur intellegam.*[2] An informed response should be always prepared to say 'whence' as well as 'what', not only in self-defence, but as an active stimulus to the perception of the 'what'.

In the present case, the need for such a stimulus is particularly clear, and correspondingly the need for a formal organization of particulars into 'theory'. In the first place, the stylistic possibilities represented by several of my categories seem hardly to figure among those recognized by current criticism. Then again, as regards Greek studies, many passages for which I claim a given kind of interaction either have not been credited with the relevant effect, even roughly, or have not been credited with a distinctive effect of any kind. For such cases, my theory is formulated to justify particular interpretations, suggestions of relation or distinction. And where there is already an adequate awareness of the general possibilities, their ramifications have not, on the whole, been realized, and it may in any case be instructive to have available a comprehensive scheme by which to discriminate between these possibilities individually and between these and others that have been less adequately comprehended.

The considerations adduced concerning prominence, intention and aesthetic status all ultimately relate to the question of *significant existence*, which is, in turn, bound up with *perceptibility*. The relations between Whitman's 'fires' may not be perceptible; if not, they may still exist in some 'objective' sense,[3] but in what other sense? The same query could apply to Norwood's Pindaric symbols. Here as elsewhere, perceptibility, not some 'objective' status, nor, again, 'intention', is the criterion of significant existence. The principal, simple and decisive objection to Norwood is that stated by Van Groningen: 'le symbole contribue en un certain sens à l'unité de l'ode, mais c'est une unité...à peine perceptible'.[4] The 'whence' need not be perceptible, the 'what' must be. The necessary attitude here is that which Abrams has called 'pragmatic'.[5] Perceptibility implies, above all, an audience to perceive, whether an actual, potential or ideal audience. The pragmatic orientation towards literature is the one which focuses primarily or ultimately on an audience; and this orientation 'has been', in Abrams' words, 'the principal aesthetic attitude of the Western world'.[6] Its 'perspective...originated in the classical theory of rhetoric';[7] and its more recent exponents have included men like Samuel Johnson.[8] Whatever other charges it may incur, a pragmatic approach to ancient literature cannot be stigmatized as inevitably a barrier to fine criticism, nor as 'modern, therefore anachronistic'.[9] And positively, to pick up my depreciatory reference to 'objectivity', it is only pragmatism, understood as above, that can decide the simple but inescapably present question: which 'objective' elements are worth talking about?

If the categories do 'make it possible to see and say things that were less possible before', the seeing and saying should bear not only on the describing of the poetry in question, but also on the evaluating of it, since description and evaluation are, for practical purposes at least, inseparable in criticism.[10] This does not mean that the categories have any straightforward evaluative status. On the one side, I would not want it said that the categories are, simply, 'good' *per se*, nor that category x is 'better' *per se* than category y. The mere presence of interaction, or of any category of interaction, is no guarantee of the quality of a passage. Such quality, if it depends directly on interaction, will depend on the precise use to which the interaction is put. A Gothic arch may be beautiful or impressive, but quite inappropriate in its context (e.g. a neo-classical building) or inappropriately big or inappropriately positioned. The same analogy may be appealed to on the other side: once beyond the rudimentary stage (a half-evaluation itself), interactions, especially interactions of certain kinds do, like Gothic arches, tend to have a certain capacity for impressiveness (or even beauty) *per se* and can at least be regarded as, potentially, *technical* triumphs, in which sense they might be 'interesting', irrespective, even, of their place in a passage or work as a whole. The general truth here is surely that interactions, like other stylistic possibilities, are sources of power and, indeed, some categories are more powerful than others; but power can be used well or abused: the value is not inherent. There is, though, another relevant truth: the categories have taken the shape they have on the basis of all apparent examples of them, but particularly the most *successful* examples, where the success in question is liable to be more than a mere *tour de force* of technique. This means, among other things, that a successful instance of a category may have helped to suggest that particular categorization, where a less successful instance might not: without that successful instance, or others equally successful, I might not have been led to postulate the category at all. The upshot is that my examples of interaction are *liable* to be examples of successful interaction.[11] Naturally, this does not obviate the reader's obligation to exercise his critical faculties independently.

The categories have been formulated on the basis of early Greek poetry. That they would have equal relevance to the practice of later Greek poets I do not doubt. Whether they would, as they stand, be equally applicable to poetry in other languages is another matter. It might be that certain typical manifestations of some categories are engendered by peculiarities of Greek expression. Again, some of the categories themselves might be rare in other literatures, though this would not in itself invalidate their potential utility: contrast is hardly less important than comparison. But the fact that I have often been able to find English parallels, to at least my own satisfaction, is some indication that such value as the categories may have is not restricted to the study of Greek poetry alone.

1 Leavis *IM* 237.
2 Cic. *Brut.*187.
3 On the 'objective' orientation to literature, see Abrams 26ff.
4 Van Groningen *CLAG* 363, on the 'Bee' in *Pythian* Eleven.
5 Abrams 14–21.
6 Abrams 21.
7 Abrams 15.
8 Cf. Abrams 19.
9 If the logic of 'modern, therefore anachronistic' is sound, which I doubt, one target for complaint would be any serious interest in the personality of an ancient author, including his 'intention' (see §25).
10 *Pace* Frye 3–29 (especially 20ff.). See Casey *passim*, especially 35–60, 165–97.
11 I note that the ancient theorists were aware of this problem. Quintilian, for one, seems to have decided that stylistic categories can have their evaluative status built into them by definition: 'tropus est verbi vel sermonis a propria significatione in aliam *cum virtute* mutatio' (8.6.1, cf. 1.5.5, 9.3.18).

PART II
THE CATEGORIES

4 Scope and Procedure

§31

It may be useful at this point to recapitulate and/or clarify the precise scope of the two chief factors in the discussions that follow, the Greek corpus and the concept of interaction.

First, the corpus. The poetry in my period extends from Archilochus at one end to Aeschylus, Pindar and Bacchylides at the other. It comprises, that is, the whole of archaic and early classical verse with the exception of the two hexametric traditions: Homer with the later hymns and epic fragments; and the Hesiodic corpus together with its distant Presocratic relatives, notably Parmenides and Empedocles. In the case of Homer, the main reason for exclusion is the peculiar difficulty of establishing standard usage for the period ('which period?'), and the situation of the other early hexametrists is comparably problematic. Their successors are omitted only for the sake of genre consistency.

Two additional points: (1) I have included early hexametric oracles, because the oracular predilection for metaphor, alliteration and ambiguity[1] results in one or two noteworthy interactions. (2) For the nonce, the final portion of the *Septem* and the whole of the *Prometheus* are treated as Aeschylean without further qualification. Likewise, the whole of 'Theognis' is counted as early lyric, irrespective of the possibility of widely differing dates for particular parts of that collection.

Secondly, interaction. By interaction I mean any local cross-terminological relation between the tenor and vehicle of an image, either aurally,

κλύδων κακῶν,

or extra-grammatically,

My way of life
Is *fall'n* into the sear, the yellow *leaf*,

or by intrusion,

ῥίзης γὰρ οὔσης φυλλὰς ἵκετ' ἐς δόμους,

or by neutral terminology,

You are too shallow, Hastings, much too *shallow*,
To sound the bottom of the after-times.

79

No other relations count as interactive. In particular, relations between one vehicle term and another ($V-V$) are not interactive relations:[2]

οἴχεται νεβροῦ δίκην
καὶ ταῦτα κούφως ἐκ μέσων ἀρκυστάτων.

Decrepit age that has been *tied* to me
As *to a dog's tail.*

The concept of interaction presupposes that every word (or smaller unit) in an image is either (1) terminologically colourless, or belongs to the terminology of (2) the vehicle, or (3) the tenor, or (4) neither tenor nor vehicle (probably because of belonging to a separate image), or (5) both tenor and vehicle, being neutral. The three main possibilities here are the second (V), the third (T) and the fifth (N). (The other two tend in practice to pass for tenor or vehicle terminology, depending on the context.) A fresh extended example may be helpful. The opening of stanza two of Keats' *On Melancholy* ('No, no! go not to Lethe...'):

> But when the melancholy fit shall fall
> Sudden from heaven like a weeping cloud,
> That fosters the droop-headed flowers all,
> And hides the green hill in an April shroud,
> Then glut thy sorrow on a morning rose...

In this passage 'the melancholy fit' is literal, T. 'Fall sudden from heaven' is N: fits 'fall on' people and may be thought to come 'from heaven'; clouds – or their contents – likewise 'fall from heaven'. The *Wiestück*, 'like... shroud', is, as one would expect, predominantly V; but 'weeping', cohering terminologically with 'melancholy' not with 'cloud', is T; and 'shroud' itself, embodying a second image within the first, is strictly, let us say, V_2, but also has a loose coherence with 'melancholy' via the missing link *suicide*, the topic the poem began with; 'shroud', then, is V_2 with a hint of T in it, although for many purposes it could be regarded simply as V. Finally, 'then...rose' is T again; and any words not otherwise accounted for are colourless, such as 'but when', to be regarded as T in conformity with its context. The passage incidentally exemplifies three of the main types of interaction: 'fall...from heaven', neutral-based; 'weeping', intrusion (along with the lesser intrusive suggestion in 'shroud'), as the above analysis indicates; and, not brought out by the analysis, an extra-grammatical interaction between the 'flowers' of the vehicle and the 'rose' of the tenor. I might add that in practice I shall not be giving such exhaustive explications for every passage discussed; and for practical purposes, it may be convenient simply to say that every N–V (or V–N) group is *ipso facto* interactive; and that some T–V (or V–T) groups are interactive, others not. Thus, 'weeping cloud' (T–V) is interactive; and likewise 'flowers' – 'rose' (V–T); but not, say, 'melancholy' – 'cloud' (T–V), which shows the ordinary, analogical kind of tenor–vehicle relation, not cross-terminological but cross-conceptual.

As regards coverage of the interactions in the corpus, the Greek examples given are necessarily a selection, albeit – if such a thing is possible – a comprehensive selection. I would not claim to have laid bare every conceivable interaction in the corpus, and, if I had, considerations of space would be prohibitive. I have, in any case, opted against a complete coverage by suppressing most of the instances I regard as dubious, whether the doubt relates to general interpretation, as often with fragments, or to substantive aesthetic status (perceptibility), or to lexical matters (leading to uncertainty about terminological status) or to text. I do not usually include examples involving unquestionably corrupt or uncertainly restored texts, unless the textual problem seems not to affect the interaction in question. As for 'lexical matters', I have tried to include only those examples of interaction which can be supported by really adequate documentation. The examples excluded on this account are quite numerous. Finally, I have passed over without comment some passages containing only very trivial interactions and others to which interaction (*vel sim.*) has been, as I see it, wrongly or questionably ascribed in earlier studies. Despite all this selectivity, there remains a sufficient number and variety of instances to make the exercise more than a *mere* exercise and, incidentally, to show up some distinct tendencies in the practice of the various poets.[3]

1 See Parke-Wormell, *Prolegomena* xxiii–xxxi; Stanford *AGL* 120ff.; cf. Plut. *Moral.*405d, 407b.
2 For a comprehensive list of V–V types, see Appendix IX.
3 See Appendix X. There are several hundred instances in all, rather less than a third in Pindar, rather more than a third in Aeschylus.

§32

A few words on procedure. Examples of interaction will usually be confined to my corpus, except for parallels and paradigms from English poetry. These were, in general, selected to illuminate the categories after the latter had already taken shape. They are not consciously the basis for the categories, although I would not want to deny the possibility of any formative influence from the poetry of my own language.

The discussions are organized by categories, not by authors. I shall, however, note in passing any apparent characteristics of particular Greek poets and summarize these later.[1] Regarding such notes, any unqualified comments of the type, 'category x only here in Pindar', are to be understood with reference to the instances excluded as dubious in addition to those discussed.

The discussions do not aspire to be commentaries on the passages in question. Comment is confined, in the main, to the interactions and to whatever is materially relevant to them.

Many passages contain several interactions, not necessarily relating to one another. If these are essentially separate interactions, they are usually discussed separately under the heading of the appropriate category. Passages with multiple interactions which deserve to be thought of specifically as such are dealt with in a later chapter.

Regarding lexical documentation, my usual practice will be as follows. If I believe a usage to be live metaphor, I cite no parallels. Where I take it to be normal (which includes cliché), I give the requisite evidence myself, citing most of it in the notes, but quoting one or more conveniently suggestive passages in the text. Only exceptionally will I be confining myself to a reference to LSJ or a commentator. Even where adequate evidence is available in such sources, the desirability of having the material of particular relevance to hand outweighs all other considerations. Some usages might actually seem to need little or no documentation, but I have preferred to err on the side of pedantry, partly for the sake of clarity, but especially where one might be fully aware that word x had meaning or connotation y, but not, for instance, know how early sense y may be taken to have been current. Fuller evidence is given where the sense proposed is at all new or controversial and where its normality, in my sense, would otherwise seem doubtful. The evidence offered will be offered as adequate, but is not to be taken as complete without an explicit statement to that effect. It will tend to be as early as possible and will almost never be later than the fourth century: Menander and Theophrastus are my effective limits. Hence 'complete' is always to be interpreted to mean 'complete as far as pre-Hellenistic Greek is concerned'; and such remarks as 'no extant parallel' mean 'no parallel sufficiently early to count'. When citing usages from a composite 'author' like Hippocrates, I shall not go into questions of authenticity or dating when the usage belongs to a work generally ascribed to the fourth century or earlier; the Aristotelian corpus is another case in point.[2] Finally, in general I let the evidence speak for itself without reference back to the particular assumption about the reliability of authors or distributional patterns to which, in the theoretical sense, it owes its relevance.

'Even where adequate evidence is available in such sources', I said in the last paragraph, with reference to 'LSJ or a commentator'. Some explanation is in order here. The simple truth is that LSJ is very often too selective for my purposes and selective in the wrong way. Part of the trouble is that our indispensable lexicon seems to have favourite authors who may not be of much help in reconstructing the norm: Plato, for one. At any rate, many normal senses, often senses of common words, are not adequately documented (i.e. sufficiently to demonstrate their normality) or are even virtually or actually ignored.[3] For instance, neither under αὐξάνω nor ἀέξω, the earlier form, is there any indication that this verb is ever used of vegetation growth, as it is in Homer (*Od.*9.111), other early hexameter poetry (*h.Cer.* 469, Hes.*Op.*394), early elegy (Mimn.2.2), early lyric (Ibyc.5.5), classical lyric and elegy (Thgn.1276, Pi.*fr.*153, B.*fr.*56), tragedy (S.*OT* 172), comedy (Ar.*Av.*1065), 'literary' prose (X.*Smp.*2.25), technical prose (Hp.*Nat.Puer.* 26) including – lo and behold! – the single most relevant source of all, Theophrastus' botanical treatises (Thphr.*HP* 2.2.5, 4.1.4 *et al.*); and this list is far from complete even for pre-Hellenistic Greek. As for the commentators, their authors are usually more interested in idiolectal or genre peculiarities than the wider norms and also in 'same ideas' rather than 'same words'. (This is truer still of special studies of imagery.[4]) The consequence is that in most cases I have had to gather 'adequate evidence' of my own. This might have meant nothing more than consulting indices to given authors (or collections of authors). In fact, some authors are fully indexed, others only partly or not at all. I have made full use of existing indices – or, as it may be, concordances or lexica – and where these are lacking, I have tried to fill the gap myself. That is, I have attempted, with specific usages in mind, to read through the whole of unindexed pre-Hellenistic Greek,[5] the authors in question ranging from philosophers like Eudemus and Aeschines Socraticus to parodists like Archestratus and Matro, from specialist writers like Hanno and Antisthenes, whose remains are neatly collected by modern or nineteenth-century scholarship, to those like Euryphon, the medical writer, whose few extant fragments have to be searched for in Galen and Stobaeus and the *Aononymus Londinensis*. But by far the most important texts in question are those that make up the Hippocratic and Theophrastean *corpora*: both of these collections are very large and, within limits, varied in content; and both contain a good deal relevant to the comprehension of classical usage – particularly so, from my standpoint, because they represent precisely the kind of 'trustworthy' Greek which is so important for questions of normality.

Thanks, therefore, to my particular orientation and the need for thorough documentation that it imposes, I may perhaps have made a minor contribution to Greek lexicography, not simply in terms of material collected, but in that some of the usages I pronounce normal are not generally regarded as such; and, more widely, in that even where the relevant evidence is available and well-known, no inference about status may hitherto have been made.

1 See Appendix x.

2 For a summary of current views and further references on Aristotle, see most conveniently Lesky 553–76 (esp. 574f.) and *Kl.P.*I.588f. As regards Hippocrates, besides brief accounts in Lesky 487ff. and *Kl.P.*II.1169ff., important modern discussions include L. Bourgey, *Observation et expérience chez les médecins de la collection hippocratique*, Paris, 1953, 27ff. and K. Deichgräber, *Die Epidemien und das Corpus Hippocraticum*, Berlin, 1933, 169ff. In his recent study, *The Pseudo-Hippocratic Tract* ΠΕΡΙ 'ΕΒΔΟΜΑΔωΝ *Ch. 1–11 and Greek Philosophy*, Assen, 1971, J. Mansfeld gives a concise account (pp.32–5 and 229–31) of the most recent findings on the later treatises in the corpus. From these various studies, I arrive at the following, extremely derivative, scheme, whereby the Hippocratic writings fall into three rough groups:

(*a*) An early group, say 400±25: *Aer.*, *Epid.*1 and 3, *Morb.Sacr.*, *Prog.* (all probably earlier than 400) and *Acut.*, *Acut.Sp.*, *Aph.*, *Art.*, *de Arte*, *Epid.*2, 4, 6, *Flat.*, *Fract.*, *Nat.Hom.*, *VC*, *Vict.*, *VM* (all probably around or later than 400). (On the affiliations and likely date of *Acut.Sp.*, see I. M. Lonie, *Archiv für Geschichte der Medezin* 49, 1965, 5off. and Joly's prefatory comments in the Budé edn, *Hippocrate* VI.2, 1972, pp.12f.)

(*b*) A late group, i.e. Hellenistic at the earliest: *Alim.*, *Cord.*, *Decent.*, *Ep.*, *Hebd.* (see Mansfeld, *op. cit.*229ff.), *Lex*, *Medic.*, *Praec.* (On purely impressionistic stylistic grounds, I would myself think *Anat.* and *Dent.* quite likely to belong here too.)

(*c*) The remaining thirty-odd treatises are fourth-century, say 345±35. Evidence from the first of these groups is obviously more valuable to me than evidence from the third, while the second group does not concern me at all. I should add that several of the treatises in (*a*) and (*c*) are more or less strongly influenced by sophistic or philosophical schools (and language) in a way that makes it misleading to think of them any longer as 'technical' treatises, with the implication of trustworthiness that the word carries. The earlier instances are *de Arte*, *Flat.*, *Nat.Hom.*, *Vict.*I. A last point worth making is that some of the treatises are almost certainly composite (e.g. *Aph.*) and therefore of varying date. But in general the tripartite scheme should be adequate.

3 See below, p. 251.

4 Taillardat is, on the whole, a valuable exception.

5 With two qualifications. First, I have not read through all of the many, scattered collections of extant prose inscriptions, a forbidding task and disproportionately unrewarding for the purpose, to judge from the meagre products got from the fairly generous selection that I have looked at. Second, not all the indices (etc.) which I have relied on are in fact complete. This applies especially to the older lexica, e.g. Bonitz's to Aristotle.

5 Neutral-based Interaction

§33

I begin with those categories that involve neutral terminology. The inherent connection of neutral terms with the ground, the likeness of an image, has been indicated already.[1] Interaction of other kinds does not have this characteristic. It is worth stressing that, in many ways, the more apparent the connection with the ground, the less interesting the interaction. This applies especially to explicit imagery, where, of course, the ground, or part of it, is usually made explicit as a matter of predictable organization. In the ' N like V ' structure of

κλάζοντες Ἄρη
τρόπον αἰγυπιῶν

or

then a soldier,
Full of strange oaths and bearded like the pard

the connection is apparent and compels little interest. Contrast

τοὶ δ᾽ ὥστε θύννους ἤ τιν᾽ ἰχθύων βόλον
ἀγαῖσι κωπῶν θραύμασίν τ᾽ ἐρειπίων
ἔπαιον, ἐρράχιζον

or

You are too shallow, Hastings, much too shallow,
To sound the bottom of the after-times

where the connection with the ground is hardly less real, but the interaction itself less predictable; in the Shakespeare, because this is metaphor, not simile; in the Aeschylus (ἔπαιον), because the simile is less predictably structured.[2]

It is pertinent to emphasize the point that neutral status is relative, not absolute. I spoke earlier of the gradation from colourlessness to pun.[3] One can distinguish also between definitive association and mere coherence. For instance, 'red' associates with 'brick' or 'wine' definitively, but merely coheres with 'book' or 'curtain'. All four objects may or may not be red – this is not the point. The point is that the first pair of associations are established associations, the other two are merely possible. Some neutral terms will involve the former kind of association, others the latter.

'Neutral' implies relativity in yet another way. Some terms are more *grammatically* neutral than others. I made it a matter of definition that inter-actions based on neutral terms are not extra-grammatical.[4] Many neutral terms, however, do operate over the grammatical structure to a degree. The ἐπέλθῃ of ὅταν κλύδων κακῶν ἐπέλθῃ is fully neutral; it can count as vehicle terminology, cohering with κλύδων, or it could stand unchanged if πλῆθος κακῶν or simply κακά were the subject. Contrast the κλάζοντες of κλάζοντες Ἄρη τρόπον αἰγυπιῶν, which, though semantically neutral, belongs, grammatically speaking, rather to the tenor, the nominative plural Atridae, than to the vehicle, the genitive plural vultures.[5] Still, this kind of assimi-lation, if one may so describe it, of neutral terminology to tenor or vehicle is not necessarily of great moment, though it may sometimes serve to give the 'neutral' term the status rather of a 'hint', whereby a vehicle term alludes to the tenor, or *vice versa*, without wholly belonging to it.

The precise functions or effects of neutral terms are often elusive. The pure ground term is the simplest manifestation, and, as intimated earlier, is especially characteristic of simile and comparison.[6] The ground term, as all neutral terminology in general, is at bottom a manifestation of what I call 'support', although individual instances will usually be better regarded under other headings. Among these, 'convergence' is to be thought of as most closely akin to support, although convergence, unlike support, is essentially formal in character. In this respect convergence stands with two other categories, 'pivot' and 'glide'. The remaining functions of neutral terms are 'explanatory' and 'specifying', neither of which entails formal properties. The exact function, to repeat, can be elusive, at least within the framework of my categories. This is simply because the categories mostly represent functions which, if not actually complementary, readily co-exist. Some categories are essentially formal, others not. Further, the chief mission of some is to serve the vehicle, that of others to serve the image as a whole, and that of one to serve the tenor. Neutral terms may have a function based on formal properties and, in addition, one or more other functions. As may be imagined, the requirements of orderly presentation will often lead to an oversimplified account.

1 Above, §12.
2 Discussions of these four passages, above, pp. 16f., 19, and Prolegom., viii. The 'N like V' structure is not in fact *entirely* predictable, since the intrusive 'T like V' ('dead as a doornail') and the non-interactive 'V like V' (εὖρις ἡ ξένη κυνὸς δίκην) are also possible.
3 Above, p. 23.
4 Above, p. 24.

5 This is obviously more likely to happen in an inflected language, like Greek, and also in simile rather than in metaphor.
6 Above, §§9, 11.

Pivot and glide
§34

The pivotal and glide functions are among those that serve the interests of the vehicle. The vehicle's extraneousness isolates it, and a reduction, more or less, of this isolation is the effect of any operative neutral term; it gives the vehicle something in common with the tenor. Such an effect is particularly characteristic of those neutral terms which have the simple formal property of preceding the vehicle.

Take first an instance of unmitigated isolation, almost studiedly exaggerated. Anacr.15:

> ὦ παῖ παρθένιον βλέπων
> δίζημαί σε, σὺ δ' οὐ κλύεις,
> οὐκ εἰδὼς ὅτι τῆς ἐμῆς
> ψυχῆς ἡνιοχεύεις.

Prominent position and a marked contrast with the bald diction of the preceding context both contribute;[1] but ultimately the isolation of ἡνιοχεύεις derives from, simply, extraneousness. Contrast A.*Ag.*5f., on the stars:

> καὶ τοὺς φέροντας χεῖμα καὶ θέρος βροτοῖς
> λαμπροὺς δυνάστας,...

Once again the vehicle, δυνάστας, is prominently stationed, though with a less definitive articulation, and the preceding diction is hardly less plain. But this time there is the significant presence of λαμπρούς. The word is neutral; it implies the kind of context represented by ἀστέρα...λαμπρόν (*Il.*4.77)[2] and, at the same time, the kind represented by οἱ δὲ 'Αλκμεωνίδαι...λαμπροὶ ἐν τῇσι 'Αθήνῃσι (Hdt.6.125.1).[3] Cohering with both terminologies, it provides a light transition from tenor to vehicle. From the standpoint of the vehicle, it has a preparatory or introductory character; it leads up to the peak. This I call a glide. Its force is light and momentary; there is no emphasis and no lingering.

In Shakespeare's *Cymbeline* (II.2), Iachimo catches sight of Imogen asleep:

> How bravely thou becomest thy *bed*, fresh lily,
> And whiter than the sheets.

The transition from 'bed' to 'lily' is comparable, but differs in a closer approximation to pun (woman's bed and flower bed) and also in syntactic organization: the operative words belong to separate units. The result is a more overt or forceful operativeness. 'Bed' is a pivot. The distinction between pivot and glide is not always easy to make. Both are momentary in effect and both have an introductory or preparatory character. Further, the extent to which the neutral term is subdued seems sometimes to override a distinction based on syntactic organization. The more subdued it is, the greater the temptation to call it a glide. But in general the factor of syntactic organization does seem central, and, in the light of the effective distinctions it implies, 'introductory' seems more aptly predicated of the glide, 'preparatory' of the pivot.

1 Cf. Bowra *GLP* 294f., Campbell *ad loc.*
2 So Arist.*Mete.*371b.24, E.*Or.*1685.
3 So Pi.*N.*8.34, E.*El.*37, Th.1.138.6.

§35

The pivotal function at its simplest is shown by the ground term in short simile and comparison, when positioned before, often immediately before, the vehicle:

Byron	a small drop of ink / Falling like dew
Shakespeare	Full of strange oaths and bearded like the pard
Anacr.92	ἔφυγον ὥστε κόκκυξ
Thgn.568	κείσομαι ὥστε λίθος
A.*Eu.*111	οἴχεται νεβροῦ δίκην
A.*Ag.*48f.	κλάζοντες Ἄρη / τρόπον αἰγυπιῶν[1]
	...white as snow
	...plain as a pikestaff
Sapph.31.14	χλωροτέρα...ποίας
Thgn.715	ὠκύτερος...Ἁρπυιῶν

These have all been cited before.[2] Other examples:

Sapph.96.6ff.	Λύδαισιν ἐμπρέπεται γυναίκεσσιν ὡς...σελάννα[3]
B.9.27f.	πενταέθλοισιν γὰρ ἐνέπρεπεν ὡς...εὐφεγγὴς σελάνα[4]
Thgn.113f.	τὸν κακὸν ἄνδρα...φεύγειν ὥστε κακὸν λιμένα[5]
Thgn.575f.	ἐχθρὸν ἀλεῦμαι / ὥστε κυβερνήτης χοιράδας[6]
Alc.369 ('wine')	ὀξυτέρω τριβόλων[7]

It is noteworthy that this essentially unsophisticated use of the pivot is particularly common in Theognis and apparently absent from Pindar.[8] In fact, pivot in general is noticeably uncommon in Pindar and common in Theognis.

Less unsophisticated and more impressive in every way is the pivotal introduction to metaphor – this being one of the occasions when the distinction between metaphor and explicit image needs to be kept in mind. Here the pivot can be, and usually is, enforced by some kind of parallel structure, as follows from its preparatory character. A beguilingly simple example is provided by Thgn.769:

χρὴ Μουσῶν θεράποντα καὶ ἄγγελον

Μουσῶν θεράπων is an absolutely conventional periphrasis for the poet;[9] Μουσῶν ἄγγελος is live metaphor; and θεράπων and ἄγγελος belong to a shared semantic field.[10] Simple as it is, the interaction has a forceful effect within its elementary structure: '*N* and *V*'. Such a structure may also be harmlessly disguised without becoming any less elementary. In A.*fr*.273.6f., the famous *Niobe* fragment, what might have been matching verbs in coordinate clauses emerges as participle and verb:

τριταῖον ἦμαρ τόνδ' ἐφημένη τάφον
τέκνοις ἐπῴζει τοῖς τεθνηκόσιν...

Vehicle ἐπῴζει. Niobe, like a hen on her eggs: ἀλεκτρυόνος... τοὺς τρόπους, ἐπὶ τῷδ' ἐπῴζουσα (Cratin.108). ἐφημένη is the pivot. We have μητέρα... βωμίαν ἐφημένην (E.*Supp*.93) and, for the vehicle, a sense best attested with ἐπικαθῆσθαι, the prose equivalent:[11] ὀρνίθων γένος... τοῦτο τίκτει δύο νεοττούς, οὐκ ἐπικάθηται δέ (Arist.*HA* 619b.14).[12]

The only example of interaction of any kind in Hipponax has the same overtly simple parallelism as was instanced by Theognis:

Hippon.50   κριγὴ δὲ νεκρῶν ἄγγελός τε καὶ κῆρυξ

The screech-owl, κριγή, is first called ἄγγελος, a conventional tag for birds: οἰωνόν, ταχὺν ἄγγελον (*Il*.24.292);[13] then, metaphorically, κῆρυξ, the two words making a natural pair in the vehicle terminology: κήρυξί τε διαχρεωμένους καὶ ἀγγέλοισι (Hdt.7.9β.2).[14]

Other instances illustrate the variety of form that the enforcing parallelism may take.

Thgn. 527f.   ὤ μοι ἐγὼν ἥβης καὶ γήραος οὐλομένοιο,
τοῦ μὲν ἐπερχομένου, τῆς δ' ἀπονισομένης.

Parallelism here extends to metre and morphology. ἀπονισομένης is the vehicle (subdued); ἐπερχομένου, which is its opposite in the concrete sense,

89

is poetic cliché in the tenor sense: γῆρας ἐπερχόμενον (Sol.14.10).[15] Theognis has a structurally comparable but much finer instance at 647f.:

ἦ δὴ νῦν αἰδὼς μὲν ἐν ἀνθρώποισιν ὄλωλεν,
αὐτὰρ ἀναιδείη γαῖαν ἐπιστρέφεται.

The description of the activity ascribed to αἰδώς involves no metaphor; ὄλωλεν and ὄλλυται with abstractions as subject are poetic cliché.[16] In contrast, ἐπιστρέφεται, ascribed to the antithetical ἀναιδείη, is the meta-phorical peak of prominence, articulated prominently as is ὄλωλεν. The double articulation, prominent positioning and the cushioning of parallelism, produces a formal poise, not as a gratuitous rhetorical trick, but in aid of an interaction, felicitous in its own right, that enacts the burden of the couplet. The menace ἀναιδείη operates figuratively, therefore unpredictably – it is 'at large' terminologically, as well as semantically; whereas αἰδώς simply ὄλωλεν, as tame as the phraseology.

Pindar's Eighth *Pythian* exemplifies again the combination of articulations (vv.92ff.):

ἐν δ' ὀλίγῳ βροτῶν
τὸ τερπνὸν αὔξεται· οὕτω δὲ καὶ πίτνει χαμαί,
ἀποτρόπῳ γνώμᾳ σεσεισμένον.

The subject, τὸ τερπνόν, is shaken and falls like a plant, perhaps specifically a tree; δρῦς...τάμνον...ταὶ δὲ...πῖπτον (*Il*.23.120),[17] σείετο ὕλη (*Il*.14.285).[18] αὔξεται is pivotal: σωφροσύνη τὰ τερπνὰ ἀέξει (Democr.211)[19] and the common δένδρον...ἀέξεται (B.*fr*.56)[20] represent the two contexts. One notes that all the operative words, the pivotal αὔξεται and the vehicle terms πίτνει χαμαί and σεσεισμένον, share a common final articulation, all gravi-tating, as it were, to the prominent place. And the parallelism serves here, as often elsewhere, not only to cushion the vehicle, but to bring each of the operative words into perceptible relation with one another, a general function of parallel structure which should not be forgotten.

Another instance with something of the double articulation, A.*Pe*.299ff. The messenger gives his announcement,

Ξέρξης μὲν αὐτὸς ζῇ τε καὶ φάος βλέπει,

and the Persian Queen her triumphantly punning thanks:

ἐμοῖς μὲν εἶπας δώμασιν φάος μέγα
καὶ λευκὸν ἦμαρ νυκτὸς ἐκ μελαγχίμου.

The vehicle, λευκὸν ἦμαρ κτλ., pivots immediately on the φάος μέγα of the previous line: 'daylight', ἡμερήσιον φάος (*Ag*.22f.), the habitual sense of the word, and 'deliverance', poetic currency: ἀπ' ἀμαχανίας ἄγων ἐς φάος τόνδε δᾶμον Pi.O.5.14.[21] But blatantly, this φάος itself takes off from the messenger's commonplace euphemism, φάος βλέπει.[22] With its doubled structuring, the interaction shows an aggressive vigour, seizing and capitalizing on its opportunity, characteristic of its author.

Blake's *A Poison Tree* offers an instance with no less force, but less formalized and, at the same time, to appreciably more ambitious effect:

> I was angry with my friend:
> I told my wrath, my wrath did end.
> I was angry with my foe:
> I told it not, my wrath did grow.
>
> And I watered it in fears,
> Night and morning with my tears;
> And I sunnèd it with smiles,
> And with soft deceitful wiles.
>
> And it grew both day and night,
> Till it bore an apple bright...

'Grow' in the fourth line, weightily placed at the end of the first stanza, is pivotal to the 'apple bright' that makes the 'tree' of the title explicit six lines later, after two substantial hints in the meantime, 'watered' and 'sunnèd'. The recapitulatory 'grew' in the ninth line gives a more constricting parallelism as the wrath irresistibly produces its poisonous fruit:

> And it *grew*...
> Till it *bore*...

The development of the vehicle from the neutral 'grow' enacts the development of the wrath from its innocent beginnings with potent simplicity.[23]

---

1 The *N* status of κλάзοντες seems to have been almost noticed by Headlam-Thomson; Fraenkel is confusing on the point; and Ole Smith 38f. explicitly takes the movement as *V–V* (metaphor-simile), instead of *N–V*. For the relevant lexicographical information, see p. 18, n.2 above.

2 Above, pp. 16f., 20.

3 Reading σελάννα *faute de mieux*; see Page *SA* 90. ἐμπρέπεσθαι occurs only here. For ἐμπρέπειν *qua T* (people in a crowd), Ar.*Nub.*605, B.9.27; so πρέπειν, *Il.*12.104. *Qua V*, with connotation of shining, often of stars etc. themselves, A.*Th.*390 and *Ag.*6 (and cf. Fraenkel on *Ag.*242); Pi.*P.*10.67; B.9.27; Hdt. 7.83.2.

4 ἐμπρέπειν as in Sapph.96 (n.3 above), which is doubtless Bacchylides' model here.

5 With additional baby-interaction from the κακόν/κακόν parallelism: 'support'. φεύγειν of people shunning the company of other people (but without any actual 'flight'): Γαράμαντες οἳ πάντα ἄνθρωπον φεύγουσι καὶ παντὸς ὁμιλίην Hdt.4.174, so E.*Med*.561, Ar.*Pl*.496, X.*Mem*.2.3.5, Hp.*Morb*.2.72, Men.*mon*. 467 and likewise (in an amatory context) Sapph.1.21, Anacr.72.2 and 92 (?), Thgn.1287 and 1302. φεύγειν of people avoiding *things*: φεύγειν δὲ σκιερούς θώκους Hes.*Op*.574, so Hp.*Morb*.2.72 (the hypochondriac τὸ φῶς φεύγει καὶ τοὺς ἀνθρώπους), *Com.Adesp*.424. (Contrast φεύγειν of *escape*, as πέτρας φύγομεν δεινήν τε Χάρυβδιν *Od*.12.260.) These senses are not in LSJ.

6 See *Od*.4.396 and 12.274 for the two senses of ἀλεῦμαι.

7 ὀξύς of wine, Hp.*Morb*.2.55, Arist.*Ph*.248b.8, Alex.141.12; of taste generally, Hp.*Vict*.2.54, Emped.90.2; cf. ὄξος, 'vinegar', first in Sol.26.7. For ὀξύς = 'sharp' to the touch, see above, p. 29.

8 Except for such a subdued instance as ἀρετάν in *I*.9.6, a comparison of the same trivial kind as Thgn.714 (see above, p. 20), or the unformalized γλυκεῖα/μελισσᾶν interaction at Pi.*P*.6.52–4, where γλυκεῖα, 'sweet-natured' (see below, p. 99), suggests also 'sweet to the taste' (as μέλιτος γλυκίων *Il*.1.249 etc.). Cf. also *P*.4.209f., where the Symplegades are κραιπνότεραι ἤ...ἀνέμων στίχες. But κρ. is not strictly pivotal here, N–V, but V–V: not neutral, but in the terminology of winds, the ἀνέμων of the vehicle (κραιπνὸν Βορέην *Od*.5.385 etc.), and not predicable of such concrete *things* as rocks, the tenor subject (albeit these rocks are ζωαί). At *N*.4.81 Pindar *does* use a neutral ground-term to comparison, but as convergence, not as pivot: στάλαν...Παρίου λίθου λευκοτέραν (see below, p. 186, n.9).

9 Hes.*Th*.100; *Margites* 1.2; *h.Hom*.32.20; *Orac*.4 (cf. Arch.293 Lasserre–Bonnard) and 74.3 (P–W); Choeril.1.2; Ar.*Av*.909 and 913; cf. B.5.14 and *fr*.63.1, E.*El*.717, Pl.*Phd*.85a (complete list).

10 See e.g. Hdt.4.71.4–72.1, B.5.14–19.

11 ἐπικαθῆσθαι not in tragedy. Conversely, ἐφῆσθαι/ἧσθαι not in prose.

12 ἐπικαθῆσθαι likewise, Arist.*HA* 558a.19. ἧσθαι and relevant compounds are used of winged creatures (mostly birds) 'sitting on' something without reference to incubation, as follows: ἐφῆσθαι A.*Ch*.501, Ar.*Av*.1066; ἧσθαι Panyas.12.17f., E.*Rh*.547; ἐπικαθῆσθαι Ar.*Eq*.1093, Arist.*HA* 625a.5; ἐπὶ...καθῆσθαι Thphr. *fr*.169. (Just conceivably, the ghostly children δόμοις ἐφημένους at A.*Ag*.1217 are likewise to be thought of, at least momentarily, as winged: 'settled on the house', Headlam–Thomson. If so, the κρεῶν and βορᾶς of 1220 would take on a related and gruesome significance: cf. Panyas. *loc. cit*. βορῆς κεκορημένον ἠΰτε γῦπα ἧσθαι). A textual note on the *Niobe* couplet is in order here (for a full discussion see Lloyd-Jones 556ff., Pickard-Cambridge 111f.). The text as given above follows the reading suggested by Hsch. who has ἐπῶζε and glosses ἐπώζειν by ἐπικαθῆσθαι τοῖς ᾠοῖς. The presence of ἐπῴζειν in this sense is certain. Hsch. is explicit and his text wholly Aeschylean (with the Fraenkelian 'intensifying contrast' – see above, p. 6, n.1 and below, p. 162); and the ἐφημένη interaction provides additional confirmation for the authenticity of the image. Hesychius' reading has a metrical gap for which Latte conjectured ζῶσα.

Despite Aeschylus *Th.*1034 (if that *is* Aeschylus), I do not find the hyperformal antithesis thereby produced wholly plausible and, in the absence of any better supplement, have simply set out the text on the lines of Hesychius' citation. The origin of the papyrus reading, ἐποιμώ3ουσα, has hardly been satisfactorily explained. Whatever it may have been, there is no justification for the *ad hoc* invention of ἐπώ3ω (or ἐπωά3ω), 'lament' (cf. Fraenkel on *Ag.*1316, p.610, n.2). Note finally that τέκνοις is also neutral, a glide (see below, p. 102, n.24).

13 So *Il.*24.296 and 310; *Od.*15.526; Hes.*fr.*60.1; Sapph.136; Stesich.32.1.3 (evidently); Simon.92; Thgn.1198; S.*El.*149 (complete list). Interpretation of this fragment has been strangely confused. Masson (p.137) is clearly right in taking κριγή as 'screech-owl'. Hsch. has κριγή· ἡ γλαῦξ and the conceptual pattern is a known one: 'It was the owl that shrieked, the fatal bellman' (*Macbeth* II.1); and, more closely, *venturi nuntia luctus...bubo* (Ovid *Met.*5.549f.).

14 Cf. *Il.*1.334, X.*An.*2.3.1–3.

15 γῆρας ἐπερχ. is dactylic cliché: *Il.*1.29, Mimn.1.5, Thgn.728 and 1132; cf. the use of the uncompounded verb thus, e.g. *Od.*13.59f.; ἐπέρχεσθαι of time in general, *Od.*2.107, Stesich.35, Hp.*Vict.*1.33 etc.

16 Thgn.291 (αἰδώς) and, comparably, *Il.*2.325, *Od.*24.196, *h.Ap.*156, Hes.*fr.*70.7 (?), Stesich.68 (?), Thgn.867, A.*Ag.*487, S.*fr.*920, E.*Med.*1035, *Trag.Adesp.* 174.2, Men.*mon.*218. Cf. ἀπόλλυσθαι (the prose equivalent) at X.*Smp.*1.15, Tyrt.8.14 (see Diehl's note) and 9.31, Thgn.677.

17 So *Il.*4.482 and 11.157; *h.Ven.*271; Thphr.*HP* 4.16.2 and *CP* 1.4.4; Men.*mon.* 185. A surprisingly ill-attested use.

18 Cf. Hes.*Sc.*299, Ar.*Pl.*213, Arist.*Mete.*368b.1.

19 So *Th.*6.40.1, A.*Pe.*756, B.14b.3, Pl.*R.*328d.

20 See above, p. 83.

21 *Il.*6.6 and 16.95; Epigr.150 F–H (vi B.C) and 837 Peek (iv B.C.); A.*Ch.*863; S.*Ant.*600. Cf. the closely related use for the human agent of deliverance, e.g. *Il.*8.282, *Od.*16.23, Anacr.35, Pi.*P.*3.75, A.*Ch.*131 (conj.), S.*El.*1354 (*pace* Jebb), E.*Hec.*841, Eubul.35.3.

22 Text as codd. (so Page, *O.C.T.*). Editors usually prefer the βλέπει φάος offered by schol. Ar.*Ran.*1028. Note the greater precision of the rhythmical structuring with φ. β.

23 Cf. Nowottny's analysis of these lines, pp.180ff., where, however, she overstates their ambivalence, taking, in particular, the *V* terms 'watered' and 'sunnèd' as *N*. This is impossible. There is no relevant context in which 'I *water x* in fears' and 'I *sun x* with smiles' could pass for non-metaphorical usage.

§36

The pivot is a conspicuous kind of interaction and in general one that operates with a plain directness. Any refraction in it tends to be correspondingly conspicuous and, in fact, to jar. So it is with the now familiar Shakespearean instance,

You are too shallow, Hastings, much too shallow,
To sound the bottom of the after-times.

'Shallow' is pivotal to 'sound the bottom' and a restrained parallelism, consisting chiefly in the metrical alignment of the first 'shallow' and 'bottom', accentuates the relationship. Along with the repetition of the pivotal word, the parallelism serves also, perhaps, to accentuate the dissonance that results from the fact that 'shallow', though clearly neutral, is not exactly the *mot iuste* for the vehicle. Instead of 'too shallow...to sound the bottom', one would expect 'too short...' or 'not long enough...' or '*in* too shallow...': 'too shallow', in other words, belongs to the vehicle *metonymically* rather than literally. One would think that the dissonant presence is well suited to the sardonic tone of the passage, and in this connection one might compare Aeschylus, *fr*.273.12f. The interaction there is broadly similar, although for once no parallel structuring stands behind it:

> Φοῖβος δὲ μῆνιν τίνα φέρων 'Αμφίονι
> πρόρριζον αἰνῶς ἐξεφύλλασεν γένος;

Niobe and her troubles. ἐξεφύλλασεν is the vehicle, πρόρριζον the pivot. The latter is normal of the 'utter' destruction of man or men: πρόρριζον, ὡς ἔοικεν, ἔφθαρται γένος (S.*El*.765);[1] and, naturally, of the destruction of a tree or other plant 'by the roots', 'root and all': τὰ δένδρα ἀνασπαστὰ πρόρριζα γίνεται (Hp.*Flat*.3).[2] But notwithstanding the elementary connection between τὰ μόρια τῶν δένδρων καὶ φυτῶν, οἷον ῥίζα καυλὸς ἀκρεμὼν φύλλον καρπός (Thphr.*HP* 1.12.3), the items are not interchangeable; and no tree or other plant can quite have its foliage[3] stripped off (ἐξεφύλλασεν) 'by the roots', 'root and all', or whatever. The dissonance is not sardonic in this case, but plaintively, and perhaps still appropriately, harsh.[4]

At the other end of the scale, it is easy to point to instances where a pivotal interaction is, for one reason or another, subdued. In A.*Ag*.32f. the slightness of the parallelism is certainly a factor:

> τὰ δεσποτῶν γὰρ εὖ πεσόντα θήσομαι
> τρὶς ἓξ βαλούσης τῆσδέ μοι φρυκτωρίας.

θήσομαι...βαλούσης is the vehicle, εὖ πεσόντα the pivot: εὖ πίπτουσιν... κύβοι (S.*fr*.895);[5] and, for the tenor context of general 'good fortune', τὰ μὲν γὰρ εὖ, τὰ δ' οὐ καλῶς πίπτοντα (E.*El*.1101) and ὅκῃ πεσέεται τὰ Μαρδονίου πρήγματα (Hdt.8.130.4).[6]

In Thgn.532, more simply, the vehicle is subdued and the pivot correspondingly:

> αὐλῶν φθεγγομένων ἱμερόεσσαν ὄπα

Vehicle ὄπα, pivot φθεγγομένων. Van Groningen *ad loc.* notes: 'ὄπα...
seulement ici pour désigner le son de la flûte.' The word is not in fact usual
of any musical instrument, whereas φθέγγεσθαι is: ὅταν...ὁ αὐλὸς φθέγ-
γηται (X.*Smp*.6.3),[7] a sense as 'proper' as the other in question, φθεγξά-
μενος δ' ὀλίγῃ ὀπί (of Odysseus, *Od*.14.492). The parallelism here is slight,
metrical only.

In Pi.*N*.8.32f. the pivot is protracted but none the less subdued:

> ἐχθρὰ δ' ἄρα πάρφασις ἦν καὶ πάλαι,
> αἱμύλων μύθων ὁμόφοιτος, δολοφραδής.

Vehicle ὁμόφοιτος κτλ., pivot ἐχθρά and ἦν (*sic*). The personification pivots
on the whole structure of the main clause, which, however, no more implies
a personification by itself than Homer's ἀλλά τοι αἰεὶ πάντας ἐπ' ἀνθρώπους
κλέος ἔσσεται ἐσθλόν (*Od*.24.93f.)[8] or ἀτασθαλίαι δέ οἱ οἴῳ ἐχθραὶ ἔσαν
(*Od*.21.146f.).[9]

In A.*Prom*.726f. a different factor is present:

> τραχεῖα πόντου Σαλμυδησσία γνάθος,
> ἐχθρόξενος ναύτῃσι...

ἐχθρόξενος vehicle, τραχεῖα pivot: γῆ...τρηχέα (Hdt.4.23.1) and μὴ
τρηχὺς ἴσθι (Eup.315).[10] The phraseology and the whole mode of interaction are reminiscent of Arch.92a:

> ὁρᾷς ἵν' ἔστ' ἐκεῖνος ὑψηλὸς πάγος
> τρηχύς τε καὶ παλίγκοτος;

But the interaction there, τρηχύς pivotal to the metaphorical παλίγκοτος, is
organized with greater clarity, enforced by the simple '*N* and *V*' parallelism
already exemplified. In the Aeschylus the unrelated metaphor in γνάθος has
a disruptive effect.[11]

My final example of the pivot involves no real parallel structure. It ranks
as pivot only because the neutral term, positionally articulated and almost
punning, has a more decisive force than 'glide' implies. A.*Th*.941ff. (beginning
of sentence):

> πικρὸς λυτὴρ νεικέων ὁ πόντιος ξεῖνος...σίδαρος.

Vehicle λυτήρ and ξεῖνος, pivot πικρός: πικρὰ βέλεμνα (*Il*.22.206)[12] and
εἶναι...ἐχθροῖσι...πικρόν (Sol.1.5).[13] But we are now certainly on the
borderland between pivot and glide.

---

1 So Hdt.1.32.9, E.*Hipp*.684, Ar.*Ran*.587, Andoc.1.146.

2 Often (as in Hp. here) destruction by the wind: so e.g. *Il*.11.157, Thphr.*HP* 3.6.4.

3 Or branches and foliage together; cf. Pickard-Cambridge 113 and LSJ *s.v.* φυλλάς 11.2.

4 Pickard-Cambridge 113 mistakenly refers to πρ. and ἐξ. as a 'mixture of metaphors' and describes the supposed mixture as 'not serious'. It *is* serious. N.B. that Hsch. ἐκφυλάσαι (i.e. ἐκφυλλ- ?)· ἐκσπάσαι may represent a well-meaning attempt to interpret this *Niobe* passage without the dissonance. ἐκσπάσαι, unlike ἐκφυλλάσαι, would go neatly with πρόρριζος: cf. the Hippocratic ἀνασπαστὰ πρόρριζα cited above, p. 94. Another dissonant instance, coincidentally still more similar to Shakespeare's 'shallow', A.*Supp*.407f.: vehicle κολυμβητῆρος κτλ., pivoting on βαθείας. *Qua T*, the word refers to mental quality (below, p. 118); *qua V*, to the 'deep' sea – except that the thing that is to be deep in this sense is the diver, deep down *in* the sea, rather than the sea itself. But in this instance, I fail to see any propriety in the dissonant effect.

5 So, with πίπτειν only, Alex.34, Pl.*R*.604c; not the sort of use for which one expects a more substantial distribution. But perhaps cf. also Epich.177 πόθεν δ' ἐολκὼς εὐπετὲς ἔβλης. (LSJ *s.v.* εὐπετής begin 'prop. of dice, *falling well*', but cite neither this passage nor any other.)

6 So, with εὖ etc., E.*Or*.603 and *Med*.55, S.*Tr*.62; cf. Ion Hist.6 Jac. (apophth. of Sophocles) κατ' ὀρθόν μοι πέπτωκεν τὸ στρατήγημα; and with πίπτειν only ('befall'), Pi.*O*.12.10, E.*Hipp*.718,Thphr.*HP* 3.5.5.

7 So Thgn.761; of other musical instruments, *h.Merc*.484; X.*An*.4.2.7, 5.2.14, 7.4.19; Archyt.1; Arist.*Metaph*.1019b.15.

8 Or Hes.*Op*.11, Pi.*N*.8.50f. Cf. also Musaeus *fr*.5 Kinkel παραιφασίη δέ τις ἔσται.

9 ἐχθρός of abstractions thus: Mimn.5.4, Thgn.270, Pi.*O*.2.59, Hdt.9.16.5, Ar.*Ran*.359.

10 τραχύς of people, human nature: also Sol.23.15, Pi.*N*.4.96, A.*Th*.1044, Hdt. 1.73.4, Arist.*Ath*.19.1, Chilo 12 (1.63 Diels–Kranz). τραχὺ ἦθος is cited as 'dead metaphor' by Demetr.*Eloc*.86.

11 A comparable interaction at Sol.3.26–8: vehicle – or rather its most striking term – ὑπέρθορεν, pivoting on ἔρχεται in parallel structure. *Qua T*, νοέω κακὸν ὕμμιν ἐρχόμενον *Od*.20.367f., so Sol.1.54, A.*Pe*.440, X.*HG* 6.5.43; *qua V*, e.g. ἐξῆλθον καὶ ὑπέρθορον ἑρκίον αὐλῆς *Il*.9.476. The distraction here is the intervention of the *V* terms οἴκαδε and ἔχειν, both implying an animate force; and this intervention, combined with the interaction's inherent restraint, makes its force slight indeed. (The effect is not to make ἔρχεται a glide to οἴκαδε: the latter is substantial enough to interfere, but not, by itself, to evoke a decisive image.)

12 So *Il*.4.118, *Od*.22.8, Mimn.13.8, S.*Tr*.681; cf. A.*Th*.730.

13 So Hdt.1.123.2, Hp.*Acut*.42, Thgn.301, A.*Prom*.739, Men.*Scut*.338; cf. Sapph. 15(*b*).9. With this interaction compare a slightly dubious instance at B.*fr*.4.61f., where μεγαλάνορα is presumably *V* (subdued personification, *pace* Campbell) and, if so, the well-placed τίκτει is pivotal to it. (τίκτειν *qua T*, of abstract

subjects, is absolutely standard, and especially well-attested in literary Ionic. To the examples in LSJ *s.v.* IV add e.g. Sol.5.9, Thgn.392, B.10.46, Democr.71 and 178, Hp.*Aph*.3.1.) Another comparable instance, Pi.*P*.3.104–6, where the vehicle is ἐπιβρίσαις, inherently unspecific, but in the context of πνοαὶ ἀνέμων inevitably coloured correspondingly: the ὄλβος becomes a wind. (For ἐπιβρίθειν of winds, see Thphr.*Vent*.34 τὸ πνεῦμα...ᾗ...ἂν ἐπιβρίσῃ, cf. Hp.*Flat*.14, *Il*.16.384.) The pivot is πολύς, in emphatic position: *qua* T, πλοῦτος γὰρ ἔσεισι πολλός Hom.*Epigr*.15.3f., ὅταν πολὺς ὄλβος ἕπηται Sol.5.9, cf. Hes.*Th*.418, *h.Merc*.117, Pi.*P*.5.14 etc.; *qua* V, οἱ ὀρνιθίαι (spring winds) ἔπνευσαν πολλοί Hp.*Epid*.7.105, so Arist.*Mete*.364b.6, Thphr.*Vent*.53, Even.2.5 Diehl, cf. D.25.57, Ar.*Eq*.760 and *Ran*.1221 (this use is most inadequately treated in LSJ).

§37

It is just possible for a simile to be introduced by a glide, rather than, or as well as, by a pivot. Keats shows this:

> But when the melancholy fit shall fall
> Sudden from heaven like a weeping cloud...

The pivot is 'fall', passably normal of 'fits' and the like – 'God caused a deep sleep to fall upon Adam' – and also in the same terminology as 'cloud', although by metonymy only: the contents of clouds fall, not usually the clouds themselves. But 'from heaven' is neutral also: rain falls 'from heaven', physically, and fits are sent 'from heaven'.

A parallel occurs in Pi.*P*.10.53f.:

> ἄωτος ὕμνων
> ἐπ' ἄλλοτ' ἄλλον ὧτε μέλισσα θύνει λόγον.

The passage, which comes from Pindar's earliest ode (498), displays what seems to me the characteristic delicacy of Pindaric style, certainly where interaction is concerned. The 'official' ground term, so to speak, θύνει, is not in the neutral terminology that one might expect of a ground term; it belongs to the vehicle: θύνειν is something a bee might do, but not a song.[1] The neutral terminology itself, the glide, is paradigmatically subdued, consisting essentially of ἐπί: ἄνειμι δὲ ἐπὶ τὸν πρότερον λόγον (Hdt.1.140.3)[2] and θρῴσκων ἄλλοτ' ἐπ' ἄλλον (*Il*.15.684). Norwood's remark on Pindar's creative use of 'the noun, the verb, even the preposition' is rightly conceived.[3]

But the characteristic use of the glide is to introduce metaphor and here one might usefully follow up Norwood's incursion into grammar. There is, in fact, a certain value in noting the particular grammatical status of a given example, in that the distinction between, say, verb-based and noun-based glides corresponds to perceptible differences in effect.⁴ An early example of the verbal glide is Tyrt.9.22:

σπουδῇ δ' ἔσχεθε κῦμα μάχης.

κῦμα vehicle, ἔσχεθε glide: σχήσουσιν πόλεμον (*Il*.14.100) or σθένος ἀνέρος... σχῶμεν (*Il*.21.309) and ἔσχε δὲ κῦμα (the river-god, *Od*.5.451).⁵
A solitary example from Pindar is *P*.5.2ff. (on πλοῦτος):

ὅταν τις...αὐτὸν ἀνάγῃ
πολύφιλον ἐπέταν.

Vehicle, subdued, πολύφιλον κτλ.; glide, equally subdued, ἀνάγῃ: ἀνήγαγε ἐς Μέμφιν τὴν Ἑλένην τε καὶ τὰ χρήματα (Hdt.2.115.1).⁶ Contrast A.*Prom.* 368:

ποταμοὶ πυρὸς δάπτοντες ἀγρίαις γνάθοις...

Vehicle γνάθοις, glide δάπτοντες. The verb is used of fire, πυρὶ δαπτέμεν (*Il*.23.183), as of destructive animals, owners of γνάθοι: λύκοι...ἔλαφον... δάπτουσιν (*Il*.16.156ff.).⁷ The sense of strength that this glide carries is primarily in the meaning, not in the stylistic mechanism, but it is surely not fanciful to appeal also to that truistic energy which the verb, above all elements of speech, can possess.⁸

The glide can, however, be much less obtrusive. One good Shakespearean instance has a phrase as the unobtrusive instrument. *Antony and Cleopatra* v.2, the queen and the asp:

Come thou mortal wretch,
With thy sharp teeth this knot intrinsicate
Of life at once untie.

Vehicle 'knot', glide 'with thy sharp teeth': teeth by which a knot might be bitten loose and which the asp actually or supposedly possesses.

Of the comparably quiet Greek instances most, as it happens, involve the adjectival glide. Aeschylus' starry potentates have already been cited:⁹

καὶ τοὺς φέροντας χεῖμα καὶ θέρος βροτοῖς
λαμπροὺς δυνάστας...

The adjectival glide is certainly less assertive than the verbal, as the examples following bear out. A.*Supp*.779 (the chorus):

μέλας γενοίμαν καπνὸς
νέφεσσι γειτονῶν Διός.

Vehicle καπνὸς κτλ., glide μέλας. The Danaids *are* black, or at least so

98

describe themselves (μελανθὲς ἡλιόκτυπον γένος, 154f.);[10] and smoke likewise (ὁ δὲ καπνὸς μέλας ὅτι..., Thphr.*Ign.*75).[11]

Anacr.3.6ff., prayer to Artemis:

> ἀνδρῶν ἐσκατορᾷς πόλιν
> χαίρουσ', οὐ γὰρ ἀνημέρους
> ποιμαίνεις πολιήτας.

Vehicle ποιμαίνεις, glide ἀνημέρους: τὰ ἥμερα 3ῷα (Pl.*Phdr.*260b) and ἄνθρωποι οὕτως ἥμεροι καὶ φιλάνθρωποι (D.21.49).[12]

Pratinas, *fr.*5 shows the glide prettily positioned before a slight rhythmic pause, but without giving the interaction any undue emphasis:

> μήτε σύντονον δίωκε
> μήτε τὰν ἀνειμέναν
> μοῦσαν, ἀλλὰ τὰν μέσαν
> νεῶν ἄρουραν αἰόλι3ε τῷ μέλει.

Vehicle νεῶν ἄρουραν, glide μέσαν: 'intermediate' (τοῖς τόνοις, οἷον ὀξείᾳ καὶ βαρείᾳ καὶ μέσῃ, Arist.*Rh.*1403b.30)[13] and ordinary concrete 'middle' (μέσσον κἀπ πεδίον...ἐσσεύοντο, *Il.*11.167).

More subdued, again, the glide at Pi.*I.*7.16f.,

> ἀλλὰ παλαιὰ γὰρ
> εὕδει χάρις.

Vehicle εὕδει, glide παλαιά. The two words jointly imply a momentary personification (γρῆυς...παλαιή, *Od.*19.346), but παλαιός is also usual enough of abstractions like χάρις.[14]

Pi.*O.*6.91 (of the chorus-master, Aeneas):

> γλυκὺς κρατὴρ ἀγαφθέγκτων ἀοιδᾶν.

Vehicle κρατήρ, glide γλυκύς. The bowl (or its contents) is γλυκύς in one sense, the man in another: εἶναι δὲ γλυκὺν ὧδε φίλοισ' (Sol.1.5).[15] At *N.*9.50 Pindar uses the same glide in reverse, speaking of the wine itself,

> ἐγκιρνάτω τίς μιν, γλυκὺν κώμου προφάταν

with προφάταν as vehicle and γλυκύν in the same rôle as before.

The nominal glide is, on the whole, more substantial. From *The Waste Land*:

> These fragments I have shored against my ruins.

The 'fragments' are the bits and pieces of the once whole literary-cultural tradition which have been insistently quoted and alluded to throughout the poem (Baudelaire, Spenser, Wagner, Augustine and so on) and the concrete bits and pieces to go with the vehicle, 'shored against my ruins'. In the Greek corpus, this kind of glide is peculiarly characteristic of Aeschylus. *Supp.*663f.:

ἥβας δ' ἄνθος ἄδρεπτον
ἔστω.

Vehicle ἄδρεπτον, glide ἄνθος: ἄνθεα δρέπομεν χείρεσσ' ἐρόεντα (*h.Cer.*425) and the universal poetic cliché, ἥβης ἄνθος.[16] *Ag.*844ff.:

τὰ δ' ἄλλα πρὸς πόλιν τε καὶ θεούς. . .
ὅτῳ δὲ καὶ δεῖ φαρμάκων παιωνίων,
ἤτοι κέαντες ἢ τεμόντες. . .

Vehicle παιωνίων κτλ., glide φαρμάκων, deploying two familiar senses, medical and non-medical: φάρμακα. . .ἐπὶ ἕλκη (Hp.*Mochl.*37) and φάρμακον κακῶν (Carc.7).[17] Conceptually and structurally similar is *Ch.*539:

ἄκος τομαῖον ἐλπίσασα πημάτων. . .

Vehicle τομαῖον, glide ἄκος: the specialized medical sense (ἰατρόμαντις. . . ἄκη τομαῖα. . .πράξας A.*Supp.*263ff.)[18] and the generalized sense (ῥεχθέντος κακοῦ. . .ἄκος *Il.*9.250).[19] From the same play, vv.661f.:

ὥρα δ' ἐμπόρους μεθιέναι
ἄγκυραν ἐν δόμοισι. . .

Vehicle μεθιέναι ἄγκυραν, glide ἐμπόρους, implying a voyager on ship[20] as well as the tenor sense, a traveller by land.[21] From the *Eumenides*, Clytemnestra to the chorus, v.137:

σὺ δ' αἱματηρὸν πνεῦμ' ἐπουρίσασα τῷ. . .

Vehicle ἐπουρίσασα, glide πνεῦμα, 'breath' and 'wind'.[22] A last instance from Aeschylus, *Ch.*67:

τίτας φόνος πέπηγεν οὐ διαρρύδαν.

Vehicle πέπηγεν κτλ. – vengeful murder 'clots' – and glide φόνος, both 'murder' and the concrete 'gore', φόνον αἵματος (*Il.*16.162), in which sense the word coheres with the vehicle: αἷμα πήγνυται (Arist.*HA* 515b.32).[23] This glide has its effect – it is extremely persuasive – rather in the unassertive manner of the adjectival.[24]

The limits of unassertiveness are reached by the prepositional glide. As it was Pindar who used this type of glide to simile (*P.*10.53f.), so it is Pindar, master of the delicate style, who instances the prepositional glide to metaphor (*O*.2.19f.):

ἐσλῶν γὰρ ὑπὸ χαρμάτων πῆμα θνᾴσκει
παλίγκοτον δαμασθέν.

θνᾴσκει κτλ. vehicle, ὑπό glide: ἐγγίνεται . . . ὕβρις ὑπὸ τῶν παρεόντων ἀγαθῶν (Hdt.3.80.3) and ὑφ᾽ Ἕκτορος θνήσκοντες (*Il*.1.242).[25]

1 θύνειν (a rare word) of animal movements, *Il*.11.73; cf. Hes.*Sc*.210 (θυνεῖν). N.B. that there is no interaction between ἄωτος and μέλισσα, as there would be if ἄω. meant 'flower'. Despite the common misapprehension that corresponds with that common mistranslation, the word has no demonstrable connection with flowers; see Appendix XI.

2 So E.*Hipp*.292, Th.2.36.4.

3 Norwood 96.

4 Such considerations seem also to mark off the practices of Aeschylus and Pindar. The noun-based glide appears to be decidedly Aeschylean, but not conspicuously Pindaric. Pindar favours, if anything, glides based on the less concrete elements like the adjective.

5 So A.*Pe*.746, cf. *Il*.21.366.

6 The relevant uses of ἀνάγειν are normal from Homer onwards: e.g. *Od*.3.272 (people), *Il*.8.203f. (goods).

7 δάπτειν of fire also at B.16.14; so A.*Eu*.1041 πυριδάπτῳ and Hsch. Ἡφαιστό-δαπτα · πυρίκαυτα. (Cf. also, eventually, E.*Med*.1189?) This evidence is not what one would normally regard as adequate, but the word itself is much rarer than one might suppose in any of its standard senses. Including the occasional derivatives and the compounds δαρδάπτειν (doubtless taken as such by folk-etymology, whether or not it was historically), διαδάπτειν and καταδάπτειν, the instances fall under five headings, all more or less uncommon, but all repre-sented in Homer and so *prima facie* normal. A number of the instances are clearly tropical and it is not always easy to see which one of the five headings they presuppose (in some cases, more than one). The whole situation is obscured in LSJ. The headings are: (*a*) Of fire, as above. (*b*) Of wild animals, as the cited *Il*.16.156ff.; also *Il*.11.481, Pi.*fr*.222; *Il*.11.479, Ar.*Nub*.711 (both δαρ-); *Il*.22.339, *Od*.3.259 (both κατα-); cf. also Emped.136 and, again, *Il*.23.183. (*c*) Of spears, *Il*.13.831; also *Il*.5.858 and 21.398 (both with διά); *P.Hib*.172.98 δορίδαπτος (item in a mid iii B.C. poetical onomasticon); cf. also, eventually, Ar.*fr*.409 (*sens. obsc.*, see Taillardat 75), A.*Supp*.70 (?), Pi.*N*.8.23 (see below, p. 165). (*d*) Of destruction of property etc., Alc.70.7 and 129.23; *Od*.14.92 and 16.315 (both δαρ-). (*e*) Of mental distress, as A.*Prom*.437 δάπτομαι κέαρ. So A.*Supp*.70ff. (καρδίαν), S.*OT* 682 and *fr*.574.10; *Od*.16.92 (κατα-); Ar.*Ran*.66 (δαρ-).

8 On such matters, see Donald Davie's very intelligent book, *Articulate Energy*, London, 1955, esp. pp.33ff.

9 Above, p. 87. Cf. my remarks on A.*Th*.941ff., above, p. 95.

10 μέλας of people's skin colour: Xenoph.14.1, Hp.*Aer.*24, Hdt.2.22.3.

11 So Arist.*Col.*791b.23, A.*Th.*494.

12 ἥμερος (the neg. is rare in any sense) of animals: also *Od.*15.162, A.*Ag.*721, Arist.*HA* 573a.31, Ctes.Hist.45K Jac. ἥμερος of men: Hom.*inc.sed.fr.*3 Kinkel (?), Pi.*P.*3.6, Hdt.2.30.5, Hp.*Aer.*24 and (the neg.) A.*Prom.*716. There may also be an allusion in Anacreon's οὐ...ἀνημέρους to Ἡμέρα, an Arcadian title of Artemis, on which see LSJ *s.v.* ἥμερος II and Jebb on B.11.39 (10.39 Jebb).

13 This parallel is not supposed to imply that Pratinas' μέσα means the same as Aristotle's – nor can it be equated with the famous *mese* in Greek music. For μέσος = 'intermediate' in general, see e.g. Hdt.4.6.1, Thgn.335, Pl.*R.*330b.

14 ἀρετή Th.3.67.2, εὐγένεια Gorg.11, φιλία Antipho Soph.64, δόξα Pi.*I.*3.16 and Lycurg.110.

15 γλυκύς of people: also Alcm.3.63 (prob.), Sapph.102.1, Thgn.301, Pi.*I.*2.36, B.*fr.*21.4, S.*OC* 106; so γλυκύθυμος, *Il.*20.467. γλυκύς of οἶνος: Xenoph.22.3 Diels–Kranz, Epich.124, Hp.*Morb.*2.64.

16 E.g. *Il.*13.484, Hes.*Th.*988, Tyrt.7.28, Mimn.1.4, Sol.12.1, *h.Merc.*375, Semon. (?).29.6, Thgn.1008, Pi.*P.*4.158, Phryn.Com.33; also two verse inscriptions of the late archaic period, Peek 1.942 and 1960a; similarly, without ἥβης, *h.Cer.*108, X.*Smp.*8.14 and (apparently) Arch.*P.Col.ined.*18. The usage is presupposed by (Taillardat's *clef*) Democr.294 γήραος ἄνθος.

17 φάρμακον thus: Hes.*Op.*485, Alc.335.3, Thgn.809, S.*Aj.*1255 (all absol.); Arist.*Pol.*1321a.16 (πρὸς τοῦτο); Hippon.42.4, Simon.87 Bergk, A.*Ag.*548, Pl.*Lg.*647e (all with gen.); Arch.7.7 (with dat.).

18 As Hp.*Acut.*1, Hdt.4.187.3 etc.

19 So Hdt.1.94.3, A.*Ch.*72, Thphr.*HP* 2.8.3 etc.

20 Whether as merchant (Hdt.4.154.3–4, Pl.*R.*371a; so ἐμπορία from Hes.*Op.*646 onwards) or passenger (*Od.*2.319, 24.300).

21 Distribution not all it might be: B.18.36, A.*fr.*17.20, S.*OC* 25, E.*Alc.*999, Pl.Com.183; so συνέμπορος A.*Supp.*939, S.*Tr.*318, E.*Ba.*57, Pl.*Phd.*108b; so ἐμπορεύεσθαι Ar.*Ach.*480 (cf. Epich.53?). Re-etymologically, cf. πόρος, 'path' (as X.*Cyr.*1.6.40), though ὁ ἐν πόρῳ seems not to be attested of land travellers. The *N* status of ἐμπόρους is noted (contortedly) by Ole Smith 33f.

22 πνεῦμα, 'breath': e.g. A.*Th.*464, Th.2.49.2, Hp.*Vict.*2.64, Archyt.1. πνεῦμα, 'wind': e.g. Emped.84.4, A.*Pe.*101, Hdt.8.13, Thphr.*Vent.*8.

23 φόνος, 'gore': also Emped.128.8, A.*Eu.*184, Hp.*Morb.*2.73, Thphr.*HP* 3.18.13. αἷμα πήγνυται: likewise, Hp.*Morb.*1.33, Meno *Iatr.*17.28, Pl.*Tim.*82d, Thphr. *Lap.*37.

24 Another restrained Aeschylean noun-glide, τέκνοις in *fr.*273.7 (on the image, see above, p. 89), the word being normal of the young of chickens and other birds (e.g. *Il.*2.311, *Od.*16.217, Epich.172.4, A.*Th.*292, Arist.*GA* 774b.30) as of people. Cf. also the quasi-nominal τέλεον at *Ag.*1504 (on the image, see below, p. 185). *Qua T*, 'adult', in antithesis to νεαροῖς (which appears to be *T*, not *N*): ἐν μὲν παισίν, ἐν δὲ ἐφήβοις, ἄλλο τελείοις ἀνδράσιν X.*Cyr.*1.2.4, so Hp.*Art.*33,

Arist.*Pol.*1259b.3, Pl.*Lg.*929c. *Qua V*, of the sacrificial victim: θύεται τὰ τέλεα
τῶν προβάτων Hdt.1.183.2, cf. *Il.*1.66 etc.
25 ὑπό, 'thanks to': also Antipho 3.3.8, S.*Ant.*221, cf. Sol.3.38. θνῄσκειν ὑπό:
Hdt.1.137.2, S.*El.*444 etc.

Convergence
§38

The category which I am calling 'convergence' involves, in the first place,
the stationing of the neutral term, or terms, after the vehicle. Its essential
property, that is, is formal, as with pivot and glide; but unlike those two, the
articulation it invites is not parallel structure but prominent position; and,
more significantly, its function is exercised not so much on behalf of the
vehicle as of the image as a whole.

Any neutral term represents a meeting of two parallel lines.[1] In κλάζοντες
"Αρη τρόπον αἰγυπιῶν and in any other instance of pivot or of glide, only
one of the lines, the tenor, is visible, known, operative at the moment when
the interaction begins. The neutral term is, for the moment, a tenor term like
any other. Inevitably, then, when the unexpected line appears, when, that is,
the vehicle is presented, it is the vehicle that is the beneficiary of the interaction. But if the neutral term follows the vehicle, when both lines are
already 'there', there may be a felt convergence of the two; the lines, which
is to say the image as a whole, are perceptibly drawn together.[2] In English
this is perhaps most familiar in the crude form of humorous punning comparisons like the following, in eighteenth-century shape: 'Why is a philosopher like a looking-glass? Because he *reflects*.'[3] The effect is violent, a
violent resolution of the disparate elements with a kind of *Q.E.D.* finality
to it; and one notes that 'reflects' is the ground term.

But the essential converging effect is not dependent on such a crude
question and answer organization. Consider the song in *Cymbeline*:

> Golden lads and girls all must,
> As chimney-sweepers, *come to dust*.

The qualitative difference is obviously considerable, but the effect is still
substantially humorous and violent – the pun is 'shocking' enough – despite
the qualifying sobriety of the 'golden'/'chimney' clash. One notes that again
the convergence consists in the official ground term.

But neither pun nor humour nor violence nor an official ground term is
essential to convergence. Consider Cleopatra's address to the 'pretty worm
of Nilus':

> Come thou mortal wretch,
>
> .   .   .
>
> Be angry and dispatch. O couldst thou speak,
> That I might hear thee call great Caesar ass,
> Unpolicied.

Charm.	O Eastern star.
Cleo.	Peace, peace.

> Dost thou not see my baby at my breast,
> That sucks the nurse asleep.

The force and pathos of the last sentence owe a good deal to a double subdued convergence. 'Baby' and 'sucks the nurse' make up the two parts of the vehicle, and each is followed, and the whole image thereby sealed, by its articulated convergence: 'at my breast', which babies are and the asp is, and 'asleep', which nurses may be and Cleopatra soon will be, 'sleep' being a stock equivalent for 'death'.

All these instances share an effect of finality, which relates simply to the common positioning of neutral terminology prominently at the end both of the image, or a main section of the image, and the syntactic unit; positional articulation is almost, though not absolutely, indispensable. Pivot and glide mitigate the extraneousness of the vehicle. Convergence, by its finality, sets the seal on the image as a whole.

1 I.e. two *otherwise* parallel lines. The model is unsophisticated. I am not suggesting that these interactions take place at infinity.
2 I cannot see that convergence has had any real recognition, but, curiously enough and quite independently, my basic analogy has a marked superficial resemblance to one of Dr Johnson's: 'a simile may be compared to lines converging to a point...an exemplification may be considered as two parallel lines' (*Life of Cowley*, 1.20).
3 The type has a Greek counterpart in the so-called εἰκάзειν, for which see e.g. A.*Ag*.1629ff. (and Fraenkel *ad loc.*), Thphr.*Char*.20.9 and McCall 13, n.1.

§39

With convergence, as with pivot and glide, an important consideration is whether the interaction is based on the 'official' ground term (which would often mean that simile, not metaphor, is involved). Another consideration is whether the formal structure is *V–N*, with the vehicle modulating into neutral, or *V–T–N*, with a return to normality before the partial recapitulation of the vehicle. The latter structure tends to be more decisive, and it is noteworthy that this more decisive type is very common in Aeschylus, but not in Pindar, while the *V–N* structure is common in both. And, as with the pivot again, Aeschylean, but not Pindaric, convergence readily employs the ground term in simile.

The simile at A.*Supp.*469 exemplifies the *V–N* structure:

κακῶν δὲ πλῆθος ποταμὸς ὡς ἐπέρχεται,

with ἐπέρχεται neutral like the paradigmatic ἐπέλθῃ in ὅταν κλύδων κακῶν ἐπέλθῃ.¹ Compare B.*fr.*56:

ἀρετὰ γὰρ ἐπαινεομένα δένδρον ὡς ἀέξεται.

Convergence on ἀέξεται: αὔξεται τὸ δένδρον (Hp.*Nat.Puer.*26)² and ἀρετὴ . . . μείζων αὔξεται τελουμένη (E.*fr.*1029.4f.).³ And again, Epich.155:

οἱοναὶ μύκαι ἄρ᾽ ἐξεσκληκότες πνιξεῖσθέ με.

'Like mushrooms, you'll. . .me', with a punning and humorous 'come to dust' convergence (without a full articulation) on πνιξεῖσθε: 'make me cross' (ἐπνιγόμην. . .κἀπεθύμουν Ar.*Nub.*1036)⁴ and 'choke me' physiologically (τὰ σιτία ἃ πρόσθεν ἐβεβρώκει πνίγει αὐτόν Hp.*Int.*27).⁵

One also finds a *V–N* structure in simile in which the interaction involves not the ground term, but a term nominally belonging to the vehicle. The resulting convergence is generally subdued. Wordsworth's much maligned *Daffodils*:

I wandered lonely as a cloud
That floats on high o'er vales and hills.

'O'er vales and hills' locates the wandering of the clouds and also, by suggestion, of the speaker. Pindar, *N.*6.27ff.:

ἔλπομαι
μέγα εἰπὼν σκοποῦ ἄντα τυχεῖν
ὥτ᾽ ἀπὸ τόξου ἱείς.

Convergence on ἱείς, nominally part of the vehicle: τοξεύειν ἄνω ἱέντες (X.*An.*3.4.17)⁶ and μᾶλλον πολλῷ ἵεσαν τῆς φωνῆς (Hdt.4.135.3).⁷ Sappho, *fr.*47:

ἔρος δ᾽ ἐτίναξέ μοι
φρένας, ὡς ἄνεμος κὰτ ὄρος δρύσιν ἐμπέτων.

Structurally part of the vehicle again, ἐμπέτων makes the convergence: ἵνα οἱ ψυχροὶ μὴ ἐμπίπτωσιν ἄνεμοι (X.*Mem.*3.8.9)⁸ and Παρμενίσκῳ καὶ πρότερον ἐνέπιπτον ἀθυμίαι καὶ ἀπαλλαγῆς βίου ἐπιθυμίη, ὁτὲ δὲ πάλιν εὐθυμίη (Hp.*Epid.*5.84).⁹

In metaphor, *V–N* convergence is often no more spectacular:

Dost thou not see my baby at my breast...

Likewise Pi.*O*.2.89f.:

> ἄγε θυμέ· τίνα βάλλομεν
> ἐκ μαλθακᾶς αὖτε φρενὸς εὐκλέας ὀιστοὺς ἱέντες;

Vehicle βάλλομεν and ὀιστούς, convergence on ἱέντες, with the same two senses as ἱείς above. Compare Bacchylides, 5.187ff.:

> χρὴ δ᾽ ἀλαθείας χάριν
> αἰνεῖν, φθόνον ἀμφοτέραισιν
> χερσὶν ἀπωσάμενον.

Vehicle ἀμφοτέραισιν χερσίν, converging on ἀπωσάμενον: χερσὶν ἀπώσασθαι λίθον (*Od*.9.305) and τὰς διαβολὰς...ἀπωσόμεθα (Arist.*Rh.Al.*1442b.22).[10] Likewise Pindar, *I*.8.51f. (Achilles):

> Ἑλέναν τ᾽ ἐλύσατο, Τροίας
> ἶνας ἐκταμὼν δορί.

Vehicle ἶνας ἐκταμών, converging on δορί: both the weapon needed to ἐκταμεῖν Troy's metaphorical 'sinews' and the actual weapon Achilles used to kill his Trojan victims;[11] a very subdued convergence, the 'lines' of the image being so close together. And likewise Aeschylus, *Ag*.827f., on the Trojan horse:

> ὑπερθορὼν δὲ πύργον ὠμηστὴς λέων
> ἅδην ἔλειξεν αἵματος τυραννικοῦ.

Vehicle ὑπερθορὼν...λέων...ἔλειξεν, converging on αἵματος and the terminologically colourless τυραννικοῦ: on the one hand, αἷμα as something that can be 'licked', τὸ αἷμα ἀναλείχουσι (Hdt.1.74.6); on the other, αἷμα as blood shed in battle, ἔκ τ᾽ ἀνδροκτασίης ἔκ θ᾽ αἵματος (*Il*.11.164).

Several of these instances involved participial convergence. Fully verbal convergence can show greater vigour. Sol.3.18f.:

> δουλοσύνην
> ἣ στάσιν ἔμφυλον πόλεμόν θ᾽ εὕδοντ᾽ ἐπεγείρει.

Vehicle εὕδοντα, converging on ἐπεγείρει: μηδ᾽ εὕδοντ᾽ ἐπέγειρε (Thgn.469, literally) and πόλεμον...ἔγειρε (*Il*.20.31).[12] Here, perhaps for the first time in the Greek instances, one sees that convergence may have an argumentative force, not merely rounding off the image in a satisfying formal way, but positively justifying it: 'εὕδοντα ??' – 'yes, because ἐπεγείρει'. Normal usage steps in firmly while the surprise caused by the image – and εὕδοντα is novel enough – is still present, and argues the image out. It now becomes clear that the essential significance of the 'philosopher/looking-glass/reflects' type, which is argumentative in just this way, is considerable.[13]

1 See above, p. 22.
2 See above, p. 83.
3 ἀρετὴ αὔξεται as a specific collocation: also Pi.*N*.8.40; so, with comparable subjects, *Il*.17.226, *Od*.2.315, Hes.*Sc*.96; more generally, Hdt.7.16α.2 (ὕβρις) etc.
4 Seemingly a colloquial use: also S.*Ichn*.393, Pherecr.51, *Com.Adesp*.336.6; ἀποπνίγειν similarly, D.19.199, Antiph.171, Alex.16.7.
5 πνίγειν, 'choke', with things as subject: also Antiph.188, prov. *ap.* Arist.*EN* 1146a.35. So ἀποπνίγειν, Pherecr.159, Alex.266, Ephipp.27, Thphr.*HP* 4.4.13.
6 So *Il*.13.650, Hes.*Th*.684.
7 So *Il*.3.221, Hes.*Th*.10, Pi.*N*.8.49. Note that in *Nemean* Six, σκοποῦ κτλ. is *V* terminology (producing *V–V*, metaphor–simile), hence provides no exception to the 'rule' (above, p. 88) that Pindar avoids the pivotal introduction to simile (*N–V*). Setting aside the stereotyped and *prima facie* normal ἀπὸ σκοποῦ (with or without a verb like εἰρῆσθαι), found at *Od*.11.344, X.*Smp*.2.10, Pl.*Tim*.25e and *Tht*.179c (cf. also μῦθος ἀπόσκοπος Emped.62.3), phrases directly comparable to Pindar's have a much more suspect distribution: Pindar himself elsewhere, *fr*.6a(g) (?) (cf. *O*.2.89 and 13.94, *N*.9.55), tragedy (A.*Ag*.628, cf. S.*Ant*.1033) and Plato (*Lg*.744a, cf. *Tht*.194a) (apparently the complete list).
8 So Hdt.2.111.1, *Il*.23.216, Hes.*Op*.511, Emped.100.21, B.17.5f., Thphr.*Vent*.34.
9 ἐμπίπτειν of emotions: also *Il*.9.436, *Od*.14.88, Hdt.4.203.3, Th.6.24.3, Asclep. Tragil.6b Jac., A.*Ag*.341, Philippid.9.1. Note that in the Sappho, as in the Pindar above, n.7, the ground term is *V*, not *N*. ἐτίναξε belongs terminologically with ἄνεμος: see *Od*.5.368, cf. Hp.*Flat*.14 and Ibyc.5.12 (conj.). This verb is not, incidentally, purely poetical, *pace* LSJ: as well as Hp. *loc. cit.* (which LSJ in fact note), there is also Thphr.*Sign*.16 (which they ignore).
10 Similarly, Arch.7.10, Sol.2.8, Stesich.33.1, Semon.7.101, Hdt.1.95.2, Th.3.39.4, Philox.8.4 Diehl, S.*Ph*.1122, E.*HF* 1152, *Trag.Adesp*.105, D.19.217 (all with abstract objects); cf. also *Il*.1.97 (act. not med.), *h.Cer*.276; but *Il*.12.276 (νεῖκος ἀπωσαμένους) and similar passages seem different, metonymic (as here νεῖκος = 'the enemy'?), with the verb genuinely physical.
11 ταμεῖν of spears, *Il*.5.73f. etc.; cf. A.*Ch*.347 δορίτμητος.
12 So *Il*.13.778, Hes.*Th*.666, Thgn.549, Hdt.8.142.2. The compound verb alludes, by right, to the usage of its elements.
13 Apropos argumentative convergence, cf. my discussion of Quintil.5.11.24, above, Prolegom.ix. But assuming that Q. is in fact thinking of interaction, which is not certain, it is much more likely to be neutral-based interaction in general than convergence specifically.

§ 40

Convergence to simile can be most decisively argumentative when the closure follows a return to the tenor (V–T–N), especially the immediate tenor:

> As flies to wanton boys, are we to the gods;
> They *kill* us *for their sport.*

The inevitable tension – 'what will the justification for bringing in flies be?' – is heightened by the intervening movement back to the terminology that does not need justification, 'we' and 'the gods'. Thus it is in the paradigmatic A.*Pe*.424ff.:[1]

> τοὶ δ' ὥστε θύννους ἤ τιν' ἰχθύων βόλον
> ἀγαῖσι κωπῶν θραύμασίν τ' ἐρειπίων
> ἔπαιον, ἐρράχιζον.

Enjambement adds to the vigour, the very Aeschylean vigour, one might add. I repeat that V–T–N convergence, not characteristic of Pindar, is especially common in Aeschylus.

A.*Ag*.1629ff. shows an instance essentially of this kind, but in analogy and with the convergence coming at the end of, rather than after, the immediate tenor. This time the effect is punning and sardonically humorous:

> Ὀρφεῖ δὲ γλῶσσαν τὴν ἐναντίαν ἔχεις.
> ὁ μὲν γὰρ ἦγε πάντ' ἀπὸ φθογγῆς χαρᾷ,
> σὺ δ' ἐξορίνας νηπίοις ὑλάγμασιν
> ἄξῃ.

'Forced βωμολοχία', Fraenkel calls it, reasonably enough; Aegisthus is not noted for delicacy. ἄξῃ is presented as neutral through the specious parallelism with ἦγε and articulated with, again, enjambement.[2]

Still humorous to a degree, but much more impressive, are two argumentative convergences in Semonides' diatribe against women, the image in each case being nominally a creation myth. Proposition one, woman as a sow (7.2ff.):

> τὴν μὲν ἐξ ὑὸς τανύτριχος,
> τῇ πάντ' ἀν' οἶκον βορβόρῳ πεφυρμένα
> ἄκοσμα κεῖται καὶ κυλίνδεται χαμαί·
> αὐτὴ δ' ἄλουτος ἀπλύτοισ' ἐν εἵμασιν
> ἐν κοπρίῃσιν ἡμένη πιαίνεται.

The woman and her doings are described variously in tenor terms (as εἵμασιν – sows don't wear clothes) or subdued neutral terms (as v.4). At ἡμένη, a human rather than an animal word,[3] the tenor seems to assert itself, but then, with a punch at the close of the section, comes πιαίνεται. This verb is regular and emotionally uncoloured of animals, ὕς... πιαίνεται (Arist.*HA* 595a.22); but, perhaps in consequence of this animal association, can be pejorative of people: ἐν τρόπῳ βοσκήματος ἕκαστον πιαινόμενον αὐτῶν δεῖ ʒῆν; (Pl.*Lg*.807a).[4] The product is a realization both of the basic analogy and its contemptuous force: she *must* be a sow if she πιαίνεται. The same sleight damns the weasel-woman (7.55f.):

κλέπτουσα δ᾽ ἔρδει πολλὰ γείτονας κακά,
ἄθυστα δ᾽ ἱρὰ πολλάκις κατεσθίει.

In this instance, as in the last, the convergence is placed at the end of the section. κατεσθίειν is 'fressen', normal of animals, pejorative of people.[5] Failure to appreciate these resolutions has contributed to the fashionable unsympathetic attitude to the poem. 'Der literarische Wert von Semonides' platter Satire auf die Frauen ist gering' is a typical verdict.[6]

Outside explicit imagery, the *V–T–N* structure tends not to be so readily distinct in effect from the *V–N*. Argumentative force is clearly not in question in A.*Pe*.598ff.,

φίλοι, κακῶν μὲν ὅστις ἔμπειρος κυρεῖ
ἐπίσταται βροτοῖσιν ὡς, ὅταν κλύδων
κακῶν ἐπέλθῃ...

in its rightful place at last.[7] Compare A.*Supp*.345:

αἰδοῦ σὺ πρύμναν πόλεος ὧδ᾽ ἐστεμμένην.

The chorus appeal for reverence to the statues of the gods, wreathed with their στέμματα. Vehicle πρύμναν, converging on ἐστεμμένην, which points both to this literal wreathing and to the figurative ship's stern, which might be wreathed also: ἡ πρύμνα ἐστεμμένη τοῦ πλοίου ὃ εἰς Δῆλον ᾿Αθηναῖοι πέμπουσιν (Pl.*Phd*.58a).[8] In convergence to metaphor, argumentative force need never be present; other instances bear this out. Thus A.*Ch*.1033 (Orestes):

τόξῳ γὰρ οὔτις πημάτων ἐφίξεται.

Vehicle τόξῳ, converging on ἐφίξεται: σφενδόνη οὐκ ἂν ἐφικοίμην αὐτόσε (Antiph.55.20)[9] and οὐδ᾽ ἂν εἷς δύναιτ᾽ ἐφικέσθαι τῷ λόγῳ τῶν ἐκεῖ κακῶν (D.19.65).[10] Likewise A.*Th*.114f.:

κῦμα περὶ πτόλιν δοχμολόφων ἀνδρῶν
καχλάζει πνοαῖς ῎Αρεος ὀρόμενον.

Vehicle κῦμα and καχλάζει, converging on ὀρόμενον (grammatically, a vehicle term, itself): ἀνδρῶν... ὀρνυμένων ἄμυδις (*Il.*20.157f.) and ὦρτο δὲ κῦμα (*Il.*23.214).[11] On the other side, consider A.*Ag.*1659f.:

> εἰ δέ τοι μόχθων γένοιτο τῶνδ' ἅλις, δεξοίμεθ' ἄν,
> δαίμονος χηλῇ βαρείᾳ δυστυχῶς πεπληγμένοι.

χηλῇ is the vehicle and the convergence is on βαρείᾳ and πεπληγμένοι: on the one hand, μή τις... ἐμὲ χειρὶ βαρείη πλήξῃ (*Od.*18.56f.); on the other, βαρεῖά γ' ἅδε συμφορά (A.*Pe.*1044) and συμφορῇ πεπληγμένον (Hdt.1.41.1).[12] It would be difficult to testify to any specifically argumentative flavour here, but the greater force of the interaction, related presumably to the doubling of the neutral term, is surely not in doubt.

It is worth noting that convergence does not always keep to the simple form shown by the instances so far discussed. The relevant point here is that it may be postponed beyond the nominal close of the image. A.*Ch.*201ff. (Electra):

> τοὺς θεοὺς καλούμεθα,
> οἷοισιν ἐν χειμῶσι ναυτίλων δίκην
> στροβούμεθ'· εἰ δὲ χρὴ τυχεῖν σωτηρίας, ...

Besides being the 'salvation' prayed for, σωτηρίας is the 'safe return' in antithesis to the figurative storm: ἐλθόντες ἐπὶ τὴν ναῦν... τηροῦντες τὴν οἴκαδε σωτηρίαν (D.50.16).[13] The recapitulatory effect seems peculiarly organic, though in fact quite unpredictable, because of its organization within what is, essentially, parallel structure. Compare A.*Ch.*466ff.:

> ὦ πόνος ἐγγενὴς
> καὶ παράμουσος ἄτας
> αἱματόεσσα πλαγά.
> ἰὼ δύστον', ἄφερτα κήδη·
> ἰὼ δυσκατάπαυστον ἄλγος.

Vehicle παράμουσος, convergence on πλαγά and, prolonged beyond the image structure, δύστονα: the former as 'disaster' (ἐν μιᾷ πληγῇ κατέφθαρται πολὺς ὄλβος A.*Pe.*251f.) and 'stroke' on the lyre (ταῖς χορδαῖς... πλήκτρῳ ... πληγῶν γιγνομένων Pl.*R.*531b);[14] the latter as δύσ-στονος, 'woeful' (δύστονα κήδεα A.*Th.*984), and δύσ-τονος, 'ill-strung', 'tuneless', antonym of εὔτονος (ἐν ταῖς χορδαῖς... εὐτονωτέρα ἡ τάσις Thphr.*fr.*89.7).[15] Compare also B.9.27ff., with a prolongation of remarkable extent that produces an effect of vivid double exposure:

> πενταέθλοισιν γὰρ ἐνέπρεπεν ὡς
> ἄστρων διακρίνει φάη

νυκτὸς διχομηνίδος εὐφεγγὴς σελάνα ·
τοῖος 'Ελλάνων δι' ἀπείρονα κύκλον
φαῖνε θαυμαστὸν δέμας
δίσκον τροχοειδέα ῥίπτων...

There is no formal closure, but in the middle of the *Sostück* a collocation of triple hints, ἀπείρονα κύκλον φαῖνε, all officially referring to the assembled crowd at the games and the athlete among them: δῆμος ἀπείρων (*Il.*24.776),[16] Περσῶν κύκλον μέγαν (X.*Cyr.*7.5.41),[17] ζώσατο...φαῖνε δὲ μηρούς (*Od.* 18.67).[18] At the same time all three words carry immediate suggestions in line with ἄστρων and εὐφεγγὴς σελάνα: ἀπείρων σφαῖρος (of the universe, Emped.28),[19] τὸν κύκλον πάντα τοῦ οὐρανοῦ (Hdt.1.131.2),[20] ἄστρα... ἀμφὶ σελήνην φαίνετ' ἀριπρεπέα (*Il.*8.555f.) – this last hint, in φαῖνε, being in one way the most apparent, in another the slightest, for obvious grammatical reasons.[21] The vehicle, well established by its own length, seems almost to envelop what is supposed, unequivocally, to be the tenor; and the protraction of the envelopment makes the convergence. The instance might profitably be used to question the received opinion that the style of the Cean nightingale is limited to producing 'a rainbow haze of verbal ornament',[22] the evasiveness of unfunctionality.[23]

1 See above, p. 19.
2 εἰκάζειν, see above, p. 104, n.3. Text as codd. (so Page, *O.C.T.*).
3 Contrast ἧσθαι/ἐφῆσθαι of *birds* (above, p. 89 with n.12).
4 πιαίνεσθαι of animals, likewise, Anan.5.9; of people, likewise (pejorative), A.*Ag.*1669, cf. Fraenkel on *Ag.*276 and πίων at e.g. Ar.*Ran.*1092 and *Pl.*560. (The verb can, of course, be used of people without the connotation, as Hp. *Mul.*1.47.)
5 κατεσθίειν of animals: *Il.*2.314, Hdt.3.16.3 (θηρίον), Arist.*HA* 568b.17, Thphr. *HP* 2.5.5. Outside comedy the word is characteristically used thus. In tragedy it is not found at all (E. only at *Cyc.*341 and 440), nor in high lyric; in low lyric, *Carm.Conv.*30, Hippon.39.4 and Semon. here. In comedy it is frequent, and frequent of people, from Epicharmus (*fr.*42.4, missing in LSJ *s.v.* 1) onwards: Ar.*Ran.*560, Alex.15.12, Ecphantid.1, Pherecr.1.1 etc. It is evident that the word had a potentially pejorative and/or vulgar tone; hence, when it *is* used of people in 'serious' literature, the situations tend to be offensive or indecorous: πουλύποδος δίκην αὐτὸς σεαυτὸν καταφαγών (*Com.Adesp.*445); likewise of Odysseus' men who ate the forbidden cattle (*Od.*1.8); of the cannibalistic Callatiae (Hdt.3.38.4); of Xerxes' men eating bark and leaves from hunger (Hdt.8.115.2); of the prisoner Aristogeiton who bit off and ate a fellow prisoner's nose (D.25.62); of the apothecaries who ate hellebore roots and took drugs for a bet (Thphr.*HP* 9.17.1f.). Cf. also the unquestionably pejorative use of the

verb for 'devouring one's substance' (LSJ *s.v.* 2, Taillardat 246). Hippon.39 is a prime example (not in LSJ): ἡσυχῇ τε καὶ ῥύδην... ἡμέρας πάσας δαινύμενος ὥσπερ... εὐνοῦχος κατέφαγε δὴ τὸν κλῆρον. Note, however, that the verb does occasionally occur in the Hippocratic corpus as a neutral equivalent to the much commoner ἐσθίειν, βιβρώσκειν etc.: thus, Hp.*Morb.*2.15 ἐπὴν δὲ κατεσθίη ἤδη τὰ σιτία ἀρκοῦντα (of a patient on a diet), so *Acut.*30, *Int.*44, *Nat.Mul.*53, *Prorrh.*2.4. Note finally that the cognate κατέδειν is comparable to κατεσθίειν – neutral of animals, pejorative of men (cf. LSJ *s.v.* and add, notably, Emped. 137.6, of cannibalism); the exceptional ὃν θυμὸν κατέδων (*Il.*6.202) should therefore have a more cutting force than is usually supposed.

6 Fränkel *DP* 236; similarly Jaeger 1.122 and Lesky 114. Campbell 184 is a little kinder. 'Flat' would better suit Phocylides' parallel attempt (*fr.*2), which also, indeed, contains a convergence (on ἐργάзεσθαι, v.7, of the bee-woman; for this verb, of bees, cf. Arist.*HA* 625b.22 and 627a.6–30); but a convergence lacking in comparable force.

7 For the lexical evidence, see above, pp. 22f.

8 The *N* status of ἐστεμμένην is noted by Weir Smyth in the Loeb.

9 Similarly *Il.*13.613.

10 So Hdt.7.9.1; cf. the simple ἱκνεῖσθαι, Parm.5, Pi.*O.*6.24.

11 ὄρνυμι of the warrior likewise, *Il.*5.17, Ibyc.1a.3, A.*Th.*91, S.*OC* 1320; with κῦμα likewise, *Il.*14.395, *Od.*5.366. Another comparable convergence occurs at A.*Eu.*765f., vehicle πρυμνήτην, converging on δόρυ: *qua T*, 'spear' (see LSJ *s.v.* II.1.a), metonymic for 'army' (as v.773); *qua V*, 'plank', the epic δόρυ νήιον (LSJ 1.1), metonymic for 'ship' (as Pi.*P.*4.27, A.*Ag.*1618, S.*Ph.*721, E.*Cyc.*15 etc.), including, specifically, 'warship' (as A.*Pe.*411). This interaction is noted by Dumortier 48.

12 βαρύς of affliction likewise, *Il.*10.71, *Od.*15.233, Thgn.1187, Pi.*P.*3.42, Th.1. 77.5. πλήσσεσθαι of misfortune likewise, A.*Ch.*31, Ephipp. 14.4, D.45.58.

13 So A.*Ag.*343, Th.7.70.7.

14 πληγή, 'disaster': likewise, Heraclit.11, *Hell.Oxy.*16.2, Arist.*Pol.*1270a.33, Aeschin.3.147; cf. also *Il.*16.816, where, though doubtless *not* original, the non-physical sense could be, and probably was, read in by later generations. πληγή of the 'stroke' on the lyre is not an officially recognized sense. Besides the Plato, note Arist.*Aud.*800a.7 τὰς...τῶν χορδῶν γιγνομένας πληγάς and *Probl.*902b.34; also, conceivably (??), Ar.*V.*1295 τὰς πληγὰς στέγειν (edd. and most mss give πλευράς), of the shell of the χελώνη, which is the original lyre (*h.Merc.*24ff.). It should be noted further that πληγή in Greek thought was a key word for explaining 'sound' (usually ψόφος) in general: οὐ δυνατόν ἐστιν ἦμεν ψόφον μὴ γενηθείσας πληγᾶς (Archyt.1); so e.g. Pl.*Tim.*67b; Arist.*de An.* 419b.10; Thphr.*Sens.*85; Euc.*Sect.Can.*init. (p.159 Menge).

15 δύστονος in any sense appears to have been coined by Aeschylus and, apart from the cited *Ch.*469 and *Th.*984, occurs again only at *Th.*998, δυστόνων κακῶν. Coinage of such a compound entails some flexibility of interpretation, which can only be in favour of the availability of the double sense here. For the 'woeful' sense, besides the two passages from A.*Th.*, one has, of course, such

parallel compounds to appeal to as βαρύστονος and πολύστονος (πολύστονα κήδεα *Il.*1.445). The musical sense, not visible in the other two δύστ. passages, is similarly supported by parallel compounds: εὔτονος, as Thphr. *loc. cit.*, cf. Arist.*GA* 786b.8, S.*fr.*966 (so codd.), Ar.*Ach.*674 (codd. plur.); σύντονον... μοῦσαν Pratin.Lyr.5, cf. Pl.*Sph.*242e, Arist.*Pol.*1342b.21; παλίντονος ἁρμονίη ὅκωσπερ...λύρης Heraclit.51 (v.l.); ἁρμονίαν χορδοτόνου λύρας S.*fr.*244; ἑπτατόνου λύρας E.*IT* 1129, so B.*fr.*20b.2, Ion Eleg.6.3; μοῦσα...ἔντονος Ar.*Ach.*665f.; and the primary τόνος itself, as τοῦ τόνου...τῶν θ' ἁρμονιῶν Ar.*Eq.*532f. (of a lyre, see Neil *ad loc.*), so Hp.*Vict.*1.8 etc. (Note in passing the later use of τόνος in a variety of technical musical senses: τόνος δὲ λέγεται τετραχῶς· καὶ γὰρ ὡς φθόγγος καὶ ὡς διάστημα καὶ ὡς τόπος φωνῆς καὶ ὡς τάσις Euc.*Harm.*12; likewise διάτονος, ὁμότονος etc.) Finally, as a parallel to δύστονος = both δύσ-τ. and δύσ-στ., cf. the two δύστομος words, one from τέμνω, one from στόμα (see LSJ *s.v.*). The δύστονος interaction and the other associated with it (πλαγά) were suggested by Tucker, albeit without any lexicography.

16 So Simon.37.38, Hes.*Sc.*472.

17 So Pi.*O.*9.93, S.*Aj.*749, Diph.55.3, Antigen.1.9 Diehl (= Simon.148.9 Bergk).

18 So Hdt.2.132.1, Thphr.*Char.*4.4 etc.

19 I am not positing a specifically 'heavenly' connotation for ἀπείρων, but merely a possible use of the ordinary spatial sense, 'endless', as *Il.*7.446, *Od.*4.510, Ar.*Av.*694; cf. ἄπειρος (of which ἀπείρων is the correlative epic form) at Anaxag.1, E.*fr.*941.

20 Cf. Emped.38.4, S.*Ph.*815, E.*Ion* 1147, Ar.*Av.*1715; and such quasi-technical uses as Arist.*Mete.*345a.25 ὁ τοῦ γάλακτος κ. and Autol.*Ort.*1 p.50 Hultsch ὁ τοῦ ἡλίου κ. (= *zodiacus*, i.e. the belt of sky within which the sun 'circles').

21 The syntactic structure φαῖνε...δέμας precludes full *N* status for the verb. Besides φαίνεσθαι of stars (standard usage, Arist.*Mete.*343a.28 etc.), cf. also the intransitive use of φαίνειν at Ar.*Nub.*586, Pl.*Tim.*39b.

22 Lesky 205.

23 Four more comparable instances (the first three being very restrained), with the convergence simply articulated 'over' a pause, instead of before it: (i) A.*Ag.* 534ff., vehicle ὀφλὼν...ῥυσίου (legal), convergence on διπλᾶ, 'twofold' and 'denoting...the *duplum*, the double value in regard to damages', as Fraenkel puts it, q.v. for details. For the legal sense of διπλᾶ, add to his citations *IG* I² 154.14 (Attic, fifth-century) and Din.1.60. (ii) B.1.161f., vehicle ὁμιλεῖ (personification), convergence on ἐθέλει, whose use with abstract or semi-abstract subjects is well attested: τριταῖος δὲ πυρετὸς...ἐθέλει μεθίστασθαι ἐς τεταρταῖον, Hp.*Aff.*18; so e.g. Hdt.7.50.3, Thphr.*CP* 2.1.1, Pi.*O.*2.97. The chiastic organization of vehicle and interactive term sharpens the relation between the two, giving the interaction greater force. (iii) Pi.*I.*6.1–9. The elaborate image of the triple libation (*V*) for a triple victory (*T*) has a kind of diffused convergence at vv.7f. with τρίτον...᾿Ολυμπίῳ (although the vehicle then reappears in σπένδειν). *Qua T*, Pindar predicts a third victory at Olympia; *qua V*, he evokes the libation to Zeus Olympios, here presented as the third after a banquet. (It is

generally supposed that it was in fact the *first* libation that was offered to this Zeus: see the scholia on this passage. But the same association is attested elsewhere: τὸ δὲ τρίτον Ὀλυμπικῶς τῷ σωτῆρί τε καὶ τῷ Ὀλυμπίῳ Διί, Pl.*R*.583b – and in a matter like this Plato's evidence is unexceptionable.) (iv) Pi.*N*.4.69–72, vehicle (the bulk of) περατόν...ναός (see below, p. 120), convergence with overspill on the neatly articulated ἄπορα and διελθεῖν. Syntactically, both words belong to the tenor and merely *hint* at a connection with the vehicle, but the connection is clear enough. ἄπορα, picking up περατόν, hints at its etymology, 'no sea-way' (the former word is in fact used in the similar, but restricted, sense 'impassable', as with the ἄπορον...πέλαγος at Pl.*Tim*.25d, also of the Atlantic 'beyond Cadiz'); while διελθεῖν, 'recount' (LSJ *s.v.* 1.6), suggests its ordinary spatial sense shown at e.g. Hp.*Epid*.5.9 Ἀθήνησιν ἄνθρωπος...διελθὼν...ἐς Μῆλον, Men.*fr*.751 διελθεῖν...διὰ θαλάττης...τόπον τινά (where, interestingly, Kock – 'fort. recte' – conjectured πόρον for τόπον).

The explanatory function

§41

Peace, peace.
Dost thou not see my baby at my breast
That sucks the nurse asleep.

I invoke Cleopatra a second time to illustrate neutral terminology in its 'explanatory' function. In 'at my breast' and 'asleep', I have said, the lines of the image are drawn together; and they are drawn together pointedly. The obvious question presents itself: in what does this 'point' consist, apart from the drawing together itself and the inevitably consequent indication of some aspect of the ground, the likeness? It consists in a simultaneous explanation, by which I mean not an explanation of the ground, nor of the vehicle, but of the tenor, and specifically, the suppressed tenor.

The explanatory function, it should be stressed at the outset, is not particularly common; or rather, not commonly dominant. Here it is dominant in 'asleep' but not in 'at my breast'. If one were barbarously to delete 'at my breast' from Cleopatra's sentence, a substantial measure of the image in all its aspects would survive, albeit with reduced efficacy. But if one deleted 'asleep', there would be an irreplaceable loss to the tenor. 'My baby...that sucks the nurse' would still be meaningful on its own terms, the terms of the vehicle; and, as regards the image as a whole, there would still be a ground to perceive. The point is simply that 'sleep' is a stock equivalent of 'death', suggests 'death' directly; that 'death' is an important part of the suppressed tenor, the literal context presupposed by the vehicle; and·that 'death' is not otherwise expressed. In crude terms, 'asleep' explains what Cleopatra is 'really' talking about, and does so by interaction. And the conjunction of the image's formal resolution with this revelation of a significant aspect of its 'real' subject contributes a good deal to the success of the whole passage.

The explanatory function, then, is exercised on behalf of the tenor, the suppressed tenor. It follows that only in those images which have a suppressed tenor can the function be exercised; i.e. in metaphor, above all,[1] and not, in general, in explicit imagery, although one can certainly point to contrary instances. One such has, in fact, been cited already:

> I wandered lonely as a cloud
> That floats on high o'er vales and hills.

The comment I made earlier on these deceptively simple lines is relevant here: '*O'er vales and hills* locates the wandering of the clouds and also, by suggestion, of the speaker.'[2] 'The speaker' naturally belongs to the tenor and this 'suggestion' is therefore clearly explanatory.

It should be stressed at the outset that the explanatory function, in no sense formal itself, may coexist with other functions, including formal functions, as in 'asleep' – and in Wordsworth's 'o'er vales and hills' – with convergence. It may, alternatively, be a neutral term's primary or, in effect, sole function.

1 πᾶν γὰρ ἀσαφὲς τὸ κατὰ μεταφορὰν λεγόμενον Arist.*Top*.139b.34.
2 See above, p 105.

§42

A paradigmatic instance of the explanatory function in a more or less pure form is Pi.*P*.2.62ff.:

> εὐανθέα δ' ἀναβάσομαι στόλον ἀμφ' ἀρετᾷ
> κελαδέων. νεότατι μὲν ἀρήγει θράσος
> δεινῶν πολέμων...

'I shall ascend a prow that is crowned with flowers, while I sound the praise of valour', says the Loeb translator. Pindar says more. The interaction concerns ἀναβάσομαι, and this word certainly does mean approximately what Sandys says it does – ἀναβάντες ἐπέπλεον (*Il*.1.312) – but also, economically and graphically, points straight to the tenor: ἀναβήσομαι ἐς τὸν κατ' ἀρχὰς ἤια λέξων λόγον (Hdt.4.82),[1] which is precisely what Pindar 'really' means and precisely what he then does. The ode began with βαθυπολέμου...Ἄρεος and ἀνδρῶν...σιδαροχαρμᾶν (vv.1f.) and now returns to that theme.

In Pi.*P*.3.75f. the image, a comparison, and the interaction itself are much less striking:

ἀστέρος οὐρανίου φαμὶ τηλαυγέστερον κείνῳ φάος
ἐξικόμαν κε...

κείνῳ is Hieron, whose health is failing, and Pindar would, if he could, have brought comfort to him. The vehicle is ἀστέρος οὐρανίου with τηλαυγέστερον, the ground term, in the same terminology: 'more *V* than *V*'. The 'explanation' is given by φάος cohering with ἀστέρος and, as common cliché, with the tenor also: αἴ κέν τι φόως Δαναοῖσι γένηαι πατρί τε σῷ (*Il*.8.282f.).[2] The indication that the 'real' subject is 'deliverance' is thus given. I might point out here that, restrained though it is, such an instance represents a much livelier and more *convincing* explanation than any non-interactive 'equivalent' – for example, the κακῶν πέλαγος type, where the explaining is done by the tenor, the defining genitive; or an epic simile, where *Wiestück* is explained by *Sostück*, so that again the tenor does the explaining. If nothing else, the interactive explanation is at least more concise and more immediate, sharing as all neutral terms may in the vehicle's inherent immediacy.

At Thgn.237f. the image is livelier, but the interaction even more subdued:

σοὶ μὲν ἐγὼ πτέρ' ἔδωκα, σὺν οἷς ἐπ' ἀπείρονα πόντον
πωτήσῃ καὶ γῆν πᾶσαν ἀειρόμενος...

The meaning of the vehicle – πτερά, πωτήσῃ, ἀειρόμενος – is clarified by ἐπ' ἀπείρονα πόντον and κατὰ γῆν πᾶσαν, both nominally referring to the range of the 'flight', essentially to the extent of the fame that ἐγώ has given σοί: τοῦ κλέος πᾶσαν χθόνα ἦλθεν καὶ ἐπ' ἔσχατα Νείλου (B.9.40f.).[3] Pi.*N*.6.48ff. is very similar (on the house of Aeacus):

πέταται δ' ἐπί τε χθόνα καὶ διὰ θαλάσσας τηλόθεν
ὄνυμ' αὐτῶν· καὶ ἐς Αἰθίοπας
Μέμνονος οὐκ ἀπονοστήσαντος ἐπᾶλτο.

πέταται, ἐπᾶλτο vehicle; ἐπί τε χθόνα καὶ διὰ θαλάσσας τηλόθεν explanatory. Pi.*I*.3/4.59f. is also similar, at least to start with, but then presents a more complex explanatory continuation:

καὶ πάγκαρπον ἐπὶ χθόνα καὶ διὰ πόντον βέβακεν
ἐργμάτων ἀκτὶς καλῶν ἄσβεστος αἰεί.

The vehicle, ἀκτίς, is prefaced by the clarifying ἐπὶ χθόνα καὶ διὰ πόντον (ἠέλιε...πᾶσαν ἐπὶ χθόνα καὶ κατὰ πόντον καταδέρκεαι ἀκτίνεσσι, *h.Cer.* 64–70) and followed by ἄσβεστος, likewise neutral, but more centrally explanatory. The coherence of ἀκτίς and ἄσβεστος involves, additionally, metonymy. ἀκτίς is a ray of the sun (φλέγων ἀκτῖσιν ἥλιος A.*Pe.*364), and the sun with its rays is terminologically just about susceptible of σβέσις: ἀποσβέννυνται πολὺ μᾶλλον τοῦ Ἡρακλειτείου ἡλίου (Pl.*R.*498a).[4] But this particular ray, like the sun itself in ordinary appearance, is not susceptible thus, hence ἄ-σβεστος. And it is ἄσβεστος that neatly indicates, or at least corroborates, that 'fame' is actually the tenor subject, by allusion to the cliché ἄσβεστον κλέος.[5]

The two interactions involved in the last instance were more or less formally organized: ἐπὶ χθόνα..., clearly, as a glide; ἄσβεστος as an unarticulated convergence. Significant formal organization of some kind is, in fact, at least as common as not, albeit sometimes more formal than significant, as at Thgn.233, a mournful tribute to the ἐσθλὸς ἀνήρ:

ἀκρόπολις καὶ πύργος ἐὼν κενεόφρονι δήμῳ...

ἀκρόπολις vehicle, πύργος explanatory. The two words are self-evidently a matching pair, but in their present application the former is novel and surprising, the latter a cliché, like our 'tower of strength'.[6] This explanatory word is structured parallel to the vehicle, but rather defensively after it, not pivotally before it.[7]

A more usual and straightforwardly effective organization at Pi.*P.*4.70f., yielding an impressive glide:

τίς γὰρ ἀρχὰ δέξατο ναυτιλίας,
τίς δὲ κίνδυνος κρατεροῖς ἀδάμαντος δῆσεν ἅλοις;

The Argonauts and a notable aspect of their enterprise. Before beginning a lengthy narrative, Pindar 'indicates at the outset the spirit in which he regards the adventure'.[8] But what are the ἅλοις, upon the underlying sense of which the interpretation of this 'spirit' depends? 'Nails of passion', suggests Gildersleeve, wrongly. Wrongly, not so much on grounds of general plausibility, but because the vehicle is introduced by a neutral term, κρατεροῖς, which, if one has eyes to see, or relevant contexts of language to draw on, interprets the suppressed tenor for us. The nails are not nails of passion but of ἀνάγκη; beside the tenor signification, σίδηρος...κρατερώτατος (Hes.*Th.*864), the collocation κρατερὴ ἀνάγκη, one of definitive familiarity in early literature, is inescapably suggested here.[9]

A comparable explanatory glide[10] is used by Pindar later in the same ode, *P*.4.291ff.:

λῦσε δὲ Ζεὺς ἄφθιτος Τιτᾶνας. ἐν δὲ χρόνῳ
μεταβολαὶ λήξαντος οὔρου
ἱστίων.

'Sails must be altered when the wind drops, a familiar figure for the impermanence of any set of conditions.'[11] Familiar (or not) as the conceptual relation may be, the explanation of the particular words that make up the vehicle is given in epitome by μεταβολαί, whose normal and common use is, precisely, 'vicissitudes'; whereas the concrete sense of material 'alteration' is uncommon,[12] though, at the lowest, available by re-etymology. Grammatically, μεταβολαί is a vehicle term, and therefore hints to the tenor without having a fully neutral status, but the pull of grammar is balanced by the pull of normal usage in favour of the tenor sense. The implicit principle is an important one: by a sort of compensation, the lexically less predictable is the contextually more predictable and *vice versa*, so that both senses are equally operative.

The explanatory function in metaphor seems to be particularly characteristic of Pindar, less so of Aeschylus. One Aeschylean instance is *Th*.592f.:

οὐ γὰρ δοκεῖν ἄριστος ἀλλ' εἶναι θέλει,
βαθεῖαν ἄλοκα διὰ φρενὸς καρπούμενος.

Here βαθεῖαν, positioned as glide, has the explanatory rôle. The ἄλοκα is βαθεῖαν in the physical sense; the sense that points to the tenor is the familiar non-physical one, 'wise': βαθείη…φρενὶ βούλευσαι (Thgn.1051f.).[13] Theognis (601f.) gives such an explanatory glide a genuinely emphatic force by thrusting the operative word out of its normal order to the head of the clause:

ἔρρε, θεοῖσίν τ' ἐχθρὲ καὶ ἀνθρώποισιν ἄπιστε,
ψυχρὸν ὃς ἐν κόλπῳ ποικίλον εἶχες ὄφιν.

Snakes are ψυχροί and so are people: ψυχρῶν ζῴων·…οἵ τ' ὄφεις καὶ αἱ σαῦραι… (Arist.*Long*.466b.20) and ψυχρὸς καὶ ἐπίβουλος (Arist.*EE* 1234a.21).[14] The latter sense is the key to the interpretation of ὄφιν. It should be added that ποικίλον also is neutral with an important explanatory function. The two senses are represented by ὄφιες…ποικίλοι τὰ εἴδεα (Hdt.3.107.2) and Προμηθέα ποικίλον (Hes.*Th*.510f.),[15] of which the latter, again, provides the key.

Let me repeat that explanation is often a part of a neutral term's total function, but is rarely the dominant part. Many of the instances of pivot, glide and convergence given in earlier sections undoubtedly have some explanatory significance, but a significance which does not, all in all, seem as decisive as that in the instances presently given. Thus, to take Aeschylus' image for the stars (*Ag*.4ff.),[16]

ἄστρων...ὁμήγυριν,
καὶ τοὺς φέροντας χεῖμα καὶ θέρος βροτοῖς
λαμπροὺς δυνάστας,

it would be a forced interpretation if one claimed for λαμπρούς, 'illustrious' (of the δυνάστας) and 'bright' (of the stars), an explanatory status by virtue of the latter sense. 'Bright' suggests nothing beyond 'stars', which we knew already; it does not suggest what, if any, the closer 'literal equivalent' for δυνάστας might be. Contrast Pi.*P*.8.96f.:

ἀλλ' ὅταν αἴγλα διόσδοτος ἔλθῃ,
λαμπρὸν φέγγος ἔπεστιν ἀνδρῶν...

Here human affairs are given in terms of 'bright' things, not *vice versa*, but this is not a relevant point of contrast. The relevant point is that Pindar's λαμπρόν deploys essentially the same senses, 'bright' and 'illustrious', but this time the tenor sense, 'illustrious', is genuinely explanatory; 'illustriousness' is evidently what, or an important part of what, the φέγγος is 'really' about. Grammatical considerations might perhaps be brought in at this point. Pindar's λαμπρόν is, in a sense, equivalent to a defining genitive noun. Is Aeschylus' λαμπρούς so equivalent? But such considerations need not be pursued here.

On leaving the topic of 'explanation' in formal structure, we may go out, as we came in, with Cleopatra's 'asleep', which did its explaining in convergence. This is a very rare conjunction in my corpus, but compare A.*Ch*.1021ff.:

ἀλλ' ὡς ἂν εἰδῆτ', οὐ γὰρ οἶδ' ὅπη τελεῖ,
ὥσπερ ξὺν ἵπποις ἡνιοστροφῶ δρόμου
ἐξωτέρω·

The charioteer is out of control; ἡνιοστρόφος ἔξω παρασπᾷ (S.*El*.731f.), but involuntarily. Meaning? Orestes is going mad, ἔξω γὰρ ἔσται τῶν φρενῶν (Men.*Dysc*.897), and the well-placed ἐξωτέρω, or its first two syllables at least, is a hint to that effect.[17]

---

1 This usage has not been properly documented. To the Pindar and the Herodotus add: (1) ἀναβήσομαι· Δημόκριτος· ἐπανεξελεύσομαι ἐξ ἀρχῆς (Democr.144a, a gloss in Photius); (2) ἐπεὶ δὲ ἠρξάμεθα ἐντεῦθεν, ταύτῃ καὶ ἀναβησόμεθα πρός... (X.*Eq*.1.4); (3) five Hippocratic instances: οὐ βούλομαι ἀποπλανᾶν τὸν λόγον...

νῦν δὲ ἀναβήσομαι τῷ λόγῳ καὶ ἐρέω περὶ... (*Gland.*7); ἀναβήσομαι δ᾽ αὖθις ὀπίσω περὶ... (*Morb.*4.45); ἀναβήσομαι δὲ αὖθις ὀπίσω ὅθεν ἀπέλιπον (*Nat. Puer.*18 and, similarly, 27); ἀναβήσομαι δ᾽ αὖθις ὀπίσω ἐς τὸν λόγον ὃν ἔλεγον (*Genit.*11). (N.B. that *Morb.*4, *Nat.Puer.* and *Genit.* are regarded by Littré and others as a single continuous treatise.) What is inescapably obvious is that the use is restricted to the first person future (which naturally makes the Pindar allusion to it the more perceptible) and is largely Ionic. We therefore have a very particularized idiom, which is not, incidentally, acknowledged to be such by LSJ: of the above nine passages, only the Democr. is cited *s.v.* (ἀναβαίνω IV).

2 φάος/φῶς of human deliverers: see above, p. 93, n.21.

3 Similarly, *Od.*7.332f., Hes.*Th.*530f. and *fr.*204.63, *h.Ap.*174 and 276, B.17.80, *Carm.Conv.*13.1 (*PMG* no.896).

4 Cf. Arist.*A.Po.*93b.6. The specific collocation ἡλίου σβέσις does not seem to be attested before Epicurus (*Ep.*2.92 and 96).

5 *Od.*4.584 and 7.333; Simon.121.1 Diehl; cf. X.*Cyr.*5.4.30 ἀποσβῆναι τὸ ἡμέτερον...ὄνομα. A modest distribution for this specific usage, but adequate in the light of the fact that the primary σβεννύναι is used of 'putting an end to' abstract objects in general, e.g. ὕβριν Heraclit.43 and Epigr.145 F-H, ἡδονήν Hp.*Genit.*4.

With the subdued type of 'geographical' explanation, cf. Pi.*N.*4.69ff., vehicle περατόν and ἀπότρεπε...ποτὶ χέρσον ἔντεα ναός, 'explained' by Γαδείρων τὸ πρὸς ζόφον (a place to sail to and a topic to invoke) and by Εὐρώπαν, likewise: *qua V*, somewhere to sail back to; *qua T*, representing the return to consideration of local matters, *viz* victories at Olympia, the Isthmus and Nemea (v.75). (The exact sense of 'Europe' in early Greek is notoriously vague: see West on Hes.*Th.*357 and, generally, the *OCD* article *s.v.* Here it seems to include mainland Greece along with the Peloponnese.)

6 πύργος thus of a person: *Od.*11.556, Callin.1.20, Alc.112.10, S.*OT* 1201 and cf. *Aj.*159 (*pace* Jebb), E.*Alc.*311 and *Med.*390.

7 Two other instances with such a structure: (1) A.*Ch.*863, πῦρ explained by φῶς, cliché for 'deliverance' (see above, p. 93 with n.21); for φῶς *qua V* (i.e. associated with πῦρ), see e.g. *Od.*19.63f., Thphr.*Ign.*12. (2) A.*Eu.*322f., ἀλαοῖσι explained as 'dead' by δεδορκόσιν, since δέρκεσθαι is a stock metonym for 'to live': ζῶντος καὶ...δερκομένοιο *Il.*1.88 (so *Od.*16.439, A.*Eu.*387, S.*El.*66).

8 Burton 154.

9 κρατερός of physical objects, also e.g. *Il.*5.386f., *Od.*24.170, Sol.5.5, Pi.*O.*1.57b. κρατερὴ ἀνάγκη: *Il.*6.458, *Od.*10.273, Hes.*Th.*517, *Cypr.*7.3, *h.Ven.*130, Orac. 33.2 P-W (vi B.C.), Parm.8.30, Thgn.195 and 387, B.11.46 and *fr.*20a.19, *Mel.Adesp.*99.2 (p.535 Page), Hp.*Septim.Sp.*122 Grensemann (*CMG* I.2.1). Cf. μοῖρα κραταιή, *Il.*5.83 etc., Hes.*fr.*212b.1, *Il.Parv.*18.5 Kinkel. That the tenor involves ἀνάγκη is recognized by Burton (p.154, n.3) and others, without reference to the interaction.

10 A rare instance of a noun glide outside Aeschylus (see above, p. 101).

11 Burton 172.

12 μεταβολαί concrete: Hp.*Prorrh*.2.6 τῶν οἴνων τὰς μ., X.*Lac*.2.1 ἱματίων μ.; abstract, see LSJ *s.v.* II.1 and add e.g. Hp.*Hum*.15.1.

13 So βαθύφρων Alcm.3.82 (?), Sol.23.1; βαθύβουλος A.*Pe*.142; βαθυμῆτα Pi.*N*. 3.53; βαθύς itself, Hdt.4.95.2, Heraclit.45, Pi.*N*.4.8, A.*Supp*.407; cf. Men.*Dysc*. 527 (conj.) and *App.Prov*.4.68.

14 So Sapph.42, Isoc.2.34, X.*Cyr*.8.4.22, cf. Pi.*fr*.123.6.

15 ποικίλος of snakes, also Alcm.1.66, Pi.*P*.8.46, cf. Hes.*Th*.300 (v.l.). ποικίλος, 'crafty', also Pi.*N*.5.28, Thgn.213, A.*Prom*.310, Ar.*Eq*.758, Alex.110.20, Arist.*EN* 1101a.8; so ποικιλομήτης *Il*.11.482, ποικιλόφρων Alc.69.7.

16 See above, p. 87.

17 ἔξω of madness is much more of a definitive usage than one could suppose from the citations in LSJ. The immediately relevant evidence, as well as some interesting marginalia, can be classified as follows: (*a*) ἔξω φρενῶν/γνώμης *vel sim.*, as Menander *loc. cit.*: E.*Ion* 926 and *Ba*.853, D.*Prooem*.42.2, cf. Pi.*I*.6.72. (*b*) Seemingly more idiomatic, ἔξω σαυτοῦ γενέσθαι Pl.*Ion* 535b, sim. D.19.198. (*c*) χειμῶνος κατακλιθείς, ἔξω ἐγένετο Hp.*Epid*.5.80: 'she went mad'. This crucial instance provides direct evidence that the signification 'madness' belongs to the adverb as of right, without the aid of any interpretative genitive. (*d*) ἔξω δρόμου etc. in other madness images, i.e. parallel instances to A.*Ch*.1022f.: A.*Prom*.883, *Com.Adesp*.474, cf. (?) Pi.*O*.7.47 (with additional metonymic rearrangement). (*e*) ἐξ ἑωυτοῦ ἐγένετο Hp.*Epid*.7.85, sim. 7.45: the same usage with the root preposition. (*f*) Likewise with other extended forms of the preposition: ἐκτὸς ἑωυτοῦ ἐγένετο Hp.*Epid*.7.46, sim. 7.90; γνώμης...ἐκτός Thgn.968, cf. S.*Aj*.640; ἔκτοσθεν ἐγένετο Hp.*Epid*.5.85. (*g*) Likewise with many ἐκ- compounds, notably ἐξίστημι, ἔκνοια, ἔκφρων. Some ἐκ- verbs are already so used in Homer: ἐκ γάρ με πλήσσουσι *Od*.18.231, φρένας ἐξέλετο Ζεύς *Il*.6.234, φρένας ἐκπεπαταγμένος *Od*.18.327. (*h*) Note incidentally a corresponding pattern in the 'sanity' word-group, formed from ἐν. Thus: ἐν ἑαυτῷ ἐγένετο X.*An*.1.5.17, sim. Hp.*Morb*.1.30. (In S.*Ph*.950, Ar.*V*.642, Pl.*Chrm*.155d, Men.*Scut*.307 and *Sam*.340, ἐν σαυτοῦ/αὐτοῦ etc. with the same meaning is the received text, although in Ar.*V*. and S.*Ph*. – cf. Jebb *ad loc*. – ἐν σαυτῷ has superior manuscript authority.) Likewise, again, ἔμφρων, ἔννοος; ἐντὸς ἑαυτοῦ γενέσθαι *vel sim*. (e.g. Hdt.1.119.6, Hp.*Epid*.7.1, D.34.20); also ἔνδον, either absol. or with ἑαυτοῦ or with φρενῶν, Antipho 5.45, A.*Ch*.233, E.*Heracl*.709. Note finally that Hp. has εἰς ἑωυτὸν παρεῖναι with equivalent meaning (*Morb*.2.22) and παρὰ ἑωυτόν and ἑωυτῷ likewise (*Epid*.7.85, *Morb*. 2.22 and *Epid*.7.48, *Prorrh*.1.78, *Coac*.345 respectively) – with the preposition curiously at odds with its well-known force in παρανοεῖν, παραφρονεῖν, παρακρούειν. (*i*) In the light specifically of the above evidence on ἔξω and ἔνδον, it seems clear that the elaborate word-play at Ar.*Ach*.395–9, mainly involving ἔνδον, but also, once, ἔξω (used absol.), presupposes the 'madness'/'sanity' use not only of ἔνδον, as commentators recognize, but of ἔξω as well.

Three other instances of explanation: (1) A.*Eu*.387f., δυσομμάτοις explained by δερκομένοισι (cf. *Eu*.322f., cited n.7 above), organized as pivot in simple parallel structure. (2) A.Th.727ff., ξένος κτλ. explained by πικρός (see below, p. 171). (3) Pi.O.9.11f., ὀϊστόν explained by πτερόεντα (glide): πτερόεντες ὀϊστοί (Il.5.171) and the widespread epic cliché ἔπεα πτερόεντα (e.g. Il.1.201, Od.1.122, h.Cer.112, h.Ap.50, h.Ven.184, h.Merc.435, Hes.Sc.117, cf. Alcm.11, Pi.I. 5.63). In itself this is as pure an instance as one could imagine, but in context the need for any explanation is largely eliminated by the prior indication that these are the arrows that go with the 'Muses' bow' (v.5).

<h1 style="text-align:center">§43</h1>

If there is any mode of imagery that positively cries out for explanation, that mode is allegory, which characteristically provides no explicit self-interpretation. It is not, however, usually the business of allegory to deceive or baffle completely, though part of its business may be to tease. Implicit interpretation may be provided by the accumulation of analogical pointers, all tending in one direction; or it may be provided by interaction, by neutral terminology in its explanatory function. Oracle to Solon (15 P–W):

> ἧσο μέσην κατὰ νῆα κυβερνητήριον ἔργον
> εὐθύνων· πολλοί τοι 'Αθηναίων ἐπίκουροι.

The transparency of the general conceptual relation – helmsman and ship: ruler and state – gives part of the interpretation; this is the analogical pointing. The remaining and perhaps most important part is given by the interactive μέσην, which, while obviously cohering with νῆα, points directly to the heart of the 'message'. μέσος θέλω ἐν πόλει εἶναι, writes Phocylides,[1] illustrating the usage in question. Solon evidently followed, or anticipated,[2] the advice, himself describing the Solonian attitude to conflicting interests thus (25.8f.): ἐγὼ δὲ τούτων ὥσπερ ἐν μεταιχμίῳ ὅρος κατέστην.

Oracular allegory is necessarily recognizable as such, although the actual interpretation may be more or less in doubt. In contrast, it may be an important feature of a genuinely poetic allegory that even the question of its status, allegorical or literal, is not immediately soluble. But built-in uncertainty of either kind can have its own potency. As Demetrius says: 'Darkly-hinting language is always more awesome, and its meaning is variously conjectured by different hearers. But that which is clear and plain is apt to be despised, like men stripped of their garments.'[3] 'Awesome' is too limited for allegory in general, but the point is just. The corollary is that if and when a similarly hinting 'explanation' is offered, its efficacy may be similarly potent. Thus Alc.326.1ff.:

ἀσυννέτημμι τὼν ἀνέμων στάσιν,
τὸ μὲν γὰρ ἔνθεν κῦμα κυλίνδεται,
τὸ δ' ἔνθεν . . .

Contemporary scholarship has established to its own satisfaction that this is an allegory and that its 'real' subject is political troubles, 'a tyrannical conspiracy'.[4] The same could be inferred, or felt, from the hint in στάσιν: the 'lie of the winds', τῶν πνευμάτων . . . τὴν στάσιν (Hp.Sacr.16),[5] and political 'faction', a usage that was doubtless as topical in seventh-century Aeolic as in all later Greek,[6] as a fragmentary collocation from Alcaeus himself indicates: . . . πόλεμον· στάσιν . . . (fr.130.26). The allegory is explained without violation of its own terms; not destroyed but enhanced.[7] Compare Archilochus, fr.56:

Γλαῦχ', ὅρα· βαθὺς γὰρ ἤδη κύμασιν ταράσσεται
πόντος, ἀμφὶ δ' ἄκρα Γυρέων ὀρθὸν ἵσταται νέφος,
σῆμα χειμῶνος· κιχάνει δ' ἐξ ἀελπτίης φόβος.

Once again the vehicle is maritime and, as the expert de-allegorizer Heraclitus puts it, the author τὸν πόλεμον εἰκάζει θαλαττίῳ κλύδωνι.[8] The explanatory items, two of them, correspond well enough to Demetrius' general characterization: 'darkly-hinting' and 'awesome'. The first is ταράσσεται: allegorically, θάλασσα ταράσσεται (Sol.11.1); but 'really', a situation like that produced by Aristagoras of Miletus, ταράξας τὴν Ἰωνίην (Hdt.5.124.1).[9] Then νέφος, which, behind its obvious meteorological significance, hints, through a literary cliché, at the enemy host: νέφος τοσοῦτον ἀνθρώπων (Hdt.8.109.2), νέφος εἵπετο πεζῶν, μυρίοι (Il.23.133f.).[10]

As a stylistic mode, allegory is not entirely cut and dried. Without actually being an allegory, an image may well have something allegorical about it and, accordingly, may be 'explained' in the same enhancing way as an allegory proper. Thus with temporary allegory at Thgn.119ff.: paratactic analogy, with enigmatic Wiestück (ohne wie) first, then the formal explanation (Sostück – ohne so), but meanwhile, in the Wiestück itself, a livelier interactive pointer to the same end:

Χρυσοῦ κιβδήλοιο καὶ ἀργύρου ἀνσχετὸς ἄτη,
Κύρνε, καὶ ἐξευρεῖν ῥᾴδιον ἀνδρὶ σοφῷ.
εἰ δὲ φίλου νόος ἀνδρὸς . . .

In fact, one hardly needs to read as far as νόος ἀνδρός to gather what the tenor is; κιβδήλοιο, a word much less common in extant literature of adulterated metal than of human dishonesty,[11] tells us in advance.[12] Another quasi-allegory of present relevance is the metaphor of the sorrowful chorus, A.*Supp*.162ff.:

ἃ Ζῆν, ᾿Ιοῦς· ἰὼ μῆνις
μάστειρ᾿ ἐκ θεῶν·
κοννῶ δ᾿ ἄταν
γαμετᾶν οὐρανονίκων.
χαλεποῦ γὰρ ἐκ
πνεύματος εἶσι χειμών.

χαλεποῦ κτλ. has, let us content ourselves with saying, something to do with the divine wrath; and χαλεποῦ itself, positioned as a glide, tells us so: not only ἄνεμοι χαλεποί (*Od*.12.286), but also χαλεπὴ δὲ θεοῦ ἔπι μῆνις (*Il*. 5.178).[13]

Part of the business of allegory, I said above, may be to tease; and, as 'tease' implies, allegory need not always be of an awesome solemnity. There is certainly nothing awesome or solemn about Anacreon's allegory (*fr*.72) that begins

πῶλε Θρηκίη, τί δή με λοξὸν ὄμμασι βλέπουσα
νηλέως φεύγεις. . .;

and ends

δεξιὸν γὰρ ἱπποπείρην οὐκ ἔχεις ἐπαμβάτην.[14]

In this instance the suggestions carried by the explanatory elements are 'suggestive' in the restricted sense. φεύγεις is mild enough. Horses do it: φεύγουσιν ἐκ τῶν ἱππασιῶν (*X.Eq*.3.4).[15] The loved one does it: καὶ γὰρ αἰ φεύγει, ταχέως διώξει (Sapph.1.21), the verb φεύγειν having perhaps a distinctive amatory flavour.[16] ἱπποπείρην is less innocent. On the one hand, ἐγώ...πεῖραν ἔχων, from Xenophon on the subject of ἱππικὴ ἄσκησις (*Eq.Mag*.1.16).[17] On the other hand, from a medical contemporary, αἱ ἑταῖραι αἱ δημόσιαι...πεπείρηνται πολλάκις (Hp.*Carn*.19).[18] Then ἐπαμβάτην, the parting shot: for the vehicle, τοὺς ἵππους...καὶ τοὺς ἀμβάτας (*X.HG* 5.3.1), ὁ ἵππος...αὐτῶν ἐπαναβεβηκότων (Hdt.3.85.1); for the tenor, ὁ δ᾿ ἄρρην ἐπαναβαίνων ὀχεύει (Arist.*HA* 540a.22), ἀναβῆναι τὴν γυναῖκα βούλομαι (Ar.*fr*.329).[19] So much for explanation.[20]

1 Phoc.12. For μέσος with political reference, cf. also Thgn.220, Pi.*P*.11.52, A. *Eu*.529, Th.3.82.8 etc.
2 The oracle may be a *post eventum* fabrication, though there does not seem to be any reason for pronouncing it post-archaic.
3 Demetr.*Eloc*.100, translation based on Rhys Roberts'.
4 Page *SA* 188.
5 So Hdt.2.26.2, Arist.*Mete*.362b.33, Thphr.*Sign*.35; cf. A.*Prom*.1087.
6 Sol.3.19, Xenoph.1.23, Thgn.781, Pi.*O*.12.16, Hdt.1.60.2 etc.

7 The equivocation has often been remarked, e.g. by G. S. Farnell 324 and Edmonds (Loeb) *ad loc.*, but I have not seen its significance spelt out. Some scholars evade the significance by an arbitrary 'either/or', not 'both/and', interpretation (so Page *SA* 187), while leaving the point of the 'or' ('strife of the winds') unexplained. This one instance should demonstrate the importance of the explanatory function in allegory, a more important one than it might seem to an age, like ours, unused to systematic allegorizing. What can happen without such explanation appears from e.g. Thgn.257ff., where there is simply no way of deciding between several alternative interpretations (listed in van Groningen *ad loc.*).

8 *Alleg.Hom.*5.2.

9 ταράσσειν of the sea: likewise, *Od.*5.291. ταράσσειν of military unrest: likewise, *Hell.Oxy.*6.3, Aen.Tact.11.8, shading off into domestic unrest, as Sol.33a West (?), Thgn.219, Lys.6.36, Ar.*Eq.*214 and ultimately *Il.*2.95.

10 Likewise *Il.*4.274 and 16.66 and, by implication, Demad.*fr.*1.15 (complete list). Cf. also the phrase πολέμοιο νέφος, *Il.*17.243, Ar.*Pax* 1090 (para-epic) and (of a person) Pi.*N.*10.9. The restrictedness of the main spread and the fact that the isolated Hdt. instance belongs to a speech ('poeticism'?) incline me to use the word 'cliché'.

For another instance of explanation in allegory – and maritime allegory once again – see Thgn.675ff., a passage that in fact contains a whole series of explanations, albeit rather flat-footed ones, the allegory being a transparent and unexciting version of the 'ship of state' and the repetition of the interactive mode becoming obtrusive. The *N* terms are: (i) φυλακήν, 676. *Qua T*, φυλακὴ πόλεως Thgn.1043; so, with various precise significations, Lys.25.28, Andoc.4.19, X.*HG* 5.4.21, Aen.Tact.3.1, *SIG* 204.20 (Eleusis, iv B.C.); περὶ φυλακῆς τῆς χώρας has the status of a separate deliberative τόπος in Arist.*Rh.*1359b.22. *Qua V*, a watch on board ship (for whatever purpose), as Arch.5a.9, Th.2.69.1, Pl.*Lg.*758a. (ii) χρήματα, 677. *Qua T*, 'property', 'money', in general: χρήματα δ' οὐχ ἁρπακτά Hes.*Op.*320. *Qua V*, specifically goods carried on board ship: χρήματ' ἐμὰ γλαφυρῆς ἐκ νηὸς ἑλόντες *Od.*13.283, so X.*HG* 1.6.37. (iii) κόσμος, 677. *Qua T*, political 'constitution' (Hdt.1.65.4, Th.4.76.2) or, less technically, political 'order': πόλις...κατὰ κόσμον οἰκεῦσα Phoc.4, so Democr.258 and cf. (εὔκοσμος) Sol.3.32. *Qua V*, 'order' on board ship: καθῖζον ἐπὶ κληῖσιν...κόσμῳ *Od.*13.76f., so Hdt.8.67.2. (iv) ἄρχουσι, 679. *Qua T*, the ordinary sense of political 'rule'. *Qua V*, the ship's command: εἰνάκις...ἦρξα...νέεσσιν *Od.*14.230, νηΐ, τῆς ἦρχε...Φάϋλλος Hdt.8.47, so Pi.*P.*4.230, Th.8.13, X.*HG* 3.4.27. The first three of these interactions are noted by van Groningen *ad loc.*, but mistakenly regarded as intrusive (i.e. he overlooks the *V* sense in each instance).

11 κίβδηλος of dishonesty: Thgn.965, Anacr.43.6, Democr.63, E.*Hipp.*616, Arist.*Rh.*1375b.6 etc.; so ἀκίβδηλος Hdt.9.7α.2, Phryn.Com.83, Isoc.1.7.

12 κ. is eventually picked up explicitly by the tenor in 'support' (v.123). Compare the interaction at Thgn.184 (analogy again) with εὐγενέας explanatory. The word is used of animals (A.*Ag.*1259, S.*El.*25, Arist.*HA* 488b.17f., so εὐγένεια

Democr.57), but is obviously commoner and more predictable of people. As such, it too explains in advance what the 'real' subject is (vv.185ff.) and the point is prominently brought out by enjambement. On this occasion, 'supporting' parallelism is confined to ἀγαθῶν/ἀγαθοῦ (184, 188). Another comparable interaction, but with less force, συμμείξεται at Thgn.1245. This verb is used of the mixture of physical elements (Hp.*Aer*.9, Heraclit.67, Pi.*N*.3.77) and also of human intercourse: ἐς πόλιν οὐ κατέρχεται οὐδὲ συμμίσγεται τοῖσι ἄλλοισι Πέρσῃσι Hdt.1.138.1, so 6.138.2, A.*Th*.611 (the active, intrans., is commoner in this sense; LSJ *s.v.* II.1).

13 χαλεπός of winds, also *Il*.21.335, Hp.*Aer*.15, X.*An*.4.5.3; of human unpleasantness, also *Od*.17.564, Thgn.638, A.*Ag*.1502, Ar.*V*.942, Hdt.3.131.1, Phryn. Com.4 Demiańczuk. Another explanatory glide to a quasi-allegorical metaphor at Pi.*N*.5.21, a slight instance: πέραν πόντοιο, cohering with the αἰετοί of the vehicle, at the same time explains that the topic is to switch from Aegina (v.16) 'across the sea' to Thessaly (vv.22ff.).

14 ἐπαμβάτην (i.e. ἐπανα-) is my own suggestion for the inherited ἐπεμ-. Whereas ἐπαμ- is lexicographically satisfactory on the two counts required, ἐπεμ- is hardly satisfactory on either – which is not readily explicable in a poem already geared to this interactive mode and, in particular, seemingly structured climactically to that end. Qua V, ἐπεμβάτης (a rare form) and the primary ἐμβαίνειν are certainly attested of horsemen, but only rarely and inadequately and the usage seems to be catachrestic from the related, but strictly irrelevant, use for riding (i.e. standing on) a *chariot* (etc.), seen in ἁρμάτων ἐπεμβάτην E.*Supp*.585 and sim.685; δίφρου ἐπεμβεβαώς Hes.*Sc*.195 and 324, sim. Pi.*N*.4.29; ἐπὶ πωλικῆς... ἀπήνης ἐμβεβώς S.*OT* 802f.; ἐμβεβὼς δίφροις E.*Ph*.2, sim. S.*fr*.672 (cf. also E.*Heracl*.845 and *Il*.23.481, ἐν...βέβηκε); and, most important, ἵπποισι καὶ ἅρμασιν ἐμβεβαῶτα *Il*.5.199. On the evidence available, it looks to be certain that in this Homeric instance ἅρμ. ἐμ. is the proper collocation and that from this passage, or from one very like it, derives the poorly attested ἵππ. ἐμ./ἐπεμ.: ἵππων...ἐπεμβάτας E.*Ba*.782 (cf. *Rh*.783) and ἵπποις ἐμβεβαώς *h.Hom*.31.9 (prob. post-archaic, cf. Allen-Halliday on the 'recondite mythology' and 'florid style' of the hymn and their note on v.18). Qua T, neither ἐπεμ. nor ἐμ. forms are attested at all. The nearest parallel is ἐπιβαίνειν (which is also used for mounting a horse) in the epic usage τῆς εὐνῆς ἐπιβήμεναι ἠδὲ μιγῆναι (*Il*.9.133 etc.), which, lacking the -εμ-, is not immediately relatable and is not itself equivalent to μιγῆναι anyway. Against my conjecture is the fact that the word ἐπαμβάτης itself is not attested; but with both the primary ἀμβάτης and the doublet ἐπαμβατήρ (A.*Ch*.280) to appeal to, this does not seem a decisive objection.

15 φεύγειν of animals: likewise, *Il*.11.477, Thgn.260, Hdt.2.68.4, Thphr.*fr*.171.2.

16 See above, p. 92, n.5.

17 So, of experience generally, Thgn.571 etc.; so πειρᾶσθαι Hes.*Op*.660, Hdt.7.125 etc.

18 πειρᾶν of sex is a widespread usage, although Anacreon's allusion to it is the earliest attested. Besides Hp. *loc. cit.*, the examples include: Pi.*P*.2.34 (med.),

E.*Cyc*.581, Ar.*Eq*.517, Th.6.54.4, Theopomp.Com.32.8, Lys.1.12, X.*Cyr*.5.2.28, Pl.*Phdr*.227c, Aristopho 4.7, Thphr.*Char*.4.7, Men.*fr*.456; also a recently discovered instance, Philaenis περὶ ἀφροδισίων, *P.Ox*.2891.1.ii.1f., δεῖ τοίνυν τὸν πειρῶντα... (advice to 'the seducer'), this being the opening of a previously lost, mid fourth century treatise (on the date, see Gow and Page 3f.). πείρασις is similarly used, Th.6.56.1.

19 The evidence for ἐπαμ. in either sense must necessarily be taken from primary or immediate cognate forms, since the conjectural ἐπαμβάτης is not otherwise attested (see n.14 above). Additional evidence, *qua V* (horse-riding): ἀναβάτης, 'horseman', X.*Eq*.3.12, Pl.*Criti*.119a; ἄμβασις S.*OC* 1070; ἀναβὰς ἐπὶ τὸν ἵππον X.*Cyr*.4.1.7, so Hp.*Int*.1, Mnesim.4.6; ἀναβαίνειν without any ἐπί, Pi.*O*.13.86, Theopomp.Hist.2. *Qua T* (sex): (ἐπ)αναβαίνειν is commoner of animals than of people, e.g. ἀναβαίνειν *Milet*.3.31a.6 (vi B.C.), Hdt.1.192.3; ἀναβ. ἐπί Arist.*HA* 539b.24; ἐπαναβ. Arist.*GA* 748a.34. Besides Ar.*fr*.329, the human sexual sense of ἀναβ. may be hinted at in Ar.*V*.398f. ἀνάβαινε... παῖε, ἤν πως...ἀνακρούσηται (for παίειν erotically, see Ar.*Pax* 899; for ἀνακρ., see Taillardat 103 on κρούειν). N.B. that βαίνειν itself is also so used: βαίνειν...καὶ παιδοσπορεῖν Pl.*Phdr*.250e; βαβαὶ βαβαί, βήσομαι γυναῖκας Hermipp.Com.98 (= Achae.Trag.28 Nauck – the words clearly come from a satyr play or a comedy); βαίνειν is used causally of animals at Thgn.185 and of the animals themselves at Hdt.1.192.3, Arist.*HA* 575a.13 (cf. Pl.*Phdr*.250e, again); cf. also νυμφόβας Achae.Trag.52 (see Lobel's *Alcaeus*, p.75); note incidentally Hes.*Op*.328 ἀνὰ δέμνια βαίνῃ, like the epic εὐνῆς ἐπιβήμεναι, discussed in n.14 above.

20 One final possibility. An important detail may be added to the immediate tenor, rather than to the suppressed tenor. Thus Pi.*I*.5.49, where Διός, while cohering fully with the vehicle ὄμβρῳ (Διὸς ὄμβρος *Il*.5.91, *Od*.9.111, Hes.*Op*. 626 etc.), suggests optimistically that the battle of Salamis was a 'divine providence' (Farnell *ad loc.*). The hint is confirmed at vv.52f., but with qualification to the optimism.

The specifying function
§44

What the explanatory function does for the tenor, the specifying function does for the vehicle. Simile, as explicit imagery generally, normally spells out what the 'real' subject is being likened to. '*T* like *V*': the vehicle is almost invariably specific, as specific, that is, as it seems to need to be. With metaphor this is not necessarily so, although there is a latent prejudice among many scholars that it is so, or, perhaps, should be so. Farnell's comment on Pi.*I*.1.4 is typical: 'We have nothing in contemporary literature to show the source of the metaphor.' Our inadequate knowledge of 'contemporary literature' and of the Greek language generally may well be in question in this and in other cases, but Farnell has evidently not even considered the possibility that any given vehicle may be inherently unspecific.

The prejudice may well be related to the dogma that imagery must be 'pictorial' and that the vehicle is therefore bound to have a certain definiteness – and this despite the well-known facts that some Greek poets in particular tend not to 'delineate the vehicle in detail',[1] and that one type of metaphor, the 'animating' type, is characteristically distinguished by its very lack of specificity. Above all, natural specificity is not inevitably a virtue in itself. The peculiar effectiveness of the metaphor in *Eleg.Adesp.*5,[2]

τοιάδε θνητοῖσ᾽ εἰσι κακῶν κακά, ἀμφί τε κῆρες
εἰλεῦνται,

lies precisely in its imprecision. The possibly relevant uses of the verb are numerous. If one asks the simple question, 'εἰλεῦνται like *what?*', all one can say is that the κῆρες are like whatever it is, presumably animate, that 'huddles' or 'winds' or 'swarms' etc. Better the devil you know; against such imponderability the victim is helpless.

But the last point should not be overstated. On the whole, the wish to pin the vehicle down is more than an academic whim, although if a cursory oversimplification is taken as 'the answer' and this as an end in itself, the wish is no better than complacent ignorance. Rather, it is often necessary to know 'like what' in order to appreciate the implications of the basic relation or even, simply, to make sense of the image at all; and the short 'answer' is merely an abbreviation of convenience. If this is recognized, the abbreviation can stand.

The specifying function, then, exists to answer the question 'like what'; it is exercised on behalf of the vehicle; and it applies chiefly to metaphor. It is also very rare; that is, the use of neutral terminology to specify the vehicle is rare. The usual method of specification is to preface the metaphor with a simile. So Cleopatra on Antony (*A/C.*v.2):

> his delights
> Were dolphin-like; they show'd his back above
> The element they lived in.

Or, still with simile, to gloss the metaphor afterwards: εὖρις ἡ ξένη κυνὸς δίκην (*A.Ag.*1093).[3] Similarly, Sapph.47:

> ἔρος δ᾽ ἐτίναξέ μοι
> φρένας, ὡς ἄνεμος κὰτ ὄρος δρύσιν ἐμπέτων.[4]

The degree to which these specifyings are 'necessary' varies. Aeschylus' εὖρις, one would have thought, was clear enough by itself. Sappho's simile, in contrast, establishes what might not otherwise have been clear and gives it in detail. And Shakespeare's simile is absolutely necessary; without it the metaphor would be baffling, quite gratuitously. But none of these instances involves interaction, and fine as the imagery is, particularly Shakespeare's, the mode of specifying itself has nothing of the economy, subtlety, immediacy that interaction, if and when used towards this end, can produce.

1 Goheen 155, of Sophocles; cf. Dornseiff 94f. on Pindar. Obviously this lack of specificity cannot be total, if the V terms mean anything at all.
2 Mimnermus? Diehl's text (given above) is far from certain; κακῶν κακά, in particular, arouses my suspicions as it did Bergk's (*PLG* III, p.689) (cf. Kock on Diocl.Com.2).
3 Ole Smith (p.38) objects to calling this kind of simile 'explanatory' (meaning 'specifying'), but does not explain why.
4 See above, p. 105 with n.9.

§45

Every neutral term is bound to add some detail, however slight, to the vehicle. Even in simile, with an instance as straightforward as οἴχεται νεβροῦ δίκην, it is undeniable that οἴχεται suggests what the νεβρός is, or would be, doing, and that this suggestion is otherwise absent. Much more delicate, and in metaphor, Pi.*N*.4.6ff.:

> ῥῆμα δὲ . . .
> ὅ τι κε σὺν Χαρίτων τύχᾳ
> γλῶσσα φρενὸς ἐξέλοι βαθείας.

Vehicle ἐξέλοι, with βαθείας, articulated as convergence, neutral. βαθεῖα φρήν is a normal collocation,[1] and, at the same time, βαθείας adds significantly to ἐξέλοι. The 'drawing out' is never fully defined, but a concrete detail is added: the whatever-it-is out of which the drawing is done is 'deep' – but the effect is too frail to stand up to such a clumsy paraphrase. Compare Pi.*P*.1.75:

> 'Ελλάδ' ἐξέλκων βαρείας δουλίας.

Vehicle ἐξέλκων, detailed by βαρείας: κακότητα βαρεῖαν (*Il*.10.71)[2] and . . . what? Once again a concrete detail is added; the whatever-it-is is 'heavy';[3] but again no fuller definition is given. It is not given to see any particular heavy thing.

Consider A.*Eu*.372ff.:

> μάλα γὰρ οὖν ἁλομένα
> ἀνέκαθεν βαρυπετῆ

καταφέρω ποδὸς ἀκμάν,
σφαλερὰ καὶ τανυδρόμοις κῶλα, δύσφορον ἄταν.
πίπτων δ' οὐκ οἶδεν τόδ' ὑπ' ἄφρονι λύμᾳ...

Archilochus' general gained praise for the ability to stay ἀσφαλέως βεβηκὼς ποσσί (Arch.60.4). The victim of the chorus, the Erinyes, has no such luck. They jump him (ἁλομένα), trip him (σφαλερά), and he falls (πίπτων). Of these three stages within the action, the latter two, and especially the last, are indicated only by interaction, while the last marks the full 'realization' of the image, aided by full convergence.⁴ σφαλερά carries its normal and predominant sense, σφαλερὰ καὶ ἐπικίνδυνα (Aeschin.2.73),⁵ and, perhaps by re-etymology, the relevant concrete sense: σφῆλαι οὔδει τε πελάσσαι (Il. 23.719).⁶ Then πίπτων; obvious in its physical sense, and equally operative in the word's secondary meaning of human ruin, τοὺς κακοὺς ὁρῶ βροτῶν πίπτοντας (E.fr.577.1f.).⁷ But once again, this is a matter of adding detail to the vehicle rather than illuminating its central aspects. And, it might be added, inasmuch as Aeschylus' interactions specify the vehicle at all, they explain the tenor in equal measure, so that without σφαλερά one would not have it actually said that the Furies' vengeance is a 'dangerous' thing nor, without πίπτων, that the victim is actually 'ruined', though both would be readily inferential. A comparable claim, if it comes to that, could be made for the interaction in Cleopatra's 'sucks the nurse asleep'. 'Sleep' is certainly less necessary to the vehicle than 'death', which it evokes, is to the tenor, but it is a distinction of degree not of kind.

This is a further illustration of the characteristic complexity of the functioning of neutral terms. It is also an indication that any instance of a genuinely specifying function in action must be radically and *effectively* different from any yet discussed.

1 See above, p. 118 with n.13; cf. also Il.19.125 ἄχος...κατὰ φρένα τύψε βαθεῖαν.
2 See above, p. 110 with n.12.
3 βαρύς of various 'heavy' objects, natural or manufactured: Il.1.219, S.fr.844, Ar.Nub.377, Hdt.8.60α, Hp.Art.40, X.Eq.10.6, Arist.Mete.340b.20, Thphr.HP 5.4.7. The usage is treated most inadequately in LSJ.
4 Both σφαλερά and (esp.) πίπτων represent convergence 'over the pause' (above, p. 113, n.23).
5 See LSJ s.v. I.
6 I.e. σφαλερά is active on both counts; so Headlam–Thomson, among others. Note the 'compensation principle' at work (see above, p. 118): the concrete sense is more likely contextually, the abstract lexicographically.
7 So A.Ch.934 and Prom.919, S.OT 50, Men.fr.740.15; cf. Hdt.7.157.2 and Th. 7.77.7 (the collective use) and perhaps Alc.380. Cf. also the commoner πίπτειν

εἰς with 'trouble' (*vel sim.*) as object: ἐς κακὸν πέσοιμι S.*Ant.*240, so Sol.1.68, Thgn.588, Th.3.82.2, Hp.*Vict.*1.32. To separate the two types inflexibly, on syntactic grounds, would be misleading for instances like this one. πίπτων in its present context is given in momentary isolation.

§46

It may seem an odd procedure to erect a category to house, substantially, a single instance, but this is what I am doing. Archilochus, *fr.*112:

τοῖος γὰρ φιλότητος ἔρως ὑπὸ καρδίην ἐλυσθεὶς
πολλὴν κατ' ἀχλὺν ὀμμάτων ἔχευεν
κλέψας ἐκ στηθέων ἁπαλὰς φρένας.

The first necessity is to appreciate that in the image of the first verse ὑπό and ἐλυσθείς make up the vehicle[1] and that καρδίην is neutral. This καρδίην is both the seat of love, ἔρως...καρδίαν ἰαίνει,[2] and a solid entity, one in which a spear can lodge – δορὺ δ' ἐν κραδίῃ ἐπεπήγει (*Il.*13.442) – and one beneath which he, she or it may be ἐλυσθείς; 'heart' both psychological and physical, in modern terms. It is no quibble to call καρδίην neutral, though in itself the word has a comparatively modest function: a measure of 'support'; a measure of introduction for the more striking part of the vehicle, ἐλυσθείς; and a measure of detail added to the vehicle, *viz* the physical base for ἔρως to ἐλύειν under.

But what is this ἐλύειν? To invoke the elementary formula again, ἐλυσθείς like *what?* 'Curled up', or the like, 'underneath'; but curled up underneath like *what?* The answer is given by a joint allusion on the part of the neutral term καρδίην and the vehicle ὑπὸ–ἐλυσθείς, allusion to a famous passage in the *Odyssey*,[3] where Odysseus, clutching the ram, is described as ὑπὸ γαστέρ' ἐλυσθείς. Any suggestion of allusion in early archaic poetry raises complex problems.[4] In general, one may say that two conditions must be fulfilled for allusion to exist as a perceptible actuality in this semi-formular[5] era. First, the phrase or whatever alluded to must be evocable; that is, known, distinctive and memorable. One could not, for instance, feasibly allude to any *particular* Homeric instance of a common Homeric formula. Second, the similarity between the phrase, if a phrase, that alludes and the phrase alluded to must be unusually marked. In this instance there is no doubt on either score. In extant epic, as elsewhere, ἐλυσθείς is a rare form[6] and distinctive on that account alone; its Odyssean context is notably memorable, and the Homeric episode was almost certainly enjoying wide circulation by the first half of the seventh century;[7] and not only is the resemblance between the

5-2

two phrases such that it could hardly be more marked short of actual identity – no other comparable phrase was ever, to our knowledge, used in any literature of the archaic or classical period.[8]

The relation of Archilochus' phrase to the Homeric is indeed widely recognized. The Teubner apparatus to Archilochus cites, without comment. Page speaks of 'adaptation' of 'Homeric phraseology'.[9] And Harvey and Webster go further, suggesting that by attributing Odysseus' action to an emotion, Archilochus evokes the whole heroic ethos. This, along with other, less striking and more or less irrelevant 'evocations' which he detects in the fragment, Harvey calls 'literary brilliance',[10] but does not attempt to explain why. Webster's contribution is: 'His love wound itself beneath his heart with the relentless intensity of Odysseus winding himself beneath the shaggy belly of the ram to escape from the Cyclops' cave' and 'small is compared to big'.[11] Despite the more specific function that Webster sees in the allusion, his explanation still seems inadequate to justify the brilliance that Harvey alleges.

The brilliance has not, I think, been fully understood. The effect of the allusion is to specify the vehicle. ἐλυσθείς like what? Quite simply, like Odysseus under the ram. Cunning, therefore; invincible in the end; subversive practitioner of violence – Polyphemus was blinded; and not at first recognized. The evident burden of this short fragment, the depiction of ἔρως as furtive menace and unrecognized agent of violence, or one not recognized until too late, is prefigured by interaction in the allusive phrase; while the allusive mode itself may seem, if not actually to 'express', at least to conform decorously to the pervasive mood of stealth. But the effect of the allusion goes still further, into the continuation of the imagery that follows. Once the decisive evocation is established, others present themselves. Odysseus under the ram was the Odysseus who outwitted and blinded Polyphemus: ὀφθαλ-μὸν...τὸν...ἐξαλάωσε...δαμασσάμενος φρένας, so cries Odysseus' victim.[12] The blinding by love,

πολλὴν κατ' ἀχλὺν ὀμμάτων ἔχευεν,

and the all too literal 'outwitting' by love,

κλέψας ἐκ στηθέων ἁπαλὰς φρένας,

are given painful particularity, informed savagely; the threat evoked by ὑπὸ καρδίην ἐλυσθείς is carried out to the letter.

This instance of the specifying function certainly depends on the evocation not of established senses of words so much as of an unusually particular context; but equally it leaves no doubt of the distinctive character and potential significance of the function.[13]

1 ὑπό here relates only to uses like Hp.*Acut*.23 ὑπὸ φρένας...τὸ ἄλγημα and, of course, the crucially relevant ὑπὸ γαστέρ' ἐλυσθείς (n.3 below) itself. There is no possibility that the word carried a simultaneous psychological sense; cf. only A.*Prom*.878, *Ag*.1215, *Ch*.272, *Eu*.159, a wholly unimpressive distribution. It is not legitimate to appeal to the usage of ὑφέρπω (LSJ II.2) etc.

2 Alcm.59(a).2; so *Od*.23.103, Sapph.31.6, Pi.*fr*.123.5, Ar.*Nu*.86, X.*Smp*.4.28.

3 *Od*.9.433.

4 See in particular Davison 125ff.

5 'Formular', but not necessarily 'oral'. See the welcome article by G. S. Kirk, 'Formular language and oral quality', in *Yale Class. Stud*.20 (ed. Kirk and Parry), 1966, 153ff. Many archaic inscriptions are formulaic; in what sense can they be called 'oral'?

6 Only *Il*.24.510 προπάροιθε ποδῶν 'Αχιλῆος ἐλυσθείς (Priam). ἐλύσθη is found at *Il*.23.393, ῥυμὸς δ' ἐπὶ γαῖαν ἐλύσθη.

7 As the proto-Attic Ram Jug suggests; see Kirk *SH* 285.

8 Cf. n.6 above.

9 Page *SA* 29.

10 Harvey 214.

11 Webster 31.

12 *Od*.9.453f.

13 For a further consideration, concerning the possible significance of τοῖος γάρ in v.1, see Appendix XII. Among the few other possible candidates (mostly problematic) for the specifying function is A.*Eu*.98off., vehicle ἁρπαλίσαι, neutral term πιοῦσα: *qua* *T*, ἡ γῆ... πίνουσα τὸ ὕδωρ Hdt.3.117.6, so 4.198.2, A.*Th*.736f. and 821, S.*OT* 1401, E.*Cyc*.305; cf. *Com.Adesp*.56.1 Demiańczuk, X.*Smp*.2.25 and ἐκπίνειν at A.*Ch*.66, S.*OC* 622, Hp.*Vict*.2.38, καταπίνειν at Pl.*Criti*.111d. ἁρπαλίζειν occurs elsewhere only at A.*Th*.243 and Arch.24.4 West, in the former case, and very possibly in the latter too (see Lasserre–Bonnard *ad loc*., p.12), of receiving news. The implicitly physical force of ἁρπαλίσαι here seems to be due to re-etymology, in line with ἁρπάζειν and other cognate or supposedly cognate forms; and the pressure to think of ἁρπάζειν etc. here comes from πιοῦσα. The phrase πιοῦσα αἷμα suggests, in particular, perhaps, the brutality of animals (cf. Weir Smyth *ad loc*.), as with κύνες...ἐμὸν αἷμα πιόντες (*Il*.22.66ff.), and this is a sense readily suggested by ἁρπάζειν: λέοντε...ἁρπάζοντε βόας *Il*.5.554ff., sim. *Od*.15.174, Hdt.2.90.1. (But it would be an overstatement to say that animal brutality is *inescapably* suggested by πίνειν and ἁρπ- in themselves: there is nothing animal about ὁ πῖνε...ἁρπαλέως *Od*.6.249f. and 14.109f. or ἡ δίψα ἰσχυρή· πιέουσα, πάλιν ᾔτει καὶ ἥρπαζε καὶ λάβρως ἔπινεν Hp.*Epid*.7.11, of a sick, but hardly brutal, woman.)

Support
§47

I have dealt with the functions so far considered at some length, not so much because of the number of examples – witness the specifying function – but because of their variety or special interest. With the last remaining function of neutral terminology, greater brevity is in order.

I have already had occasion to refer in passing to the 'supporting' function. Shakespeare, Sonnet 30:

> When to the sessions of sweet silent thought
> I summon up remembrance of things past. . .

Of 'summon up' Mrs Nowottny says: 'the familiarity of the phrase. . .acts as a guarantee of the propriety of the metaphor of the sessions of thought. . . supports it. . .'[1] The function is adequately indicated, except that 'the metaphor' rather obscures the distinction between image and vehicle. Like convergence, the supporting function is exercised on behalf of the image as a whole. Unlike convergence, however, it involves no full resolution of the image, and in any case has no formal property, except that of not preceding, and thereby presumably introducing, the vehicle. It is, I suppose, the residual function of all neutral terminology, and if I am judged to have seriously overstated the effects of any interactions discussed above, it may well be to this category that such passages should be referred.

'Residual' is not a eulogistic epithet; nor do I think the supporting function deserves any special eulogy. A characteristically unremarkable instance is Pi.*O*.13.93ff.:

> ἐμὲ δ᾽ εὐθὺν ἀκόντων
> ἱέντα ῥόμβον παρὰ σκοπὸν οὐ χρή
> τὰ πολλὰ βέλεα καρτύνειν χεροῖν,

where ἱέντα has the same neutral status as the converging ἱέντες of *O*.2.89f.[2]

> τίνα βάλλομεν. . .εὐκλέας ὀιστοὺς ἱέντες;

What it does not have is the articulation, and the articulation seems to me to make all the difference.

The function is not confined to metaphor. Perhaps its purest form, indeed, is casual parallelism in analogy or epic simile, as in my paradigm[3]

> οἱ δ᾽ ὥς τ᾽ αἰγυπιοὶ. . .κλάζοντε μάχωνται,
> ὣς οἱ κεκλήγοντες. . .

134

A comparable effect results in the short simile at A.*Pe*.126ff., where the ground term is set inside the *Wiestück*,

πᾶς γὰρ. . .λεὼς
σμῆνος ὣς ἐκλέλοιπεν μελισσᾶν
σὺν ὀρχάμῳ στρατοῦ,

the operative word being ἐκλέλοιπεν: ἐκλελοιπότων τῶν Βουδίνων καὶ κεκενωμένου τοῦ τείχεος πάντων (Hdt.4.123.1)[4] and γόνος μελιττῶν ἐκλείπει (Arist.*HA* 625b.28).[5] And when organized neither pivotally nor in convergence, the ground term in comparison will have the same residual function. Thus Thgn.805f.:

τόρνου καὶ στάθμης καὶ γνώμονος ἄνδρα θεωρόν
εὐθύτερον χρὴ ἔμεν. . .

where inasmuch as εὐθύτερον, 'straighter' geometrically and morally, has the felt force of enjambement behind it, it approximates to convergence, and inasmuch as it does not, it approximates to support.[6] It is clear that support is more akin to convergence than to any other function; these two, and only these two, act for the image as a whole.

As far as metaphor is concerned, some instances of support could simply be regarded as unarticulated convergence – like Shakespeare's 'summon'; or like Pindar, *I*.3/4.39ff.,

τόνδε πορὼν γενεᾷ θαυμαστὸν ὕμνον
ἐκ λεχέων ἀνάγει φάμαν παλαιὰν
εὐκλέων ἔργων,

where παλαιάν (cohering both with φάμαν and a hypothetical γραῦν) supports ἐκ λεχέων ἀνάγει.[7] It might be worth distinguishing such instances from those where the support is merely incidental, like Pindar's ἱέντα,

ἐμὲ δ' εὐθὺν ἀκόντων
ἱέντα ῥόμβον. . .,

which stands between the two vehicle terms ἀκόντων and ῥόμβον.[8] In favour of the former type, there is at least one instance notable for a peculiar effect of fading away – the figurative dissolving barely perceptibly into the larger literal reality. At Pi.*I*.6.74f., the poem's closing image, and with it the poem itself, is exquisitely undone in this way:

πίσω σφε Δίρκας ἁγνὸν ὕδωρ, τὸ βαθύζωνοι κόραι
χρυσοπέπλου Μναμοσύνας ἀνέτειλαν παρ' εὐτειχέσιν Κάδμου πύλαις.

πίσω vehicle, Δίρκας...ὕδωρ κτλ. support, Dirce being a plausible poetic symbol for Thebes.[9] The image was nicely analysed by Norwood: 'In the last sentence of *Isthmian* VI he praises Lampon as a man of integrity and an inspiration to others, adding...I will give him to drink of Dirca's sacred water, meaning (no doubt) I will pour forth in his honour my Theban minstrelsy: but the next words refer to the literal fountain of Dirca, for it springs beside the fair-built gate of Cadmus...'.[10]

But this said, there is little left to say. The variations noted are not considerable, and there seems no ground for attempting any larger distinctions.

1 See above, Prolegom. viii.

2 See above, p. 106.

3 *Il.*16.428ff. (see above, p. 16). The parallelisms in the 'short' similes at *Il.*13.389 (above, p. 16) and Thgn.113f. (above, p. 88 with n.5) belong here, along with those in the analogies at E.*fr.*1047 (above, p. 15) and Thgn.119ff. and 184 (above, p. 123 with n.12). Another example, involving analogy, is *Carm.Conv.*21, where the parallelism is in fact the point of the poem.

4 So Hdt.4.158.1, *Com.Adesp.*1239.

5 So X.*Oec.*7.38.

6 For εὐθύς *qua* *V* (physical), see LSJ *s.v.* A.I. εὐθύς *qua* *T* (morally 'straight') is common from Tyrt.3.6 onwards; cf. Εὐθύδικος, a VI B.C. proper name (see Fraenkel on *Ag.*761); so ἰθύς, the epic form, from *Il.*23.580 onwards; more references in LSJ *s.vv.* A.2 (εὐθύς), A.I.2 (ἰθύς). Alc.372, cited above, p. 20, is presumably another instance of support in comparison.

7 παλαιός as at *I.*7.16 (see above, p. 99). Other instances of support of this kind: (i) A.*Prom.*1015f. Vehicle χειμών and τρικυμία; support ἔπεισι, a second parallel to ἐπέλθῃ in ὅταν κλύδων κακῶν ἐπέλθῃ (see above, p. 105), but unarticulated. (ii) Pi.*I.*8.43. Vehicle πέταλα; support ἐγγυαλιζέτω, both a physical 'putting into the hands' (Hes.*Th.*485, *h.Merc.*497, Hegem.Parod.12) and an abstract 'bestowing' (*Il.*15.644, *Od.*23.140, Pi.*fr.*52f.133); *Il.*9.98 seems to imply both uses. In the tenor sense, the abstraction 'bestowed' is usually a benefit; hence a certain irony here. (iii) A.*Th.*62f., a comparable instance with simile, support from φράξαι: φράξαντο δὲ νῆας ἕρκει χαλκείῳ *Il.*15.566f. (so *Od.*5.256, Alc.6.7, cf. ναύφαρκτος A.*Pe.*951 etc.) and φραξάμενοι τὴν ἀκρόπολιν θύρῃσι Hdt.8.51.2 (sim. Th.3.3.5, A.*Th.*798). φρ. is wrongly taken as pure *V* by Ole Smith, p.59. (iv) Mimn.2.1–3, a comparable instance with *epic* simile, support from ἄνθεσιν: *qua* *T*, the collocation ἥβης ἄνθος is venerable cliché, as already noted (p. 100 with n.16).

8 Other instances of incidental support: (i) Thgn.839, vehicle ἄν and στρωφήσομαι, support from τὸ μέσον (*N* like μέσος in Pratinas 5, see above, p. 99 with n.13). (ii) A.*Ch.*775 (effectively classifiable here), vehicle τροπαίαν, support from Ζεύς: both god of the winds (*Il.*12.252f., *Od.*15.297 etc.) and controller of good or bad fortune (*Il.*24.529f., *Od.*4.237 etc.). (iii) Alcm.1.51, where the protracted woman/horse comparison is supported by χαίτα: horses' *mane*

(*Il.*17.439, X.*Eq.*5.5, cf. Semon.7.65) as well as human hair. The *N* status of χαίτα is noted by Page *AP* 88. (iv) Pi.*O.*3.43f., vehicle πρὸς ἐσχατιάν... ἱκάνων ἅπτεται... Ἡρακλέος σταλᾶν, support from οἴκοθεν: *qua V*, 'from home' (LSJ *s.v.* 1); *qua T*, 'by one's own powers' (LSJ *s.v.* 2). The two possibilities have been recognized (see e.g. Farnell), but here, as often, tidy-minded scholars have yet to learn the basic truth of literature, that 'alternatives' are not necessarily, or even usually, mutually exclusive. (v) Pi.*I.*3/4.29f., with image and interaction very similar to those at *O.*3.43f. above. Vehicle ἐσχάται-σιν...στάλαισιν ἅπτονθ' Ἡρακλείαις, supported, as before, by οἴκοθεν. Note that ἐσχάταισιν is *V* (not *N*) here, corresponding to ἐσχατιάν at *O.*3.43. ἔσχατος (and derivatives) cannot signify the 'height' of achievement. In such a context the word is pejorative (τὸ ἔσχατον κακοῦ Hdt.8.52.1, sim. Hp.*Vict.* 3.72, Aen.Tact.10.23, S.*Ant.*853 etc.), implying an *extreme*, which, in accordance with the 'Apolline' Hellenic ideal, is necessarily something to be deplored (cf. in this connection some interesting uses at Hp.*Aph.*1.3). The only contrary evidence consists of uses elsewhere in Pindar (*O.*1.113, *N.*10.32, cf. *I.*7.36) and Sophocles (*fr.*907), all to be regarded as tropical. Pindar's curious penchant for this usage is associated with the connection he makes between this same word ἔσχατος and Heracles (see above, p. 35 with n.5) and his preoccupation with the imagery of 'the limits of human attainment' (see below, p. 194 with n.4). (vi) Note also ἔξω...φέρομαι and the -δινεῖται of τροχοδινεῖται at A.*Prom.*882f. (see Appendix IX).

Note finally that a supporting term may be ostensibly part of a simile's *Wiestück*. Thus with 'Love's feeling is more soft and sensible / Than are the *tender* horns of cockled snails' (*Love's Labours Lost* IV.3). 'Tender' = 'gentle' from the fourteenth century onwards: 'tender of hert', 'O Lorde, thy tender mercies...' (see *NED s.v.*).

9 As also at A.*Th.*307 and Pi.*I.*1.29.
10 Norwood 98. Cf. A.*Th.*690f., with its dissolution of the metaphorical ἴτω κατ' οὖρον into the mythical κῦμα Κωκυτοῦ (i.e. on the assumption that γένος is subject of the sentence; cf. Tucker *ad loc.*).

6 Intrusion

§48

Intrusion, the second main type of interaction, has comparatively few distinct varieties. The chief reason for this would seem to be that for once considerations of word order or structuring hardly arise. Another contributory factor is that in general the distinctions between the different forms of imagery have little practical relevance here. In particular, the distinction between implicit imagery (i.e. metaphor) and explicit (e.g. simile) is not of much consequence in most cases – with one exception.

The exceptional case has already been treated, albeit briefly.[1] In its most rudimentary form, intrusion is confined to comparison and short simile, where a predictable 'N as V' (or 'more N than V') is replaced by 'T as V' ('more T than V'). Thus it was with the fossil, 'dead as a doornail', and thus it may be with live imagery as well:

> I wandered lonely as a cloud...

Terminologically speaking, clouds cannot 'wander' nor be 'lonely'; Wordsworthian poets can do either or both. Again, Shelley, *The Cenci*, III.1.255ff.:

> beneath this crag
> Huge as despair, as if in weariness,
> The melancholy mountain yawns.

Crags or mountains may be 'huge', but not despair. In both instances, the intrusion has a mutedly frigid effect; in the Wordsworth, rather distractingly so; in the Shelley, with a certain stylized *decorum* in keeping with the awesome mood ('despair', 'weariness', 'melancholy', 'yawns'). This kind of intrusion would not appear to be of much potential, and the few possible Greek instances confirm the impression.[2]

Much more usual and, at the same time, more creative are the cases where the intruder displaces *vehicle* terminology. Here, intrusion is widely known and as widely misunderstood; known, because its manifestations are usually very striking; misunderstood, because of preconceived ideas. The preconceptions are at bottom, perhaps, derived from the belief that imagery aspires to be 'pictorial' and that 'pictorial' is to be interpreted as 'representational' in the best stag-at-bay tradition. Hence anything that 'interferes' with the clear lines of the 'picture' is to be censured. Whether this is a complete explanation of the misunderstanding or not, there is no doubt that many Hellenists in particular are subject to it, and the still current phraseology by which intrusion is known bears witness to it. Consider A.*Ag.*1005ff.:

> καὶ πότμος εὐθυπορῶν
> ἀνδρὸς ἔπαισεν ἄφαντον ἕρμα.
> καὶ πρὸ μέν τι χρημάτων
> κτησίων ὄκνος βαλὼν
> σφενδόνας ἀπ᾽ εὐμέτρου,
> οὐκ ἔδυ πρόπας δόμος
> πλησμονᾶς γέμων ἄγαν...

By way of complement to his translation Weir Smyth notes: 'The house of Agamemnon, full of calamity, is likened to an overloaded ship, which will founder if some part of its freight is not jettisoned...', and adds, 'By confusion of the symbol and the thing signified, δόμος is boldly said to "sink its hull".'[3] I suppose that 'boldly' is not pejorative, but 'confusion' is, and its main implication as well as its pejorative tone is quite mistaken.

There is no mystery about the character of δόμος. Within the image there is, if one cares to say so, a second image that peremptorily reverses the first's terms. More simply, δόμος is a tenor term where one would expect a word in the terminology of the vehicle; the suppressed terminology suddenly reasserts itself, intrudes. And the effect of the intrusion should be no mystery either. δόμος is, in the first place, explanatory. It tells you what the 'real' subject is, tells you what is not, in fact, otherwise given at all, inside or outside the above quotation. Weir Smyth is right to say 'the house of Agamemnon', but it is only the intrusion that fully entitles him to say it. It would, of course, be presumed in any case that in this context the ship must 'really' mean the house of Agamemnon, but δόμος ('boldly') pushes aside the need for presumption. To the extent that this is so, the function of the intrusion, on behalf of the tenor, is comparable to the explanatory function of neutral terminology, and the suggestion of 'confusion' is comically misleading. But there is both more and less to it than this. There is not the painless and easy allusion that neutral terminology permits; instead there is a certain disharmony. The image is stood on its head. δόμος has, in an obvious sense, no right to be there, though in another sense it has every right to be there: it is the 'real' subject. Yet this 'real' subject is given force as the object of surprise: disharmony, unexpected, compels attention. Further, the sudden inversion of the image, in a way that preserves the basic analogical relation, produces a certain feeling of *enactment*, to use a rather overworked expression.[4] The whole image is affected, although assuredly the enactment is not compelling in this instance. But the implication is important. Intrusion does not serve a single master: the tenor, characteristically (by giving its 'real' subject); the whole image, more or less, often (by enactment); and even, sometimes, the vehicle.[5]

The enacting potential of intrusion is susceptible of a very complete realization. Thus with the friar's comment on Romeo's idea of a precipitate marriage (*Romeo and Juliet*, II.6):

> These violent delights have violent ends,
> And in their triumph die; like fire and powder,
> Which, as they *kiss*, consume.

Any more complete, and the enactment is in danger of overbalancing into self-parody. Shelley:

> And the hyacinth, purple and white and blue,
> Which flung from its bells a sweet peal anew
> Of music so delicate, soft and intense,
> It was felt like an *odour* within the sense.[6]

'But it *was* an odour', is the obvious comment.

Commonly, though, enactment goes more soberly in hand with explanation, as in Aeschylus' δόμος–ship paradigm; and likewise in this characteristic Shakespearian instance from *II Henry VI*, III.3 (Beaufort, recalling the murder of Gloucester):

> He hath no eyes, the dust hath blinded them.
> Comb down his hair; look, look – it stands upright
> Like lime-twigs set to catch *my* winged *soul*.

And likewise in another Aeschylean δόμος-instance, already briefly discussed,[7] *Ag*.966ff.:

> ῥίζης γὰρ οὔσης φυλλὰς ἵκετ᾽ ἐς δόμους,
> σκιὰν ὑπερτείνασα σειρίου κυνός.
> καὶ σοῦ μολόντος δωματῖτιν ἑστίαν...

The intrusive element, the phrase ἵκετ᾽ ἐς δόμους, carries a certain proleptic force in anticipation of the 'real' subject, and is accordingly picked up by the 'official' tenor two lines later: ...μολόντος δωματῖτιν....[8] But the conjunction of the interactive and the plain 'explanations' serves only to show up the almost absolute difference in effect. The latter is ordinarily inert; the former, with its enactment, pointedly upsetting. Beneath Clytemnestra's overt loyalty, her obsession with the single crucial fact is dramatically vivid. He's *got home*, is therefore vulnerable: πόσιν χρόνιον ἱκόμενον εἰς οἴκους. . . ἔκανεν αὐτόχειρ (E.*El.*1156ff.).⁹

Less enacting and more explanatory again, Pi.*P.*2.79f.:

> ἅτε γὰρ ἐννάλιον πόνον ἐχοίσας βαθύν
> σκευᾶς ἑτέρας, ἀβάπτιστος εἶμι. . .

Fishing tackle doesn't feel 'pain' and can't get into 'trouble'.¹⁰ The human subject can, and it is his situation that πόνον points to. Compare another Shakespearian instance, from *Richard II*, iii.3:

> See, see, King Richard doth himself appear
> As doth the blushing *discontented* sun.

Elizabethan suns do, by poetic convention, 'blush', but the discontent belongs exclusively to the king.

Explanation may be regarded as intrusion's central function, but it should also be said that the range of this category is not negligible and extends, at times, to the suggesting of what one might well think of as intellectual 'points'. Some such suggestion was, indeed, operative in Clytemnestra's ἵκετ' ἐς δόμους, discussed above. A straightforward and impressive instance from the beginning of the second stanza of Keats' *On Melancholy* shows a suggestion of the same intellectual kind predominating over any other effect:

> But when the melancholy fit shall fall
> Sudden from heaven like a weeping cloud,
> That fosters the droop-headed flowers all. . .

'Weeping' is intrusive, belongs by rights with 'melancholy', or with the sufferer from melancholy, not with the 'cloud'. It associates the action of the cloud with that of melancholy in such a way as to suggest – reinforcing a paradox central to this poem – the utter indissociability of melancholy and joy, melancholy and beauty, melancholy and the creation of beauty: the beauty the cloud creates is itself dependent on 'weeping'. And this, in terms of the poem, is the whole and plain truth. The intensely subjective Keatsian 'beauty' has its fullest existence only for the fully suffering beholder, just as – the explicit converse – the melancholic suffering truly exists only for the sensibility most keenly affected by joy and by beauty. 'She' – that is, Melancholy – 'dwells with beauty', and

> Ay, in the very temple of Delight
> Veil'd Melancholy has her sovran shrine,

141

> Though seen of none save him whose strenuous tongue
> Can burst Joy's grape against his palate fine.

But the interactive suggestion that this is so is still, let it be noted, given through the disharmony characteristic of all intrusion – aptly enough for such a paradox.

Keats' 'weeping cloud' consists, structurally, of an intrusive tenor adjective attached to a vehicle noun. This particular structure is a well-established one. At its lowest, it has the effect of isolating the vehicle, throwing the extraneous into relief, and, at the same time, indicating vigorously that what is being thrown into relief is indeed extraneous. So it is at Pi.P.1.8, where sleep is called

$$γλεφάρων ἁδὺ κλάϊθρον$$

with ἁδύ intrusive (ἡδέϊ...ὕπνῳ Il.4.131).[11] Likewise, from a very youthful Keats (I stood tip-toe),

> The clouds were pure and white as flocks new shorn,
> And fresh from the clear brook; sweetly they slept
> On the *blue* fields of heaven...

And likewise, Pindar again (O.4.6f.),

$$Αἴτναν...$$
$$ἷπον ἀνεμόεσσαν...Τυφῶνος,$$

and again (O.9.11f.),

$$ἵει γλυκὺν$$
$$Πυθῶνάδ' ὀϊστόν,$$

where γλυκύν belongs not with the *arrow* of song, but the song itself: γλυκεῖ' ἀοιδά Pi.N.5.2.[12] Note, above all, Pascal's superb use,[13]

> L'homme n'est qu'un roseau, le plus faible de la nature; mais c'est un roseau pensant,

where the terminological incongruity of the 'thinking reed' correlates with the stated paradox: both the lowest, yet the highest. With the given word order, the crucial 'pensant' gets the isolation in this instance.[14]

---

1 See above, pp. 20 and 23f.
2 Four in all, none quite certain (*ex silentio*). A proverbial flavour might be claimed for any or all of them. (i) Alcm.3.61f. τακερώτερα δ' ὕπνω καὶ σανάτω ποτιδέρκεται. The adjective τακερός is not common and especially uncommon (and only poetical) in a non-physical context. It is attested of erotic 'looks' (Ibyc.6.2, Philetaer.5) and of Eros himself (Anacr.114), but not of anything like

'sleep' or 'death'. (ii) A hyperbole in honour of one of the fair sex, ῥόδων ἁβροτέρα, very likely by Sappho (on the authorship see Lobel–Page's *apparatus* on Sapph.156, also Page on Anacr.143, and cf. Philostr.*Epist.*71 ἡ Σαπφὼ τοῦ ῥόδου ἐρᾷ . . . ἀεὶ τὰς καλὰς τῶν παρθένων ἐκείνῳ ὁμοιοῦσα). ἁβρός is standard of people (LSJ *s.v.*), but is not used of vegetation: cf. only ἁβρότονον (earliest occurrence, apparently, Hp.*Mul.*2.201), without aspiration, but evidently sometime folk-etymologized as ἁβρο-; also the ἁβρόκαρπον recorded in Hsch. with the same meaning. (iii) Epich.153 πραΰτερος ἐγών γα μολόχας. πρᾶος/ πραΰς is, again, standard of people (LSJ *s.v.* 1.2), but not of food. (iv) Anacr.82 μηδ' ὥστε κῦμα πόντιον λάλαζε. There seems to be no other example of any λαλ- word of water from any period, but it must be said that the only other known instance of λαλάζειν itself is apparently Call.*fr.*191.11 γέρων λαλάζων.

Note incidentally that the type represented by the *mot* in Quintil.6.3.64, *libidinosior es quam ullus spado*, is 'more *N* than *V*', not 'more *T* than *V*'. The semantic field of a word, which is what is implied by 'its terminology', includes its antonyms: 'black' is obviously part of the field of 'white' etc. *Libidinosior . . . spado* is a physical incongruity, but not a terminological one.

3 Cf. Fraenkel *ad loc.*, without 'confusion', but with 'even at the expense of the pictorial effect', in corroboration of my remarks above.

4 Compare incidentally S.*OT* 422, where δόμοις is intrusive 'equivalent' to νηΐ. Misunderstanding of this has led to misunderstanding of the syntax: δ. goes with ἄνορμον; it does not go with εἰσέπλευσας, nor is it some self-sufficient 'locative', as edd. have variously supposed.

5 See p. 142.

6 *The Sensitive Plant*, 1.25ff.

7 See above, p. 24.

8 The intrusion, along with the pick-up, is repeated in miniature at 971f. with δόμοις and δῶμα. For a less formalized equivalent to such 'prolepsis', cf. B.5.29f., where ἀρίγνωτος μετ' ἀνθρώποις, closing the long eagle *Wiestück* (*ohne wie*), implies a *human* subject, a *man* among men, just as at *Il.*5.1ff. Διομήδεϊ . . . δῶκε μένος . . . ἵν' ἔκδηλος μετὰ πᾶσιν Ἀργείοισι γένοιτο, it is implied that Diomedes is an Argive. (Cf. Jebb's evident feelings of discomfort about the words' aptness for an eagle.) As such, the words do in a way signal the forthcoming resumption of the tenor, albeit not persuasively: they cut too close.

9 ἱκέσθαι *qua T*: likewise, *Il.*15.58 πρὸς δώμαθ' ἱκέσθαι, *Od.*7.76 etc. *Qua V*, ἱκέσθαι might just conceivably stand by itself: ἐλάτην . . . ἢ μακροτάτη πεφυΐα δι' ἠέρος αἰθέρ' ἵκανεν *Il.*14.288 (cf. ἐφ-ικέσθαι of plants, Thphr.*HP* 5.1.8, *CP* 2.4.10), but although the verb is very common, the Homer is an isolated example and not fully parallel in construction.

10 Although πόνος is not entirely restricted to people. The word is used, for instance, with reference to plants (as at Thphr.*HP* 4.14.7 and *CP* 1.15.1) and to fish (as at Hp.*Vict.*2.48).

11 ἡδύς of sleep; likewise, *Od.*1.364, S.*El.*781, Hp.*Vict.*3.71.

12 Cf. specifically *Il.*1.249; B.5.4; Pi.*P.*10.56, *N.*9.3, *I.*2.7; *Mel.Adesp.*36a (p.513 Page); and generally LSJ *s.v.* γλυκύς I.a.

143

13 *Pensées* 347 in the Brunschvicg numeration.

14 In the Greek corpus, the *T* adj. + *V* noun structure seems to be purely Pindaric. (Farnell, with quaint stolidity, pronounced such interaction a 'sin' – this on *N*.8.46f., in contemplation of another conceivable instance.) The type is superficially, but only superficially, similar to the structures involving a limiting or privative explanatory epithet discussed in Appendix VII, e.g. Διὸς...πτηνὸς κύων (A.*Prom*.1021f., of the eagle). In intrusion, the epithet (or whatever) is terminologically unexpected; in these structures, terminologically predictable. More generally, contrast, though not always so decisively, such parallel or parenthetic explanation in the tenor as is associated with the γρῖφος in Aeschylus (see Fraenkel on *Ag*.133 στρατωθέν and 136).

§49

The explanatory function of neutral terminology has been shown to be of special importance in allegory,[1] and the same is true of intrusion. Alcaeus (6.1f.)[2] provides an excellent example:

> τόδ' αὖτε κῦμα τὼν προτέρων ὄνω
> στείχει,...

στείχει is intrusive. The word is not current of physical inanimates.[3] What it is current of is soldiers on the march: στείχειν ἐς πόλεμον (*Il*.2.833), θωρηχθέντες ἔστιχον (*Il*.16.258), στίχοντας ἐπὶ τοὺς ξείνους (Hdt.9.11.2), στρατὸν στείχοντα (S.*fr*.502.3). The allegory, whose reference to 'the soldier on the eve of battle'[4] might have been, indeed has been, taken anyway, interprets itself for us through the interaction; and not merely interprets, but genuinely enacts. What lies behind the allegory can be *felt*.

Another fine instance is Pi.*P*.4.263ff., Pindar's famous allegory of the oak beam with – as he subsequently makes clear – underlying reference to a certain exiled nobleman:[5]

> εἰ γάρ τις ὄζους ὀξυτόμῳ πελέκει
> ἐξερείψειεν μεγάλας δρυός, αἰσχύνοι δέ οἱ θαητὸν εἶδος,
> καὶ φθινόκαρπος ἐοῖσα διδοῖ ψᾶφον περ' αὐτᾶς,
> εἴ ποτε χειμέριον πῦρ ἐξίκηται λοίσθιον,
> ἢ σὺν ὀρθαῖς κιόνεσσιν δεσποσύναισιν ἐρειδομένα
> μόχθον ἄλλοις ἀμφέπει δύστανον ἐν τείχεσιν,
> ἑὸν ἐρημώσαισα χῶρον.

The intrusion here is in fact multiple and is combined, very felicitously, with convergence. The allegory, at first sustained without interruption, is displaced by, to begin with, μόχθον...ἀμφέπει δύστανον, an obviously intrusive word group: μόχθος is a *man's* μόχθος. ἐν τείχεσιν too is intrusive, but more subtly. τείχεα are not building walls, but *city* walls;⁶ '*within* city walls' most naturally implies *people* within the walls (Νικίας δὲ ἐν τοῖς τείχεσιν ὑπελέλειπτο Th.7.43.2);⁷ and, above all, ἄλλοις gives the phrase an emotive nuance proper only to the exile who has had to move *from one city* to another. Compare Lycurgus 143 on Leocrates, the deserter, who 'will beg his city to let him οἰκεῖν ἐν τοῖς τείχεσι τῆς πατρίδος. Which τείχη? Those he failed to defend.' Next, ἐρημώσαισα, though nominally – syntactically – cohering with the vehicle and its feminine subject, δρῦς, is terminologically intrusive, pointing to a *person* leaving a place: τὴν πόλιν ἐκλιπόντες καὶ ἐρημώσαντες Συρακούσας (Th.5.4.3).⁸ And last, χῶρον resolves the whole image with a subdued convergence: the oak tree's 'ground' and the exile's 'country', χῶρον ἀν' ὑλήεντα (*Od*.14.2) and οἰκήσαντας τοῦτον τὸν χῶρον τὸν καὶ νῦν οἰκέουσι (Hdt.1.1.1).⁹

One very distinctive exploitation of the enacting potential concerns the omen, which, as a literary mode, bears obvious affinities to allegory. Consider Pindar's Sixth *Isthmian*. Heracles prays for a son to be born to Telamon, a son and a hero (45ff.):

> λίσσομαι παῖδα θρασὺν ἐξ Ἐριβοίας
> ἀνδρὶ τῷδε...θυμὸς δ' ἐπέσθω.

The god gives his answer (49f.):

> ταῦτ' ἄρα οἱ φαμένῳ πέμψεν θεός
> ἀρχὸν οἰωνῶν μέγαν αἰετόν...

And Heracles interprets:

> ἔσσεταί τοι παῖς, ὃν αἰτεῖς, ὦ Τελάμων ·
> καί νιν...κέκλευ...εὐρυβίαν Αἴαντα, λαῶν
> ἐν πόνοις ἔκπαγλον Ἐνυαλίου.

The key to the 'code' is the aural similarity of αἰετόν/Αἴαντα, but the force of the interpretation offered depends largely on intrusion: ἀρχόν. In literature ἀρχός usually means a military commander, and has an overwhelmingly epic flavour:¹⁰ εἷς δέ τις ἀρχὸς...ἢ Αἴας ἤ... (*Il*.1.144f.).

Isthmian 6 is customarily dated to 484 or 480. If rightly so, it antedates Aeschylus' *Agamemnon* by a considerable period. Whether this speaks for or against the possibility of Pindar's interaction having exercised influence on *Ag*.108ff., I would not presume to say:

> Ἀχαιῶν δίθρονον κράτος...
> πέμπει σὺν δορὶ καὶ χερὶ πράκτορι

θούριος ὄρνις Τευκρίδ᾽ ἐπ᾽ αἶαν,
οἰωνῶν βασιλεὺς βασιλεῦσι νεῶν ὁ κελαινός,
ὅ τ᾽ ἐξόπιν ἀργᾶς,
φανέντες...

The literal βασιλεῦσι are the Atridae; the other 'monarchs', βασιλεὺς...ὁ
...ὅ τε..., are the eagles that represent them only too ominously. Unlike
Pindar, one notes, Aeschylus is not content to let the 'real' significance of his
omen be felt out – he produces the most assertive juxtaposition imaginable.[11]

Earlier in the same play Aeschylus gives us a remarkable series of intrusions. The image in question is the simile of the vultures that hangs on the
pivotal κλάζοντες (Ag.48ff.). The Atridae

Μενέλαος ἄναξ ἠδ᾽ Ἀγαμέμνων

have raised their army and

μέγαν ἐκ θυμοῦ κλάζοντες Ἄρη
τρόπον αἰγυπιῶν
οἵτ᾽ ἐκπατίοις ἄλγεσι παίδων...

This last word, παίδων, is widely recognized for what it is.[12] In itself it
represents a rather different kind of intrusion from any yet discussed, partial
rather than full. The birds' situation is given in specifically human terms,
where the tenor is itself human but is not immediately concerned with the
aspect of humanity that παίδων evokes.[13] Fraenkel's interpretation of the
effect, to 'intensify the feeling of grief' and to form 'a further link' between
tenor and vehicle, is worth recording. The intensification stems from the
'link', one might add, and the 'link' is essentially a form of enactment. A
qualification added by Fraenkel errs in a way that focuses attention on
another aspect. 'Naturally it occurs to no one that the Atridae have lost
children' – but Agamemnon...? This faint and slightly surreal 'proleptic'
evocation of Iphigenia, however, involves no specific interaction; she does
not form the official topic for some time.[14] The passage continues

οἵτ᾽ ἐκπατίοις ἄλγεσι παίδων
ὕπατοι λεχέων στροφοδινοῦνται
πτερύγων ἐρετμοῖσιν ἐρεσσόμενοι

with a further intrusion in λεχέων,[15] nominally referring to the empty nest.
λέχος of the marriage-bed is one of the predominant uses of the word,[16] and
this time there is no doubt of the full relevance to the tenor. The painful
significance of the word is echoed by the chorus in later retrospect (v.411):

ἰὼ λέχος καὶ στίβοι φιλάνορες.

146

The vividness of the effect makes 'explanatory' seem a poorly inadequate description; the antecedents of the drama seem to be coming back to life. So too with ἐρετμοῖσιν ἐρεσσόμενοι, yet another intrusion.[17] Headlam notes that 'as the kings launch forth in ships, so fly the eagles πτ. ἐρ.', but subsumes this under discussion of the Aeschylean 'carrying a figure through'.[18] If by 'figure' he means vehicle, this is plainly the exact opposite of the truth: λεχέων leads to ἐρεσσόμενοι, the rape to the expedition. And the expedition is a mission of revenge. The image closes:

> ὕπατος δ' ἀίων ἤ τις 'Απόλλων
> ἤ Πὰν ἤ Ζεὺς οἰωνόθροον
> γόον...
> πέμπει παραβᾶσιν 'Ερινύν.
> οὕτω δ' 'Ατρέως παῖδας...
> ἐπ' 'Αλεξάνδρῳ πέμπει...
> Ζεὺς πολυάνορος ἀμφὶ γυναικός...

Terminologically, 'Ερινύν is alien to the animal world;[19] its applicability is to the actual situation of Paris and Helen, description of which follows at once. The rôle of the interaction is almost enunciatory, directly 'proleptic', to authorize, as it were, the progression of ideas into what Fraenkel reasonably calls 'a much deeper level', from 'crying and lamentation' to the central theme, 'the just vengeance'.[20]

---

1 §43.

2 V.1 contains a notorious crux, though one that hardly looks likely to affect the interaction. The text above (as Seidler and Bergk) is given *exempli gratia*.

3 Unless of the movement of the sun (*Od.*11.17, cf. A.*Supp.*769, Critias 25.35, E.*Rh.*992). Miscellaneous metaphorical uses at A.*Prom.*1090, *Th.*534, *Eu.*906 (ἐπι-), E.*Cyc.*648, *Trag.Adesp.*611 Nauck–Snell (περι-).

4 Page *SA* 184.

5 One Damophilus: see vv.279ff., 293ff.

6 So Gildersleeve; most commentators evidently miss the point. τείχη μέν ἐστι τὰ τῶν πόλεων, τειχία δὲ τὰ τῶν οἰκιῶν, Ammonius (*Diff.*468 Nickau).

7 So D.23.155 and Eup.7.13 Demiańczuk (dual) (E.*Ion* 206 looks different, but is generally reckoned corrupt); so ἐν τείχει *Il.*13.764 and 22.299, Hdt.5.64.2 and 9.118.1, Th.2.78.4, E.*Rh.*879, Andoc.1.45, X.*Cyr.*7.5.13. It is true that physical 'things' *may* be located likewise 'within city walls' (e.g. Hdt.7.107.2, Th.3.68.3, both ἐν τῷ τείχει), but it is only in marginal circumstances that any thing is likely to be so described. In itself, of course, the phrase ἐν τείχεσιν might mean 'in, i.e. *as physical part of*, city walls', as with the ὀρσοθύρη...ἐνὶ τοίχῳ of *Od.*22.126; but this is clearly not what σὺν ὀρθαῖς κιόνεσσιν suggests, quite apart from ἄλλοις.

INTRUSION (§49)

8 See further LSJ *s.v.* ἐρημόω III.

9 On χῶρος, cf. my remarks below, p. 200 with n.1.

10 There are some thirty references in Ebeling's *Lex.Hom.*; the word occurs once in Hesiod (*fr.*204.53), once in Archilochus (*fr.*113.7 West); not again in literature before Pindar, except at Anacr.107.2 Diehl (elegiacs). It does occur, however, in early inscriptions in the sense 'magistrate' (e.g. *SIG* 47.42, Locrian, early v B.C.) or, apparently, 'ruler' (*SIG* 3d, Miletus, vi B.C.). Not in Aeschylus, unless one accepts the speculative conjecture of Fritsch to fill a papyrus gap at *fr.*225.14 or the reading ἀρχούς at *Ag.*125, which, oddly enough, is connected with the eagle omen there.

11 Another quasi-allegorical mode is the dream. The queen's dream in Aeschylus' *Persians* contains one straightforward intrusion, εὔαρκτον at v.193: ἐν ἡνίαισί τ' εἶχεν εὔαρκτον στόμα (the good horse). 'Easily managed', renders Broadhead, but ἄρχειν does not mean 'manage' in this sense; and Ole Smith's assurance (p.23) that -αρκτος is a 'technical term from the horse race' seems to be a mere guess. (The only evidence in favour is (1) the horsey φρένες δύσαρκτοι at A.*Ch.*1024; (2) Pl.*Theag.*123d ἵππων ἐπιστάμεθα ζεύγους ἄρχειν, which is not even Plato, but pseudo-Plato and, incidentally, appears to be a piece of linguistic trickery designed to 'prove' the analogy between politics, the real sphere of ἄρχειν, and various other fields, of which ἡνιοχεία is one.) The normal and obvious meaning, 'easily ruled', points unambiguously to the suppressed tenor in this political 'allegory'. Persia, like the Erinyes, stands in horror of the ἄναρκτον βίον (A.*Eu.*526). The political sense is, as one would expect, reliably attested in the -αρκτος formations, rare as they are (and apparently confined to v B.C. Athens): νησιώτας...ἀνάρκτους (Th.5.99).

12 Most recently by Smith 55.

13 The continuation of the Keats lines quoted above, p. 141 (and quoted in full on p. 80), provides a comparable instance of 'partial' intrusion: 'and hides the green hill in an April shroud'. This 'shroud' is obviously closer to the 'melancholy' terminology, without really belonging to it, than to the 'cloud...flowers... hill'. Its terminological status is more elusive than that of 'weeping' and its effect much vaguer and, bearing in mind the meaning, more sinister.

14 Not until v.151 (θυσίαν ἑτέραν).

15 Noted by Fraenkel and Smith (p.55) but without full interpretation. Fraenkel reasonably compares λεχαίων at A.*Th.*292 (so too Smith 61), though there the intrusion is partial, as with παίδων at *Ag.*50. Cf. also ἶνιν and τοκέων at *Ag.*717 and 728 respectively, the former noted by Fraenkel on *Ag.*50. There is certainly a remarkable amount of intrusion of one sort or another in the play.

16 See LSJ *s.v.* 3.

17 So, apparently, Smith 56.

18 Headlam 436.

19 So, apparently, Smith 55f. and Fraenkel. Denniston–Page, *contra*, cite *Il.*19.418, but the parallel is not close (the Erinyes checking the voice of the exceptional *human*-speaking horse, Xanthus) and, in any case, is perhaps the only parallel.

20 There is one other notable intrusion in the *Agamemnon* in the quasi-allegorical

148

omen at v.137: οἴκτῳ γὰρ ἐπίφθονος Ἄρτεμις ἁγνὰ / πτανοῖσιν κυσὶ πατρὸς / αὐτότοκον πρὸ λόχου μογερὰν πτάκα θυομένοισι. The intrusive element is θυομένοισι, which suggests not murderous killer animals but human sacrificers, hence points directly to the sacrifice of Iphigenia which is the tenor of the omen. As such, it explains/enacts the omen in the characteristic way. The terminological shift is supported by the neutral term αὐτότοκον, a word probably coined for this passage, which plays on two equally available senses of the αὐτο-compounds, the two represented by (a) αὐτόπρεμνα (sc. δένδρα), 'trunk and all', S.Ant.714 (cf. LSJ s.v. αὐτός v.6), (b) τῷ Διὸς αὐτόπαιδι, 'own child', S.Tr.826 (cf. LSJ s.v. αὐτός v.1). αὐτότοκον correspondingly suggests both the hare 'with her young' (for τόκος of animals see LSJ s.v. II.1) and Iphigenia, the 'own child' of the θυσία ἑτέρα (151). The N status of αὐτότοκον has been recognized by Lawson, Headlam–Thomson and Stanford AGL 143f. and GM 148, but Stanford, following Lawson, unwarrantably sees N terminology also in θυομένοισι (T only), in πτάκα (V only, A.Eu.326 and Lyc.944 being wholly inadequate to suggest that πτάξ/πτώξ could be normally used of a person in classical Greek) and in πρὸ λόχου. The terminology of this last item is doubtful: certainly T ('in front of the host') and maybe also V ('before birth'), but this sense of λόχος is not ordinarily normal, but at most due to Aeschylus' own re-etymological invention (see Fraenkel).

7 Interaction outside the grammar

§ 50

It is convenient to regard neutral-based interaction as, so to speak, the nominative kind and, accordingly, define extra-grammatical interaction with reference to it, as I in fact did, to some extent, in the case of intrusion. In the exposition that follows, this is done without further argument.

Whatever minor qualifications must be made, it is clear that on the whole neutral terms operate within or through the grammatical structure of the sentence to which they belong. I say and have said 'grammatical', although it may appear that what I am ultimately appealing to is not grammar but logic. But whether the structure is better regarded as logical or grammatical, there is the fundamental distinction to be made between interactions that work within it and interactions that work outside and obliviously of it.

This distinction, however, does not imply that the various effects created by the two kinds must be radically different. My paradigm of interaction outside the grammar was Stesich.8.2f. on ʼAέλιος,[1]

ὄφρα δι' ὠκεανοῖο περάσας
ἀφίκοιθ' ἱαρᾶς ποτὶ βένθεα νυκτὸς ἐρεμνᾶς,

in which the interactive relation is that between the tenor ὠκεανοῖο and the vehicle, βένθεα. It should not be difficult to see that the character of the relation is preparatory: ὠκεανοῖο leads up to and prepares βένθεα. As such, the relation is comparable with pivotal interaction, for whose characteristic effect I have already invoked the tag 'preparatory'. Comparable, but different, and the difference must be referred to grammatico-logical factors. There is no other way of explaining the perceptible difference in kind between Stesichorus' interaction and, for instance, that in

ἐν δ' ὀλίγῳ βροτῶν
τὸ τερπνὸν αὔξεται· οὕτω δὲ καὶ πίτνει χαμαί...[2]

In the latter case, even though the interaction takes effect over clearly separate syntactic units, there remains an intimate structural relation between αὔξεται and πίτνει. The structures are aligned, and it is this that invites us to think, half-rightly, of αὔξεται as 'part of the image'. One could not think of ὠκεανοῖο in this way.

There are three main categories of extra-grammatical interaction. One is preparation. The other two are 'anticipation of a theme' and 'link'. There is also a subsidiary type that I shall refer to as 'retrospective imagery', which is best thought of as a particular type of preparation, but will be discussed after the group of three. As regards this group, the distinction between preparation and anticipation of a theme does not require immediate clarification. All that need be said for the moment is that these two stand essentially together as distinct from the link, and it is this distinction that may conveniently be clarified here. The first point is that linking is usually found as an additional function of a preparation or an anticipation, whereas those two categories may more readily stand by themselves. The second is that linking implies effects that appeal much more to the intellect, much less to the aesthetic faculty, in the limited sense of the word 'aesthetic'.

With Stesichorus' pure preparation contrast two Shakespearian instances of preparatory link. First, lines from *Antony and Cleopatra* (II.2):

> Our courteous Antony
> Being barbered ten times o'er, goes to the feast,
> And for his ordinary pays his heart
> For what his eyes eat only.

'Eat' is prepared by 'feast'. It is also linked to it in such a way that the association is felt to be significative. We are invited to take or make a point involving, in relation, the feast – with all that 'feast' presupposes in the way of social function and appetite – and the personal preoccupation, the diferent appetite, of Antony. Now, from *Macbeth* (v.3):

> My way of life
> Is fall'n into the sear, the yellow leaf.

'*Fall'n* into' is, of course, normal usage. ('I am fallen in to pouerte and mysery', writes Lord Berners in the mid sixteenth century.[3]) It prepares 'the sear, the yellow *leaf*' and indeed subtly activates it; and also, again, forms a link with it, but a much less overt and assertive one. 'Change and decay', to take the infinitely cruder cliché as paraphrase, are inseparably associated: the ageing ('yellow leaf') is already implicit in the becoming ('fall'n into'). What I wish to stress is that even though this link is less overt and less assertive, its presence differentiates the interaction sharply from Stesichorus' ὠκεανοῖο ...βένθεα, where there is, apparently, no intellectual point at all, but simply an invitation not to be surprised by the inherently surprising, the vehicle.

1 Above, p. 24.
2 Pi.*P*.8.92f. (above, p. 90).
3 See further *NED* s.v. 'fall'. The *Macbeth* instance has already been cited (above, pp. xi and 24).

Preparation
§51

The general character of 'preparation' has been sufficiently indicated. From what has already been said it is obvious that the beneficiary is always and only the vehicle. Take Pi.*fr.*52a.6ff.:

῏Ωραι. . .ἐπῆλθον
Ἀπόλλωνι δαῖτα φιλησιστέφανον ἄγοντες·
τὰν δὲ λαῶν γενεὰν δαρὸν ἐρέπτοι
σώφρονος ἄνθεσιν εὐνομίας.

The words ἐρέπτοι and ἄνθεσιν make up the vehicle, and the vehicle is prepared by φιλησιστέφανον; both the vehicle and the operative part of the tenor relate to a common field, στεφάνοισιν ἀνθέων. . .ἐρεφθείς (B.13.69f.).[1] Only the vehicle gains; nothing is done for the suppressed or immediate or wider tenor, nor for the tenor–vehicle relation itself. Simply, the extraneous is put 'at issue'.[2]

Like the pivot, preparation is naturally amenable to enforcement by parallel structure. Stesichorus' preparation shows a slight enforcement of this sort, δι' ὠκεανοῖο. . .ποτὶ βένθεα, 'from *T* to *V*', as it were. At B.5.24ff. the parallelism takes a more decisive form, 'neither *T* nor *V*'. The subject is the eagle:

οὔ νιν κορυφαὶ μεγάλας ἴσχουσι γαίας,
οὐδ' ἁλὸς ἀκαμάτας
δυσπαίπαλα κύματα. . .

Waves 'rugged and steep'. The vehicle is δυσπαίπαλα and the preparation comes from κορυφαί: βήσσας ὀρέων δυσπαιπάλους (Arch.116),[3] οὔρεος ἐν κορυφῆς (*Il.*2.456).[4] Compare Pi.*O*.2.12f., 'both *T* and *V*', with an incidental but irrelevant verbal resemblance to the last instance:

ἀλλ' ὦ Κρόνιε παῖ ʽΡέας, ἕδος Ὀλύμπου νέμων
ἀέθλων τε κορυφάν. . .

Vehicle κορυφάν, prepared by ἕδος Ὀλύμπου, the collocation κορυφὴ Ὀλύμπου being familiar enough.[5] This example, like the others above, involves metaphor, but it is worth noting that where preparation is concerned – and all extra-grammatical interaction in general – the distinction between metaphor and explicit imagery is insignificant.[6]

1 The Bacchylides is a reconstructed text. For the associations, cf. likewise Pi.*P.* 4.240, Cratin.98, B.4.16, Hes.*Th.*576, *Cypr.*5.2, Sapph.98(a).8f., Anacr.51, Ar. *Ach.*992, Thphr.*HP* 4.2.8.

2 Other instances of straightforward preparation: (1) Pi.*O.*1.12f., δρέπων prepared by πολυμάλῳ, 'much-fruited' (the predominant MS reading, though rejected by Snell, among others). For the connection cf. Sapph.105 (μαλοδρόπηες) and δρέπειν of fruit-picking at Alc.119.15, Pi.*frr.*6b(f) and 209, Hes.*Op.*611 (ἀπο-), Pl.*Tim.*91c (κατα-). The verb is commoner of flowers, leaves etc. (2) Pi.*O.* 13.86–95, ἀκόντων κτλ. prepared by ἐνόπλια... τοξόταν. The interaction is noted by Gildersleeve *ad loc.* ('the figures grow out of...'). (3) A.*Prom.*1048–52, δίναις prepared by κῦμα κτλ.; cf. *Il.*21.239f. (ἐν δίνῃσι...κῦμα) etc. A similar preparation is apparent at A.*Ag.*984ff.–997 over a greater distance.

3 δυσπαίπαλος is a very rare word. Cf. ὄρεος παιπαλόεντος at *Il.*13.17; also παιπαλόεις as epithet of named peaks at *h.Ap.*39 and, probably, at Hes.*fr.*150.25, also Id.*Th.*860 (where cf. West, who should, however, have noted Arch.116 before discarding the reading βήσσῃσιν...παιπαλοέσσῃς).

4 So *Od.*2.147, Pi.*P.*1.27, Hdt.8.32.1.

5 *Il.*1.499, 8.3; Hes.*Th.*62; Pi.*fr.*52f.92. On the *V* status of κορυφάν, cf. above, p. 35.

Other instances of preparation in parallel structure: (1) Arch.81, σκυτάλη prepared by Κηρυκίδη. (Parallelism somewhat specious – the two are not in apposition.) For the connection cf. Th.1.131.1 πέμψαντες κήρυκα οἱ ἔφοροι καὶ σκυτάλην. Interpretation of the image has sometimes been unnecessarily diffident. G. S. Farnell (p.301) paraphrases, 'I, an angry messenger, will tell a tale to you, O Cerycides', and adds, 'the metaphor in σκ. is of course suggested by K., "Herald's son"'. This is surely right in the main, though it should be said that σκ. refers essentially to a dispatch or message in cipher, hence implies information conveyed covertly or indirectly. (Cf. Plut.*Lys.*19 on the use of the σκ.: ὅταν...ἀπόρρητόν τι καὶ μέγα φράσαι βουληθῶσι....) This is in full accord with the implication of αἶνον in v.1: νῦν δ' αἶνον βασιλεῦσιν ἐρέω φρονέουσι καὶ αὐτοῖς (Hes.*Op.*202). (2) A.*Th.*681f., γῆρας prepared by θάνατος. Parallelism slight (subjects of successive clauses). Association obvious: εἰς ὅ κε γῆρας ἔλθῃ καὶ θάνατος (*Od.*13.59f.). (3) A.*Th.*1076f., κύματι...κατακλυσθῆναι prepared by ἀνατραπῆναι, seemingly the only interaction in the suspected part of this play. For the association cf. ἀνατραπῇ...πλοῖον (Alex.76.3, so Pl.*Lg.*906e, Arist.*HA* 606b.14, D.9.69, Aeschin.3.158) and also ἀνατρέπεται ἡ θάλαττα (Arist.*HA* 600a.4, sim. 616a.29). This preparation, of course, involves only a connotation of the preparatory word, ἀνατραπῆναι here being used denotatively in its ordinary sense, ὀντρέψει τάχα τὰν πόλιν (Alc.141.4, so Hdt.8.62.1, E.*Ph.*888, Ar.*V.*671, Diph.24.3, Aeschin.1.190). Such preparation tends, naturally, to be more restrained. Cf. (without parallelism) (4) Pi.*N.*7.52f., vehicle μέλι (analogy), prepared by γλυκεῖα, 'delightful', suggesting the γλυκεῖαι μέλιτος...ῥοαί (E.*Ba.* 711; cf. *Il.*1.249 μέλιτος γλυκίων, Ar.*fr.*587, Arist.*HA* 488a.17). Again (5),

Pi.*I.*2.1f., vehicle δίφρον, prepared by χρυσαμπύκων, via the association of -αμπύκων with horses (see above, p. 45). And (6) Sol.23.1ff., vehicle περιβαλών κτλ., prepared by βαθύφρων via the association of βαθύ- with the sea. And (7) A. *Ag.*847ff., vehicle παιωνίων κτλ. (see above, p. 100), prepared by χρονίζον with its strong medical flavour: παθήματα...χρονίσαντα Hp.*Mul.*1.28 (likewise from Hp., *Aph.*3.28, *Coac.*396, *Epid.*4.56, *Morb.*4.54, *Nat.Puer.*15; cf. Arist.*HA* 638b.17). This interaction was spotted by Ole Smith 35. (8) In Pi.*P.*3.48–54 it is, *vice versa*, a connotation of the vehicle δέδεται that is in question, the preparation here stemming from a series of innocent tenor terms (ἑλκέων...τετρωμένοι... ἐπαοιδαῖς...φάρμακα...τομαῖς) evoking its common, but irrelevant, medical sense: ὠτειλήν...δῆσαν...ἐπαοιδῇ δ᾽ αἷμα...ἔσχεθον Od.19.456ff., ἐπὴν δέ, ὅταν τοῖσι νάρθηξι δεθῇ,...ἄλλο τι ὀχλέῃ τὸν τετρωμένον Hp.*Fract.*7; likewise, from the Hippocratic corpus, *Off.*18 (δεθέντα/ἀνελκέα), *VC* 13 (ἕλκος/ἐπιδεῖν/ τομῆς), *Nat.Mul.*108 (φάρμακον/δήσας/ἕλκος). Cf. (9) Pi.*N.*5.42, where ἐν ἀγκώνεσσι πίτνων can hardly be claimed to suggest the victor actually making love to Nike, but is prepared as such by the strong erotic tendency of the ode hitherto (Peleus and Thetis), especially the account of Hippolyte's designs on Peleus (26–33). ἐν ἀγκώνεσσι has, that is, a marked erotic flavour – or rather the phrase itself does not recur elsewhere, but the closely related epic phrase ἐν ἀγκοίνῃσι has such a flavour: Hes.*fr.*252.5f. Θηρὼ δ᾽ Ἀπόλλωνος ἐν ἀγκοίνῃσι πεσοῦσα γείνατο..., *Od.*11.268 ἐν ἀγκοίνῃσι Διός...μιγεῖσα, cf. *Il.*14.213, *Od.*11.261, Hes.*fr.*43a.81, Matro.*Conv.*39. At h.*Cer.*141 and 264 ἐν ἀγκοίνῃσι is used of a baby/child in arms, the usual phrase for which is ἐν ἀγκάλαις (A.*Ag.*723, Hdt.6.61.4, E.*Ion* 280, Pl.*Lg.*790d), so ἐν ἀγκαλίδεσσι *Il.*22.503 and ἐν ἀγκῶσι E.*Supp.*817. ἐν ἀγκῶσι (the alternative – and more usual – dative plural of ἀγκών) occurs in other connections at Hp.*Prorrh.*2.15 and Archestr.9.3f.

6 Note as a further, marginal, possibility that preparation may carry a specifying force for the vehicle (see below, p. 197 on Pi.*N.*11.19ff.) and in fact such a force can subsist *without* preparation at all (see below, p. 165 on Pi.*N.*8.22f.). Two other possible instances (both preparatory): (1) A.*Supp.*1045ff., ἀπέρατος vehicle, specified as maritime by εὔπλοιαν. By itself, ἀπέρατος is in fact reasonably likely to be maritime anyway (see LSJ *s.vv.* περατός, περάω A.1.2), but εὔπλοιαν makes it inevitable. For the specific collocation, cf. Hes.*Op.*650ff. ἐπέπλων... ἐπέρησα. (2) Pi.*N.*3.60ff.: πάξαιτο vehicle, specified by ὑπὸ Τρωΐαν δορίκτυπον κτλ. As Fennell says, ἐν φρασὶ πάξαιτο is a 'strong variation' on ἐνθέσθαι τι θυμῷ, and the tone of πάξαιτο is more than 'strong': it is fiercely insistent. This is determined by the general Iliadic context in which the vehicle operates and particularly the quasi-heroic epithets that delineate Achilles' world of battle. The words δορίκτυπον and ἐγχεσφόροις readily evoke typical epic contexts, e.g. Τρῶας δ᾽ ἔκλιναν Δαναοί...πρῶτος δὲ...Ἀγαμέμνων...μεταφρένῳ ἐν δόρυ πῆξεν *Il.*5.37–40 (sim. *Il.*5.616, 11.572, 13.570, 15.314f., *Batr.*207) with the super- ficially innocent ἐν φρασί adding to the impression: note the μεταφρένῳ in *Il. loc. cit.* and cf. Pi.*N.*7.26 ἔπαξε διὰ φρενῶν ξίφος. As in (1), however, it is clear from the general use of the compound in earlier literature that the locating done by the interaction amounts to a confirmation of what is undoubtedly a likely possibility anyway.

Anticipation of a theme
§52

I have pressed this cumbrous phrase into service to avoid confusion between preparation and what is functionally its exact opposite. By 'anticipation of a theme' I mean a movement which is in all other respects of the preparation type, but goes from vehicle to tenor and effects the foreshadowing of some substantial topic or consideration within the tenor, 'theme' in a loose sense. Swinburne, *Laus Veneris*:

> Ah yet would God this flesh of mine might be
> Where air might wash and long leaves cover me,
> Where tides of grass break into foam of flowers,
> Or where the wind's feet shine along the sea.

'Wash' and 'tides' and 'foam' to 'sea'. It is clear, and given by definition, that the function is exercised purely on behalf of the wider tenor. The new topic, the next item, the coming theme is delivered painlessly, unless indeed, like Swinburne's 'sea', its first breath is smothered by an excess of consideration.

Anticipation pure and simple is not especially common in my corpus, but is most characteristic of Pindar. At *N.*4.11ff. Pindar prays that Aegina accept his ode, composed in honour of its citizen Timasarchus, son of Timocritus:

> δέξαιτο δ' Αἰακιδᾶν
> ἠύπυργον ἕδος, δίκᾳ ξεναρκέι κοινόν
> φέγγος. εἰ δ' ἔτι ζαμενεῖ Τιμόκριτος ἁλίῳ
> σὸς πατὴρ ἐθάλπετο. . .

Aegina is a φέγγος, and φέγγος leads on to the new topic, 'were Timocritus alive today. . .', where 'alive' is given metonymically through ἁλίῳ. . . ἐθάλπετο. It hardly needs saying that the collocation φέγγος ἡλίου is a familiar one.[1] The association of Aegina, the φέγγος, with the sun is entirely casual – 'yes, and talking of φέγγος. . .' – and there is no link, no invitation to see significance in the association.

Anticipation, like preparation, is not a type that presents much variety. Within its limits, Pi.*P.*4.244ff. is as fine an instance as any, in the service of a narrative of major significance, Pindar's *Argonautica*. Jason has accomplished all his tasks but the last. The dragon guards the fleece:

> δράκοντος. . .
> ὃς πάχει μάκει τε πεντηκόντερον ναῦν κράτει,
> τέλεσεν ἂν πλαγαὶ σιδάρου.

With this comparison, in terms that recall the good ship *Argo* herself,[2] the main part of the saga – all 170 verses of it – is brought to a sudden close:

μακρά μοι νεῖσθαι κατ' ἀμαξιτόν. . .

The story itself, however, is not complete, and Pindar resumes it, summarily:

κτεῖνε μὲν γλαυκῶπα τέχναις ποικιλόνωτον ὄφιν. . .

But this postponed and climactic detail is already anticipated in the last and prominent phrase of the image that preceded the interruption. πλαγαὶ σιδάρου – these words would no doubt pass in shipbuilding,[3] but by themselves would naturally, more naturally, suggest the murder stroke, as Pindar himself shows elsewhere: πλαγαῖς τε σιδάρου. . .εἰς ὀχετὸν ἄτας ἵ͜ζοισαν. . . πόλιν (*O*.10.37f.).[4] The transition is expertly made.[5]

Both anticipation and preparation, more often than not, carry a link, a category that presents greater variety and so requires fuller discussion.

1 E.g. B.5.161f., A.*Pe*.377, S.*Tr*.606, E.*fr*.316, Ar.*fr*.188. Cf. Arist.*Mete*.370a.21 etc.

2 Cf. Gildersleeve *ad loc*. This relation between ναῦν of the vehicle and the *Argo* belongs to a well-known type which I exclude from present discussion. If it is interaction at all, it is interaction with the tenor at its widest, and is not strictly a relation between word and word, but one between word (ναῦν) and *idea* currently presupposed. Cf., for instance, χαλκοῦ βαφάς in A.*Ag*.612. The image 'in the mouth of Clytemnestra...conveys some hint of the murder' (Fraenkel). This is a matter of 'supporting or reflecting action by cognate imagery' (Stanford *AS* 100) – and doing so 'macro-contextually'. The technique is especially familiar in creative drama. Cf. e.g. Macbeth's 'come, seeling night,...and with thy bloody and invisible hand...' (*Macb*.III.2), with painful evocation of murder already committed (see e.g. Empson *ST* 23). It is also common in various forms in Pindar: see e.g. Fennell's notes on *N*.1.7, 4.93ff., *I*.2.2; Burton 17 on *P*.6.7, 187 on *P*.8.77 (where the frequency of such relations in Pindar leads him to 'expect' one). Keith 86 calls it 'relevant metaphor'.

3 πληγή in the context of shipbuilding, Thphr.*HP* 5.1.7; Aristopho 4 (ὑπομένειν πληγὰς ἄκμων) and Arist.*de An*.419b variously attest the use of the word in comparable contexts. σίδηρος of building tools, Hdt.2.125.7.

4 Similarly E.*Ph*.1393. πληγή by itself thus, A.*Ag*.1343, Hp.*Art*.30, X.*Cyr*.5.4.5; σίδηρος of weaponry, *Od*.16.294, Acus.22 Jacoby, Th.1.6.3, E.*Or*.966. Note the compensation principle in operation (see above, p. 118).

5 With this analysis compare Gildersleeve's remarks *ad loc*., but he does not comment specifically on the interaction. Some other instances of anticipation may be noted here: (i) Pi.*O*.6.100ff., ἄγκυραι to πλόον. (ii) Pi.*O*.7.45-9, νέφος to νεφέλαν (see below, p. 166). (iii) Pi.*P*.2.56, πιαινόμενον to πλουτεῖν (for the association, see below, p. 194 with n.3). (iv) Pi.*P*.3.36ff., πῦρ to σέλας. . . Ἁφαίστου.

(v) Pi.*P*.4.3ff., οὖρον to ναύταις κτλ. (v.12). (vi) Pi.*P*.4.210ff., where στίχες, the winds' 'battle-lines', anticipates the theme of the new episode, Κόλχοισιν βίαν μεῖξαν (general association as at *Il*.15.614f.). (vii) Pi.*P*.10.29ff., πλόον to ναυσί and the Perseus myth (cf. Burton 7). (viii) A miniature instance, Pi.*P*. 12.10, λειβόμενον to δυσπενθέϊ σὺν καμάτῳ. The interactive sense of the vehicle is a connotation, via the epic phrase δάκρυα λείβειν (cf. e.g. ἀργαλέῳ καμάτῳ... δάκρυα λεῖβον *Il*.13.85–8). (ix) Pi.*N*.1.5ff., ὁρμᾶται to ἵππων...ἅρμα (ἵππον θυμοειδῆ...εἰς τὸ τάχιστον ὁρμᾶν Χ.*Eq*.9.8). (x) Pi.*N*.1.13ff., σπεῖρε to εὐκάρ-που...πίειραν. (xi) Ibyc.1(a).24–7 ἐμβαίεν to ναῶν (ἔμβη νηΐ *Od*.4.656, so Lys. 2.40 etc.). (xii) A.*Supp*.127ff., κῦμα to the next new topic, πλάτα κτλ. (134ff.). None of these instances carries any appreciable link, but several are complicated in a different way, in that they involve preparation as well as anticipation, with the two combining to form an interactive theme in which more than one image may be involved. Thus with (vi) Pi.*P*.4.210–13, στίχες (*V*) to K. βίαν μεῖξαν (*T*) to βελέων (*V₂*) (cf. contexts like *Il*.13.286–9, 15.727 etc.). Three successive episodes in the *Argonautica* – the Symplegades, battle with the Colchians, Aphrodite's intervention to win Medea for Jason – have their transitions facilitated in this way. Again with (vii) Pi.*P*.10.27ff., ἀμβατός and περαίνει (*T*) (see below, p. 194) to πλόον (*V*) to ναυσί and Perseus (*T*); with (ix) Pi.*N*.1.5–7, ὁρμᾶται (*V*) to ἵππων...ἅρμα (*T*) to ζεῦξαι (*V₂*); and with (xi) Ibyc.1(a). 18–27, νᾶες (*T*) to ἐμβαίεν (*V*) and back to ναῶν (*T*). With or without this additional preparation, Pindar's propensity for anticipation is evident.

Link

§ 53

The first thing to say about linking is that, as a significant possibility, it is a possibility of extra-grammatical – or extra-logical – interaction only. It is not a possible function of neutral terms, or, to put the matter differently, neutral terms – *all* neutral terms – carry an *automatic* association of an essentially different kind. All neutral terminology follows an intimate preexisting relation without affecting it, and the relation it follows is that given by the grammatico-logical structure. In λαμπροὺς δυνάστας...ἀστέρας, to take a clear-cut and now familiar instance,[1] there is an automatic relation between adjective and noun, λ. and δ., which the interaction neither creates nor intensifies. Whereas in '...goes to the feast and...pays his heart for what his eyes eat only', there is no comparable relation between 'feast' and 'eat'. The relation that there is here is *created* by the interaction. If one replaced δυνάστας with some literal 'equivalent', presumably a noun, that equivalent would still be in intimate structural relation with λαμπρούς. If one replaces 'eat' with 'look at' or, to make it tolerable, 'his eyes eat' with 'he looks at', the relation disappears.

157

Both my Shakespearian instances were preparatory links. The type is familiar enough in the Greek corpus. Pi.*P*.4.14ff.:

φαμὶ γὰρ τᾶσδ' ἐξ ἁλιπλάκτου ποτὲ γᾶς 'Επάφοιο κόραν
ἀστέων ῥίζαν φυτεύσεσθαι μελησιμβρότων
Διὸς ἐν "Αμμωνος θεμέθλοις.

Vehicle ῥίζαν φυτεύσεσθαι, prepared by and linked to γᾶς, the link constituting an enforcement of the 'cause and effect' (or rather, origin and effect) logic: from the *land* of Thera, Libya shall be *planted* with a *root* of cities. The interaction involves only a connotation of the preparatory term – its agricultural sense, as against the national sense that is overtly operative. The terminological relation between tenor and vehicle is close: γῆ πεφυτευμένη (Hdt.4.127.2), ἀφίησι ῥίζας ἐς τὴν γῆν (Hp.*Nat.Puer.*26); so close, as almost to create the impression that γᾶς is not a tenor term at all, but neutral. It *is* a tenor term, though, and in its restraint recalls the more subtle Shakespearian instance:

My way of life
Is fall'n into the sear, the yellow leaf.

Both links involve a restrained enforcement of underlying logic and, in this, both manifest an essential characteristic of linking, which is to relate tenor to tenor. This could be demonstrated from any instance, but it is conveniently apparent from the mode of paraphrase used above for the Pindar ('cause and effect') and likewise from the paraphrase used previously for the Shakespeare.[2] 'Change and decay', I said, 'are inseparably associated'; where 'decay' is a crude de-figurative equivalent for 'leaf', in terms of its suppressed tenor, and 'change' an opportunistic substitute for 'fall'n', which belongs to the tenor (wider tenor) anyway.

A more vigorous link in Pi.*O*.6.45ff., on the divine favour shown to the infant Iamus:

δύο δὲ γλαυκῶπες αὐτὸν
δαιμόνων βουλαῖσιν ἐθρέψαντο δράκοντες ἀμεμφεῖ
ἰῷ μελισσᾶν καδόμενοι.

The character of the link here inclines one to speak of 'logical' function, misleading as that might be. ἰῷ, the vehicle, has a self-evident relation with δράκοντες, a strict association whose significance is flatly contradicted by ἀμεμφεῖ. The paradox of beneficent serpents is lucidly enforced by recall of the familiar pattern, δρακόντων ἰός (E.*Ion* 1015),[3] which is here *not* the pattern. Comparably palpable but quite different in tone is the ironic pick-up at A.*Ag*.479ff.:

τίς ὧδε παιδνὸς ἢ φρενῶν κεκομμένος
φλογὸς παραγγέλμασιν

νέοις πυρωθέντα καρδίαν ἔπειτ'
ἀλλαγᾷ λόγου καμεῖν;

The significance of the relation between φλογός and πυρωθέντα is too transparent to need much comment. 'Mockingly', says Fraenkel, which sums it up.[4]

It is to be noted that preparatory link implies a gain for both tenor and vehicle. The latter is prepared, while specific elements within the tenor are brought into significant relation. If the linking combines with anticipation rather than with preparation, the vehicle naturally stands to gain nothing. Thus with the 'flowers' and 'rose' in Keats' *On Melancholy*:

> But when the melancholy fit shall fall
> Sudden from heaven like a weeping cloud,
> That fosters the droop-headed flowers all,
> And hides the green hill in an April shroud,
> Then glut thy sorrow on a morning rose...

The anticipation and the link do nothing for the vehicle, everything for the tenor. Beauty or the perception of beauty (flowers and rose) is intensified by melancholy (as the cloud fosters the flowers) and thereby – this is the momentary hope – can be the solace of self-indulgent melancholy itself. The hope, if nothing else, is consummated by the interaction.

Consummation more of another kind in Pi.*fr.*52f.134ff.,

> Κρόνου παῖς... ἀνερέψατο παρθένον
> Αἴγιναν· τότε χρύσεαι
> ἀέρος ἔκρυψαν κόμαι
> ἐπιχώριον κατάσκιον νῶτον ὑμέτερον,
> ἵνα λεχέων ἐπ' ἀμβρότων...

at which point the papyrus coyly breaks off. The vehicle is χρύσεαι κόμαι, virtually a single unit like the compounds χρυσοκόμης[5] and χρυσεοκόμης.[6] The topic to which the vehicle looks ahead is that given by λεχέων, though the connotation of χρύσεαι κόμαι that creates the interaction is not one, I think, that has been recognized. The poetic associations of this phrase and its compounded equivalents, the contexts, that is, in which they occur, are very specific. They are two only: that of Ἀπόλλων χρυσοκόμης,[7] which is irrelevant here, and that of any male deity (*vel sim.*) in erotic contexts, as if 'golden hair' were a symbol or correlative of male virility. So we find Ἶρις χρυσοκόμα Ζεφύρῳ μίγεισα (Alc.327.3), χρυσοκόμης...Διώνυσος...Ἀριάδνην...ποιήσατ' ἄκοιτιν (Hes.*Th.*947f.), and significantly χρυσοκόμης ἔρως

(Anacr.13.2, E.*IA* 548).[8] Possessed of this erotic suggestion, the χρύσεαι κόμαι anticipate the impending λεχέων and corroborate the cooperation of the elements (ἀέρος) in the elemental act.[9]

1 See above, p. 87.
2 See above, p. 151.
3 Although the antiquity of ἰός (venom) is guaranteed by etymology (ἰός = Lat. *virus* = Skt *viṣá-* < *wiso-*), the word seems not to be attested before the fifth century.
4 Other instances of preparatory link: (i) A.*Th*.495–503, ὄφεων το δράκοντα, an ironic relation like that at *Ag*.479ff. (ii) A.*Ag*.1395–7, ἐπισπένδειν το κρατῆρα, a slightly dubious case. That the words belong to the same terminology is indisputable: ἐπισπένδει ὁ ἱερεὺς τούτοις οἴνου κρατῆρας τρεῖς *SIG* 1025.39 (Cos, c.300 B.C.), cf. *Il*.9.175–7, *Od*.7.179–81, Thgn.490–3, Ion Eleg.2.2–5, Th.6.32.1, E.*Ion* 1195–1202. Likewise, it seems evident that the relation can only be interactive and, specifically, a preparatory link, but the notorious doubts about the text and interpretation of this passage make further comment unwise.
5 As Hes.*Th*.947 etc. N.B. that the status of χρύσεαι is unclear (see above, p. 32). For convenience, I take it as pure *V*.
6 As *Mel.Adesp*.32 (p.511 Page).
7 So Tyrt.3a.1f., Pi.*I*.7.49, B.4.2, *Carm.Conv*.3, *Mel.Adesp*.32, E.*Supp*.975, Ar. *Av*.217; there is also reason to believe that the collocation occurred in the epic Cycle (see Lorimer 15; her article contains a fairly thorough survey of the use of the word, primarily vis-à-vis Apollo, but gives no hint of any erotic association). Note also χρυσοκόμ' Ἄπολλον *SEG* 10.327 (Attica, vi B.C.).
8 Two other extant instances show a combination of the two types, i.e. the golden hair belongs to Apollo in erotic contexts. Thus Pi.*O*.6.35ff., ὑπ' Ἀπόλλωνι... ἔψαυσ' Ἀφροδίτας (Evadne)...τᾷ μὲν ὁ χρυσοκόμας..., and similarly E.*Tro*. 254f. There are also instances of 'golden hair' in erotic contexts, but with different compounds or phrases, e.g. Philox.8, E.*Ion* 887. I have found no evidence that might suggest that the erotic association has any ritualistic standing. The one apparent exception to the 'rules' above is Hippolytus' allusion to Artemis' χρυσέας κόμης at E.*Hipp*.82, which is also peculiarly deviant as involving a *female* deity. (Barrett makes no comment on the point.) Is it too much to suggest that the phrase must carry its erotic-male undertone, ironically enough, here too? If so, it would operate in implicit contrast to the keynote of chastity that characterizes H.'s address to his goddess, vv.73–87 (overtly, ἀκήρατος 73, 76; αἰδώς 78 – see Barrett; also the symbolic value of the meadow, for which cf. Ibyc.5 and Bowra *GLP* 261f.). That the irony, in its proclamation of perversion, would be 'dramatic', not conscious, goes without saying.
9 A motif in itself familiar enough; cf. e.g. *Il*.14.350f. Note also the sensuous impression created by the sequence κόμαι...κατάσκιον νῶτον (cf. e.g. Arch.25, Pi.*P*.4.82f.). This is one of those Pindaric passages (as *P*.4.14f.) in which a nymph is simultaneously a place (cf. ἐπιχώριον), and the created impression is bound up with this almost metaphysical duality in such an intimate way that it is hardly given to say whether interaction is involved a second time.

One other instance of anticipatory link: Pi.*P*.8.9ff., vehicle ἐνελάσῃ, linked to the assertion that Peace will overcome Hybris and to the instances of Porphyrion and Typhos. The interpretation of ἐνελ. as 'driving in a nail or bolt' (Fennell, Gildersleeve) is wholly arbitrary and goes against the evidence. The compound – including its equivalent with the two elements separate – is not common and seems to be characteristically used of weapons: ἐν...σάκει ἤλασεν...ἔγχος *Il*.20.259, ἄκοντι...ἤλασε...ἐν πλευραῖσι χαλκόν Pi.*N*.10.70 (cf. *Il*.5.400, 17.519, 24.421). The word thus associates itself with the general ὑπαντιάξαισα κράτει and the particular violent fates of P. and T., as if to say: violence begets violence; the κότος that leads to ὕβρις is itself a violence; the sequence of violence, from initial act to retribution, is already implicit in the conception of κότος.

§54

Since a word must either precede or follow another, it is obviously likely that linking will involve either preparation or anticipation of a theme. But it can happen that a nominal preparation or anticipation, usually the latter, is hardly to be felt as such, leaving in effect a pure link. This is the characteristic situation with imagery geared to explicit, and therefore dominant, antithesis. Thus with A.*Eu*.935ff.:

> σιγῶν δ' ὄλεθρος
> καὶ μέγα φωνοῦντ'
> ἐχθραῖς ὀργαῖς ἀμαθύνει.

Vehicle σιγῶν, link with μέγα φωνοῦντα. Thus, again, with what looks almost like an interactive *topos*, first attested in Theognis, vv.877f.:

> ἥβα μοι, φίλε θυμέ· τάχ' αὖ τινες ἄλλοι ἔσονται
> ἄνδρες, ἐγὼ δὲ θανὼν γαῖα μέλαιν' ἔσομαι.

Vehicle ἥβα, link with θανών. Compare A.*Supp*.774f.:

> ἄγγελον δ' οὐ μέμψεται
> πόλις γέρονθ', ἡβῶντα δ' εὐγλώσσῳ φρενί.

Vehicle ἡβῶντα, link with γέροντα. Compare, likewise, A.*Ag*.584:

> ἀεὶ γὰρ ἥβη τοῖς γέρουσιν εὐμαθεῖν.

Vehicle ἥβη, link with γέρουσιν. In each of these instances, the interaction is as transparent as the imagery is quiet.[1]

Another source of an effectively pure link is implicit and partial antonymy: not a formal antithesis, but an informal, dissonant clash. This is a livelier matter altogether, to be thought of as an exploitation of the 'unlikeness' that we have allowed to be a necessary factor in the success of an image.[2] The characteristic effect of such an exploitation is a strong irony or pathos. Both notes are struck in Aeschylus, *fr*.273.6f., a passage already discussed in a different connection.[3] Niobe, the hen on her eggs:

> τριταῖον ἦμαρ τόνδ᾽ ἐφημένη τάφον
> τέκνοις ἐπῴζει τοῖς τεθνηκόσιν . . .

The idea of the dead as unhatched carries at once an obvious likeness and an obvious unlikeness. The latter, the unlikeness, is brought out poignantly by the interactive link between ἐπῴζει, the vehicle, and τεθνηκόσιν, the tenor. καὶ γὰρ – as Epicharmus reminds us (*fr*.172.3ff.) – τὸ θῆλυ τῶν ἀλεκτορίδων γένος. . .οὐ τίκτει τέκνα ζῶντ᾽, ἀλλ᾽ ἐπῴζει καὶ ποιεῖ ψυχὰν ἔχειν. Fraenkel's principle of the Aeschylean 'intensifying contrast' could hardly be better exemplified.[4]

An intensifying contrast comparable in vigour, this time from Pindar, *I*.3/4.34ff.:

> ἀλλ᾽ ἀμέρᾳ γὰρ ἐν μιᾷ
> τραχεῖα νιφὰς πολέμοιο τεσσάρων
> ἀνδρῶν ἐρήμωσεν μάκαιραν ἑστίαν . . .

The vivid νιφάς jars against ἑστίαν: war's 'snowstorm' and the hearth and home. The hearth-fire warms the house in cold weather – ἐὰν δὲ νείφῃ, πρὸς τὸ πῦρ καθήμενος (Ar. *V*.773) – and, in Nilsson's words, 'the hearth is the centre of the house and the symbol of the family'.[5] Slight as it is, the link is poignantly evocative. Against the hearth that, with its fire, symbolizes the household's continuing existence, is set war that destroys the family, ἀνδρῶν ἐρήμωσεν, takes away the guardians of the fire. Compare the still more bitter effect at A.*Ag*.658ff.:

> ἐπεὶ δ᾽ ἀνῆλθε λαμπρὸν ἡλίου φάος,
> ὁρῶμεν ἀνθοῦν πέλαγος Αἰγαῖον νεκροῖς
> ἀνδρῶν Ἀχαιῶν . . .

Here the link depends on the unlikeness as brought out in the active contrast between νεκροῖς and the vehicle, ἀνθοῦν. Like the noun ἄνθος, the verb ἀνθεῖν, one should make clear, does not have the associations of 'prettiness' of its English equivalents that might seem to be the source of the link.[6] The actual source, more decisively relevant in any case, is the inescapable associations the word has with growth, not merely the growth of vegetation[7] but of human youth, like ἄνθος ἥβης,[8] and, most telling of all, of prosperous livelihood on a collective human scale: ἀνθεύσης γὰρ τῆς Ἀσίης ἀνδράσι (Hdt.4.1.1), λαοὶ δ᾽ ἀνθεῦσιν. . .εἰρήνη δ᾽ ἀνὰ γῆν (Hes.*Op*.227f.).[9] The whole context is informed with cutting irony.[10] Life, growth and prosperity – the dead have only the appearance.

A link may be made by repetition of the same word, or of close cognates, once literally, once figuratively. Othello's famous speech (v.2):

> Put out the light and then put out the light:
> If I quench thee, thou flaming minister,
> I can at once thy former light restore,
> Should I repent me; but once put out thy light,
> Thou cunning'st pattern of excelling nature,
> I know not where is that Promethean heat
> That can thy light relume.

The interaction, in the opening verse, involves the parallel structure of overt antithesis; this initial rhetorical association then serves as the basis for an inexorably logical dissociation.

A.*Ag*.184ff. has greater bite. Agamemnon at the fatal moment of choice:

> καὶ τόθ' ἡγεμὼν...
> ἐμπαίοις τύχαισι συμπνέων,
> εὖτ' ἀπλοίᾳ κεναγγεῖ βαρύνοντ'
> Ἀχαιικὸς λεώς...
> πνοαὶ δ' ἀπὸ Στρυμόνος μολοῦσαι
> κακόσχολοι...
> τρίβῳ κατέξαινον ἄνθος Ἀργείων...

The connection between συμπνέων and the ἄπλοια is self-evident in the given situation, already described as ἀντιπνόους...ἀπλοίας (v.147), but in any event the πνοαί are brought back as specific reminder. The link created, συμπνέων–ἀπλοίᾳ–πνοαί, superbly 'places' the character of the hero's decision. On his response to ἐμπαίοις τύχαισι depends the πλοῦς. By taking on himself the colour of the τύχαι themselves, the πνοαὶ κακόσχολοι, he commits himself prefigurationally to the – what shall one say? – compulsive choice.[11] This raises, needless to say, the delicate issues of 'responsibility' in Aeschylus. Lesky's formulas are the ones I would appeal to: 'in Agamemnon...compulsion and volition are one', but 'that double motivation – divine decree and human will – which we saw to be a characteristic element in Homeric psychology' is no longer 'a simple unity', but 'the field of a deep tragic conflict'.[12]

The specifiable characteristic of these interactive repetitions is simply their conspicuousness. This makes it likely that the linking force will again overshadow any preparatory or anticipatory significance; and that the links themselves, if successful, will be substantial and lucid.[13] Paradigmatically substantial and straightforwardly lucid, Antony's interactive riposte in *Antony and Cleopatra* IV.4:

> Ant. Eros, mine *armour*, Eros.
>
> · · ·
>
> Cleo. Nay, I'll help too, Antony,
> What's this for?
>
> Ant. Ah let be, let be, thou art
> The *armourer* of my heart.

Likewise the play on λατρεία/λατρεύειν at A.*Prom.*966ff. Prometheus and Hermes:

> Πρ. τῆς σῆς λατρείας τὴν ἐμὴν δυσπραξίαν,
> σαφῶς ἐπίστασ', οὐκ ἂν ἀλλάξαιμ' ἐγώ.
>
> Ep. κρεῖσσον γὰρ οἶμαι τῇδε λατρεύειν πέτρᾳ
> ἢ πατρὶ φῦναι Ζηνὶ πιστὸν ἄγγελον;

In a celebrated passage from *Paradise Lost*, the interaction is much sweeter, yet potently persuasive. *PL* IV.268ff.:

> Not that fair field
> Of Enna, where Proserpin *gathering flowers*,
> Herself a fairer *flower*, by gloomy Dis
> Was *gathered*...
> ...nor that sweet grove
> Of Daphne ...
> ...might with this Paradise
> Of Eden strive.

Strictly speaking, the repetition of 'gather' is what matters here, since the repeated 'flower' hardly involves more than cliché. As Dr Leavis wrote, admiringly: 'It is in the repeated verb that the realizing imagination is irresistibly manifested; it is the final "gathered" that gives concrete life to a conventional phrase and makes Proserpin herself a flower. And to make her a flower is to establish the difference between the two gatherings: the design – the gathered gatherer – is subtle in its simplicity.'[14]

Equally fine and not dissimilar in feeling, Simonides, *fr.*38.21f.:

> κέλομαι δ' εὖδε βρέφος,
> εὑδέτω δὲ πόντος, εὑδέτω δ' ἄμετρον κακόν.

Danae, Perseus, and the sea – plus the famous 'Simonidean pathos'. Danae's repetitions, poignantly recalling the patterns of a lullaby,[15] associate, first, child with sea, a genuinely pathetic contrast of unequals, then the whole 'immeasurable trouble' with the two things, this child and this sea, that define for her its present terms.

One final variety. A link, as it can still be called, may be less intellectual in its force and more *energizing*: the vehicle, that is to say, *activates* the tenor.[16] *Macbeth* I.7:

> If it were done when 'tis done, then 'twere well
> It were done quickly: if the assassination
> Could *trammel* up the consequence and catch,
> With his surcease, success; that but this blow
> Might be the be-all and the end-all, here,
> But here, upon this bank and shoal of time,
> We'd jump the life to come.

'Trammel' means, among other things, to bind a corpse within the shroud,[17] and, as such, inevitably forms a link with 'assassination', two words before it. An interpretation of the 'meaning' of the link might run, a little laboriously: 'if the assassination could only put an end to, not just the corpse, but the consequence of making it a corpse; if only *this* was as circumscribed as *that*'. But in the given heightened context and especially at the speed with which this reflection proceeds, one feels the link as something more immediately concrete: *visualizing* the actual visualizable consequence of the actual murder, the 'binding-up', and feeling the visualization, in its swift vividness, striving to distract from the consequences that dare not be visualized, the 'life to come'. Compare Pindar, *N*.8.22f., on envy. In this remarkable instance, the activating that the vehicle does to the tenor is matched by the specifying the tenor does to the vehicle.[18]

> ἅπτεται δ' ἐσλῶν ἀεί, χειρόνεσσι δ' οὐκ ἐρίζει.
> κεῖνος καὶ Τελαμῶνος δάψεν υἱὸν φασγάνῳ ἀμφικυλίσαις.

δάψεν is unspecific. 'Envy destroyed the son of Telamon...causing him to fall upon his sword' (Donaldson). 'Destroyed', though, like *what*? Like fire (πυρὶ δαπτέμεν *Il*.23.183)? Like animals (λύκοι...ἔλαφον...δάπτουσιν *Il*.16.159)? In fact, as φασγάνῳ irresistibly suggests (especially as the syntax of the noun is momentarily equivocal), *like a stabbing weapon*: δόρυ...ὅ τοι χρόα δάψει (*Il*.13.831).[19] And the complementary link: stab of envy leads to suicide stab: the causal sequence is enforced strongly – and, along with it, the subtle notion of this self-destructive envy chasing its own tail (the choice of the idiomatic turn of phrase by which 'envy' is subject of ἀμφικυλίσαις is felicitous in the extreme); and at the end of it all, the actual stroke of the suicide itself is conveyed, thanks to the energizing force of δάψεν, with a dramatic power.

1 Another such link, A.*Ch.*915: vehicle ἐπράθην, linked to ἐλευθέρου (for the association, cf. D.18.46, Sol.24.8–15, E.*fr.*775). Orestes was not literally 'sold' (any more than Electra, cf. *Ch.*132), but ἐλευθέρου πατρός is literally true and this pained collocation testifies to the feeling behind, though not in itself the accuracy of, αἰκῶς. Cf. also the slightly sardonic Pi.*N.*5.1: vehicle ἐλινύσοντα, linked to ἐργάζεσθαι (for the association see e.g. Hdt.8.71.2 ἐλίνυον οὐδένα χρόνον...ἐργαζόμενοι). Pindar is *not* a sculptor who 'works' in objects that go 'on holiday'. The interaction recurs at *I.*2.46.

2 See above, p. 5.

3 See above, p. 89 with nn.11 and 12.

4 See above, p. 6, n.1.

5 Nilsson 73. Cf. Fraenkel on the πῦρ ἐφ' ἑστίας ἐμῆς and Aegisthus as 'protector of the family' at A.*Ag.*1435.

6 So, notably, Stanford *GM* 112ff. The sense 'flower' is also only one among several (cf. Stanford *loc. cit.* and J. M. Aitchison, *Glotta* 41, 1963, 271ff.), though perhaps the 'primary' sense from a fifth-century standpoint.

7 First at Hes.*Op.*582.

8 See above, p. 100 with n.16. ἀνθεῖν thus is much less common than ἄνθος, but may well be fifth/fourth-century cliché: Pi.*P.*9.110, Isoc.5.10, Pl.*R.*475a, Anaxandrid.9, Timocl.30.

9 Cf. Hdt.6.127.4, Pi.*P.*10.18, E.*El.*944, *Iamb.Adesp.*5 Diehl.

10 The irony was uncomfortably evident to Stanford (*GM*112ff.) who found it too horrific to credit; but both his discomfort and his scepticism concerned only the verb's supposed association with 'prettiness', which he rightly rejected. (He later retracted his scepticism, *AS* 95, but without reinterpreting the irony.) Evident also to Denniston–Page, whose response was more bemused than sceptical: '*blossoming with corpses,* an exceptionally incongruous metaphor'.

11 This analysis is not, of course, wholly original; cf. notably Fraenkel *ad loc.* Ole Smith (p.25) rightly associated this interaction with that at *Ag.*479ff. (see above, p. 158), both being extra-grammatical links, but without formally recognizing a category.

12 Lesky *JHS* 1966, p.85 and *Hist.Gr.Lit.*261. I note that even the supposedly unequivocal phrase ἀνάγκας ἔδυ λέπαδνον (*Ag.*218) is double-edged. It *was* ἀνάγκη and yet Ag. also, *actively*, 'put it on', ἔδυ. This active tone is not characteristically found with the 'yoke of necessity': cf. the essential passivity in e.g. *h.Cer.*217, Pi.*N.*7.6, B.11.45, A.*Prom.*108, S.*fr.*591.5, E.*Heracl.*886, Hdt.8.22.2 (but note A.*Ag.*1071). 'A man who acts under Necessity is not acting voluntarily', say Denniston–Page (intro., xxvii); good Aristotelian logic, but, from Aeschylus' standpoint, simplistic.

13 Significantly, there are a few instances of 'substantial' repetitions without any evident linking force which seem (literally) *pointlessly* conspicuous: Pi.*O.* 7.45–9, νέφος (*V*)/νεφέλαν; [Pi.]*O.*5.10–13, ἄλσος/ἄλσος (*V*) and, less per-

ceptible, *ibid.* 12–23, ἄρδει/ἄρδει (*V*); B.16.5–9 (very fragmentary), ἀνθεμό-εντι/ἄνθεα (*V*). Those who relate success to intention would no doubt put such repetitions down to careless accident. It is noteworthy that none of the four instances is from Aeschylus, whereas most of the available examples of such repetition *with* a linking force *are* Aeschylean. Besides (i) *Ag.*187–92 (above, p. 163) and (ii) *Prom.*966ff. (above, p. 164), note: (iii) *Ag.*811–13, δίκη... δικαίων to δίκας (*V*) (legal image). The repetition is very obvious, especially as δίκας is emphatic (*sic*), but the link itself is devious, as if Ag. were using specious rhetoric to bolster a none too sure argument: a dramatic use of a stylistic feature, *not* another example of 'carelessness'. (iv) *Ag.*1257–9, Λύκειε to λύκῳ (*V*), a pained association of the healing god of light and the hateful Aegisthus. (v) *Ch.*1011–13, ἔβαψεν (*V*) to βαφάς, a straightforward enforcement of the overt argument, almost antithetical: the 'dye' of blood takes the place of any natural dye. (vi) *Ch.*1047–50, δρακόντοιν (*V*) to δράκουσιν, a link that illuminates the truth of the heightened moment. To the chorus the horror is over, the snakes are dead. That the horror still exists as a personal horror for the killer is seen only by the killer. Orestes sees the snakes back already: as before, only worse; not δυοῖν now, but πυκνοῖς. (Note the enforcing metrical parallelism.)

14 Leavis *R V* 63. The idea of the flower-gathering Persephone as herself a flower seems to go back to *h.Cer.*8 καλυκώπιδι κούρῃ.

15 Cf. Theoc.24.7–9. A much less distinguished interaction is that in Alcm.89, a passage which may have influenced Simonides here. The Alcmanic link between εὕδουσι δ' ὀρέων κορυφαί... and εὕδουσι δ' οἰωνῶν φῦλα, though not negligible, is less pointed and heightened in all respects. As far as our fragment goes, a limitation that should not be forgotten, the product of the link seems to be a confirmation of the feeling of nocturnal 'oneness' that the parallelizing catalogue engenders.

16 Contrast the *Macbeth* paradigm discussed above, p. 151, where *fall'n* (*T*) 'activates', as I put it, *leaf* (*V*).

17 See Hulme 21ff.

18 See above, p. 154, n.6.

19 *Pace* Donaldson, who plumped, gratuitously, for animals. On the various senses of δάπτειν, see above, p. 98 with n.7.

Retrospective imagery
§55

An effect broadly comparable to that produced by preparation can be produced without the aid of what is obviously preparation or obviously interaction at all. The apparent means is simply a word order whereby the image, though it 'turns out' to be such in retrospect, does not seem such at the time. The vehicle appears for the moment to be literal – and unexceptionable.

> Nor suffer thy pale forehead to be kissed
> By nightshade,

to take an instance from Keats. For 'kissed' to be able to seem, as it does, momentarily literal, it must seem 'in question', and the capacity to seem this symptomatizes, in the present instance, a degree of terminological coherence of the vehicle with its context. 'Thy pale forehead' is actually a sequence of very subdued neutral terminology. But other instances show that essentially the same effect may be traceable to similarly subdued preparation, as in Pi. *P*.1.61f., where the sentence begins τῷ πόλιν κείναν θεοδμάτῳ σὺν ἐλευθερίᾳ ...ἔκτισσε. The exact significance of θεοδμάτῳ is not clear until ἐλευθερίᾳ. For the moment it seems to hang vaguely with πόλιν and does so because it is 'the sort of word' that might be used as epithet of that noun and, indeed, actually is so used: θεόδματον πόλιν (B.12.7)[1] like ἐυδμήτοιο πόληος (*Il.* 21.516).[2]

But the source of the effect is a secondary matter. The primary point is the distinctiveness of the effect itself and, in particular, a special feature which is not shown by 'normal' preparations. This feature can be seen in sharper focus when the organization is such that the signal that an image is or has been in operation is further delayed. Pi.*O*.10.52ff.:

> παρέσταν μὲν ἄρα Μοῖραι σχεδόν
> ὅ τ' ἐξελέγχων μόνος
> ἀλάθειαν ἐτήτυμον
> Χρόνος.

It is only the announcement of the subject of ἐξελέγχων that indicates that the activity is being ascribed not mythically to a deity (as to Μοῖραι) but metaphorically to an abstraction, that, in fact, 'time' is being personified. The particular effect, the special feature of which I spoke, is to take the force of surprise off the vehicle, where it properly belongs, and throw it emphatically on to the tenor, the word that reveals the image, Χρόνος. But Χρόνος, being the tenor, is itself unassailable; it is there by right; it can bear the closest scrutiny. In short, the vehicle's natural prominence is redistributed and transferred to the tenor in a way that gives the tenor a peculiar emphasis (which one hopes it deserves) and allows the vehicle to do its work without any questioning.

The technique appears to be favoured especially by Pindar.[3] But other poets exploit it to a lesser extent. Thus Thgn.409f.:

> οὐδένα θησαυρὸν παισὶν καταθήσει ἀμείνω
> αἰδοῦς.

Once again, it is only with αἰδοῦς, or strictly ἀμείνω αἰδοῦς, that it becomes clear that θησαυρόν was figurative; and again all the weight goes on to αἰδοῦς, whose enjambement is not irrelevant. It is evident that the effect is likely to involve postposition of a noun. So again in A.*Ag*.648ff., in the herald's speech,

> πῶς κεδνὰ τοῖς κακοῖσι συμμείξω, λέγων
> χειμῶν' Ἀχαιῶν οὐκ ἀμήνιτον θεοῖς;
> ξυνώμοσαν γάρ, ὄντες ἔχθιστοι τὸ πρίν,
> πῦρ καὶ θάλασσα,

where the 'conspiracy' takes on an almost sinister flavour from the sudden revelation of its unexpected membership.[4] And again at Pi.*O*.12.1f.:

> Λίσσομαι, παῖ Ζηνὸς Ἐλευθερίου,
> Ἱμέραν εὐρυσθενέ' ἀμφιπόλει, σώτειρα Τύχα.

The personification of Τύχα might be taken for an invocation to a 'real' daughter of Zeus until the postponed subject releases the tension and so, as before, attracts the emphasis.[5] In this, as in many of the instances, the imagery is subdued; personification at its barest.

The type clearly presents little variation. The following instances conform to the now familiar pattern: postposition, emphatic release of tension and a more or less subdued image. Pi.*P*.3.28f.:

> Λοξίας, κοινᾶνι παρ' εὐθυτάτῳ γνώμαν πιθών,
> πάντα ἰσάντι νόῳ·

Vehicle κοινᾶνι, postponed release on νόῳ.[6] Pi.*P*.3.84ff.:

> τὶν δὲ μοῖρ' εὐδαιμονίας ἕπεται.
> λαγέταν γάρ τοι τύραννον δέρκεται,
> εἴ τιν' ἀνθρώπων, ὁ μέγας πότμος.

Vehicle δέρκεται, release on πότμος. A.*Th*.66f. (Eteocles' scout):

> κἀγὼ τὰ λοιπὰ πιστὸν ἡμεροσκόπον
> ὀφθαλμὸν ἔξω.

Vehicle πιστὸν ἡμεροσκόπον, release on ὀφθαλμόν. A.*Th*.793f., the same scout after the defeat of the enemy force:

> πόλις πέφευγεν ἥδε δούλιον ζυγόν·
> πέπτωκεν ἀνδρῶν ὀβρίμων κομπάσματα.

Vehicle πέπτωκεν, appearing to imply some such non-figurative use as ὁ...στρατὸς...ἔπιπτε (Hdt.8.16.2); release on κομπάσματα.

The type is not entirely invariable in its use, however. At A.*Ch.*983ff., Orestes, displaying the robe that was used to help kill his father, contrives to make poignant capital out of an essentially straightforward instance:

> ἐκτείνατ' αὐτὸ καὶ κύκλῳ παρασταδὸν
> στέγαστρον ἀνδρὸς δείξαθ', ὡς ἴδῃ πατήρ –
> οὐχ οὑμός, ἀλλ' ὁ πάντ' ἐποπτεύων τάδε
> ἥλιος – ἄναγνα μητρὸς ἔργα τῆς ἐμῆς...

Orestes has no real father left to show the robe to. πατήρ (a title reserved for Zeus among divinities[7]), vehicle; οὐχ οὑμός, a negative gloss; positive release, as usual, on the postponed noun, ἥλιος, characteristically enjambed.

Pindar has a comparably creative use at *P.*9.23ff., not a matter, this time, of pathos, but of wit. The virgin Cyrene, παρθένος ἀγροτέρα (v.6), is soon to be carried off by Apollo. Meanwhile she lives a solitary life at home, but spurns such usual occupations of a young woman as weaving,

> οὔθ' ἱστῶν παλιμβάμους ἐφίλησεν ὁδούς (v.18),

and gregarious entertainment with her own sex, even,

> οὔτε δείπνων οἰκοριᾶν μεθ' ἑταιρᾶν τέρψιας (v.19).[8]

By day, she hunts the animals that menace her father's cattle,

> ...κεράϊζεν ἀγρίους
> θῆρας, ἦ πολλάν τε καὶ ἡσύχιον
> βουσὶν εἰρήναν παρέχοισα πατρῴαις (vv.21ff.),

and by night...

> τὸν δὲ σύγκοιτον γλυκὺν
> παῦρον ἐπὶ γλεφάροις
> ὕπνον ἀναλίσκοισα ῥέποντα πρὸς ἀῶ (vv.23ff.).

'Her elected virginity is suggested most delicately by the opening words of the last clause in v.23: her only bed-fellow is sleep.'[9] Right: σύγκοιτον is the vehicle, a figurative σύγκοιτον only. But the effect of the word order is to suggest the opposite, that there *is* a σύγκοιτος, and to create a momentary melodramatic tension ('who can the fellow be?'), which drops bathetically, on ὕπνον, a few words later. The poetic organization is indeed 'delicate' and a fine humour informs it.[10]

In one final instance from Pindar, which has not gone unremarked,[11] the usual emphatic release is absent. Instead there is an almost imperceptibly gradual revelation. *O.*6.22ff.:

ὦ Φίντις, ἀλλὰ ζεῦξον ἤδη μοι σθένος ἡμιόνων,
ᾇ τάχος, ὄφρα κελεύθῳ τ' ἐν καθαρᾷ
βάσομεν ὄκχον, ἵκωμαί τε πρὸς ἀνδρῶν
καὶ γένος.

Phintis is the victorious charioteer, who, it seems at the outset, is being invoked 'legitimately' in the way that the triumphant athlete of an ode sometimes is: νίκαις τρισσαῖς, ὦ 'Αριστόμενες, δάμασσας (*P*.8.80). But as the sentence proceeds, it gradually emerges that the invocation is a pretext for something else, that we are on a purely metaphorical 'journey'. The opening phrase, ὦ Φίντις, clearly has a main rôle in the interaction, acting rather as a glide, though one hesitates to call it that.[12]

1 So B.13.163.
2 So Hes.*fr*.235.4, B.9.54.
3 In line with a more general habit of postponing the grammatical subject or other 'explanatory' element. See e.g. Gildersleeve on *O*.10.34.
4 One's initial impression was perhaps that certain deities had settled their differences (e.g. Artemis and Zeus, cf. vv.135f.).
5 Cf. a miniature version at Alcm.57, οἷα Διὸς θυγάτηρ ἔρσα τράφει / καὶ Σελάνας. But with the postposition on such a small scale, both tension and release are almost negligible.
6 Cf. Young 37f.
7 The point is made by Rose *ad loc*.
8 Moschopoulos' text (οἰκουρ- codd.).
9 Burton 42.
10 For more humour in this ode, see Burton 41. Note that σύγκοιτον in its retrospective rôle is abetted by γλυκύν in *N* terminology, applicable both to people (above, p. 99) and to sleep (γλυκὺς ὕπνος, *Il*.1.610, *Od*.2.395, *h.Ven*.170, *h.Merc*.8, Sapph.63.3, Alcm.3.7). As such, γλ. gives nothing away but hardly retains any but the faintest sense of support for the image when the image comes to be seen for what it is. Compare the rôle of πικρός at A.*Th*.730, 'sharp' of σίδαρος, 'cruel' of the ξένος (see above, p. 95). But here the image (727ff.), though not formally announced as such until σίδαρος, is effectively recognized as soon as Χάλυβος is given. The function of πικρός is in fact explanatory, rather than evasive like Pindar's γλυκύν; it helps to confirm what Χάλυβος suggests, that this is an image and that its tenor is 'steel'. Contrast altogether the superficially similar image, again with πικρός, at *Th*.941ff. The very similarity of this passage to the earlier, combined with reasonable proximity to it, acts as an indication that imagery is about. Hence there is little feeling of postponed revelation, and this πικρός has the more 'orthodox' function of a glide or pivot (see above, p. 95). In neither passage, at all events, is the imagery truly 'retrospective' as in the Pindar.
11 Dornseiff 66 refers to Pindar's 'hovering' between tenor and vehicle, using this passage as example.

12 Two further instances of retrospective imagery, both slight: (i) B.15.44, vehicle διέδραμεν, postponed release on λόγος. In context one has a momentary impression of an actual *human* runner. (ii) A.*Th*.343f., vehicle μαινόμενος δ' ἐπιπνεῖ κτλ. In this passage it is in fact evident almost at once that the opening words must be figurative, probably evident as soon as ἐπιπνεῖ, and this being so, the postponed subject, Ἄρης, is hardly the object of much released tension. (Ἄρης, one can note in passing, is not strictly a tenor term. It is neutral, albeit very subdued, and makes a slight convergence: the conventional metonymy for 'war' and the animate subject of the animate activities in the vehicle.)

Note finally the distinction between retrospective imagery and the kenning (as at A.*Ag*.494f.). In the latter case it is usually obvious from the start that there *is* an image; what is uncertain is its tenor. Similarly with, for instance, the analogy at Thgn.1245. When a poem begins οὔποθ' ὕδωρ καὶ πῦρ..., the natural presumption is that this is an image. The surprise would be if water and fire were the *real* subject.

8 Aural interaction

Alliteration and assonance: preliminaries

§56

Any detailed discussion of alliteration and assonance in Greek must take account of certain general considerations.[1] The most general, I suppose, is the question – if it is worth calling a question – whether alliteration, in particular, existed as a significant possibility in Greek poetry at all. As is well known, alliteration was not formally recognized by the ancient Greek stylisticians, although they did, of course, recognize under various names several of the forms of sound-patterning and sound-repetition of which alliteration is a particular type.[2] Most modern Hellenists have shown the good judgement that they have shown elsewhere – in regard to the ancients' inattention to epic formulaism, for instance – in declining to interpret such a silence as the voice of authority, and have sensibly allowed their aesthetic faculties rather than dogmatic preconceptions to pronounce on the question of significant existence, although there have been complete sceptics.[3] A few types of marked exploitation of alliteration in Greek will be noted later,[4] and this evidence can serve as adequate for an answer, if evidence is still thought necessary.

Denniston defines assonance as 'the recurrence of a sound in such a measure as to catch the ear', but adds, 'we do not know with any accuracy what ancient Greek sounded like'.[5] The definition is plausible enough, but the qualification is ill-judged. We *do* know with surprising accuracy a good deal about what ancient Greek sounded like,[6] but in fact we do not need to know nearly as much as we do know in order to detect 'recurrence of a sound'. We do not need to know what the Greek kappa sounded like in order to recognize its recurrence in κλύδων κακῶν. We only need to know that there was, as one would hope, a high rate of correspondence between the Greek phonological and alphabetic systems.[7]

Stanford has a different caveat: 'these sound patterns may occur accidentally and unintentionally'.[8] But this merely takes us back to Denniston's 'to catch the ear'. As usual, we cannot guarantee the accuracy of the intention or the insignificance of the accidental, nor are we called upon to make the attempt. The point is simply that it is perceptibility (ear-catching) that is in question, and that recurrence of sound is not necessarily perceptible. Some limiting factors are obvious, even in theory: recurrence over a longer space tends to be less perceptible; intermediate distractions similarly reduce perceptibility.[9] More important, a less predictable recurrence is more perceptibly a recurrence than a more predictable. Thus the nominal alliteration in stock phrases like 'Cheshire cheese' and 'high hopes' probably passes unnoticed; these are virtually 'dead' alliterations. It is pertinent to note that a tenor–vehicle collocation is necessarily less predictable: κλύδων κακῶν.

It will appear that for present purposes I am, on the whole, restricting 'assonance and alliteration' to word-initial or – where the second element in a compound is in question – morpheme-initial alliteration; and this, as it happens, is usually consonantal alliteration. My reason concerns initial alliteration's greater prominence, and by this I mean in the first instance not phonetic but *psychological* prominence. The initial phoneme is peculiarly associated with its word or its morpheme;[10] a fact which, for Greek, receives corroboration from, and itself helps to explain, the instinctive (?) inclination of the professional etymologists of a somewhat later period towards pairs that 'get the first letter right';[11] and a fact which, as will appear, is of some significance where interactive alliteration is concerned.

As for phonetic prominence, the nature of the Greek pitch accent was presumably such that it could not give alliteration the kind of support that accentual stress is capable of. But even under a pitch accent, syllable-initial consonants (which are, in phonetic terms, fully articulated) will have greater prominence than syllable-final (which are unreleased).[12] In the case of Greek, then, it is no more arbitrary than it would be in that of English to recognize the greater prominence of initial phonemes,[13] and it is these that will provide most of the instances that follow.

These few introductory remarks should suffice. Let me merely restate a point made earlier, that the functions I shall claim for alliteration are not the private property of interaction. Rather, the given instances of particular functions are paradigms of some of the uses to which alliteration may be put in any connection.

---

1 For discussion of Greek assonance and alliteration and references to further literature, see, *inter alia*, Defradas 36ff., Herescu 129f., Caplan 271, Opelt 205ff., Groeneboom on A.*Prom.*131f., Fraenkel on *Ag.*268, Porzig 76ff.

2 See Lausberg 885.

3 See Denniston *GPS* 126f. and Opelt 206.

4 Appendix IV.

5 Denniston *GPS* 124.

6 See Allen *VG* 145ff. and *passim*.

7 See Allen *VG* 6f.

8 Stanford *AS* 81.

9 There is also the presumption that a less common recurrence (e.g. χ–χ) is more striking than a more common (e.g. π–π); cf. Porzig 77. (On the great frequency of π–π alliteration in Greek cf. Porzig 81; Stanford *AS* 82, n.21; Denniston *GPS* 129; Opelt 214.) But the difference in perceptibility must be marginal.

10 'Psychological prominence...morpheme'; I am indebted for the formulation of this point to conversation with Professor W. S. Allen.

11 See Allen *AIL* 54 on the principle of *compositio*. I say 'professional etymologists' advisedly. Poetic 'etymologies' do show a similar inclination, but their status and function usually differ in such a radical way from those of etymologies proper that an easy association of the two kinds, in this or any other connection, is to be avoided. Given the specific technical meaning that 'etymology' now has, it pains me that we persist in using the word to describe, say, Aeschylus' Διòς κóρα–Δíκα (*Ch.*948). 'Etymology' – now – means the study of *origins*. Aeschylus' word play has nothing to do with origins but with perceptible *significance* (cf. Dodds on E.*Ba.*367).

12 Here again I acknowledge the informal comments of Professor Allen.

13 Cf. Porzig 77, also Defradas 40, n.2 (modifying his earlier statement, p.38). But one must, of course, beware of a mental Anglicization (Germanization etc.) that might, for instance, elevate consonantal alliteration over vocalic (cf. Defradas 38). Note incidentally that, contrary to what is sometimes asserted, in a language with an English-type stress accent it is not a condition of alliteration's perceptibility that it must take place between stressed syllables (cf. 'cábin'd, críb'd, confín'd', or made up instances like 'hoárse hyéna' etc.). And if alliteration needs no stress to exist (though, naturally, stress can support it), there is no theoretical foundation for the suggestion that Greek, lacking a stress accent, must have lacked alliteration too (see Appendix IV).

Alliterative link

§57

The alliterations that concern interactions are largely 'associative'. In Hopkins' lines

> Thou mastering me
> God! giver of breath and bread;
> World's strand, sway of the sea,
> Lord of living and dead...

alliteration marks off 'full' words (as 'sway' and 'sea') from 'empty' words (as 'of the') and associates these particular 'full' words with each other. An extreme contrast is provided by S.*OT* 371,

τυφλòς τά τ' ὦτα τóν τε νοῦν τά τ' ὄμματ' εἶ,

where empty words alliterate with full and it is entirely irrelevant *which* words have the tau. Nothing is associated with anything: the effect is not associative but 'expressive', in this instance an aural intensification correlative to heightened emotion.[1] The effect might also be thought emphatic, but the relation between alliteration and emphasis needs careful formulation. In 'whether 'tis nobler in the mind to suffer / The slings...', it is not true that 'slings' is more emphatic than it would be if the words ran 'endure / The slings'. Nor is 'suffer' more emphatic thus, obviously. Emphasis – or shall we once again say 'prominence'? – is given only to the whole alliterative unit, by virtue of its distinctive alliterative structure. Alliteration, in fact, may be thought of as a type of parallel structure, and as such produces no prominence – or emphasis – for *particular* constituent terms.[2] In the Sophocles it is the whole line that stands out; that τόν and τε etc. get nothing out of it hardly needs saying. And to return to the earlier point, these are 'empty' words, and such words are terminologically colourless. It is not words of this kind that play a significant part in interaction, and so it is the Hopkins type of alliteration rather than the Sophoclean that I shall be looking to.

The expressive function of alliteration is the function with which Greek scholarship has been preoccupied. A wholly representative comment is that made by Fraenkel on a line of Aeschylus.[3] The suggested function of 'the piling up of the p-sounds' is to 'express the breathless excitement of the questioner'. I am not, I should stress, wishing to criticize the particular interpretation, but merely noting that when Hellenists comment on alliteration, it is usually along these lines that their comments run; and, further, that when faced with instances which are hardly or not at all amenable to such interpretation, they tend either to 'note the alliteration' without interpretative comment or to say nothing at all. But the associative use is sometimes admitted, though perhaps more in theory than in actual practice. Empson's classic statement, 'its most important mode of action is to connect two words by similarity of sound so that you are made to think of their possible connections',[4] is phrased more decisively than most Hellenists would venture, but note Porzig's remark, 'Die Alliteration...verkörpert...die enge Zusammengehörigkeit der betreffenden Wörter';[5] or another scholar's more modest conception of the function, 'den syntaktischen Bezug der alliterierenden Wörter hervorzuheben';[6] and Fraenkel himself elsewhere remarks on the common use of the 'Klangfigur' in Greek tragedy as 'Bezeichnung reziproker Verhältnisse'.[7]

This associative function I shall call 'alliterative link',[8] which is in a sense, as its name is meant to suggest, a counterpart of link proper, although it does not necessarily serve the tenor in the same clear-cut way. κλύδων κακῶν is a simple instance, the link enforcing the obvious logical – and grammatical – relation between tenor and vehicle, binding the vehicle to its immediate context. It should now be evident why the special status of the initial phoneme (and so of alliteration between initial phonemes) is particularly important for alliteration-based interaction. The initial phoneme is *the* phoneme of a word[9] and the word[10] is the terminological unit. Alliteration between initial phonemes is, or may be, a semantic carrier.[11] If the alliteration does not take place between initial phonemes, it is not so decisively associated with, and does not in turn decisively associate, the words whose co-presence creates it. This is especially true if the alliteration is multiple, as in Sophocles' τυφλός. . . . Multiple alliteration, even if initial, tends not to be associative.[12] There is usually no possibility of associating so many words and no incentive to decide which should be associated with which. The link, therefore, tends to involve simple initial alliteration.[13]

1 On the insignificance of 'empty' words for associative alliteration cf. Opelt 208. N.B. that the associative/expressive distinction (my own) is not supposed to cover the whole field; nor is it implied that a given alliteration must be one or other; it may be both. I might note here that I know of no adequate typology of the poetic functions of alliteration or of sound patterning generally. The most elaborate scheme I have seen is that of D. I. Masson (pp.785f.), who lists eighteen 'functions of sound manipulation', ranging from 'structural emphasis' to 'incantation'. The subtlety of some of his distinctions must be seen to be believed, but despite this and the length of his list he has little to offer the present discussion, primarily, it seems, because he makes no distinction between alliteration and assonance and concentrates on highly patterned 'manipulations'.
2 See above, §29.
3 A.*Ag.*268.
4 Empson *ST* 12. I am inclined to agree that it is the most important function, though others are certainly not negligible. Some expressive uses are of pervasive significance, e.g. that discussed by Spearing 19f.: 'when Chaucer wants to express violent physical action, he normally does so directly through violence of sound...makes use of alliteration for this purpose.' This admirably fits passages like Pi.*P.*1.21–4, Alc.326.3–5, *Mel.Adesp.*11(c).1 (p.496 Page), B.5.104–6, Hom.*Epigr.*14.9–12.
5 Porzig 86; cf., for instance, his discussion of A.*Ch.*846 (p.92).
6 Opelt 207.
7 Fraenkel *PP* 364. The remark, however, was made apropos full verbal repetition.
8 Which of course is also the function of the 'Klangfigur' in poetic 'etymologies' (above, p. 175, n.11).
9 Or morpheme.
10 Or morpheme.
11 Cf. Opelt 209, n.2.

12 Cf. Opelt 211.

13 I have not thought it necessary to discuss at length the question of the degree of kinship required between the 'recurring sounds' to constitute alliteration. π–π, for instance, are twins, π–φ less closely related (phonemically distinct). My instances will be confined to the former kind.

§58

It will be clear from the instances that follow that exploitation of alliterative linking was common in my period. It will also be clear that on the whole the creativity involved was of a very limited kind. The commonest use of the link is as structural reinforcement, and in particular reinforcement of the relation between vehicle and immediate tenor. Any kind of image may be involved. In English verse one is familiar with such reinforcement in simile: 'the barge she sat in, like a burnish'd throne'; 'his delights were dolphin-like'; 'and fleckèd darkness like a drunkard reels'.[1] Correspondingly in short simile, A.*Supp*.469:

κακῶν δὲ πλῆθος ποταμὸς ὣς ἐπέρχεται.

The same in comparison, Epich.44.1:

κορακῖνοί τε κοριοειδέες.[2]

And the same on a grandiose (mock-grandiose?) scale in epic simile, Phryn. Trag.3 Bergk,

σχήματα δ᾽ ὄρχησις τόσα μοι πόρεν, ὅσσ᾽ ἐνὶ πόντῳ
κύματα ποιεῖται χείματι νὺξ ὀλοή,

with complex patterning, τόσα...πόρεν versus ὅσσα...πόντῳ, plus the assonance of σχήματα...κύματα enforced by parallel metrical positioning.[3]

But there is no doubt that in the corpus it is more often metaphor that is favoured with this reinforcement. Several different formal structures may be involved, appositional nouns, for instance, as at Pi.*N*.3.1

Μοῖσα, μᾶτερ ἁμετέρα

and at A.*Ag*.494f.

κάσις / πηλοῦ ξύνουρος, διψία κόνις,

where the link has somewhat greater importance, bridging the separation of the two words, κάσις...κόνις. Or noun and adjective, as at A.*Ag*.132f.

στόμιον μέγα Τροίας στρατωθέν,

178

where the στόμιον...στρατωθέν relation is roughly comparable to the appositions above (as if στόμιον..., στρατός), although much more lively than those; στρατωθέν feels almost intrusive.[4] But neither of these formal structures is commonly reinforced by link. On simple numerical criteria, the almost definitive form for the reinforcement is that exemplified by κλύδων κακῶν, embodying a specialized genitival relation of an instantly recognizable kind. However, this comparative frequency is due almost entirely to Aeschylus, whose partiality for the type, one would note, is a partiality for what might almost be reckoned a formula, lacking both depth and flexibility. With κλύδων κακῶν (Pe.599f.) compare the reinforced genitives of 'contents' or 'material' (etc.) at

Prom.368	ποταμοὶ πυρός
Prom.1015	κακῶν τρικυμία
fr.237	πεδίον πόντου
Eu.516	δόμος δίκας

and with slight separation

Supp.135	δόμος...δορός
Th.758	κακῶν...κῦμα
Ag.872	χθονὸς...χλαῖναν
Ag.1397	κρατῆρα...κακῶν

a tally that may come as a surprise.[5] Outside Aeschylus we find only[6]

B.fr.4.63	ἀοιδᾶν ἄνθεα
Pi.P.1.21f.	πυρὸς...παγαί ('streams' of fire, of Etna)[7]
Pi.fr.70a.16	ἕρκος ἅλμας (apparently periphrastic for 'the sea')[8]
Pi.fr.124.6	πελάγει δ' ἐν πολυχρύσοιο πλούτου

in the last of which the directness of the link is weakened by the intervening πολυ- (πελ- πολ- πλ-).

Genitival links may, naturally, involve genitival relations of other kinds, which characteristically imply a marginally less intimate connection of the tenor term with the vehicle. Once again Aeschylus shows the way:

Supp.345	πρύμναν πόλεος
Th.2	πρύμνη πόλεως
Th.760f.	πρύμναν πόλεως
Pe.814f.	κακῶν κρηπίς
Th.661	φοίτῳ φρενῶν
Prom.109f.	πυρὸς πηγήν (the 'fount' of fire Prometheus stole)
fr.530.21	δέλτῳ Διός

Ch.211   φρενῶν καταφθορά (as if 'death of the mind'; not cliché)
Eu.1001   Παλλάδος...πτεροῖς

and, with a neat use of articulation to give prominence to the alliterative pair,

Supp.329   πόνου δ' ἴδοις ἂν οὐδαμοῦ ταὐτὸν πτερόν.[9]

All the comparable instances this time are Pindaric and, all in all, rather tame:

O.2.17   χρόνος ὁ πάντων πατήρ
O.7.4   κορυφὰν κτεάνων
P.6.1   'Αφροδίτας ἄρουραν
fr.134   εὐδαιμόνων δραπέτας

and, phraseologically very like A.Eu.1001 above, but with the operative words apart,

I.1.64f.   πτερύγεσσιν ἀερθέντ' ἀγλααῖς Πιερίδων.[10]

Aeschylus' peculiar predilection for the genitival link takes on a further significance when one finds that simple enforcing links of other kinds are much better represented in the œuvres of other poets. A bare list will suffice:

Arch.92a   πάγος...παλίγκοτος
Sapph.22.11f. πόθος...ἀμφιπόταται
Anacr.3.8   ποιμαίνεις πολιήτας
B.3.13   πυργωθέντα πλοῦτον
5.9f.   ὑφάνας ὕμνον[11]
Pi.O.5.16   κινδύνῳ κεκαλυμμένον
O.8.25   ἁλιερκέα (h–h) (apparently a Pindaric coinage, recurring at
              P.1.18, I.1.9)[12]
O.13.57   τάμνειν τέλος
N.7.53   ἄνθε' 'Αφροδίσια
I.6.40   φιάλαν χρυσῷ πεφρικυῖαν
fr.6b(f).1   ἄρδοντ' ἀοιδαῖς
fr.78.3   ἱρόθυτον θάνατον (the 'sacrifice' of death)
fr.150   μαντεύεο, Μοῖσα ('you be the prophet')
fr.185   κακίει καπνός ('oozes')
A.Pe.613   παρθένου πηγῆς
Pe.714   διαπεπόρθηται τὰ Περσῶν πράγματα
Supp.618   πόλιν παχῦναι
Th.594   βλαστάνει βουλεύματα
Prom.88   ταχύπτεροι πνοαί
Prom.651   ἀπολακτίσῃς λέχος
Ag.155   μνάμων μῆνις[13]

Ag.299   πομποῦ πυρός (the 'courier' beacon)
Ag.997   κυκλούμενον κέαρ
Ag.1005 πότμος εὐθυπορῶν
Eu.466   ἀντίκεντρα καρδίᾳ
fr.419   πόνου πλουτοῦντα

1 *Antony and Cleopatra* II.2 and V.2, *Romeo and Juliet* II.3.
2 I shrink from offering an interpretation of these words. Can κοριοειδής really mean 'like the pupil of the eye, dark-gleaming' (LSJ)? At all events, it can hardly be formed directly from κόρη, though it might be formed from its diminutive, κόριον.
3 Cf. κύματος...πήματος at A.*Ag*.1181f., a kind of parallelism visible elsewhere in Aeschylean imagery; see Johansen *SS* 52f. Note the extent of marked sound-patterning in the very few scraps of Phrynichus now extant: *fr*.1 Bergk Παλλάδα περσέπολιν...πολεμαδόκον...παῖδα Διός...παρθένον, *fr*.5.3 Nauck πεδία δὲ πάντα καὶ παράκτιον πλάκα. (Schmid–Stählin 1.2.177, n.8 note only the latter instance in this connection. It is true that the ascription of the Bergk fragment is not beyond dispute, but Ph. is definitely the most likely candidate; see Page *PMG*, p.379, Dover on Ar.*Nub*.967, Wilamowitz *TGL* 84f.) One other instance of the enforcement of the vehicle/immediate tenor relation: Thgn.535ff. (analogy), δουλείη/σκολιή/σκίλλης/δούλης with metrical parallelism, more or less, in chiastic structure.
4 See above, p. 144, n.14.
5 It is not without significance that four of the above instances share a κ- κακῶν structure (least perceptible at *Th*.758 thanks to the invervening *V* term, θάλασσα); compare also the κακῶν κρηπίς (if sound) of *Pe*.814f., embodying a different kind of genitival relation. See further Appendix IV.
6 'Only': these two lists are complete (within the limits outlined above, p. 81, as usual).
7 LSJ are surely mistaken in placing this usage under πηγή II, 'source'.
8 Contrast the obscure ἕρκος at Pi.*P*.2.80 which may mean 'net' (see Farnell *ad loc*.) in the same terminology as ἅλμας.
9 Note also: (i) *Supp*.556f. βέλει βουκόλου, where the 'tenor' (βουκόλου) is in fact the vehicle of a second image (*V₁* of *V₂*). (ii) *Ag*.820 πλούτου πνοάς, in isolation a genitive link like the others; but in context πν. is neutral (see below, p. 185). (iii) *Ag*.897f. στέγης στῦλον, where στέγης is in fact neutral (see below, p. 187).
10 Add perhaps Pi.*P*.2.80 (see n.8 above). Note incidentally that Brooke-Rose 146ff. uses the expression 'Genitive Link' for simple '*V* of *T*' structures without reference to alliteration, e.g. for Blake's 'clouds of reason' (p.155).
11 ὑφαίνειν thus is not to be thought a cliché. The evidence is limited and of a suspect kind: only *Il*.3.212, Pi.*fr*.179, B.19.8, *Mel.Adesp*.37 *PMG* (conj.), Anon.Parod.*ap*.Ath.5.187a (Brandt, *Parod.Epic.Graec*., p.96).
12 Cf. Pindar's ἕρκος ἅλμας at *fr*.70a.16 (above, p. 179).

13 This image – or most of it – could be, and has been, regarded as involving metonymy rather than metaphor, with 'wrath' standing for 'the wrathful Clytemnestra'. On this type of 'conditional metaphor', see Appendix XIII.

§59

'To connect two words...so that you are made to think of their possible connections.' Few if any of the links cited so far have been serious candidates for the Empsonian 'mode of action'. In every case it has been a pre-existing relation that the link has enforced: a matter of urging the reader to dwell on connections he must have taken in anyway, rather than one of prompting him to consider additional possibilities. A transparent instance from Milton may help to clarify what kind of effect such prompting might involve. *Paradise Lost* I.749, on Mulciber's fall:

> he with this rebellious rout
> Fell long before; nor aught availed him now
> To have built in Heaven high towers...

Ricks' comments are to the point: 'alliteration...can tie together things which are not tied together in the plain statement....Alliteration and word order tie "Heaven" and "high" together, though the plain sense is "high towers".... The feeling of *high Heaven* is important to the sense of Mulciber's fall from that height, Mulciber who fell headlong down to Hell. To say that Heaven is high would be to risk cliché, but to suggest it while saying something else is a different matter.'

The Miltonic paradigm, though pleasingly effective, hardly provides a particularly spectacular demonstration of the creative possibilities of an aural link. Even so, it represents a marked contrast to a reinforcement of a pre-existing relation – and the more conspicuously because, like most of the simple reinforcements, it involves actual juxtaposition. Even with these simple types, a link will in fact tend to have some extra importance when the operative words are separated, as in, for instance, A.*Prom.*275f.:

> ταὐτά τοι πλανωμένη
> πρὸς ἄλλοτ' ἄλλον πημονή...

But the relation enforced is still a pre-existing one; the interaction confirms without decisively adding.

Consider A.*Eu.*427:

> ποῦ γὰρ τοσοῦτο κέντρον ὡς μητροκτονεῖν;

Alliteration connects κέντρον and μητροκτονεῖν and thus brings into focus the very association – provocation and matricide – that the speakers, the Erinyes, refuse to accept as meaningful. The interaction still adds to a pre-existing relation, but one can feel that the addition, the sharper focus, is significant and, in a measure, creative. Contrast, for instance, the plain enforcement at *Eu.466*:

ἄλγη προφωνῶν ἀντίκεντρα καρδίᾳ.

More unequivocally creative, the assonantal link between ὠδῖνα and ἐπῳδόν at A.*Ag*.1418 (Clytemnestra speaking):

ἔθυσεν αὑτοῦ παῖδα, φιλτάτην ἐμοὶ
ὠδῖν', ἐπῳδὸν Θρῃκίων ἀημάτων.

The metaphorical ἐπῳδόν with its contemptuous associations[1] –

λέγουσι δ' ὥς τις εἰσελήλυθε ξένος,
γόης ἐπῳδὸς Λυδίας ἀπὸ χθονός,
ξανθοῖσι βοστρύχοισιν εὐοσμῶν κόμην

(E.*Ba*.233ff.)

– collides with the metonymic ὠδῖνα: the personal, natural pain of her daughter's birth, the alien nonsense of her death.

Consider now Eteocles' prayer at A.*Th*.69ff.:

ὦ Ζεῦ τε καὶ Γῆ καὶ πολισσοῦχοι θεοί
Ἀρά τ' Ἐρινὺς πατρὸς ἡ μεγασθενής,
μή μοι πόλιν γε πρυμνόθεν πανώλεθρον
ἐκθαμνίσητε δηάλωτον...

πρυμνόθεν and ἐκθαμνίσητε make up the vehicle, the former word being a derivative of πρυμνός/πρυμνόν: ὕλην πρυμνὴν ἐκτάμνοντες (*Il*.12.148f.). This πρυμνόθεν is joined by alliteration to πανώλεθρον, a link that suggests nothing in particular, and to πόλιν, a link that suggests a good deal. 'You are made to think of their possible connections' and, specifically, invited to re-etymologize πρυμνόθεν in the light of πόλιν. Eteocles is concerned for the city above all others because he is its head, or, as he phrased it himself shortly before (vv.2f.), ἐν πρύμνῃ πόλεως οἴακα νωμῶν. The link, in short, conjures up a second image of complete propriety. With the best will in the world, it is not easy to find more than one or two links of comparable efficacy within the corpus.[2]

---

1 Cf. Fraenkel *ad loc.* and Dodds on E.*Ba*.234.
2 Most of the best instances of creative link comes from Aeschylus, like the three discussed here. Two more: (i) *Th*.244, βόσκεται...βροτῶν, a collocation vividly

suggestive of perversion (*animals* feeding on men; see LSJ *s.v.* βόσκω II.1).
(ii) *Th.*382f., σοφόν/σαίνειν, slightly argumentative. σαίνειν is the reported
accusation, σοφόν the editorial comment which, by the link, takes up and counters
the accusation at the outset. Other instances on various levels of creativity:
(iii) Semon.7.105, μῶμον...μάχην, cause (or pretext) and effect. (iv) Thgn.19,
σοφιζομένῳ...σφρηγίς, associating the poet's 'seal' with his poetic skill, σοφία.
Cf. the emphases in Woodbury's intelligent paraphrase of Theognis' claim:
'when I compose my verses...such is my skill that I only have to seal them
with my name in order to win a universal and undying reputation' (L. Woodbury,
The Seal of Theognis, in *Studies in Honour of Gilbert Norwood*, ed. M. E. White,
Toronto, 1952, p.27). (Needless to say, this interpretation of the 'seal' – the poet's
name – is still controversial, although it hardly affects my point. It is, in fact,
probably the prevalent modern interpretation: see e.g. Lesky 170, van Groningen
ad loc., Campbell 347ff.) (v) Pi.*fr.*180.3, κέντρον...κρατιστεύων, an enforcement
of a less predictable relation: even the *best* λόγος....

Alliteration as enforcement for interaction
§60

Alliteration can be a source of interaction in its own right. It can also enforce
a given interaction by linking the operative, interactive words. Thus, it may
link pivot to vehicle in simile, as

Arch.79a.9	κροτέοι δ' ὀδόντας ὡς κύων[1]
Arch.98	πτώσσουσαν ὥστε πέρδικα[2]
Mimn.5.1	(ἥβη) ὀλιγοχρόνιον...ὥσπερ ὄναρ[3]
Thgn.939	οὐ δύναμαι...ἀειδέμεν ὥσπερ ἀηδών[4]
A.*fr.*630	ἐτονθόρυζε ταῦρος ὥς[5]
A.*Ag.*2f.	κοιμώμενος...κυνὸς δίκην[6]
A.*Eu.*131f.	κλαγγαίνεις δ' ἅπερ κύων[7]

a list more notable for its length than for any subtlety of procedure within
it.[8] Alliteration may be used in similar fashion to link pivot to vehicle in
comparison: 'plain as a pikestaff', 'good as gold' and so on. In Greek, as in
English, there is good reason for regarding this type as essentially popular
and subliterary in character, and it rarely surfaces in the corpus.[9]

There is no need to linger over this enforcement function. Any kind of
interaction may be so enforced, though none so commonly as the pivot in
simile. Aeschylus (*Ag.*818ff.) provides a good instance with convergence to
metaphor:

καπνῷ δ' ἁλοῦσα νῦν ἔτ' εὔσημος πόλις.
ἄτης θύελλαι ζῶσι· συνθνήσκουσα δὲ
σποδὸς προπέμπει πίονας πλούτου πνοάς.

The intensive π-alliteration culminates with the interactive phrase, πλούτου πνοάς. The vehicle is συνθνήσκουσα with πνοάς neutral: 'breath', οὔπω τεθναότ' ἄσθματι δὲ φρίσσοντα πνοάς Pi.N.10.74f.; and 'hot vapour', ὁκόταν δὲ ὁ χύτρινος ζέση καὶ ἡ ἀτμὶς ἐπανῇ, ἢν μὲν ᾖ λίην θερμὴ ἡ πνοή, ἐπισχεῖν... Hp.Mul.2.133.[10] This particular alliteration is hardly to be thought of as purely enforcing. Over and above its enforcement duty, it has an obvious 'expressive' rôle and discharges it vigorously. The difference between this and a pure enforcement is clear if one recalls the alliterative structure of Cleopatra's words:

> Dost thou not see my baby at my breast,
> That sucks the nurse asleep.

'Baby' and 'breast', 'sucks' and 'asleep': the double convergence is pointed most compellingly.

Aeschylus (Ag.1501ff.) provides another good instance with preparatory link:

> ὁ παλαιὸς δριμὺς ἀλάστωρ
> Ἀτρέως χαλεποῦ θοινατῆρος
> τόνδ' ἀπέτεισεν
> τέλεον νεαροῖς ἐπιθύσας.

Agamemnon dead, Clytemnestra invokes the spirit of vengeance. The vehicle is ἐπιθύσας, articulated at a stanza's end. One need hardly say that there is no question of a literal 'sacrifice'.[11] Rather, ἐπιθύσας, evocative in its own figurative right, is linked still more evocatively to θοινατῆρος, the 'banqueter' Atreus, through the organic connection of sacrifice and feasting:[12] ἐπὶ θοίνην ἢ θυσίαν (Arist.Pol.1324b.39). The alliteration, without doubt, helps significantly to confirm the link between the operative words, widely separated as they are. And the link itself is pointed. Atreus' sense of sociability to Thyestes is matched now, impeccably, with the welcome given to Atreus' son.[13]

1 The Archilochian authorship of this fragment may be acceptable on other grounds, but without stressing the point, one might note that whereas interaction of this and other types is well attested in Archilochus, the other candidate, Hipponax, has but one instance of any sort (pivot in fr.50 – see above, p. 89).
2 Subject presumably human. πτώσσειν of men, in various senses, Il.4.371, Hes.Op.395, Hdt.9.48.3; of birds etc., Il.21.14, Od.22.304.
3 Copied verbatim by Theognis (1020).
4 'Etymology.' The nightingale ἀείδει at e.g. Od.19.519, Arist.HA 536a.29.
5 It is only a presumption that the verb is neutral. The available parallels all show it used of people, not animals: Ar.Ach.683, Ran.747, Vesp.614. (So, later,

Herod.6.7, 7.77, 8.8.) If the word is not *N* but *T*, the result would be alliteratively enforced intrusion, intrusion of the type discussed above, p. 138.

6 κοιμᾶσθαι of animals, *Od.*14.411, Arist.*Somn.Vig.*454b.19, Thphr.*Sign.*41. N.B. that κ. and κ. are in parallel metrical structure.

7 κλαγγαίνεις is apparently (and wrongly) taken as *V* (not *N*) by Ole Smith 41. The verb seems to occur only here, so that appeal must be made to the evidence of cognates. *Qua T*, κυνῶν. . .κλαγγήν X.*Cyn.*4.5, cf. Hes.(?)*P.Ox.*2509.21; so κλάζειν at *Od.*14.30, X.*Cyn.*3.9, Ar.*Vesp.*929f. (explained by v.916). *Qua V*, of the human voice, κλαγγή at A.*Ag.*1152; κλαγγώδης Hp.*Prorrh.*1.17 and *Coac.*550; for κλάζειν thus, see above, p. 16 with n.2.

8 Note also one dubious instance, A.*fr.*702 παύσυβριν δίκην πυρός (conj. text), and two trivial ones: Thgn.56 ἔξω δ᾽ ὥστ᾽ ἔλαφοι and Arch.40 ἐπίκουρος ὥστε Κάρ. Likewise A.*Supp.*223f., where the ground term is not pivotal but supporting: ἑσμὸς ὡς πελειάδων ἵζεσθε (*h–h*); for ἰ3. of birds, see Hdt.2.55.2, Ar.*Av.*742. The comparative frequency of the enforcement in Archilochus is striking, as is its frequency in general (in all authors) when compared with enforcement of any other kind of interaction; both points may be thought to add weight to the theory that the type is a more or less literary extension of the essentially popular schema involving comparison (see n.9 below). Note that the alliterations discussed in this section differ from κλύδων κακῶν etc. in that they link words whose relation is not inherently surprising. This lessens the force of the link, but there is no reason why it should negate it altogether. Even though 'sweet cider' is not live alliteration, the same words, with only a slight structural dislocation of the relevant kind, may alliterate perceptibly: 'Ida, sweet as apple-cider'.

9 Apart from an 'etymological' use at A.*Pe.*82, δέργμα δράκοντος (for the association cf. *Il.*22.93ff.; Hes.*Th.*825ff. and *Sc.*233ff.), the only instances are trivial in the extreme: Alcm.100 μεῖον ἢ κοδύμαλον and A.*Supp.*760 κρείσσονας λύκους κυνῶν. There is also an instance of convergence to comparison enforced thus, Pi.*N.*4.81 στάλαν. . .Παρίου λίθου λευκοτέραν (*more Pindarico*, not as simple as it looks: the image is retrospective and λίθου is only shown to be figurative by λευκ.; the effect is an ingeniously double hyperbole). The pattern is sufficiently established to exert influence even on 'literal' comparisons: A.*Prom.*922f. κεραυνοῦ κρείσσον᾽. . .φλόγα, βροντῆς θ᾽ ὑπερβάλλοντα. . . κτύπον, with the alliterative schema intact in both phrases; the parallel comparison at Pi.*I.*8.34 also has κεραυνοῦ. . .κρέσσον. On the popular character of the type, see Appendix IV.

10 πνοή of breath, likewise: *Il.*20.439, E.*Or.*421, Thphr.*Vent.*20. Of 'hot vapour', likewise: Eub.75.8, Antiph.217.7 and also Hp.*Nat.Puer.*24, where πν. = διαπνοή. . .τοῦ θερμοῦ (from the soil), apparently in accordance with the principle mentioned above, p. 50, n.2; add also the closely related sense of 'fiery heat' (σποδός being 'embers'), as πυρὸς. . .πνοαί E.*fr.*1059.2 (so E.*Tro.* 815; cf. *Il.*21.355 πνοιῇ. . .Ἡφαίστοιο) and cf. πύρπνοον. . .λιγνύν A.*Th.*493f. (so A.*Prom.*371 and 917). The documentation for these senses of πνοή in LSJ is inadequate and the organization (*s.v.* II, III) misleading, but the grossest

failing of the article is the parting shot: 'poet. (Pl.*Cra*.419d is no exception), once in Th. and freq. in later prose (v.supr.) for πνεῦμα.' The Platonic passage is certainly no exception (an incidental etymology; and Plato is virtually 'poet.' anyway), and 'later prose' is not relevant for us, but in addition to the Thucydides passage (Th.4.10.4, of the 'wind' from the bellows) there are (at least) about fifty instances of the word in the *classical* prose of Theophrastus and the Hippocratic corpus, *viz*: in Theophrastus, *HP* 3.4.2; *CP* 2.7.5, 3.13.2, 5.11.3, 5.12.2, 5.12.4, 6.11.7; *Ign*.28, 39; *Vent*.1, 11, 20, 21 (*bis*), 24, 29, 33, 35 (*bis*), 37, 39, 41 (*bis*), 43, 46, 48; also a Theophrastean passage in Porph.*Abst*.2 (*fr*.4 in J. Bernays, *Theophrastos' Schrift über Frommigkeit*, Berlin, 1866). And in Hippocrates: *Epid*.5.42 (dub.), 6.5.1, 7.98; *Morb*.2.6, 2.33, 2.59, 4.47, 4.57; *Mul*.2.133; *Nat.Puer*.12, 13, 14 (*bis*), 15 (*ter*), 17 (*ter*), 18 (*s.fin*.), 24, 29, 30. At Hp.*Nat.Puer*.24 and *Mul*.2.133, as stated, the word means 'hot vapour'; in the other passages, either 'breath' or 'blast of wind' (of which Th. *loc. cit.* and also Thphr.*Ign*.28 and 39, 'air current for a fire', are presumably to be regarded as special instances). Note finally that in a few of its prose occurrences the word is printed as πνοιή (the epic form) by some edd. (see e.g. Hp.*Mul*. 2.133 in Littré).

11 Nor is there any likelihood that ἐπιθύειν or the uncompounded θύειν can in normal usage denote simply *homicide*. Apparent instances are to be explained otherwise; θύειν at Hdt.1.216.2–3 and 3.99.2, for instance, refers to *cannibalistic* slaughter, i.e. killing for food, with sacrifice involved.

12 Cf. Rose *ad loc.*

13 Other instances of alliterative enforcement of interaction: (i) A.*Ag*.897f. στέγης στῦλον, with στῦλον the vehicle and στέγης an Aeschylean noun-glide: the place where pillars are and the place where Agamemnon is (στέγαις Ἀτρειδῶν, v.3). (ii) Simon.37.1–3, τετράγωνον vehicle, converging on τετυγμένον, a word as apt for the artefact, or whatever, that τετρ. implies (ἱμάτιον τετράγωνον Arist.*fr*.500, εἵματα...τετυγμένα *Il*.22.511; ἱρὸν τετράγωνον Hdt.2.91.2, νηὸς...ἐτέτυκτο *Il*.5.446) as for the ἄνδρ᾽ ἀγαθόν himself (ἄνδρα...ὃς ἄριστος ...τέτυκτο *Il*.6.7) or for his physical and mental faculties (εἰσί μοι...πόδες... καὶ νόος...τετυγμένος οὐδὲν ἀεικής *Od*.20.365f.).

Aural preparation and isolation

§61

Two contrasting possibilities of alliterative or assonantal interaction are worth recording. The first is 'preparation'. As alliterative link is a counterpart of link proper, so preparation proper has its counterpart on the aural level. In 'plain as a pikestaff' there is a link, enforcing, in this instance, a preexisting interactive relation between pivot ('plain') and vehicle ('pikestaff'). There is also an element of preparation: 'pikestaff', the vehicle, is made to chime in with its context, with something that is not the vehicle. It does not take much effort to see that, for instance, 'slings' is prepared in a comparable way in 'whether 'tis nobler in the mind to *s*uffer / The *s*lings...'. Contrast Thomas Lodge's 'love in my *b*osom like a *b*ee'. Here there is still, surely, the 'chime' of preparation, but no link. There is neither a pre-existing relation to enforce nor a new relation to create.[1]

Pure preparation is not particularly common in the corpus, at least with simple alliteration, the obvious reason being that words close enough for alliteration to be perceptible between them usually have some inherent relationship which the alliteration, in its linking capacity, will bring out. Among the instances of link given above, or those of them in which the vehicle picks up rather than initiates the alliteration,[2] a good few have a preparatory flavour, particularly those in which the vehicle (or its alliterative mate as well) is prominently articulated. So A.*Supp*.329:

πόνου δ' ἴδοις ἂν οὐδαμοῦ ταὐτὸν πτερόν.

Articulation seems to give the alliteration greater penetrability, helps it to 'stand up'.[3]

Preparation is not, by itself, associative. In Lodge's simile, 'love in my bosom like a bee', it matters neither which word carries the preparatory *b* nor what that word means; it matters only that there should be such a word. Nor, if the *b* is effectively detached from its carrier in this way, does it matter so much whether it is initial or not; and further, multiple alliteration – and/or assonance – might well be the likeliest way of introducing the aural character of the key word or words,[4] the vehicle. The result is that the most striking instances of preparation in the corpus involve a more intensive or elaborate patterning than linking requires or even permits. Thus Pi.*P*.10.71f.

ἐν δ' ἀγαθοῖσι κεῖται
πατρώιαι κεδναὶ πολίων κυβερνάσιες,

where the ode closes on the metaphorical κυβερνάσιες, prepared κ–π–κ–π–**κ**.[5] Again, A.*Ag*.390ff.

κακοῦ δὲ χαλκοῦ τρόπον
τρίβῳ τε καὶ προσβολαῖς
μελαμπαγὴς πέλει δικαιωθείς, ἐπεὶ
διώκει παῖς ποτανὸν ὄρνιν...

where the whole phonetic composition of διώκει παῖς is prefigured almost anagrammatically by δικαιωθεὶς ἐπεί and this whole enveloped by more π-alliteration. And again, Thgn.177f.

καὶ γὰρ ἀνὴρ πενίῃ δεδμημένος οὔτε τι εἰπεῖν
οὔθ' ἔρξαι δύναται, γλῶσσα δέ οἱ δέδεται

where δύναται...δέδεται involves alliteration, homoeoteleuton and isorrhythm, supported by syntactic parallel structure.

Such elaborate patterning is not in fact essential for a strong preparatory effect. Parallel structure on its own may be adequate; even a merely specious parallelism, as at A.*Ag*.1164ff., where an alliterative pair is placed on either side of a pause:

πέπληγμαι δ' ὑπ' αὖ δήγματι φοινίῳ
δυσαλγεῖ τύχᾳ μινυρὰ θρεομένας,
θραύματ' ἐμοὶ κλύειν.

For a more powerful impetus, rhythmical parallelism is a prerequisite. At A.*Ch*.149f., the vehicle ἐπανθίζειν is prepared in this way by ἐπισπένδω (with repetition of the prefix in lieu of alliteration):

τοιαῖσδ' ἐπ' εὐχαῖς τάσδ' ἐπισπένδω χοάς.
ὑμᾶς δὲ κωκυτοῖσ' ἐπανθίζειν νόμος.

And at A.*Pe*.747, where πέδαις is alliteratively prepared likewise, the innate drive of the trochaic metre is an additional factor:

καὶ πόρον μετερρύθμιζε
καὶ πέδαις σφυρηλάτοις
περιβαλὼν πολλὴν κέλευθον
ἤνυσεν πολλῷ στρατῷ.

In all such instances, the vehicle profits from the preparation in a way in which, of course, any word or word-group might – but, as usual with inter-action, the vehicle of an image is peculiarly well suited to profit: aural preparation, like other preparation, is a natural complement to its inherent prominence.[6]

The exact opposite of preparation is 'isolation', opposite, that is, except that the vehicle is still the beneficiary. The vehicle, possibly in prominent position, is set in relief by a sound pattern which precedes it and in which it does not itself take part. The consequent aural isolation simply gives the vehicle further prominence. Once again the function is one that seems better suited to other sound patterns than simple alliteration. In *Blood and the Moon* Yeats achieves such isolation by aural contrast between vehicle and a preceding triadic structure, where the triad is held together by homoeo-teleuton, developing into full rhyme, and isorrhythm. Such pronounced structuring makes any other articulation for the vehicle unnecessary:

I declare this tower is my symbol: I declare
This winding, gyring, spiring *treadmill* of a stair is my ancestral stair.[7]

Isolation is not the most powerful weapon in the poetic armoury, and, as one might predict, it is but rarely exploited in the corpus. One instance will suffice. Xenoph.7.1f.:

ἤδη δ' ἑπτά τ' ἔασι καὶ ἑξήκοντ' ἐνιαυτοὶ
βληστρίζοντες ἐμὴν φροντίδ' ἀν' Ἑλλάδα γῆν.

The only articulation for βληστρίζοντες ('tossing about')[8] that might support the isolation is initial position in the verse. Even so, the contrast between a string of vowel-initial or aspirate-initial words and the explosive cluster βλ- is arresting enough, particularly as neither of the cluster's constituent sounds occurs at all, initially or non-initially, in the preceding verse. The aural contrast, one notes, plays a co-operative part with the contrast of diction and tone between vehicle and the preceding context, the latter being as plain and matter-of-fact as it could possibly be.[9]

1 Cf. A.*fr.*461 ἔδυ δ' ἐς ἄντρον ἀσχέδωρος ὥς, *Supp.*223f. ἐν ἁγνῷ δ' ἑσμὸς ὡς πελειάδων... (*h–h*).
2 Presumably an alliteration involving *V* and *T* in that order might achieve a perceptible 'anticipation', though no significant instances are to hand. The use of sound patterning for preparatory purposes is not actually my own 'discovery', although I had formulated the principle before coming across what remain the only relevant remarks I know of, those of Porzig 76 (on A.*Supp.*40–8), made incidentally to a discussion of 'thematic' alliteration in Aeschylus (pp.76–81) – a discussion, however, that seems vastly to overrate the importance of such 'themes' and is also open to criticism on other grounds (notably imperceptibility; cf. Stanford *SG* 91f.). But Porzig's anticipation of the preparatory principle ('zunächst die einzelnen Leitlaute gegeben und erst am Schluss der Strophe das Thema' – i.e. the word prepared – 'eingeführt wird') deserves credit.
3 Cf. Porzig 77.
4 As is indeed the case with Porzig's instance (n.2 above).
5 The studied alliterative pattern is akin to other manifestations of hyperformality in this, Pindar's earliest ode: v.10 ἀνθρώπων τέλος ἀρχά τε δαίμονος (where δαίμονος is not, despite the chiasmus, dependent on ἀρχά), v.66 φιλέων φιλέοντ', ἄγων ἄγοντα (on which cf. Fennell).
6 Another instance of preparation enforced by parallelism, Pi.*O.*10.103f. ἰδέᾳ τε καλόν / ὥρᾳ τε κεκραμένον, but although the parallelism is intensively rhythmic as well as syntactic, the vehicle (κεκραμένον) is tame and the interaction, correspondingly, lacking in force. Note that inasmuch as alliteration is itself a kind of parallel structuring (above, p. 176), the two alliterative functions of preparation and link correspond to the two rôles of parallel structure remarked on earlier: to 'cushion' and to 'set up an association' (above, p. 72).
7 One might note that '*tread*mill' interacts with 'stair', as Mr A. G. Lee has observed to me.

8 Why LSJ give a 'metaph.' to Xenoph.45 (Diels–Kranz) but not to this usage, I cannot imagine.

9 Another comparable instance of isolation, A.*Ag.*1268 ἄλλην τιν' ἄτης ἀντ' ἐμοῦ πλουτίζετε (text as Page, *O.C.T.*). There is an early example, outside the corpus, Hes.*Op.*413 αἰεὶ δ' ἀμβολιεργὸς ἀνὴρ ἄτῃσι παλαίει. (The resemblance between these two self-contained verses could conceivably be due to more than coincidence.) Note also B.*fr.*14, where the two sections of an analogy have their beginnings demarcated Λυδία...λίθος and ἀνδρῶν...ἀρετάν, and finally Sol.3.28, where the extended vehicle (or the active part of it – see above, p. 96) is slightly energized as well as isolated by its unpredictable *h*-alliteration: οὔτω δημόσιον κακὸν ἔρχεται οἴκαδε...ὑψηλὸν δ' ὑπὲρ ἕρκος ὑπέρθορεν, ηὗρε δὲ πάντως....

Aural suggestion
§62

Finally, some marginal and rare possibilities, not so much of alliteration as of aural suggestivity in general, under which heading one may reasonably include *rhythmic* as well as phonetic manifestations. Several authors are represented, although Pindar is conspicuous by his absence. First, A.*Eu.*181, an oracular periphrasis from Apollo to the chorus of Furies. The Furies are to leave his precinct forthwith, under threat of a

πτηνὸν ἀργηστὴν ὄφιν.

ὄφιν is metaphor for 'arrow' and ἀργηστήν, 'flashing', aurally suggests ἀργῆς, 'serpent': the phrase ὄφις ἀργῆς actually occurs at Hp.*Epid.*5.86.[1] The effect is approximately that of a glide.[2]

A.*Prom.*902ff., the chorus, contemplating Io's distress, in prayer that no such fate overtake them:

μὴ
κρεισσόνων ἔρως ἄφυκτον ὄμμα προσδράκοι με.
ἀπόλεμος ὅδε γ' ὁ πόλεμος, ἄπορα πόριμος· οὐδ'
ἔχω τίς ἂν γενοίμαν.

The linguistic boldness of ἄπορα πόριμος ('source of resourceless ill'[3]) is noteworthy but almost pales beside the aural progression (in parallel structure) from the metaphorical πόλεμος to the literal πόριμος. The articulation of πόριμος contrives to give it something like the flavour of convergence, while the progression's irresistible fullness invites interpretation as an enactment: overwhelming force, feebly opposed. Compare a superficially quite different Shakespearian passage, the flagrantly well-knowr image from Enobarbus' account of Cleopatra on the river:

I will tell you:
The barge she sat in, like a burnish'd throne,
Burn'd on the water: the poop was beaten gold,
Purple the sails...[4]

In this instance, the interaction is in fact organized as if for convergence proper: 'the barge..., like..., burn'd...', as if '*T*, like *V*, *N*'. But 'burn'd' is *not* neutral, not in the same terminology as 'barge' (*T*) or 'throne' (*V*). 'Burn'd' is, of course, a separate metaphor, whose own immediate plausibility, as well as the impression of convergence to the simile, depends to an audacious extent on the aural logic of the 'burnish'd'/'burn'd' progression: granted 'burn-ish'd', then also 'burn'd'. (Elementary pedagogy: for 'burnish'd' read 'polish'd' and see the difference.) The effect, extraordinarily vivid when felt at all, is easier to define negatively than positively: not purely formal, certainly; not exactly argumentative, though pointed assertively like a convergence or even a link; enacting, conceivably – but it would be hard to say precisely what is being enacted. The most certain thing is that the overfamiliarity of the lines, without ultimately diminishing their power, tends to preclude a properly surprised response to what is, taken seriously, very surprising.

Sappho, *fr.*158, features a less surprising kind of enactment:

σκιδναμένας ἐν στήθεσιν ὄργας
μαψυλάκαν γλῶσσαν πεφύλαχθε.[5]

μαψυλάκαν...πεφύλαχθε: the repeated -υλακ- element creates an onomatopoeic effect in favour, not of the tenor, human feelings and reactions, but the vehicle, the barking dog. Effects of this kind are more commonly associated with patterning of rhythm than of 'sound' narrowly understood. Enjambement is one likely mechanism, as with Sol.23.1ff.:

οὐκ ἔφυ Σόλων βαθύφων οὐδὲ βουλήεις ἀνήρ·
ἐσθλὰ γὰρ θεοῦ διδόντος αὐτὸς οὐκ ἐδέξατο.
περιβαλὼν δ' ἄγραν ἀγασθεὶς οὐκ ἐπέσπασεν μέγα
δίκτυον,...

The rhythmic stretching-over and pulling-back on δίκτυον mimes the hauling in of the net – that would be the natural interpretation. For such an effect to materialize, 'energetic' subject matter and a rhythm to match are requisite, as here. Compare Arch.58.1ff., a disquisition on the gods:

πολλάκις μὲν ἐκ κακῶν
ἄνδρας ὀρθοῦσιν μελαίνῃ κειμένους ἐπὶ χθονί,

πολλάκις δ' ἀνατρέπουσι καὶ μάλ' εὖ βεβηκότας
ὑπτίους, . . .⁶

The over- (or up-)turning is presented with a still greater mimetic vividness: the regular syncopation entailed by the transition from one ordered rhythmic run to another corresponds with the movement of sense from εὖ βεβηκότας to ὑπτίους precisely.⁷

The aural effects discussed in this section are mostly of a kind that notoriously rouses a lack of response in certain readers. I can only say that the foregoing instances seem to me as persuasive as any.

1 ὄφιν for 'arrow' is itself oracularly metaleptic: ἰός, both 'venom' and 'arrow', is the missing link.

2 Compare the aural play from the 'real' Apollo at Orac.7.1 P–W: αἰετὸς ἐν πέτρῃσι. . . . The allegory alludes to Ἠετίων. . .ἐκ Πέτρης (Hdt.5.92β.1), and the fact that it does so allude is revealed, as is generally recognized, by the aural suggestion; its function is explanatory. Partly parallel, but rather more tenuous, A.Supp.283, where the V term τεκτόνων plausibly evokes one of its possible tenor 'equivalents', namely (τῶν) τεκόντων. The image to which the interaction belongs (begetting and family resemblances: coin striking) is not in fact allegorical, though not exactly transparent either, and the effect is not so much to explain what the 'real' subject is as to give the vehicle an obscure rightness, a kind of restricted support.

3 Plumptre's translation.

4 *Antony and Cleopatra* II.2.

5 Text as suggested (one suggestion among several) by Bergk. Doubt surrounds the word order of the second verse and the part of φυλάσσω involved (see Bergk's apparatus). Neither problem seems likely to impinge on the interaction, and so I have simply adopted what I take to be the most attractive *exempli gratia* restoration.

6 Punctuation as West (*fr.*130 in his numeration).

7 Especially as εὖ βεβηκότας and ἀνατρέπουσι are in fact neutral, hence differ from ὑπτίους in immediacy, albeit only slightly (see Appendix XIV). Archilochus' placing of ὑπτίους may be supposed to have been influenced by *Il*.24.10f. ἄλλοτ' ἐπὶ πλευρὰς κατακείμενος, ἄλλοτε δ' αὖτε/ὕπτιος, ἄλλοτε δὲ πρηνής: ὕπτιος does not usually occupy the first foot in early epic, but the fourth.

9 Combinations

Preparation
§63

I have reserved for discussion here certain passages containing more than a single interaction. Not all combinations are significant, though. For instance, in Aeschylus' ὅταν κλύδων κακῶν ἐπέλθῃ, one would not be justified in seeing anything but an arbitrary conjunction of aural link and subdued convergence.[1] The significant combinations in the Greek corpus are of several kinds, of which the best attested and conceptually simplest comprises those instances with a broadly or cumulatively *preparatory* effect in favour of the vehicle.[2]

Pi.*P*.4.148ff., Jason to Pelias:

> μῆλά τε γάρ τοι ἐγὼ
> καὶ βοῶν ξανθὰς ἀγέλας ἀφίημ' ἀγρούς τε πάντας, τοὺς ἀπούρας
> ἁμετέρων τοκέων νέμεαι πλοῦτον πιαίνων.

Vehicle, the expressive and nicely articulated πιαίνων. Preparation, extragrammatical and multiple: a shower of hints from μῆλα (πίονα μῆλα *Il*.12. 319), from βοῶν (βοῦν...πίονα *Il*.2.402f.), from ἀγρούς (πίονες ἀγροί *Il*.23.832), and climactically, with alliterative enforcement, from πλοῦτον (πλουσίοιν καὶ πίονοιν Pl.*R*.422b).[3]

Pi.*P*.10.27ff., the first extant expression (498 B.C.) of one of Pindar's favourite topics for imagery, the limits of human attainment:[4]

> ὁ χάλκεος οὐρανὸς οὔ ποτ' ἀμβατὸς αὐτῷ ·
> ὅσαις δὲ βροτὸν ἔθνος ἀγλαΐαις ἁπτόμεσθα, περαίνει πρὸς ἔσχατον
> πλόον.

'Voyage of life': vehicle πλόον, again nicely articulated; preparation outside the grammar from ἀμβατός, then from περαίνει. As regards ἀμβατός, the preparation comes not from the denotation, 'climbable', but from a well-established connotation: ἀναβάντες ἐπέπλεον (*Il*.1.312).[5] With περαίνει, the preparation, alliteratively enforced, is again through a connotation – the associations of sea-faring, derived, as if by re-etymology, from the verb's cognates, πέραν ('*across*,...esp. of water')[6] and περάω ('*traverse*, freq. of water').[7]

COMBINATIONS (§63)

Pi.*O*.12.1ff.:

> Λίσσομαι, παῖ Ζηνὸς Ἐλευθερίου,
> Ἱμέραν εὐρυσθενέ' ἀμφιπόλει, σώτειρα Τύχα.
> τὶν γὰρ ἐν πόντῳ κυβερνῶνται θοαὶ
> νᾶες, ἐν χέρσῳ τε λαιψηροὶ πόλεμοι
> κἀγοραὶ βουλαφόροι. αἵ γε μὲν ἀνδρῶν
> πόλλ' ἄνω, τὰ δ' αὖ κάτω
> ψεύδη μεταμώνια τάμνοισαι κυλίνδοντ' ἐλπίδες.

Multiple preparation with some specifying force. The vehicle, τάμνοισαι κυλίνδοντ' (maritime), is prepared first, extra-grammatically, by ἐν πόντῳ... νᾶες, which provides also the concrete ('specifying') detail of the location and essential elements of the scene; prepared likewise and further detailed by μεταμώνια, meaning 'vain' or 'idle', but re-etymologized as connected with ἄνεμος;[8] and introduced by an explanatory glide, ἄνω...κάτω. These last words suit the tossing waves well enough (ἄνω τε καὶ κάτω ῥεῖ Pl.*Phlb*.43a), but are commonly used as proverbial of violent change in human affairs: τὸ λεγόμενον ἄνω κάτω πάντα (Pl.*Tht*.153d).[9]

A.*Supp*.996ff., Danaus to his daughters:

> ὑμᾶς δ' ἐπαινῶ μὴ καταισχύνειν ἐμέ,
> ὥραν ἐχούσας τήνδ' ἐπίστρεπτον βροτοῖς.
> τέρειν' ὀπώρα δ' εὐφύλακτος οὐδαμῶς·
> θῆρες δὲ κηραίνουσι...

The analogy vehicle, whose key term is ὀπώρα, pivots on ὥραν, suggesting equally a season of the year and a period of human life, ἢ ὥρην τινὰ τοῦ ἐνιαυτοῦ ἢ τῆς ἡλικίης τῆς τοῦ ἀνθρώπου (Hp.*Nat.Hom*.2); and, within 'a period of human life', focusing specifically on the beauty of youth, τῆς σῆς ὥρας ἀπολαύσονται, ἀλλά...πρεσβυτέρῳ γενομένῳ... (Pl.*Phdr*.234a);[10] and, within 'a season of the year', focusing specifically on fruit in its season: ὃς ἄν...ὀπώρας γεύσηται...πρὶν ἐλθεῖν τὴν ὥραν (Pl.*Lg*.844d). At the same time, ὥραν prepares ὀπώρα, extra-grammatically, by virtue of the sense 'summer' (or 'autumn') held by the latter, albeit held here only as an otherwise irrelevant connotation: τῆς ἀμπέλου τῆς ἀγρίας ῥίζα...τέμνεται...πᾶσαν ὥραν ὀπώρας δὲ μάλιστα (Thphr. *HP* 9.20.3).[11] Finally, τέρεινα is a glide: τερένας ἄνθος ὀπώρας (Alc.397) and παρθένος...τέρεινα (Hippon.79).[12]

Pi.*fr*.75.6:

> ἰοδέτων λάχετε στεφάνων τᾶν τ' ἐαριδρόπων ἀοιδᾶν...

195   7-2

Garlands and songs; the songs are the dithyrambs of Athens. The -δρόπων of ἐαριδρόπων is the vehicle[13] and the beneficiary of diverse preparation and introduction. In the first place ἰοδέτων, in meticulously parallel structure, is preparatory, -δέτων aurally and ἰο- semantically: ἄνθεα δρέπομεν (*h.Cer.* 425).[14] Then the ἐαρι- of ἐαριδρόπων itself yields a glide of effortless simplicity: the actual season when the songs are sung[15] and the season of flowers, ἦρος ἀνθεμόεντος (Alc.367).[16]

Pi.*N.*11.19–32:

> Ἀρισταγόραν...
> ἐστεφάνωσαν πάλᾳ καὶ μεγαυχεῖ παγκρατίῳ.
>
> ·　·　·
>
> ἀλλὰ βροτῶν τὸν μὲν κενεόφρονες αὖχαι
> ἐξ ἀγαθῶν ἔβαλον· τὸν δ' αὖ
> 　καταμεμφθέντ' ἄγαν
> ἰσχὺν οἰκείων παρέσφαλεν καλῶν
> χειρὸς ἕλκων ὀπίσσω θυμὸς ἄτολμος ἐών.

The account of the wrestling match between Odysseus and Ajax in *Iliad* 23 is not long, but suffices to authorize for Pindar, and to illustrate for us, the technical vocabulary alluded to here:

23.714　τετρίγει δ' ἄρα νῶτα θρασειάων ἀπὸ χειρῶν
　　　　ἑλκόμενα στερεῶς...
719　οὔτ' Ὀδυσεὺς δύνατο σφῆλαι οὔδει τε πελάσσαι
　　　οὔτ' Αἴας...
727　κὰδ δ' ἔβαλ' ἐξοπίσω· ἐπὶ δὲ στήθεσσιν...
　　　κάππεσε...

It does not seem to have been recognized that Pindar's image is a wrestling image, the reason presumably being that the technical use of certain operative words has itself not received full recognition. The vehicle is χειρὸς ἕλκων ὀπίσσω, of which χειρός and ὀπίσσω (cf. Homer's ἐξοπίσω) are clear enough. For ἕλκων, primary revealing passages are Homer's νῶτα...ἀπὸ χειρῶν ἑλκόμενα and ἀκροχειρισμός ('finger-wrestling')...τὰς σάρκας ἕλκει ἄνω (Hp.*Vict.*2.64). Presumably from such usages developed the generalized sense of the verb visible here and visible also at Pi.*N.*4.94 ἀπάλαιστος... ἕλκειν, with which compare Hes.*Sc.*301f. ἐμάχοντο πύξ τε καὶ ἑλκηδόν, evidently equivalent to the ἢ πύξ ἠὲ πάλῃ of *Od.*8.206.[17] ἕλκων, then, is a main term of the vehicle, and ἐξ...ἔβαλον is preparatory to it. The denotation is 'deprive of', much as in ὕβρις...ἐξ ἀγαθῶν ἐς κακότητ' ἔβαλεν (sc. ἡμᾶς) (Thgn.836),[18] and at the same time the verb alludes to the arena, as we see from Homer's ἔβαλ' ἐξοπίσω and from ἐκβάλλει in Sophocles' question on the love goddess: τίν' οὐ παλαίουσ' ἐς τρὶς ἐκβάλλει θεῶν; (fr.941.13).[19] The preparation adds a vivid detail, and a comparable particularization results from παρέσφαλεν, whose primary sense here, in accordance with the grammatical construction, is like that of the uncompounded verb in σφαλέντες...τῆς δόξης (Th.4.85.2),[20] or the otherwise compounded verb in μὴ...σφᾶς ἀποσφήλειε πόνοιο (Il.5.567). A connotation of the verb points again to the wrestling; Homer's σφῆλαι οὔδει τε πελάσσαι and Aristophanes' σφαλείς...παλαίσμασιν (Ran.689) are to hand.

One further interaction is involved, in fact the primary one, the form of my interpretation being dictated by the present state of comprehension, not by the actual order of events. Despite the analysis given above, the words that denote or connote wrestling might, by themselves, conceivably suggest other spheres, horse riding for instance: ἔλασε...ἐκ δ' ἔβαλ' ἵππων (Il. 11.109),[21] καὶ εἰ ἕλκοι τις αὐτόν (the rider), ἧττον ἂν σφάλλοιτο (X.Eq. 7.7).[22] It is simply the recent invocation[23] of the literal πάλᾳ καὶ...παγκρατίῳ that directs us, extra-grammatically, to the 'right' location of χειρὸς ἕλκων ὀπίσσω, genuinely specifies the vehicle.[24]

A.Ag.1178ff.:

καὶ μὴν ὁ χρησμὸς οὐκέτ' ἐκ καλυμμάτων
ἔσται δεδορκὼς νεογάμου νύμφης δίκην·
λαμπρὸς δ' ἔοικεν ἡλίου πρὸς ἀντολὰς
πνέων ἐσᾴξειν...

The interaction has received much attention but never, seemingly, a fully adequate interpretation. There are, of course, two separate images and two separate vehicles, ἐκ καλυμμάτων... and ἡλίου.... The interaction concerns λαμπρός and, remarkably enough, four separate senses of that word. For the first image λαμπρός has the senses 'clear', of the χρησμός (λαμπρῶς κοὐδὲν αἰνικτηρίως A.Prom.833),[25] and 'bright', like the bride's uncovered face: νυμφίον...λαμπρόν (Ar.Pax 859), τᾶς...ἐρατόν τε βᾶμα κἀμάρυχμα λάμπρον...προσώπω (Sapph.16.17f.).[26] The product is postponed convergence to this first image and, as it turns out, a bridge to the next,[27] whose vehicle λαμπρός prepares, outside the grammar, and introduces by a glide. λαμπρός is now 'keen' like the wind, πνέων (ὅταν νότος λαμπρὸς πνεύσῃ Thphr.HP 6.3.4);[28] 'bright' like the sun (ἥλιος...λαμπρός Thphr.Sign. 50);[29] and, as before, 'clear' like the subject, χρησμός. One is rarely tempted to invoke characterization, in the full sense, as a function of style in earlier Greek poetry, but this intense concentration seems not merely apt for a prophetess versed in oracular equivocations, but somehow suggestive of her unique access to the complexities of the events that are now reaching their fulfilment.

1 See above, pp. 109 and 179. As it happens, even this arbitrary conjunction (aural link and subdued verbal convergence) has its interest, being, apparently, the object of a uniquely Aeschylean predilection:

Pe.599f. ὅταν κλύδων κακῶν ἐπέλθῃ

Supp.345 πρύμναν πόλεος ὧδ' ἐστεμμένην (see above, pp. 109 and 179)

Supp.469 κακῶν δὲ πλῆθος ποταμὸς ὡς ἐπέρχεται (pp. 105 and 178)

Prom.1015f. κακῶν τρικυμία ἔπεισ' ἄφυκτος (unarticulated; see above, pp. 136, n.7 and 179).

The predilection prompts the thought that the textually suspect Pe.814f. may conceal another instance:

κοὐδέπω κακῶν κρηπὶς ὕπεστιν.

But no existing interpretation of this text nor any suggested alternative text is wholly adequate.

2 Even here I have thought it best to treat some 'combinations' under separate headings. E.g. at A.Ag.847–50, the conjunction of preparation (χρονίζον, see above, p. 154) and glide (φαρμάκων, see above, p. 100) for παιωνίων does not seem to me a genuinely creative combination, in which the whole is more than the sum of its proverbial parts.

3 So, respectively, e.g. Od.9.217; Anan.5.9, Arist.HA 595b.6ff.; Od.4.757; and, vis-à-vis πλοῦτος, cf. Hes.Th.969ff. Πλοῦτον ἐγείνατο...Κρήτης ἐν πίονι δήμῳ (the only proper place), Phoc.7.1, A.Ag.820 and the interactive rôle of πιαινό-μενον at Pi.P.2.56, anticipating τὸ πλουτεῖν (see above, p. 156, n.5).

4 And a favourite topic for interaction too; cf. O.3.43f. and I.3/4.29ff. (see above, p. 137, n.8) and N.4.69ff. (above, p. 120, n.5).

5 ἀναβαίνειν, 'embark': likewise, Pi.P.2.62, Th.4.44.6 etc.

6 LSJ s.v. I.1.

7 LSJ s.v. περάω (A) I.1. The denotative sense of Pindar's περαίνει is actually problematic. The verb cannot and does not mean 'travel' or 'pass over', pace Bowra (Pindar 305) and others. The mistake perhaps derives from Arat.288f. οὔτε κεν ἠοῖ / πολλὴν πειρήνειας... (referring to a journey by sea) and an ill-judged scholion thereon: οὔτε γὰρ πολλὴν θάλασσαν δυνατὸς εἶ διαπερᾶσαι διὰ μιᾶς ἡμέρας – whereas the unexpressed noun is surely ὁδόν (cf. Ar.Ran.403 and, for the ellipse, e.g. X.An.6.3.16), not the θαλάσσην of v.287. What the verb can and does mean is 'accomplish': πάντα πεπείρανται Od.12.37, οὐδὲν περανῶ Hp.Vict.1.1 (so Pi.I.8.24, S.Aj.22, X.Cyr.4.5.38 etc.). The sense is therefore: 'whatever we put our hands to, he accomplishes (it) – right to the end of the voyage' (cf. Schroeder ad loc.). The odd epexegesis may, however, additionally evoke the separate and not inapt construction περαίνειν πρός, with its idea of physical limit: Melissus 5 εἰ μὴ ἓν εἴη, περανεῖ πρὸς ἄλλο, 'if it were not one, it would have a limit, would be bounded by something else' (cf. Hp. Vict.1.10, Arist.Ph.203b.21, Eudem.19.15–17 Spengel). 'To the edge of the world and no further', would be the implication, but activated.

8 See LSJ s.v.

9 Cf. A.Eu.650, Hdt.3.3.3, Ar.Nub.616, Dinarch.3.17, D.9.36, Men.fr.7.

10 So ὥρα at Mimn.2.9, Pi.O.10.104, Ar.Av.1724, Th.6.54.2.

11 So Alcm.20.1f., Ar.Av.709.

12 τέρην of soft fruit, vegetation: likewise, *Od*.9.449, Hes.*fr*.70.21, Pi.*N*.5.6, Melanipp.1.6. Of girls: likewise, Thgn.261, E.*Cyc*.515, also Arch.*P.Col.ined*.4; the sense is effectively metonymic from τέρενα χρόα (*Il*.4.237 etc.), cf. Cratin. 302 τέρεν τὸ χρωτίδιον (of a girl). The word is not found in prose in any sense.

13 Not a cliché. δρέπειν in this context only at Pi.*fr*.6b(f).3 and 52m.5, Ar.*Ran*.1300 (Aeschylus talking), Pl.*Ion* 534b.

14 Cf. A.*Supp*.663, Pi.*fr*.52m.4f., E.*IA* 1299, Hdt.2.92.2.

15 Note ἔαρ in v.15 and cf. Pickard-Cambridge–Webster 21.

16 Cf. the stock ἄνθεσιν εἰαρινοῖσιν, *Il*.2.89, *Cypr*.4.2, *h.Cer*.401, Thgn.1276, Simon.76.2. For a direct association of δρέπειν (not a very common word) and 'spring', cf. the flowers in Hippolytus' garden of innocence (E.*Hipp*.73ff.), frequented by the ἠρινὴ μέλισσα (v.77) and to be picked (δρέπεσθαι, v.81) by the pure alone.

17 The technical sense of ἕλκειν is recognized by, among others, Rumpel (p.151), Slater (p.165), and Fennell on Pi.*N*.4.94 and Russo on Hes.*Sc*.302, but neither the Hippocratic nor the present Pindaric passage seem to have been adduced. Slater adduces also ἑλκύσαι at Pi.*N*.7.103, which is possible, despite a lack of any decisive contextual support; the present ἕλκων, however, he is content to render merely by 'drag' and misguidedly glosses the two wrestling instances that he does recognize with βιάζεσθαι, a word with no wrestling associations. In an article on Greek wrestling in *JHS*, 1905, 14ff., E. N. Gardiner knew of no authority for the verb's technical use 'except a wrong reading in a passage of Lucian' (p.28) and contrived to cite the *Iliad* passage without relevant comment.

18 So ἐκβάλλειν at X.*Cyr*.1.3.9, *An*.7.5.6; S.*Aj*.808, *El*.649; E.*Or*.168; cf. also Isoc.4.70, A.*Prom*.203, 910.

19 On ἐκβάλλει Pearson notes, 'seems to be a technical term...for a decisive throw', but knows no Greek parallels.

20 So Th.7.66.3, A.*Eu*.717, E.*Ph*.758. παρασφάλλειν is rather rare.

21 So *Il*.5.39, 8.403, 417.

22 Cf. X.*Eq*.3.9, 8.11; *Il*.16.409.

23 A strictly unpredictable one. The poem is not an epinician but an ode in honour of Aristagoras' installation as *Prytanis* at Tenedos.

24 For this extra-grammatical specifying, cf. above, p. 154, n.6.

25 So Hp.*Art*.58 προρρήματα λαμπρά, Th.8.67.3, E.*Heracl*.864.

26 λαμπρός is standard of human complexion (as Hdt.4.75.3, Hp.*Aer*.24 and *Mul*.2.184) and seems to be specially associated with the good looks of youthful or prenuptial complexion; cf., besides Ar. and Sapph. cited above, Ar.*Nub*.1011 (χροιὰν λαμπράν, aligned with, among other things, πόσθην μικράν), Th.6.54.2 ('Αρμοδίου ὥρᾳ ἡλικίας λαμπροῦ), Chaerem.1.3f. The word cannot of itself mean 'uncovered', as Fraenkel translates. He and others are oddly vague about its connection with the vehicle of the first image.

27 For this bridging function, which is not strictly interaction in my sense, see Appendix IX.

28 So Hdt.2.96.3; Alex.46.2; Arist.*Mete*.361b.8; Thphr.*CP* 4.13.4, *Vent*.8, 28 and

passim; cf. Ar.*Eq*.430 and 760, D.25.57. The operativeness of this sense here is widely recognized, e.g. by Headlam 437, Fraenkel, Smith 60.

29 Not exactly a rare collocation (likewise, *Il*.1.605, A.*Ag*.658 etc., etc.). Yet its relevance for this passage is generally ignored (but noted by Smith 60).

Pivot and convergence
§64

To be effective, a combination need not consist in functions operating alike in favour of the whole image or of one of its components. One effective combination is that of pivot, or glide, and convergence. Both ends of the image, so to speak, are favoured; the vehicle is introduced at the beginning and the whole image resolved at the end. Paradigm, A.*Th*.412f.:

σπαρτῶν δ' ἀπ' ἀνδρῶν, ὧν Ἄρης ἐφείσατο,
ῥίζωμ' ἀνεῖται, κάρτα δ' ἔστ' ἐγχώριος.

Eteocles, in a proud and colourful speech in favour of the warrior Melanippus, moves forcefully into the vehicle, ῥίζωμ' ἀνεῖται, and out from the vehicle to a majestically punning closure. The organization is meticulous, with σπαρτῶν pivotal in parallel (metrical) structure to ῥίζωμ', both being in positions of prominence, and ἐγχώριος in articulated convergence. In the first place, Melanippus can claim two related distinctions: that of his heroic ancestry, from the (literally) 'sown' men, οἱ σπαρτοί, and that of being a true native in the country, ἐγχώριος in its usual sense. Secondly, σπαρτῶν, ῥίζωμα and ἐγχώριος allude in the most overt manner possible to a common sphere: ὅτι ἄν...σπαρῇ διείρει τὴν ῥίζαν (Thphr.*HP* 1.7.3) and – ἐγχώριος by re-etymology rather than actual usage – πίονα χῶρον...σπείρειν (Hes.*Op*.390f.), συμβάλλεται πρὸς βαθυρριζίαν...ἡ τῆς χώρας φύσις (Thphr.*HP* 1.7.1).[1] The pivot functions with the certainty of genuine simplicity, and the triumphant 'argument' is carried through with evident relish.

A similar combination characterizes A.*Ag*.524ff., though the tone of this passage is greatly different:

ἀλλ' εὖ νιν ἀσπάσασθε, καὶ γὰρ οὖν πρέπει,
Τροίαν κατασκάψαντα τοῦ δικηφόρου
Διὸς μακέλλῃ, τῇ κατείργασται πέδον.

Vehicle μακέλλῃ, introduced by κατασκάψαντα: τὸ ἀστὺ κατέσκαψε (Hdt. 7.156.2)[2] and κατασκάψαντα ἐπὶ θάτερα τῆς ἀμπέλου (Thphr.*HP* 4.13.5).[3] Then κατείργασται πέδον as convergence, the verb in its senses 'subdue', as νῆσον... ὑποδεξάμενος κατεργάσεσθαι (Hdt.6.2.1),[4] and 'cultivate', as κατεργαζομένη...ἡ γῆ (Thphr.*CP* 3.1.3);[5] the noun in its particular uses 'physical site', πέρσαι...τὸ Δαρδάνου πέδον (S.*Ph*.69),[6] and scene of vegetation or object of cultivation, ξηρὸν πέδον ἄκαρπον αὐχμῷ (E.*fr.* 898.7f.).[7] The neutral terms here have a certain specifying significance beyond their formal functions, μακέλλη being set inescapably in its full agricultural context, so that the destruction of Troy should be felt to be given in terms of cultivation with the implicit promise of growth. This said, the irony is too apparent to need further comment.

It is worth noting that the pivot/convergence combination can occur, still recognizably, in miniature. The simile at A.*Supp*.429ff. provides one instance. The whole thing is enormously simpler; but there is no loss of overall coherence, rather (εὐσυνόπτως) the opposite:

> ἀπὸ βρετέων βίᾳ
> δίκας ἀγομέναν
> ἱππαδὸν ἀμπύκων,

ἱππαδόν vehicle; ἀγομέναν pivot: τὴν δ᾽ ἀεκαζομένην ἦγεν (*h.Cer*.30) and οἴχεται ἵππον ἄγων (*Il*.23.577);[8] and convergence on ἀμπύκων, the word for a woman's headband and a horse's headband.[9] Compare a cameo in metaphor, Xenoph.1.5 (preparations for the banquet):

> ἄλλος δ᾽ εὐῶδες μύρον ἐν φιάλῃ παρατείνει·
> κρατὴρ δ᾽ ἕστηκεν μεστὸς εὐφροσύνης·
> ἄλλος δ᾽ οἶνος ἑτοῖμος, ὃς οὔποτέ φησι προδώσειν.

Vehicle οὔποτέ φησι (*sic*); pivot ἑτοῖμος, implying the types ὀνείαθ᾽ ἑτοῖμα (*Il*.9.91)[10] and ὁ μὲν...ἦν ἕτοιμος (Hdt.1.10.1); convergence on προδώσειν, the verb having an idiomatic use for the 'failure' of things, including the running dry of liquids: οὐδέν μοι θῶμα...προδοῦναι τὰ ῥέεθρα (Hdt. 1.187.1).[11]

At the opposite pole, Theognis 213ff., an ostentatious set-piece:

> Θυμέ, φίλους κατὰ πάντας ἐπίστρεφε ποικίλον ἦθος,
> ὀργὴν συμμίσγων ἥντιν᾽ ἕκαστος ἔχει·
> πουλύπου ὀργὴν ἴσχε πολυπλόκου, ὃς ποτὶ πέτρῃ
> τῇ προσομιλήσῃ τοῖος ἰδεῖν ἐφάνη.
> νῦν μὲν τῇδ᾽ ἑφέπου, τοτὲ δ᾽ ἀλλοῖος χρόα γίνου.
> κρέσσων τοι σοφίῃ γίνεται ἀτροπίης.

The interaction is actually more striking than the image itself. The vehicle is – primarily and principally – πουλύπου, to which ποικίλον is pivotal:

'crafty' (Προμηθέα ποικίλον Hes.*Th*.510f.) and 'many-coloured' (πολυπόδων...ἄλλοι...ποικίλοι Arist.*HA* 525a.13ff.).[12] One does not have to be particularly sensitive on the aural dimension to perceive that the interaction, ποικίλον/πουλύπου, is strongly enforced by alliteration[13] and that the sound-patterning is continued massively in πολυπλόκου, where it again enforces interaction, this time the convergence: 'full of tricks' (φρένας ἔχουσα καὶ πολύπλοκον αὖ νόημα Ar.*Th*.463)[14] and 'of many convolutions' (δράκοντα...σπείραις πολυπλόκοις E.*Med*.480f.).[15] '*The* convergence' is in fact an overstatement. This elaborate image is finally and formally resolved, after a due return to the tenor and its σοφίη, on the cheerfully argumentative ἀτροπίης, a rare formation presumably coined *ad hoc* to yield the senses 'inflexibility, lack of savoir-faire' (μήποτε...τρόπος...σημαίνει τὸ ἦθος Antisth.51 Caizzi)[16] and 'no change of colour' (τὸ σῶμα ἀλλοιοτροπέει καὶ γίνεται ὠχρόν Hp.*Int*.37).[17]

1 χωρ- may not be quite as 'earthy' as γῆ, but χώρα in particular is commonly used of soil, e.g. at A.*Eu*.817, *SIG* 22.25 (*Darei epistula*, early v B.C.), Thphr. *HP* 8.6.2; LSJ ignore the use. ἐν χώρᾳ would by itself doubtless suggest 'on the spot' or 'in the place' or 'in the country', but obviously could mean 'inside...' rather than 'on the surface of...'. Thphr.*HP* 1.7.1, quoted above, continues: ἐν γὰρ ταῖς τοιαύταις (sc. χώραις) πορρωτέρω καὶ μείζους αἱ αὐξήσεις (of roots).

2 The usual sense of the verb; see LSJ *s.v.* The *N* status of κατασκάψαντα is noted by Ole Smith 27f., though the notice is misleadingly included in a discussion of *V–V* structures (pp.13–32).

3 For the grammatical construction of soil dug as direct object, cf. Philem.71.6, E.*fr*.188, X.*Oec*.16.15, Thphr.*CP* 3.20.4.

4 See LSJ *s.v.* 1.2.b. For κατεργάζεσθαι passive in this sense, cf. Hdt.1.201.

5 So ἐργάζεσθαι Hdt.1.17.3, X.*Cyr*.1.6.11, Hp.*Vict*.4.90.

6 Similarly Pi.*fr*.52i(A).22f.; A.*Prom*.1; Ar.*Nu*.573. The evidence for πέδον in any sense is, of course, purely verse and largely post-epic.

7 Similarly *h.Cer*.455, B.9.5, A.*Eu*.786; cf. n.6 above.

8 So, respectively, *Il*.20.194, Hdt.1.5.2; X.*Eq*.6.4, A.*Prom*.465.

9 ἄμπυξ of a woman's headband: *Il*.22.469, E.*Hec*.465; so χρυσάμπυξ Hes.*Th*. 916, Pi.*P*.3.89, B.5.13; εὐάμπυξ Pi.*fr*.70a.13; λιπαράμπυξ Pi.*N*.7.15 (and cf. *fr*.52b.99); ἱμεράμπυξ B.17.9. For the horse-ἄμπυξ, see above, p. 51, n.11. The neutral status of the word is recognized by Dumortier 155, Stanford *AS* 77. (Contrast incidentally the similar image at A.*Th*.326ff. τὰς δὲ κεχειρωμένας ἄγεσθαι...ἱππηδὸν πλοκάμων, where interaction is confined to the pivotal ἄγεσθαι.) Another instance of the combination, but with only a light convergence, A.*Eu*.155ff.: vehicle διφρηλάτου; pivot ἔτυψεν (τύπτε δὲ κέντρῳ Thgn.847 and τὸν δ' ἄχος...τύψε *Il*.19.125, so Hdt.3.64.1, Pi.*N*.1.53, E.*Ion*776, Thphr.*Lass*.18); convergence on φρένας (*qua T*, 'mind'; *qua V*, relevantly concrete, as in τυπτόμενοι εἰς τὰς φρένας γελῶσιν Arist.*Probl*.965a.15f., cf.

*Od.*9.301, *Il.*16.481 etc.), but fading away at λοβόν, which is not immediately operative in tenor terms.

10 So e.g. ἕτοιμον ἔστω τὸ κλύσμα Hp.*Morb.*3.14; not an especially well-attested use.

11 So Hdt.8.52.1 and (trans.) Philyll.18, X.*HG* 5.2.5, D.52.13, cf. Ar.*Nub.*1500.

12 See above, ooo. The neutral status of ποικίλον is noted by Campbell *ad loc.* Note that the 'official' ground term here is ὀργήν in 215.

13 Alliteration seems to have been traditionally associated with the poulp; see Appendix iv.

14 So Ar.*Th.*435; πολυπλοκία Thgn.67; δολοπλόκος Sapph.1.2, Thgn.1386, Simon.36.9; δολοπλοκία Thgn.226; πλέκειν Ar.*V.*644, A.*Ch.*220, Pl.*Smp.*203d.

15 Sim. Hp.*Oss.*17 πολυπλόκους φλέβας (πλέκειν likewise, Pl.*Tim.*77e); πλέκειν of body movements, Hp.*Mochl.*25 (where πλέξαντα is apparently equivalent to ἐνείραντα τὸν πῆχυν μεσηγὺ τῶν μηρῶν in the corresponding passage in *Art.* 70), Anacr.94, A.*Eu.*259; cf. πουλύπους. . . πλεκταῖς ἀνάγκαις Xenarch.19. The neutral status of πολυπλ. is noted by van Groningen and Campbell. Note that (as van Groningen perceives) προσομιλήσῃ is intrusive, albeit clumsily so. The word is used for *human* associations: X.*HG* 1.1.30 οἱ πρὸς Ἑρμοκράτην προσομιλοῦντες. Pindar's parallel image (*fr.*43) has the uncompounded verb in this sense: ποντίου θηρὸς πετραίου χρωτὶ μάλιστα νόον προσφέρων πάσαις πολίεσσιν ὁμίλει. LSJ's rendering for Thgn.'s use, 'cling to' (*s.v.* προσομιλέω ii) is wholly arbitrary; the 'parallels' cited there are a millennium later and worthless. The nearest thing to a real parallel is Simon.88 ἄνθεσιν ὁμιλεῖν ὁ Σιμωνίδης φησὶ τὴν μέλιτταν (Plutarch), where it is not even certain that ὁμ. belongs to the poet.

16 'Lack of savoir-faire' seems to me nearer the likely meaning; I interpret the ἀτρόποισι. . .ἔπεσι of Pi.*N.*7.103f. similarly. ἀτροπίη is therefore opposite to πολυτροπίη, 'cunning' (Hdt.2.121ε.3), from πολύτροπος, 'ingenious' (*Od.*1.1, *h.Merc.*13 and 439, Th.3.83.3), and aligned with δύστροπος in Democr.100 (cf. van Groningen) ὅτεῳ μὴ διαμένουσιν ἐπὶ πολλὸν οἱ πειραθέντες φίλοι, δύστροπος. Also related are κακοτροπία at Th.3.83.1 ('depravity') and ἤθεος εὐτροπίη at Democr.57. Antisthenes' remark about τρόπος quoted in the text continues, εὔτροπος γὰρ ἀνὴρ ὁ τὸ ἦθος ἔχων εἰς τὸ εὖ τετραμμένον, this being said apropos his discussion of the ἦθος interpretation of *Od.*1.1. The modern consensus that by πολύτροπος *ipse Homerus* actually meant 'much-travelled' (see Stanford *UT* 98f. and 260f., Pfeiffer 4) is irrelevant here, even if correct: the ἦθος interpretation was *available* at an early period (attested implicitly by *h.Merc.ll.cc.* and explicitly by the Platonic Hippias at *Hipp.Min.*364c–365d, as well as by Antisthenes), whereas there is no such evidence in favour of the 'travel' interpretation. τρόπος = ἦθος is attested as such at Pi.*P.*10.38, Thgn. 964, Hdt.1.107.2 etc.

17 Cf. τρέπεται χρώς *Il.*13.279, *Od.*21.413, Hes.*Op.*416, Ar.*Lys.*127, Hp.*Mul.* 2.113; ἡ χροιὴ τρέπεται Hp.*Mul.*2.122 and *Int.*31. Cf. also Heraclit.31 πυρὸς τροπαί· πρῶτον θάλασσα κτλ., the 'changing forms' of fire; but the association in Arist.*GC* 316a.1 (Δημόκριτος. . .χροιὰν οὔ φησιν εἶναι· τροπῇ γὰρ χρωματίζεσθαι) is presumably fortuitous. The neutral status of ἀτροπίη is noted (without discussion) by Campbell.

Link

§65

Combinatory interactions involving a link tend to be dominated by its characteristic intellectuality, which sets the tone almost irrespective of the make-up of the rest of the combination in question. The three passages discussed in this, the final section, bear out the point variously.

B.*fr*.4.71ff., a vision of peace:

ἔγχεά τε λογχωτὰ ξίφεά
τ' ἀμφάκεα δάμναται εὐρώς.

. . . . .

χαλκεᾶν δ' οὐκ ἔστι σαλπίγγων κτύπος,
οὐδὲ συλᾶται μελίφρων
ὕπνος ἀπὸ βλεφάρων...

On συλᾶται Campbell comments: 'apt, since often found in the context of war'. For the association compare, for instance, ἔλασε ξίφει...ἐσύλα τεύχεα (*Il*.11.109f.), ἐρύσσατο χάλκεον ἔγχος...τεύχε' ἐσύλα (*Il*.22.367f.). 'Apt', as often, says little or nothing of the specific effect. συλᾶται is in fact prepared by its martial context, and not merely prepared but specified. 'Strip off armour' is the characteristic epic – Iliadic – use of the verb; in contemporary Greek it had other uses.[1] The specifying preparation carries a link: war envelops everything, even sleep. One thinks, perhaps, of the butchery of the sleeping Thracians in *Iliad* 10; and on the other side, one recalls Hesiod's Golden Age (*Op*.112ff.): ὥστε θεοὶ δ' ἔζωον...ἄτερ τε πόνων καὶ ὀιζύος... θνῆσκον δ' ὥσθ' ὕπνῳ δεδμημένοι. Untroubled sleep, defencelessly opposed to 'war's alarms', is invaded before our eyes. And on the aural level one notes the place of συλᾶται in an extended assonantal sequence: χαλκεᾶν... σαλπίγγων...συλᾶται μελίφρων...βλεφάρων. The sequence is partly preparatory for the vehicle, more particularly – dare one say? – euphonic, with its plangent lambda: τὸ λ̄...ἔστι τῶν ἡμιφώνων γλυκύτατον.[2] The effect is a peculiar energizing. The sweetly inexorable progression bodies forth the spirit *not* of συλᾶται and war, but of peace, thereby counterpointing the effect of συλᾶται itself: sleep is 'despoiled', but spoliation in turn flows easily, mellifluously, away, negated overtly by the οὐδέ, but *effectively* by the subtle interactive manoeuvre.

A.*Pe*.426ff.:

οἰμωγὴ δ' ὁμοῦ
κωκύμασιν κατεῖχε πελαγίαν ἅλα,
ἕως κελαινῆς νυκτὸς ὄμμ' ἀφείλετο.
κακῶν δὲ πλῆθος, οὐδ' ἂν εἰ δέκ' ἤματα

στοιχηγοροίην, οὐκ ἂν ἐκπλήσαιμί σοι.
εὖ γὰρ τόδ' ἴσθι, μηδάμ' ἡμέρᾳ μιᾷ
πλῆθος τοσουτάριθμον ἀνθρώπων θανεῖν.
– αἰαῖ, κακῶν δὴ πέλαγος ἔρρωγεν μέγα
Πέρσαις...

The interaction, one might have thought, would be too striking to be missed. πέλαγος picks up – is prepared by and linked to – πελαγίαν ἅλα, while aurally the whole image κακῶν δὴ πέλαγος,[3] vehicle and immediate tenor, has a corresponding relation to κακῶν δὲ πλῆθος, whose πλῆθος is repeated three lines later. The total effect is at the same time so simple and so comprehensive that one hardly cares to gloss it: the scope, the scene, the issue, the whole texture of the event in one disastrous unity.

This study has not aspired to distinguish and contrast essential characteristics of the poets whose works make up its material, and interaction is merely one among many creative aspects that might be called upon if such an aspiration were to be realized. But the essence can only be seen through particulars, and each must be taken on its merits. Perhaps, then, I may be allowed to set against Aeschylus' massive show of force an instance, as it seems to me, of the Pindaric delicacy I have invoked on several occasions. 'The image', one will see, is not unrelated to Aeschylus', is as commonplace or as uncommonplace; the instance would do as well as any to expose the vanity of concentrating critical comment on the generalized conceptual plane. The categories of interaction manifested are themselves similar in type; the instance would serve also to suggest the dangers inherent in the irresponsible 'application' of a typology. Pi.*N*.7.25ff.:

ὅπλων χολωθεὶς
ὁ καρτερὸς Αἴας ἔπαξε διὰ φρενῶν
λευρὸν ξίφος· ὃν κράτιστον Ἀχιλέος ἄτερ μάχᾳ
ξανθῷ Μενέλᾳ δάμαρτα κομίσαι θοαῖς
ἂν ναυσὶ πόρευσαν εὐθυπνόου Ζεφύροιο πομπαὶ
πρὸς Ἴλου πόλιν. ἀλλὰ κοινὸν γὰρ ἔρχεται
κῦμ' Ἀίδα...

From ναυσί to κῦμα, preparation with link; from specific instance to general statement. This voyage and sea were indeed a voyage and sea of death for Ajax. Even for Ajax, κράτιστον Ἀχιλέος ἄτερ, the sea was inescapable. And undemonstrative alliteration carries the proposition through; κοινόν... κῦμα, even for Ajax as for all. The proposition, someone will say, is a truism. But a truth with particular substance, enforced, is not a truism.

1 E.g. of plundering of temple property (ten references thus in Powell's *Lex. Herodot.* alone).
2 D.H.*Comp.*14. See further Stanford *SG* 52.
3 Strictly speaking, the main *part* of the image, since the vehicle in fact continues with ἔρρωγεν: cf. e.g. ῥήξας...ὁ ποταμός Hdt.2.99.3, τὰ ῥεύματα πρὸς τὰς ἀνατολὰς τοῦ ἡλίου ἐρρώγασι Hp.*Aer.*7, with the verb used intransitively in the sense attested also with the passive (κῦμα θαλάσσης ῥήγνυτο *Il.*18.66f. etc.).

APPENDICES

APPENDIX I

'*Work on interaction to date*'

Strictly speaking, there has been no such thing, for lack of the relevant concept. However, various partial anticipations deserve a mention. Due notice has already been given of comments on particular instances. Beyond these, there are a few anticipations of single categories and some discussions of given aspects of imagery (often, the imagery of a single author) which contain allusions to one or more types of interaction along with (and usually in confusion with) one or more types of other thing.

The most discussed categories have probably been pivot (and/or, but more rarely, glide) and intrusion, albeit in both cases only vis-à-vis metaphor: the interactive presence of N or T terminology in explicit imagery usually goes unremarked (although cf. Johansen's comments on some rudimentary instances involving parallelism in paratactic analogy, *GR* 22ff. and *SS* 20; cf. also *GR* 104). The pivot is recognized and discussed by Ole Smith 33–7 and 71, following Headlam (see above, p. 32 with n.2). Among non-classicists, Clemen, dealing with the 'associative rise of the image' in Shakespeare (pp. 74–80 and 89–105), discusses some instances along with, and without distinguishing them from, other kinds of interaction and also V–V relations. For Mrs Nowottny's contribution, see the Prolegomenon. On a wider and more theoretical level, Koestler's 'bisociation' (32ff. and *passim*) has much relevance to the essential character of neutral terms in general and pivot in particular. On a more bemusing 'grammatical' level, Brooke-Rose (212–17 and elsewhere in 206–86) touches on certain kinds of subdued neutral terminology that often characterize the glide, without, however, identifying any distinct categories; in this connection cf. also Leisi's principle of 'semantic congruence', briefly reported by Ullmann *PS* 316.

As regards intrusion, see pp. viii and 138f. and Smith 52–7, who calls intrusion 'fusion' and regrettably (pp.57ff.) associates it with a quite unrelated V–V structure (simile to metaphor, as A.*Ch*.505f.); references to earlier scholarship, *ibid.* 54f. Outside Greek studies, intrusion seems to have less formal recognition. When e.g. Ricks tells us (apropos Milton) that 'there is something wrong with a metaphor in the course of which we have to switch back abruptly to the tenor of what is said' (p.51), employing a formulation that would tend to disqualify all intrusion, it would appear that he is speaking *ad hoc*, without knowledge of any reason for qualification (i.e. knowledge of any respectable stylistic entity).

Regarding other categories, instances of link are sometimes commented on and, less often, instances of preparation/anticipation, though the two kinds tend to be confused with each other and with pivotal and V–V relations: so e.g. Clemen 74ff. and 89ff., Smith 34, Johansen *GR* 25. The latter actually uses the word 'preparation' to cover at least one genuine though trivial instance (A.*Th*.582ff. πατρῷαν to μητρός), but also V–V relations (see Johansen *SS* 19–23). Comparably indiscriminate, but often interesting, discussions of interaction (i.e. of a given kind *plus* things of other kinds): D. West, 'The Imagery and Poetry of Lucretius', Edinburgh, 1969, pp. 43–8, 89, 98–102 ('transfusions'); Ricks 47–66 (on Milton);

Dornseiff 66 (who perceives an instance of retrospective imagery in Pindar – see above, p. 170 with n.11 – but then associates it with 'Vermischung der Bilder', i.e., mostly, conjunctions of unrelated metaphor plus cliché). In classical studies, the most ambitious attempt to deal with interaction and, in particular, to provide some kind of theoretical framework is Ole Smith's work on Aeschylus; but the result is little more than a synthesis of previous knowledge (including previous confusions), or rather such of it as has been available to Hellenists.

APPENDIX II

Catachresis (see above, p. 6, n.6)

The difficulty about catachresis (never really faced?) arises from a combination oʌ (i) deficiency in the definitions and exemplifications offered by those (later) ancients who first used the term and (ii) an apparent widening of meaning in the use of the term at least as early as the Renaissance. Anyone conscientiously perusing the evidence and references given by e.g. Lausberg 288ff., Tuve 59f., 104, 130ff. and Wellek–Warren 198 must conclude that it is not possible to elicit anything from either ancients or moderns (let alone *both*) that would yield a generally acceptable definition of catachresis as an *independent* trope. All one can say is that the modern examples contrive to make catachresis sound more interesting than those of the ancient theorists did. Example given include:

(*a*) *minutum* animum (Cicero, *Orat.*94).

(*b*) *grandem* orationem (Cicero, *de Or.*3.169).

(*c*) ὀφθαλμὸς ἀμπέλου (Trypho, *Trop.*192).

(*d*) τράχηλος ὄρους (*ibid.*).

(*e*) '*mow* a beard' and '*shave* the grass' (Pope *ap.* Wellek–Warren).

(*f*) il *neige* des feuilles (Hugo *ap.* Wellek–Warren).

(*g*) Inside my brain a dull *tom-tom* begins (Eliot *ap.* Tuve).

(*h*) My spirit is not *puffed up* with fat fume
    Of slimy ale (Marston *ap.* Tuve).

(*i*) To know and feel all this, and not to have
    Words to express it, makes a man a *grave*
    Of his own thoughts (Donne *ap.* Tuve).

(*j*) *Shrill* green grass (Edith Sitwell *ap.* Tuve).

The ancient definitions are spoiled by persistent dependence on the idea that catachresis, but not metaphor, involves a transference to something as yet unnamed in ordinary language (so Trypho and others cited in Lausberg). Metaphor itself characteristically involves this: there is no name, as Stanford notes (*GM* 20), which covers precisely and accurately the 'something' pointed to in 'the barge she sat in...*burned* on the water'; or the 'something' in 'a *sea* of troubles' and so on (cf. Demetr.*Eloc.*82, Nowottny 60). (The suggestion recurs in Quintil.8.6.34–6, a passage betraying a high degree of confusion: *nam...poetae* removes any justification for the notion; note also the disparity between 8.6.35 and 8.6.5–6.) The ancients themselves, one could add, were not unanimous on the question of the trope's independent existence. Cicero (*Orat*.94) remarks that Aristotle counted it as metaphor (which, granted the latter's expansive conception of μεταφορά, is hardly significant in itself) and elsewhere himself inclines towards this view (*de Or*.3.169). The former passage, incidentally, at least indicates the respectability of the trope (sometimes doubted): its use is acceptable, *si opus est vel quod delectat vel quod decet*. The modern definitions (see Tuve, Wellek–Warren) tend to overlap or differ bewilderingly. (Add to these also Lausberg's distinction between what he calls 'metaphorische Katachrese', pp.288ff., and 'metonymisch-synekdochische Katachrese', 297f.)

APPENDIX III

The characteristic quality of various authors' usage ('normal' or 'abnormal'): ancient testimony

1. On prose and verse in general

Isocrates' point about the much greater freedom of verse as opposed to prose (see above, p.35 with n.9) is corroborated or amplified by Aristotle *Rh*.1404b.10–15, Lucian *Hist*.8, Aristides 45.8–13. Isocrates' suggestion that metaphor is unavailable for prose carries, as already noted, the particular implication of *oratorical* prose. Exaggerated though it may be, the implication is endorsed explicitly by Cic.*de Or*. 1.12 (*in dicendo...vitium vel maximum...a vulgari genere orationis atque a consuetudine communis sensus abhorrere*) and, blatantly so, Sch.in Dionys.Thr.p.14 Hilgard (ταύτῃ οὖν τῇ εἰρωνείᾳ κέχρηνται οἱ ῥήτορες· ἄλλοις δὲ τρόποις οὐκ ἐφικτὸν αὐτοῖς κεχρῆσθαι..., the remark coming straight after a discussion of metaphor). In support of the Aristotelian point that 'metaphor is poetic' (above, p.35), cf. Plutarch *Mor*.747c–d, Cicero *Orat*.202, Philodemus *Rh*.1.175.xvi. The point is actually built in to the later definitions of the tropes (among which metaphor was always regarded as pre-eminent). Thus Trypho *Trop*.III.191 τρόποι δέ εἰσιν... τέσσαρες καὶ δέκα, μεταφορά, κατάχρησις... τούτους δὲ ποιητικοὺς καλοῦσιν, ἐπεὶ κατά γε τὸ πλεῖστον ἡ τούτων χρῆσις παρὰ ποιηταῖς... and likewise Anon.*Trop*.III.207 and 228, Choerob.*Rh*.III.244; cf. D.H.*Comp*.25.195 ὀνομασία ποιητική... τροπικῶν..., οἷς ἡδύνεται ποίησις and *Vett.Cens*.VIII, p.214 Usener-Radermacher.

2. On the normality of Homer (see above, p. 41 with n.19)

There is not much evidence to hand. *Ex silentio*: Dio Chr.55.9 comments on the simile as a notable feature of Homeric verse (Σωκράτης τε καὶ Ὅμηρος... εἰκάσαι καὶ παραβαλεῖν ἱκανώτατοι), but makes no mention of metaphor; and Dionysius Hal. at *Comp*.3.15 characterizes a representative piece of Homer (*Od*.16.1–16) as having οὔτε...μεταφοραὶ...εὐγενεῖς...οὔτ' ἄλλη τροπικὴ διάλεκτος. *Contra*, Aristotle claims (*Po*.1459b.34ff.) that τὸ ἡρωικὸν...μεταφορὰς δέχεται μάλιστα, which is suspect, being (i) quasi-prescriptive rather than descriptive of actual (i.e. Homeric) practice; (ii) in pretty flat contradiction to his statements at *Rh*. 1406b.1ff. and *Po*.1459a.9f. that metaphor is peculiarly suited to *iambics*. One assumes that A. is in fact thinking of *simile* here (see Lucas *ad loc*. and cf. *Rh*.

1411a.1–3 and b.21–9 where A. uses μεταφορά for similes, albeit short ones; on A.'s terminology in general, see McCall 24–53). But whatever A. thought he meant, he undoubtedly seems to have meant it: cf. his remark at *fr.*70 that Empedocles was Ὁμηρικὸς. . . καὶ δεινὸς περὶ τὴν φράσιν. . . μεταφορικός τε ὢν καί. . . .

3. *Normality of Lysias*

I have already (above, p. 43) cited Dionysius' comprehensive claim for Lysias' pre-eminent normality. The key words are ἥκιστα γὰρ ἄν τις εὕροι τὸν Λυσίαν τροπικῇ καὶ μεταφορικῇ λέξει κεχρημένον (*Vett.Cens.*IX Usener–Radermacher), words which recur almost verbatim (but without καὶ μεταφορικῇ) at *Lys.*3. The point is denied by no one and corroborated by Longinus (the real Longinus), *fr.*1, 1.325 Spengel; by the anonymous *Vita Isaei*, p.261.17ff. Westermann; and, more circumstantially, by the choice of Lysias to exemplify κυρία λέξις in Demetrius (*Eloc.*190) and by the progression of ideas and names in Longinus (ps.-Longinus) ch.32, on metaphor, where the examples feature, among others, Plato, the discussion of whom prompts reference to Caecilius' contrast of the philosopher with Lysias (32.8). The evidence for Lysias is, in fact, conveniently one-way. The only problem, again already mentioned (above, p. 44), concerns the authenticity of the Lysias-corpus; in particular, where Dionysius is concerned, it must be borne in mind that any given work now attributed to L. may not have been so recognized by Dionysius. K. J. Dover, *Lysias and the Corpus Lysiacum*, California, 1968, gives a lengthy and generally depressing discussion of this and other problems concerning the authenticity of the corpus. But Dover's enquiries (especially pp.193ff.) seem to point to the conclusion that some works belonging to the extant corpus will in fact be by L. and that the others are either partly by L. or not by L., but either way are approximately of his time and in his manner (cf. also pp.91ff.). It may surely therefore be presumed that, even on Dover's severe terms, categorical assertions, like those by Dionysius, concerning L.'s avoidance of metaphor have a general applicability to the present corpus; and despite Dover's arguments, there would still seem to be room for informed critics to hold to what one of his reviewers called 'the rational belief. . . that Lysias was the author of the majority of the speeches ascribed to him in the *Corpus Lysiacum*' (S. Usher, *JHS* 1971, 150).

4. *Normality of Isaeus*

D.H.*Is.*2–3 indicates the close relation of Isaeus' style to Lysias' (including, explicitly, the crucial item, κυρία. . . λέξις, ch.3). Likewise *Vita Isaei*, p.261.17ff. Westermann.

5. *Comparative normality of Isocrates*

Two remarks by Dionysius seemingly point to a Lysias-like avoidance of metaphor on Isocrates' part, but a less consistent avoidance. Thus (*Dem.*4), ἡ Ἰσοκράτους λέξις. . . πέφευγε τὴν τροπικήν, ὥσπερ ἐκείνη [sc. ἡ Λυσιακή], φράσιν. . . although it might be more strictly true to say that (*Isoc.*2) τὴν τροπικὴν φράσιν ὀλίγον τι διαλλάττει τῆς Λυσίου καὶ κέκραται συμμέτρως. In general, then, Isocrates, on this reckoning, would be practising what he preached (above, p. 35).

6. Normality of technical prose in general

The evidence here comes again from Dionysius. Discussing those stylistic virtues which Lysias brought to perfection, he ascribes them (*Dem.*2) to the earlier technical prose writers generally, more or less: οἱ τὰς γενεαλογίας ἐξενέγκαντες καὶ οἱ τὰς τοπικὰς ἱστορίας πραγματευσάμενοι καὶ οἱ τὰ φυσικὰ φιλοσοφήσαντες [i.e., presumably, the more prosaic of the Presocratics] καὶ οἱ τῶν ἠθικῶν διαλόγων ποιηταί, ὧν ἦν τὸ Σωκρατικὸν διδασκαλεῖον πᾶν ἔξω Πλάτωνος, καὶ οἱ τοὺς δημηγορικοὺς ἢ δικανικοὺς συντατόμενοι λόγους ὀλίγου δεῖν πάντες. Although no specific mention is made of tropical or metaphorical language, the non-metaphorical tendency of such writing in general may be inferred from the association with Lysias and the contrast with Plato. In this same passage D.H. evinces acceptance of the fundamental truth that technical prose tends to depart least, in relevant respects, from the norms of ordinary speech: τὴν πρὸς ἰδιώτην…λόγον… ὁμοιότητα characterizes the writers just listed. Writing elsewhere, D.H. explicitly invokes the literalness of one group on the list, the early historians. Hellanicus and the other ἀρχαῖοι συγγραφεῖς, he says, employed a λέξιν…κοινήν (*Th.*5); and, more specifically, οἱ πρὸ τοῦ Πελοποννησιακοῦ γενόμενοι πολέμου…οἵ τε τὴν Ἰάδα προελόμενοι διάλεκτον…καὶ οἱ τὴν ἀρχαίαν Ἀτθίδα…πάντες…περὶ τὴν κυρίαν λέξιν μᾶλλον ἐσπούδασαν ἢ περὶ τὴν τροπικήν (*Th.*23) – although he does add as a rider that these historians did admit the latter ὥσπερ ἥδυσμα, 'as a seasoning', but without specifying *which* historians and under *what* circumstances and, most important, *which* tropes (an imprecision that recurs apropos Thucydides, see below).

7. Normality of Aristotle

One witness here, Ammonius *in Cat.*36b.25ff.: ἐν μὲν γὰρ τοῖς ἀκροαματικοῖς… ἐστι…κατὰ τὴν φράσιν ἀπέριττος…ἐν δέ γε τοῖς διαλογικοῖς ἃ πρὸς τοὺς πολλοὺς αὐτῷ γέγραπται καὶ ὄγκου φροντίζει τινὸς καὶ περιεργίας λέξεων καὶ μεταφορᾶς…. In other words: in his popular works (dialogues), *none of which now survive*, Aristotle's Greek is comparatively heightened and, *inter alia*, makes use of metaphor. But in his technical writings (lectures etc.), he writes 'normal' Greek. All the extant works (apart from a few fragments) must be assigned to this latter category.

8. Normality of the Hippocratic Corpus

It would be pleasant to be able to cite a pithy characterization of the Hippocratics. There is indeed a relevant testimony, but one inconveniently untidy, in Erotian's preface to his *Glossary of Hippocratic Usage* (τῶν παρ' Ἱπποκράτει λέξεων συναγωγή). The relevant part of this preface (pp.3f. Nachmanson) may be interpreted as follows: among the usages of Hippocrates (i.e. the authors of the bulk of the fifth and fourth century treatises now extant) are expressions described as ἀσαφεῖς καὶ κατὰ πολὺ τῆς κοινῆς ἀνακεχωρηκυίας ὁμιλίας…λέξεις ('obscure and remote from common usage'). But contrary to one prevalent belief, this ἀσάφεια is not the result of a studied disdain for clarity; nor (so the vindicatory tone of the preface suggests) does it call for unfavourable explanations of any kind. It is in fact the result of a mode of language common to ⟨at least some of⟩ his contemporaries: πάλαι αἱ συνήθειαι ταύτῃ κέχρηνται τῇ περὶ τὴν διάλεκτον φορᾷ, which appears to mean 'the earlier convention was to use his kind of flexibility (range? tendency?) of idiom'. Whatever precisely it might be, the quality in question is, anyway, ascribed to the writers of Old Comedy, to Democritus, to Thucydides and Herodotus and virtually the whole collection of ancient συγγραφέων (which presumably means *historians*, rather than *prose authors* in general). Hp. himself is credited with certain particular characteristics which may be assumed to relate both to the preceding argument – and therefore to be, *inter alia*, defensible or even meritorious characteristics – and to the compilation of a glossary. The characteristics (given in obscure Greek) are itemized thus: Hp. is (i) Ὁμηρικὸς τὴν φράσιν, i.e. 'is archaic'; more precisely, 'like Homer, uses obsolete vocabulary' or, specifically, 'uses obsolete vocabulary preserved by Homer' or both; (ii) καὶ τὴν ὀνοματοποιΐαν εὐχερής, i.e. coins words or invents new word-formations, especially new compounds or derivatives; (iii) περιγράψαι τε διάνοιαν ἱκανός, i.e. 'encapsulates' his thought (cf. LSJ *s.vv.* περιγραφή II.3 and περιγράφω II.2, *s.fin.*)? Almost 'compresses' his thought, 'packs thought into his words'. In this context, it can hardly mean 'defines his meaning'. (iv) καὶ τῆς κοινῆς καὶ εἰς πολλοὺς πιπτούσης λέξεως ἐκλέξασθαι τὴν κυριωτέραν. This means either 'his λέξις is more κυρία, literal, than the common, everyday λέξις' or 'he chooses from the common, everyday λέξις the more κυρία element'. The passage is difficult and perhaps corrupt (see Danielsson 8ff., whose exposition, however, is incomplete and sometimes implausible), but the second interpretation is more easily ascribed to the Greek as it stands and certainly squares no less well with the *raison d'être* of Erotian's compilation, an exegesis of obsolete or rare expressions (ἠβουλήθην τὰς... ἀσαφεῖς καὶ κατὰ πολὺ τῆς κοινῆς ἀνακεχωρηκυίας ὁμιλίας ἐξηγήσασθαι λέξεις). The opposition between 'literalness' and 'common usage' and the equation between 'literal' and 'obsolete and rare' present no great problem, if we assume, as we must, that the idea of 'literalness' presupposed is the one involving 'natural' or 'primary' usage (see Appendix v). Admittedly, it can hardly be claimed that Hp. *is* peculiarly 'literal' in this sense, nor do the items in Erotian's list appear to bear it out: e.g. p.14 N., ἀνθεῖν of disease, or p.62 N., νεφέλαι on excreta, on which the glossarist himself comments μεταφορικῶς...κληθεῖσαι. But other interpretations are even more problematic and in any case my argument does not require a decision between them. It is surely clear, on the evidence of the preface, that the Hippocratic deviations from popular usage that E. is considering are not deviations from *normal* usage in my sense. They involve e.g. archaism and have nothing to do with ('live') tropes: his discussion of the Hippocratic ἀσάφεια (a term, incidentally, that recurs in the *Vita Hippocratis* of 'Soranus', *CMG* IV.177.16) contains no mention of tropes and the use of the word κυριωτέρα should preclude any implication of tropes. For even though κυριωτέρα here implies no contrast with a hypothetical τροπικωτέρα, the special element in Hippocratic idiom could not be metaphorical and κυριωτέρα at the same time, irrespective of what it might be κυριωτέρα *than*. In the end, then, Erotian's tortuous argument is to be regarded as confirmatory of the normality (in *my* sense) of Hippocratic usage.

9. *Normality of Herodotus*

In *Th*.5 Dionysius Hal. explains that the ἀρχαῖοι συγγραφεῖς (Hecataeus etc.) used a style largely free from live metaphor: λέξιν ὡς ἐπὶ τὸ πολὺ τὴν αὐτὴν ἅπαντες ἐπιτηδεύσαντες . . . τὴν σαφῆ καὶ κοινὴν καὶ καθαράν. . . . A later discussion in ch.23 spells out the implications of κοινήν: οἱ δὲ πρὸ τοῦ Πελοποννησιακοῦ γενόμενοι πολέμου καὶ μέχρι . . . Θουκυδίδου . . . οἵ τε τὴν Ἰάδα προελόμενοι διάλεκτον . . . καὶ οἱ τὴν ἀρχαίαν Ἀτθίδα . . . πάντες . . . περὶ τὴν κυρίαν λέξιν μᾶλλον ἐσπούδασαν ἢ περὶ τὴν τροπικήν . . . (although they do use the latter 'as a seasoning'; see above, p. 213). The discussions in chapters 5 and 23 show that in D.H.'s view Herodotus *supplemented*, rather than altered, the stylistic practices of these earlier authors. From ch.5: Ἡρόδοτος . . . τῇ λέξει προσαπέδωκε τὰς παραλειφθείσας ὑπὸ τῶν πρὸ αὐτοῦ συγγραφέων ἀρετάς (i.e. his style was still σαφὴς καὶ κοινὴ καὶ καθαρά . . . but not only these). And, in more detail, from ch.23: 'the earlier historians all περὶ τὴν κυρίαν λέξιν . . . ἐσπούδασαν . . . τὰς μὲν οὖν ἀναγκαίας ἀρετὰς ἡ λέξις αὐτῶν πάντων ἔχει . . . with the result that they all lack that 'inessential' but highly prized quality, δεινότης· πλὴν ἑνὸς Ἡροδότου. . . .' That κυρία λέξις is still being ascribed to Hdt. as to his predecessors is clear from the placing of the phrase πλὴν ἑνὸς Ἡροδότου ('they all had κυρίαν λέξιν but no δεινότητα – all except Hdt., who had both') and from the continuation of ch.24, in which it is evident that (in D.H.'s view) the first historian to use τὴν τροπικὴν λέξιν . . . ἀντὶ τῆς κοινῆς καὶ συνήθους was Thucydides (see below, p. 216).

Some further corroborative evidence exists. Elsewhere (*Pomp*.4 and *Vett.Cens*. VI.3 Usener–Radermacher) D.H. suggests that Hdt.'s historiographical style was the model for Xenophon's, the normality of which is likewise not in question (see below). Finally, for what it may be worth, the suggestion in Marcellinus, *Vit.Thuc*. 41 (below, p. 216) that Thucydides used μεταφοραῖς τισίν by implication excludes such use for Hdt.

10. *Xenophon*

As remarked above (last paragraph), D.H. regards Herodotus as Xenophon's model in historiography, which is itself a sign of the latter's presumptive reliability; and Marcellinus' suggestion about Thucydides (*ibid*.) carries the same implication of normality for X. as for Hdt. Demetrius, *Eloc*.80, is more explicit: X. (unlike Plato) does not usually show a predilection for metaphor, although he does use simile (Πλάτων ἐπισφαλές τι δοκεῖ ποιεῖν μεταφοραῖς μᾶλλον χρώμενος ἢ εἰκασίαις, ὁ μέντοι Ξενοφῶν εἰκασίαις μᾶλλον). In contrast, note that Longinus' chapter on metaphor (*Subl*.32) contains a notable specimen from a Xenophon dialogue (*Mem*.1.4.5: *Subl*.32.5). As with Aristotle (above, p. 213), and in accordance with the prevailing tendency of 'literary' speech in Greek, X.'s practice here will have been predictably different from his usual sobriety.

11. *Thucydides*

A cursory glance at the ancient witnesses to the character of Thucydidean usage might suggest that here is a prose writer as unreliable as any poet. The most straightforward piece of evidence, already mentioned apropos Hdt. and X., comes from Marcellinus' *Life of Thucydides*, a late source, admittedly, but one that may derive much of its material from Caecilius of Calacte, a contemporary of D.H. (see Lesky 607). What Marcellinus tells us (*Vit.Thuc.*39–41) is that 'Thucydides uses some metaphors': τριῶν δὲ ὄντων χαρακτήρων φραστικῶν, ὑψηλοῦ ἰσχνοῦ μέσου... μέσῳ μὲν Ἡρόδοτος ἐχρήσατο...ἰσχνῷ δ' ὁ Ξενοφῶν. διά γ' οὖν τὸ ὑψηλὸν ὁ Θουκυδίδης καὶ ποιητικαῖς πολλάκις ἐχρήσατο λέξεσι καὶ μεταφοραῖς τισίν. Superficially straightforward, fundamentally problematic: (i) τισίν is vague. It presumably implies 'few' rather than 'many', but leaves it quite open where those 'few' might be found. In, for instance, speeches rather than narrative? (ii) The phrase καὶ μεταφοραῖς τισίν is entangled in an appeal to the famous 'three styles' formula, a formula which, as I shall argue below (pp. 222f.), is not utilizable for present purposes. In particular, the cast of the crucial sentence allows a suspicion that the specific quality of style (including καὶ μετ. τ.) is not merely related to the general formula, but mechanically *inferred* from it (διά γ' οὖν τὸ ὑψηλὸν...ἐχρήσατο... μεταφοραῖς) – and such mechanical procedures are certainly not uncommon among the theorists in later antiquity.

Marcellinus' testimony should surely be set beside – or against – some more substantial ancient evidence; and such is provided, yet again, by D.H. This superior witness might in fact be taken to confirm Marcellinus' assertion. One modern analyst of Thucydidean style writes as follows of his author and D.H.'s comments on him: 'Darum gebraucht er wie Gorgias, obgleich weniger als dieser, neben tropischen und metaphorischen Wendungen, vielfach poetische, veraltete, ausser Gebrauch gekommene Wörter und Ausdrücke. Daher auch das wiederholt sich findende Urteil des Dionysios...über die λέξις des Thuk., die er nennt γλωττηματική, ξένη, ἀπηρχαιωμένη, ἐκ τοῦ συνήθους ἐξηλλαγμένη, τροπική, zusammengefasst in dem Ausdruck τὸ ποιητικὸν τῶν ὀνομάτων..., d.h. poetische Ausdrucksweise' (Ros 2f.). Closer scrutiny, however, reveals further problems. The Greek words quoted are certainly Dionysius' words (albeit composite) and do concern Th., but Ros is guilty of misrepresentation. In particular, D.H. says τροπική; Ros says 'tropischen *und metaphorischen Wendungen*' (my italics); and there is a difference. All metaphors are tropes, but most tropes are not metaphors. Which sort or sorts of trope, then, does D.H. have in mind? The Dionysian treatises that Ros cites in support of his remarks are two, the *de Thucydide* and the *Second Letter to Ammaeus*. But though D.H. there discusses Th.'s stylistic peculiarities at considerable length, nowhere does he give any definite indication that the tropes in question include metaphor.

In *Th.*24 (substantially repeated in *Amm.*2.2), D.H. explains that Th. was the first historian to develop an idiosyncratic style. He classifies the idiosyncrasies under three headings, (i) ἡ ἐκλογὴ τῶν ὀνομάτων, (ii) ἡ σύνθεσις, (iii) οἱ σχηματισμοί. It is under the first heading that he ascribes to Th. a τροπικὴν καὶ γλωττηματικὴν καὶ ἀπηρχαιωμένην καὶ ξένην λέξιν, but it is to the third group, σχηματισμοί (= 'figures', like σχήματα, or 'constructions'), that most of Th.'s individualistic energy is devoted (ἐν οἷς μάλιστα ἐβουλήθη διενέγκαι τῶν πρὸ αὐτοῦ, πλείστην εἰσενεγκάμενος σπουδήν). And it is to this third group that most of his many illustrations of Thucydidean style belong (*Th.*25–49, *Amm.*2.3–17). So substantial, in fact, is the imbalance between his treatment of the three headings that the τροπική part of the ἐκλογή formula is never directly explained.* In *Th.*50, after twenty-five Teubner pages of discussion and examples, he repeats the formula in a more comprehensive form that would seem to involve σχηματισμοί as well as ἐκλογή (τὴν φράσιν τὴν γλωττηματικήν τε καὶ ἀπηρχαιωμένην καὶ τροπικὴν καὶ ἐξηλλαγμένην τῶν ἐν ἔθει σχημάτων ἐπὶ τὸ ξένον καὶ περιττόν), but again without any direct comment on τροπικήν. In the course of the examples (ch.35), he in fact offers another, *less* comprehensive, version of the formula: αἱ γλωττηματικαὶ καὶ ξέναι καὶ πεποιημέναι λέξεις...καὶ τὰ πολύπλοκα καὶ ἀγκύλα καὶ βεβιασμένα σχήματα. The chief point of interest here is obviously the omission of the now predictable καὶ τροπικαί.† Are the tropes to be thought of as only a minor or marginal source of idiosyncrasy? Another noteworthy point is provided by the present context of the formula: he is now dealing specifically with Th.'s *speeches* (περὶ τῶν δημηγοριῶν, ch.34, *init.*) and has recently remarked (ch.33, *fin.*) that in narrative (ἐν τοῖς διηγήμασιν) Th. may be free from his idiosyncrasies altogether (ὅταν ἐν τῷ συνήθει καὶ κοινῷ τῆς διαλέκτου χαρακτῆρι μένῃ).

The *Second Letter to Ammaeus* is a kind of illustrative appendix to the *de Thucydide*. In *Amm.*2.2, D.H. quotes the formula unchanged from *Th.*24 and when he comes to illustrate his generalities, gives first (*Amm.*2.3 *init.*) a brief list of (*inter alia*) γλωσσηματικά...καὶ ἀπηρχαιωμένα and ποιητικά‡ without any mention of τροπικά; then, under the heading ἡ ἐν τοῖς σχηματισμοῖς καινότης τε καὶ πολυτροπία (which means 'variety' and has nothing to do with τρόπος, 'trope') καὶ ἡ ἐξαλλαγὴ τῆς συνήθους χρήσεως (ch.3 *fin.*), a long list of instances (ch.4ff.) which purportedly, therefore, are instances of 'figures' or 'constructions' (σχηματισμοί) and/or of the ἐξαλλαγὴ τῆς συνήθους χρήσεως, 'deviation from normal usage'. Although this ἐξαλλαγή could be regarded as a vague umbrella term to cover almost any of Th.'s idiosyncrasies, its association with σχηματισμοί as against γλωσσηματικά κτλ. indicates that it should have nothing to do with ἐκλογή and hence nothing to do with tropes. This is confirmed by the fact that the heading ἡ ἐν τοῖς σχηματισμοῖς καινότης...καὶ ἡ ἐξαλλαγή... is qualified with the words ἐν ᾗ μάλιστα διαφέρειν αὐτὸν ἡγούμεθα τῶν ἄλλων, 'the sphere in which, above all, he seems to us to differ from other authors', which correspond closely to those used in *Th.*24 of the Thucydidean σχηματισμοί: ἐν οἷς μάλιστα ἐβουλήθη διενέγκαι τῶν πρὸ αὑτοῦ, πλείστην εἰσενεγκάμενος σπουδήν. Here, therefore, is another indication that tropes must represent a minor aspect of Th.'s deviations, so minor that for a second time D.H. passes over the word – and any explicit illustration of it – without comment.

Let me at this point anticipate a possible objection. Is the foregoing argument

---

* Although in *Amm.*2, at least, this must be partly due to a lacuna in the text (see below, footnote to p. 219).

† Likewise another summary formula in ch. 52, τὴν γλωσσηματικὴν καὶ ἀπηρχαιωμένην καὶ ποιητικὴν καὶ ξένην λέξιν, with the σχηματισμοί duly mentioned afterwards. (Other shorter phrases occur in various parts of the *Th.*)

‡ He has already (*Amm.*2.2, following *Th.*24) used τὸ ποιητικὸν τῶν ὀνομάτων as apparently an equivalent to ἐκλογή. This ποιητικά appears to represent a separate heading *within* ἐκλογή, not an inclusive equivalent for it.

perhaps guilty of manipulating the technical terms of Greek stylistics with an anachronistic punctiliousness? Surely not. It can easily be shown that D.H. was well aware of the meaning of 'trope' and 'figure' and so on. Cf. the precise distinctions and associations in a passage from *Comp.*3, for instance: οὔτε γὰρ μεταφοραὶ...οὔτε ὑπαλλαγαὶ οὔτε καταχρήσεις οὔτε ἄλλη τροπικὴ διάλεκτος οὐδεμία, οὐδὲ δὴ γλῶτται...οὐδὲ ξένα ἢ πεποιημένα ὀνόματα. He was, in fact, among the first theorists to be quite clear about the difference between trope and figure (cf. Schenkeveld 147), although he does not, as it happens, offer a pithy definition like his contemporary Cicero (*Brut.*69): *verborum immutationibus...quos appellant* τρόπους *et sententiarum orationisque formis quae vocant* σχήματα. But notwithstanding this capacity for precision, there is, it must now be said, a practical proviso: the fact is that among the instances of σχηματισμοί, or whatever, listed in *Th.*25–49 and *Amm.*2.4–17, there *are* a few tropes. One might reasonably describe the Thucydidean 'treating things as persons and persons as things' as a species of the trope metonymy: τὸ γὰρ ὑμέτερον ἀντὶ τοῦ ὑμεῖς (*Amm.*2.14, *fin.*) is a very clear instance. In *Th.*29, again, D.H. cites instances of what is arguably the trope periphrasis, as he himself is aware: περιφράσεως ποιητικῆς ἐστιν οἰκειοτέρα 1.375.7 Usener–Radermacher (cf. 378.1 and, again, ch.31, involving metalepsis). Metaphor, however, is conspicuous by its absence.

One final complication. During Dionysius' protracted discussions, the *word* μεταφορά does crop up once. The word occurs, but *not* in the course of the illustrations, and *not* in the sense 'metaphor' – this much can be confidently asserted, although the Teubner editors evidently thought otherwise. The passage in question comes in *Amm.*2.2, as part of what is purportedly a verbatim quotation from *Th.*24, and the phrase in question reads – in the inherited text – καὶ τοπικῶν σημειώσεων μεταφοραῖς, with reference to, as Roberts put it, 'strained use. Here used in much the same sense as διαφορά, which is found in the parallel passage',* that is, in *Th.*24. The manuscript reading in the 'parallel passage' in *Th.*, καὶ τοπικῶν σημειώσεων διαφοραῖς, was in fact 'emended' by Reiske to...μεταφοραῖς to conform with the reading in *Amm.*, and Usener–Radermacher, following Krüger, further 'emended' τοπικῶν in both passages to τροπικῶν. The result is nonsense: 'metaphors involving tropical expressions' is worse than tautological, irrespective of context. And in fact the context, which I have not yet mentioned, almost precludes any allusion to tropes or metaphor proper and surely puts the necessary interpretation beyond any doubt. Dionysius is briefly summarizing *Th.*'s σχηματισμοί, and while it is true that the extended illustrations of σχήματα/σχηματισμοί in both *Amm.*2 and *Th.* do, as I have shown, contain a few tropes, this summary is a much more tightly organized affair. I quote from Roberts' translation of *Amm.*2.2: 'He takes the greatest trouble to vary his constructions (ἐπὶ δὲ τῶν σχηματισμῶν), since it was in this respect chiefly that he wished to excel his predecessors. At one time he makes a phrase out of a word...again, he converts a noun into a verb...interchanges common with proper nouns and active with passive verbs. He varies the normal use of the plural and the singular.... He

---

* Roberts 196. He goes on to say, '...the parallel passage of the *de adm. vi dic. in Dem.*', evidently a mistake for *Th.*24.

combines feminines with masculines. . . . He wrests the cases of nouns. . . from the expression to the sense. . . . In the employment of conjunctions and prepositions, and especially of the particles which serve to bring out the meanings of individual words, he allows himself full poetic liberty. There will be found in him a large number of constructions which by changes of person and variations of tense, and *by the strained use of expressions denoting place*, differ from ordinary speech and have all the appearance of solecisms. Further, he frequently substitutes things for persons and persons for things. In his enthymemes and his sentences the numerous parentheses. . .' (Roberts 135). This is unquestionably a summary of σχηματισμοί and although tropes of certain kinds (periphrasis etc.) might on occasion pass for σχηματισμοί (as they do in the full, illustrative lists), it is not credible that metaphor should be so designated, with or without the conjectural τροπικῶν σημειώσεων as well.* If metaphor *was* to have been mentioned, it would have been mentioned *before* (in fact immediately before) this summary of constructions, under the heading of 'choice of words' – i.e. it would have come in as part of the formula that I have discussed at length already: ἐπὶ μὲν τῆς ἐκλογῆς τῶν ὀνομάτων τὴν τροπικὴν καὶ γλωττηματικὴν καὶ ἀπηρχαιωμένην καὶ ξένην λέξιν παραλαμβάνων πολλάκις ἀντὶ τῆς κοινῆς καὶ συνήθους τοῖς καθ᾽ ἑαυτὸν ἀνθρώποις, [after which we come on to the constructions with] ἐπὶ δὲ τῶν σχηματισμῶν. . . .

The inferences to be drawn from this confusing evidence from D.H. are: (i) Of the various formulae for Th.'s deviations, the ἐκλογή formula *without* τροπικὴ λέξις is to be taken as applying chiefly to Th.'s speeches, as opposed to his narrative (*Th.*33–5). *A fortiori*, this should hold good for the same formula *with* τροπικὴ λέξις, although D.H. is not explicit. (One might note incidentally that in *Lys.*3 he refers to the ποιητικὴ κατασκευή as specifically characteristic of Thucydidean speeches.) (ii) The tropical component of Th.'s idiosyncrasy must be a minor one, as is shown by D.H.'s lack of interest in illustrating it (in *Th.*) and his readiness to omit the word τροπικός from the general formula used to characterize Th.'s ἐκλογή (*Th.*35 and 52, *Amm.*2.3). He certainly makes it clear that ἐκλογή is *itself* only a minor element in the idiosyncratic whole (the major element being σχηματισμοί, *Th.*24, *Amm.*2.3). As an additional point in this connection, it may be mentioned that characterization of Th.'s style given elsewhere by D.H. makes no mention of tropes: so *Dem.*1 and *Vett.Cens.*VI.3 Usener–Radermacher. (iii) In any case, it is not evident that D.H. means τροπικός to include metaphor specifically, in contra-distinction to the metonymies and periphrases (etc.) instanced in *Th.* and *Amm.*2.

I think it is fair to conclude that D.H. hardly gives much support to Marcellinus' assertion about μεταφοραῖς τισίν. One may suppose that in general Thucydidean narrative is as reliable (in my sense) as any; Thucydidean speeches – as one would expect of literary speeches – that much less so. Marcellinus' 'metaphors' may be presumed to belong, if anywhere, to the speeches.

* For further argument in favour of τοπικῶν, the manuscript reading, see Roberts 176. It might also be that διαφοραῖς, the reading in *Th.*24, should actually be restored (*lectio difficilior*) in *Amm.*2.2: μετα- could be an unfortunate gloss. I should mention that none of this speculation would be needed, but for a lacuna in the text at the end of *Amm.*2.13, where D.H. was (presumably) due to exemplify the feature in question.

12. *Other 'reliable' authors*

There are certainly some candidates for reliability for whom there is no adequate ancient testimony, direct or indirect, and therefore nothing but *a priori* principle to turn to: Democritus is a good example (see only some inconclusive remarks by Cicero, *Orat*.67). In passing, I note that there is further testimony extant concerning prose authors too late to concern me – most notably, Epicurus, to whom Diogenes ascribes λέξις κυρία and who had his own, apparently corresponding, theory about literal language (see D.L.10.13, Epicur.*Ep.ad Hdt*.38 and *de Natura* 28.5 Vogliano, also A. A. Long, *BICS* 1971, pp.114–34).

13. *On the abnormality of particular poets*

Various statements exist testifying to the use of metaphor made by particular poets of the archaic or classical periods. Most of these statements are short and self-explanatory and so can simply be cited without lengthy discussion. (i) Oracles and (?) choral lyric: Plut.*Moral*.405d. (ii) Pindar and tragedy: Hermog.*Id*.248f. Rabe (*tropes*). (iii) Dithyramb: almost proverbial for highly wrought language. Cf. notably Demetr.*Eloc*.78 μεταφοραῖς χρηστέον..., μὴ μέντοι πυκναῖς, ἐπεί τοι διθύραμβον ἀντὶ λόγου γράφομεν. See also D.H.*Pomp*.2 τροπικήν τε καὶ διθυραμβικὴν φράσιν (of Plato), where, as the context makes clear, tropes include metaphors. (iv) Aeschylus: *Vit.Aesch.* p.118 Westermann. (v) Tragic iambics: Arist.*Po*. 1459a.9f. and *Rh*.1406b.1ff. (both passages, however, have a dangerously quasi-prescriptive tone). (iv) Comic iambics: Arist. *Rh*.1406b.7 (ditto). (vii) Parmenides: Procl.*in Prm*.1.665.17ff. Cousin. (viii) Empedocles: Arist.*fr*.70 (= D.L.8.57); cf., conceivably, Philodemus (quoting the fourth century philosopher, Nausiphanes?), *Rh*.2.27f., col.18 on some unspecified (and perhaps unspecific) φυσιολόγος, a word used by Aristotle, for one, of Emped. (φυσιολόγον μᾶλλον ἢ ποιητήν *Po*.1447b.19).

14. *Abnormality of Heraclitus*

There seems to be no consequential Greek testimony, but N.B. that Lucretius 1.642 stigmatizes H.'s *inversis verbis*. Bailey *ad loc.* plausibly quotes Quintil.8.6.44, ἀλληγορία *quam inversionem interpretantur*, but hedges on L.'s exact meaning here. It is at least *possible* that metaphor (of a particular, protracted, kind) is one of the stylistic features in question.

15. *Abnormality of Plato*

The most explicit statement comes from Demetrius (*Eloc*.80): Πλάτων ἐπισφαλές τι δοκεῖ ποιεῖν μεταφοραῖς μᾶλλον χρώμενος ἢ εἰκασίαις. Add D.H.*Comp*.25 (II.124 U–R) on the frequency of P.'s use of tropes in general, τροπικῶν..., οἷς ἡδύνεται ποίησις, εἰς κόρον ἐγκαταμιγέντων τῇ ἀμέτρῳ λέξει, ὃ ποιοῦσιν ἄλλοι τε πολλοὶ καὶ οὐχ ἥκιστα Πλάτων – a remark which, in the light of comments made by Dionysius elsewhere, is to be understood with reference to, 'not least', metaphor: cf. *Dem*.5 and 32 and the associations between Plato, 'dithyrambic' style, tropes and metaphor at *Pomp*.2. Cf. likewise Longinus' configuration in his ch.32, discussed above (p. 212). D.H. pointed out (at e.g. *Dem*.5) that P. was capable of using the most straightforward Greek – a fact that does not make Platonic usage in general any more reliable, since one has, as usual, no internal basis on which to decide the straightforwardness of any given usage. Note finally that the ancient comments on the general metaphoricality of P.'s style are to be related to those on the style of the dialogues of Xenophon and Aristotle (see above, pp. 213 and 215 and cf. also D.L.2.63 on Aeschines Socraticus, μάλιστα μιμεῖται Γοργίαν, the likely implication of which is clear).

16. *General abnormality of sophistic and oratorical prose*

Despite the claims and prescriptions made by or on behalf of orators that there was no particular place for metaphor in oratory (see above, pp. 35, 37, 211), it was widely understood that in fact oratorical prose, and likewise its parent/cousin, sophistic prose, made use of metaphor on a large scale. A good example is provided by Phld.*Rh.*1.149–81 (fragmentary), where 1.175.xvi.8ff. apparently ascribes to 'the orators and especially the sophists' a greater use of metaphor than that shown by poets (cf. also 1.149.iv); a mention of Alcidamas, among others, at 1.180.xxi and an allusion to Pericles (1.181.xxii) in the context of the same discussion serve to show that the orators and sophists in question include those of the classical period as much as any other. (For the Greco-Roman rhetorical world of Phld.'s own time, the notion is certainly a commonplace and likewise the corresponding prescription: *translatis utamur frequenter* Cic.*de Or.*3.201.) More generally: although one properly hesitates to infer description from prescription in points of detail, it is an inescapable lesson of every rhetorical handbook from Aristotle onwards that orators are expected to include metaphor in their armoury, especially public orators: Plut.*Moral.*803a δέχεται δ' ὁ πολιτικὸς λόγος δικανικοῦ μᾶλλον...μεταφοράς (cf. Isocr. *Antid.*47, where public oratory is characterized as having a λέξει ποιητικωτέρᾳ).

17. *Gorgias*

The tropicality and, especially, metaphoricality of Gorgias' style were notorious. The Suda sums it up (*s.v.*): Γοργίας...πρῶτος τῷ ῥητορικῷ εἴδει τῆς παιδείας δύναμίν τε φραστικὴν καὶ τέχνην ἔδωκε, τροπαῖς τε καὶ μεταφοραῖς καὶ ἀλληγορίαις καὶ ὑπαλλαγαῖς καὶ καταχρήσεσι...ἐχρήσατο. Cf. D.H.*Lys.*3 (citing the authority of Timaeus) and *Vett.Cens.*VIII–IX Usener–Radermacher. Note further that ('frigid') metaphorical conceits were peculiarly associated with Gorgias: so e.g. Arist.*Rh.*1406b.4ff. and Hermog.*Id.*248f.Rabe.

18. *Abnormality of other specific orators*

No specific testimony seems to exist for several of the orators. There is some for Demosthenes: D.H. speaks of his μυρίοις...τρόποις (*Dem.*48); Hermogenes (*Id.*248f.Rabe) uses him to illustrate tropes (although he always prefers to use Demosthenic examples anyway); and D. is likewise among the select group of prose authors on whom Longinus draws to illustrate his discussion of metaphor (*Subl.*32).

19. *Dubious and irrelevant evidence*

Some dubious or dubiously relevant items have already been discussed. I add here a further sample and a few general thoughts.

(i) Some evidence is pitched at too high a level of generality. Statements to the effect that 'author *X* is poetical', for instance, are of little value in themselves. In particular, many remarks made about the poeticality of a given prose writer's style are probably concerned not with *how* words are used (literally, tropically, metaphorically) but with *what sort of* words they are (high-flown, archaic, vulgar etc.). A good example: Longinus, *Subl.*31 on colloquialism in Herodotus and Theopompus (see Russell *ad loc.*).

(ii) Many remarks on metaphor that might be taken to concern the *frequency* with which an author uses it in fact concern the *boldness* of his metaphors, which is quite different. One cannot infer from e.g. D.H.*Dem.*18 (on Isocrates), ἄτολμός ἐστι περὶ τὰς τροπικὰς κατασκευάς, whether Isoc. uses tropes seldom or often.

(iii) Metaphor is a *trope*, not a *scheme*. Remarks on σχήματα are irrelevant: thus e.g. Plut.*Moral.*835b (on Andocides) ἐν τοῖς λόγοις ἀφελής τε καὶ ἀσχημάτιστος. Even so experienced a scholar as Jebb was not free from confusion here: witness his discussion of Dionysius' phrase ποικίλη περὶ τοὺς σχηματισμούς (*Comp.*22, 1.98 U-R, used of writers in the 'austere style'), which he translates as 'fanciful in imagery' (see Jebb *AO* 1.23 and 27ff.). (For information on σχήματα and σχηματισμοί besides e.g. Volkmann 456ff., see D.S.12.53 on Gorgias; further references in Russell 126-8; cf. also my remarks on Thucydides above, p. 218.)

(iv) The Three Styles formula (χαρακτὴρ ἰσχνός, μέσος, ὑψηλός).* Mention has already been made of the formula apropos Marcellinus' comments on Thucydides (above, p.216). Although the formula evolved comparatively late, it might be thought that reasonable inferences about metaphoricality could be drawn from its applications by ancient theorists. Since e.g. Lysias wrote in the 'plain' style and Gorgias in the 'grand' style, one might presume that if a writer is said to write in the grand style, he will probably be a user of metaphor; if in the intermediate style, he will be less likely to be a user of metaphor; if in the plain style, not likely at all. But such inferences would only be reasonable if it were clear (*a*) that the criteria by which the styles were assigned to authors necessarily included scale of metaphoricality; and (*b*) that any author could be acceptably assigned to one of the styles. In fact, neither condition is fulfilled.

On the first point, Marcellinus serves to show that the ancient verdicts about χαρακτήρ and metaphoricality may have little or nothing to do with each other. On the evidence available, one would not suppose that antiquity distinguished greatly between the metaphoricality of Thucydides, Herodotus and Xenophon; yet for Marcellin. (*Vit.Thuc.*39-41) they exemplify the ὑψηλός, μέσος and ἰσχνός χαρακτήρ respectively. Again, D.H. plausibly ascribed to Plato a combination of the ὑψηλός and ἰσχνός (*Dem.*5), which ought to imply, very implausibly, that Pl. must have been less metaphorical than Thucydides, who is simply ὑψηλός (*teste Marcellino*, cf. D.H.*Dem.*1-3, Demetr.*Eloc.*38-49). And again, Gellius tells us (6.14.7) that different speakers in Homer exemplify the different styles: *magnificum*

---

* For a good brief discussion see Russell xxxiv-xxxvii. It is worth mentioning here that there is actually a considerably greater scarcity of ancient material (especially Greek material) about, or based on, the formula than its notoriety would lead one to suppose.

in Ulixe..., *subtile in Menelao...*, *mixtum...in Nestore*. But would anyone care to ascribe a greater use of metaphor to Odysseus than to Nestor, or to Nestor than to Menelaus? Finally, there is evidence to show that there could be formal disagreement between theorists as to the implication of a given style. Thus with the prescriptive interpretations* of the plain style by Demetrius (*Eloc.*190) and Cicero (*Orat.*81). For Cic. metaphor is allowable, albeit in small doses; for Demetr. it is not allowable at all. It would be surprising if comparable disagreements did not arise all along the line, but the more insidious for being unspoken.

On the second point, one can begin by noting that, on the evidence just given, Plato and Homer supposedly exemplify more than one style. This might be taken to mean only that certain authors have an unusual range; and it is certainly true that Plato in particular is sometimes credited with such a range: Demetrius ascribes all the styles† to him (see Schenkeveld 58) and at least one source even attempts to tell us in which dialogues Pl. inclines more towards which χαρακτήρ (see *Proleg.Plat. Philosophiae* 211f. in *Platonis Dialogi* ed. C. F. Hermann, Leipzig, 1884, vol.VI). Demosthenes, likewise, is said to possess all three styles by Cicero (*Orat.*20–3). But the truth goes uncomfortably deeper. As Quintilian saw, *any* author may be expected to vary his choice of style (*utetur...*, *ut res exiget, omnibus, Inst.Orat.* 12.10.69, specifically of the orator) and the tidy picture of three styles is, in any case, only a convenient fiction: there are endless gradations (*innumerabiles species reperiuntur*, 12.10.67). In consequence, the assignment of an author to a single style is a drastic (let alone, for us, irrelevant) oversimplification. Operating with the few fixed styles of theory and yet confronted with the complexities of practice, the ancient theorist was liable to come up with bizarre results. A recent student of Demetrius provides a suggestive example, remarking that for him, 'even viewed from the same aspect, a passage may belong simultaneously to several types of style' (Schenkeveld 55f.).

It is evident, then, that the Three Styles formula cannot help us. And one can say this, notwithstanding the fact that (say) D.H. sometimes uses the formula in connection with testimony which is in fact acceptable in its own right. The point is not that the formula can *never* be correlated with metaphoricality, but that in a doubtful case one cannot know *when* it can.

* Prescriptive testimony is, of course, suspect in its own right, independently of the Three Styles, inasmuch as one cannot infer a description from a prescription. Take e.g. *Proleg. Syll.* (*Rhet.Gr.*XIV) 13, p. 207 Rabe: τὸ μὲν προοίμιον σαφὲς...ἐστὶ καὶ λέξιν μεταφορικὴν οὐχ ἔχον, ὁ δὲ ἐπίλογος σαφὴς μέν ἐστιν...δυνατὸν δὲ καὶ λέξει μεταφορικῇ χρήσασθαι (cf. Quintil.11.1.6). One cannot infer that any Greek orator's practice specifically corresponded with this – let alone infer *which* orators that would mean.

† In Demetrius' case, four styles, not three.

APPENDIX IV

Some notes on alliteration in Greek

These notes instance only a few of the manifestations of 'significant' alliteration in popular and literary Greek.

1. It is generally accepted, for Greek as for other languages, that whatever its current literary applications, alliteration is a characteristic feature of 'popular' genres. (So Parke–Wormell xxiv, Strömberg 12, Defradas 43, Opelt 208f.) Where Greek is concerned, there is indeed abundant evidence to substantiate the tendency, principally from proverbs, also from the few surviving folk songs. A third potential source, liturgy, cannot now be tapped. (The pitiful fragments may be found in Dieterich 213ff. One has occasional echoes in lines like A.*Ag.*1485f. ἰὼ ἰή, διαὶ Διὸς παναιτίου πανεργέτα, which Pfeiffer, p.4, rightly calls 'hieratic'.)* Notable proverbial examples (from Leutsch–Schneidewin) are:

ἀγαθοὶ δ' ἀριδάκρυες ἄνδρες
γεννητὸς γεγονὼς τήρει τὴν τάξιν
εὖ κείμενον κακὸν κινεῖς
καὶ κεραμεὺς κεραμεῖ κοτέει   (= Hes.*Op.*25)
κακοῦ κόρακος κακὸν ᾠόν
λεχὼ λέαιναν καὶ κακὸς κύων φοβεῖ
μετὰ Μαραθῶνα μάχη
μήτε μοι μέλι μήτε μέλισσα   (= Sapph.146)
μία μέλισσα μέλι οὐ ποιεῖ
πολλαῖσι πληγαῖς δρῦς δαμάζεται
ποταμὸς τὰ πόρρω ποτίζων
πτωχοῦ πήρα οὐ πίμπλαται
τὰ Ταντάλου τάλαντα τανταλίζεται   (= Anacr.10)

(The fact that several of these are metrical, i.e. – in extant shape – literary, is of little moment.† The fact that it was alliterative phrases, whether literary or not, that took root is what matters.‡) Naturally, there are simpler types as well: ἀρότρῳ ἀκοντίζεις, βίος βαλανίτης, δακτύλῳ δείκνυται, ἐν Καρὶ τὸν κίνδυνον, μὴ κάρφος κινεῖν, μὴ κίνει Καμάριναν, λίθῳ λαλεῖς, λύω λέσχας, μία Μύκονος, πλίνθον πλύνεις.§

* Cf. the list of aural (but rarely alliterative) effects associated with parallel structure given by Kranz 127–34 under the heading, 'das alte Lied: kultische Elemente'. The popular provenance of 'symmetrical repetitions' (again without reference to alliteration as such) is discussed by K. J. Dover, *Theocritus, Select Poems*, London, 1971, xlvii–lxii.

† The examples from Sapph. and Anacr. are cited above in their literary forms. (As is, of course, the Hesiod instance, which is, presumably, original to him and proverbial only thereafter.)

‡ Whether the proverbs are literary or not, one can seldom know when they took root. Proverbs are often wholly undatable. Some of those discussed here may well be later than 'early Greek', although 'late' linguistic features are not necessarily a guide: old proverbs may at any time be *slightly* up-dated.

§ The alliterative structure of πλίνθον πλύνεις corresponds to that of Terence's *laterem lavem* (*Phormio* 186), which might be based on this very phrase (both refer to 'lost labour'): see Kock

Add also κυσὶ κανθαρίς from Miller, *Mélanges* 374 and τὸ παρὸν εὖ ποιεῖν from Pl. *Grg.*499c (explicitly referred to as a proverb). From folk-songs, note the following: *Carm.Pop.*17 (Page *PMG*) ἄρχει μὲν ἀγών...καιρὸς δὲ καλεῖ μηκέτι μέλλειν, 18 πόρρω παῖδες μετάβατε πόδας (*vel sim.*; see Page's apparatus), 35 ἐκκόρει κόρη κορώνην (ditto).*

2. Alliteration in parallel structure ('to have and to hold') is surprisingly rare in Greek proverbs, although parallel structure itself is common enough there (cf. Strömberg 12). A few instances from Leutsch–Schneidewin:

> ἄλλοισι μὲν γλῶττα, ἄλλοισι δὲ γομφίοι
> ἄμ' ἔπος, ἄμ' ἔργον
> ἢ κρίνον ἢ κολοκύντην
> σκιὰ ἀντὶ σώματος

In contrast, a good number of simple proverbial comparisons are supported in this way ('plain as a pikestaff'):

> ἀκαρπότερος ἀγρίππου
> ἀκαρπότερος Ἀδώνιδος κήπου (ἀ-κ. Ἀ.κ.)
> κωφότερος κίχλης
> λεπτότερον λεβηρίδος
> λιπαρώτερος ληκυθίου
> λιπαρώτερος λύχνου
> μολύβδου μαλθακώτερον
> μωρότερος Μορύχου
> Παύσωνος πτωχότερος
> πραότερος περιστερᾶς
> συστομώτερος σκάφης.

Strömberg (p.8) suggests also as proverbial πηλοῦ παχύτερος from Eunapius (without reference to the prevalence of the type in 'official' proverbs). Cf. also A.*Supp.*760 κρείσσονας λύκους κυνῶν, expressly called a φήμη. The question arises: are comic examples of this kind, as Diph.78 πόρκων πυκνοτέρους, borrowed directly from popular usage or are they modelled on it? For it is clear that the type is essentially non-literary; it is much less common in my corpus (see above, pp.184, 186) than in the proverbial collections, despite the much greater bulk of the former.†

3. The intensive alliteration of Thgn.213ff., φίλους κατὰ πάντας ἐπίστρεφε ποικίλον ἦθος...· πουλύπου ὀργὴν ἴσχε πολυπλόκου, ὃς ποτὶ πέτρῃ τῇ προσο-

on Com. *Adesp.*891. If so, this would incidentally suggest that one Roman, at least, was sensitive to alliteration in Greek.

* It is noteworthy how few non-consonantal alliterations there are in this list. I have not thought it proper to include 'imperfect' instances (such as αὐτὸς αὐτὸν αὐλεῖ, from Leutsch–Schneidewin).

† The equivalent '*N* like *V*' in simile, common in the corpus (see above, pp.184–6), does not seem to occur in proverbs, although it is attested elsewhere in what might be popularisms: Lysipp.8 κύων...ἐβόα...ὥσπερ Βούδιος, Hp.*Mul.*1.61 μαλθακὸς ὡς μνοῦς ('soft as down', of the σπλήν).

μιλήσῃ..., is paralleled on a lesser scale by Ar.*fr*.191 πληγαὶ λέγονται πουλύπου πιλουμένου, by Pl.Com.173.17 πουλύποδος πλεκτὴ δ', εἰ πιλήσεις..., by Eup.101 ἀνὴρ πολίτης πουλύπους, and most significantly by Pi.*fr*.43 ποντίου θηρὸς πετραίου χρωτὶ μάλιστα νόον προσφέρων πάσαις πολίεσσιν ὁμίλει.* Pindar does not, apparently, use the actual word πουλύπους, but employs the same π-alliteration as the other writers who do use the word. The quotations above, one notes, vary greatly in particular subject, the only common feature being allusion to the poulp. The only plausible inference is that π-alliteration and the poulp were traditionally associated; whether in imitation of some definitive description one cannot say.†
The predominantly comic character of the passages may indicate a popular etymon.

4. The manifest structural kinship of Aeschylus' κλύδων κακῶν, κ. κρηπίς, κ. τρικυμία, κ. ...κῦμα,‡ and κρατῆρα...κακῶν (above, p. 179 with n.5) acquires a special significance in the light of related phrases elsewhere. There seems to have been an almost formulaic structure consisting of κ- κακῶν, where κ- is a metaphorical noun and κακῶν its dependent genitive. The etymon of these phrases may be lost, but Aeschylus appears to have been a key figure in the development, and his are the first extant examples. In the whole of post-Aeschylean literature (prose included), I have found fourteen more instances. It appears that after Aeschylus the tradition develops along two lines. (1) The actual Aeschylean phrases are copied without substantial change: κακῶν...κῦμα (E.*Ion* 927), κλύδωνα...κακῶν (E. *Med*.362), κλύδωνι κακῶν (Hld.*Aethiop*.2.17), κῦμ' ἐπέκλυζεν κακῶν (Lyc.228) and κρατὴρ κακῶν (Ar.*Ach*.937, of a person, unlike A.*Ag*.1397). (2) Apparently new phrases are generated with the alliterative structure intact, but with greater variety of genitival relations. Some of the instances may be cliché rather than live metaphor, especially, for obvious reasons, the proverbs cited last: κηλὶς κακῶν (S.*OC* 1134), μοῖρα κεδνῶν καὶ κακῶν κυνηγέτι (*Trag.Adesp*.504), πλοῦτος...παρακάλυμμα τῶν κακῶν (Antiph.167), πλοῦτος...πολλῶν ἐπικάλυμμ'...κακῶν (Men.84), τὸ κεφάλαιον τῶν κακῶν (of avarice, Apollod.Gel.4 and Anon.*Vita Thucydidis* p.201, 54 Westermann), and three proverbs from Leutsch–Schneidewin, κύρβεις κακῶν (see LSJ κύρβεις III), κορωνίδας κακῶν, κολοφὼν κακῶν (for the last two see L–Schn. on Greg.Cyp.2.86). Consider the following facts: (i) there seems to be no other extant instance of alliterative link in Aeschylus – or elsewhere? – with a comparable history. (ii) There are only two other comparable examples of interactive alliterative link in the whole of the proverbial collections, νὶς μέλιτος μυελός and – derivatively parallel to the κ. κακῶν type? – ἀγαθῶν ἀγαθίδες (a 'bags of luck' kind of phrase, ἀγαθίς being a ball of thread). (iii) The distribution of those instances not, to our knowledge, formally identical with Aeschylus' shows a distinct popular bias:

* Cf. also Archestr.53.

† It can at least be said that the 'definitive description', if any, does not appear to have been the epic 'Αμφιαράου ἐξέλασις, whose *content* may lie behind the pareneses of Pindar and Theognis (see I. U. Powell, *Collectanea Alexandrina*, Oxford, 1925, p. 246, no. 2 and van Groningen on Thgn.215).

‡ This particular association may be responsible for the phraseology of A.*Ag*.653 δυσκύμαντα δ' ὠρώρει κακά, where the waves are literal waves. I note also, for what it may be worth, that Mette conjectures another interactive κῦμα κακῶν ('beispielshalber') at A.*fr*.223a.8.

three proverbs and three occurrences in comedy among only nine instances. It is hard to avoid the inference that Aeschylus established a poetic structure which thereby and thereafter acquired a possibly unparalleled generative capacity; and either that the structure pre-existed as a popular, presumably proverbial, form, of which we have three, presumably later, manifestations, or that Aeschylus himself was a formative influence on proverbial structure.* The latter conclusion may seem the more plausible in view of the fact that these alliterative interactions (with genitive links) are not otherwise characteristic of those Greek proverbs that survive,† whereas they are peculiarly characteristic of Aeschylean style (see above, p. 179).

5. There is such a thing as creative invention based on alliterative association. At *IT* 1394ff., Euripides, through the mouth of a messenger, describes Iphigenia's ship in a rough sea:

> δεινὸς γὰρ ἐλθὼν ἄνεμος ἐξαίφνης νεὼς
> ὠθεῖ παλίμπρυμν' ἱστί'· οἱ δ' ἐκαρτέρουν
> πρὸς κῦμα λακτίζοντες· ἐς δὲ γῆν πάλιν
> κλύδων παλίρρους ἧγε ναῦν.

The phrase πρὸς κῦμα λακτίζοντες graphically suggests painful labour; and the hopelessness of that labour is implicit in the inevitable – alliterative-enforced – association with the proverb for lost causes, πρὸς κέντρα λακτίζειν (see e.g. Dodds on E.*Ba.*795), on which the phrase is based.

6. Rhythmically structured alliteration has a character all of its own, as any reader of G. M. Hopkins can attest. I do not think that there are many instances in (earlier) Greek poetry, but there are certainly some and these seem to pass unnoticed. A good instance occurs in the lyrical section towards the end of the *Choephori*. The first strophe of that section begins (936)

> ἔμολε μὲν **δ**ί**κα**...ἔμολε δ' ἐς **δ**ό**μον**,

the first antistrophe (946)

> ἔμολε δ' ᾧ **μ**έ**λει**...ἔθιγε δ' ἐν **μ**ά**χ**ᾳ.

7. A note on a representative unbeliever. Denniston's moderate scepticism towards the existence of significant alliteration in Greek (above, ooo, n.3) rests on the insubstantial foundations of (1) intentionalism and (2) obliviousness to the necessity of thinking out what 'significant' might imply in the way of function. He

---

* The comic instances doubtless derive directly from the proverbial structure, irrespective of the latter's origin.

† Although attested in comedy: μέλιττα Μούσης (of love) Ar.*Ec.*974, σοφιστῶν σμῆνος Cratin.2 (whence σμῆνος σοφίας Pl.*Crat.*401e?). There is also evidence of the type in Orphic sources, which might, like liturgy, be taken to be a possible representative of the stylistic modes of popular, rather than literary, Greek: δάκρυα Διός ('rain') *Orphica* 22 Diels–Kranz; cf., conceivably, ἀνάγκης ἄτρακτον Pl.*R.*616c (in the Orphic-influenced myth of Er).

does not reject alliteration outright. He recognizes and stresses its existence in the Presocratics (where it is, indeed, often so intense that even a computer could detect it); he is impressed by Sophocles' τυφλός...; but he decides, no doubt rightly, that there are few exactly comparable instances in Greek *poetry*, and concludes that therefore (the logic is his, not mine) even in the case of Sophocles' τυφλός... 'we must refrain from seeing design in this assonance'. Which, for Denniston, apparently closes the matter; there is *no* significant alliteration in Greek poetry. Where does one start? Having accepted alliteration for one genre (the Presocratics), it is not open to Denniston to deny it to other genres on theoretical grounds (grounds like Wölfflin's, below). Nor does he. He denies it primarily on grounds of relative infrequency (impressionistically judged) and the 'it' that he denies is essentially the τυφλός kind of multiple 'expressive' alliteration. The logic in full is:

because   (*a*) there are few poetic parallels to τυφλός...
therefore   (*b*) alliteration is uncharacteristic of Greek poetry
and   (*c*) if uncharacteristic, therefore unintentional in all cases.

Of these (*a*) is, I believe, true; (*b*) is false, relying on an arbitrary assumption that multiple (expressive) alliteration is the only kind that counts; and (*c*) may be true (though why it *must* be true is not clear) but, where significant existence is concerned, is irrelevant.

8. Finally, the superficially impressive argument, accepted by Wölfflin among others (see Opelt 206), that alliteration cannot exist in a language that lacks a stress accent, becomes less plausible as soon as one recalls the ease with which aural structures can be imposed wholescale on supposedly 'alien' language systems, as, for instance, quantitative metrics were imposed on Latin. For the association between alliteration and stress is no more necessary than that between quantity and non-stress (see above, p.175, n.13).

APPENDIX V

Confusion in ancient stylistics between metaphor and 'dead metaphor' (see above, p. 52 with n.5)

Instances of cliché or 'dead metaphor' cited simply as metaphor are not difficult to find. Another good instance: Phld.*Rh*.1.179 (xx.17ff.) cites νῆσον τὴν πέρι πόντος ...ἐστεφάνωται (*Od*.10.195) despite e.g. *Il*.15.153, Hes.*Th*.382, *h.Ven*.120, Hp.*Aer*.19, Hdt.7.130.1, Ar.*Pl*.787. Such confusion at its most grotesque permits acknowledged 'dead metaphors' to be quoted as instances of *bold* usage. Thus Cicero (*Orat*.81f.) uses *audacter* of *laetas segetes* and other usages which, as he says, *frequentissime sermo omnis utitur non modo urbanorum sed etiam rusticorum*.

Some scholars would think it perverse to speak of 'confusion' as I have, on the grounds that the distinction in question was not recognized as such in ancient theory, which had, instead, the notion of an unchanging κατὰ φύσιν χρῆσις. Cf.

Russell on Longinus (p.127): 'One basic assumption of the whole theory must be emphasized – namely that there really is a κατὰ φύσιν χρῆσις, deviations from which can be recognized. This was L's assumption; in reading him – and indeed all the writers on figures – we must remember that they think of this φύσις as something immutable and that they are quite without the historical sense of modern scholarship, which recognizes from the start that "natural expression" varies from age to age... – if indeed there is such a thing at all.' So the norm would be permanent and deviations permanently deviant: once a trope or figure, always a trope or figure. But in fact this simple picture of ancient theory involves a large oversimplification. It is certainly true that there was this notion of 'natural' usage; and correlatively, although remarks acknowledging the inevitability of linguistic change can be pointed to (e.g. Varro *LL* 9.17), there *was* a reluctance to admit formally the idea that such change, especially if *semantic* change, could be permanent (cf. generally Waldron 113ff.); accordingly, instances of the confusion like those cited above were bound to arise. But it would be quite false to suggest that no ancient theorist was aware that the point from which deviations actually (i.e. perceptibly) operate is normal usage (which changes from time to time) and not 'natural' usage (which cannot change); or that every comment on tropical or figurative deviations presupposes the concept of 'natural' usage rather than that of normal usage. When Aristotle says that 'we all use μεταφοραί in our ordinary discourse' (*Rh.*1404b.22), he is obviously presupposing the concept of 'natural' usage, deviations from which remain deviations however accepted they may become. But when D.H. says that 'Lysias hardly uses tropes and metaphors' (*Vett.Cens.*IX U–R), he can only be presupposing the other (superior) concept of normal usage, usage from which, he assures us, Lysias almost never deviates: that Lysias must have used 'dead metaphors' ('dead metonymies' etc.) as much as anyone else is obvious and must have been obvious to D.H. (because, as Aristotle says, we *all*...). And likewise when D.H., elsewhere (*Comp.*3), singles out a Herodotean passage for its 'extreme literalness', despite the presence of several likely candidates for 'dead metaphor' (συνεκδύεται...τὴν αἰδῶ, ἀπεμάχετο = 'argued', and λόγον ὑγιᾶ, see above, p.54, n.6). Again, on occasion the theorists specifically and correctly note that a particular instance of a trope or figure may come to be normal usage and thereby lose its tropical or figurative status. So e.g. Quintil.9.3.4, *quamquam sunt quaedam figurae ita receptae, ut paene iam hoc ipsum nomen effugerint*; and 9.3.13, *quae ille quidem fecerit schemata, an idem vocari possint videndum, quia recepta sint* ('these instances may have been figurative when he [sc. Sallust] used them; the question is whether they can [sc. still] be called figurative, having passed into general usage').

Ancient theory, then, was fluid or, more accurately, permitted a constant, if usually unexpressed, tension between the rival pulls of perception and dogma. A graphic instance is the definition of trope in Cocondrius περὶ τρόπων III.230 Spengel, τρόπος ἐστὶ φράσις ἐκβεβηκυῖα τὴν κοινὴν καὶ πρωτότυπον τοῦ λόγου χρῆσιν...ἢ λέξις ἢ φράσις ἐκ τοῦ συνήθους παρατετραμμένη..., which would seem to have it both ways. Some theorists, notably D.H., were admirably alive to the practical implications of the normal usage principle, but in general the unsatisfactory tension simply persisted. What was lacking was not Russell's 'historical sense', which by itself is as likely as not to perpetuate an obsession with origins at the expense of current status, but the strength of mind to counter a limp tendency to subordinate experience to 'reason'. (Cf. the tendency of ancient science to elevate speculative theory above concrete experiment.)

APPENDIX VI

Apologetic ὥσπερ (see above, pp. 52, 55)

Like τις (cf. above, p. 55, n.10), ὥσπερ can certainly 'apologize for' much else besides metaphor, though even when one can be sure that a given instance does not involve metaphor, it may still be unclear precisely what is involved (as with the Xenophon instance quoted on p. 52). The crucial problem can be seen for what it is in the following list (mostly drawn, as it happens, from Thphr.*HP*), in which none of the items involves live metaphor (as is clear from independent evidence), though some might be thought to involve 'dead metaphor'. (i) It appears that ὥσπερ (or ὡσπερεί) can qualify other tropes, e.g. metonymy. *HP* 1.4.2, 'some plants like dry soil', ἔνια δὲ ὡσπερεὶ κάθυγρα καὶ ἕλεια, καθάπερ ἰτέα – i.e. *wet* soil/soil *with* water in it, but not actually *watery* soil/soil *in* water, as the word might suggest. (ii) Or simple overstatement. *HP* 6.8.2 ταῦτα μὲν οὖν ὥσπερ ἐαρινὰ φαίνεται, 'these, then, are the plants of spring, so to speak', the point being that some of them actually appear in winter (see 6.8.1 *init.*). (iii) Or vagueness. *HP* 7.9.3 αἱ μὲν γὰρ λευκαί, αἱ δὲ μέλαιναι...αἱ δ᾽ ὥσπερ ξανθαί, 'some are white, some black, some a kind of yellow'. (iv) Or technicality? *HP* 1.12.2, on the relation between fruit's physical make-up and its flavour: δεῖ γὰρ ὥσπερ τὸ μὲν ὕλην ὑπολαβεῖν τὸ δὲ εἶδος καὶ μορφήν, 'we must consider the one [sc. τὰ περικάρπια] as *matter*, the other [sc. flavour] as *form*'. These are Aristotelian technical terms and ὥσπερ seems equivalent to an italicization or a use of inverted commas. Cf. perhaps Ar.*Nub.*1276 τὸν ἐγκέφαλον ὥσπερ σεσεῖσθαί μοι δοκεῖς, 'in my judgement, you're suffering from concussion', where there is no question of a live metaphor being qualified, since σείεσθαι is the normal medical *technicality* for the affliction in question (Hp.*Morb.*1.4 ἢν ὁ ἐγκέφαλος σεισθῇ τε καὶ πονέσῃ, so *Aph.* 7.58, *Coac.*163 and 489, *Prorrh.*1.143; cf. Ar.*Ach.*12, Thphr.*Vert.*8, Hp.*Epid.*5.103 and 7.49, *Art.*48, *Mochl.*36). Starkie, however, takes ὥσπερ as equivalent to a mannered 'I think', while Dover, less plausibly, seems to imply that this is *simile*. (v) And some instances suggest other possibilities. One example: D.3.7 ἐπράξαμεν ...εἰρήνην· ἢν τοῦθ᾽ ὥσπερ ἐμπόδισμά τι τῷ Φιλίππῳ καὶ δυσχερές, 'we made peace: which was an obstacle to Philip...'. There can be no doubt that the whole ἐμποδ- word-group, used of non-physical obstacles, is normal usage by the fourth century: so ἐμποδών A.*Prom.*13, Ar.*Lys.*1161, Lys.13.88 etc.; ἐμπόδιος Hdt.5.90.1, E.*Ion* 862, Arist.*EN* 1175b.2 etc.; ἐμποδίζειν Ar.*Av.*965, D.24.94, Aeschin.3.223, Arist.*EN* 1100b.29 etc.; ἐμποδιστικός Arist.*EN* 1153b.2, al.; ἐμπόδισμος Arist.*Rh.* 1378b.18, al.; and ἐμπόδισμα itself, Pl.*Plt.*295b, *Phlb.*63d, *Crat.*413d. The last three formations are both the least common and the latest attested of the group; ἐμπόδισμα itself is attested only in the Demosthenes (*Olynthiac* III, 349/8 B.C.) and in

Plato as indicated. (It should be remembered that none of these words is attested in any sense before the mid fifth century anyway: the earliest occurrences of the primary ἐμποδών are at Hdt.1.80.3, al., A.*Prom.* (*loc. cit.*), A.*Th.*1016 (the suspect part of the play), S.*OT* 128.) It is, accordingly, possible that the ὥσπερ is qualifying a *neologism*. Another possibility is that the cast of the sentence is what needs the apology: it is fairly rare for an abstract noun in -μα to be subject of the copula (see A. A. Long, *Language and Thought in Sophocles*, London, 1968, p.75). Alternatively, we might simply have a mannerism here, a studied vagueness, conceivably amounting to a bland litotes: 'this was a sort of – well – *obstacle* (shall we say?) to Philip'.*

I would not wish to deny that ὥσπερ *can* qualify metaphor. Pl.*Smp.*219b ταῦτα ἀκούσας τε καὶ εἰπὼν καὶ ἀφεὶς ὥσπερ βέλη is surely one instance. Cf. e.g. Thphr. *HP* 1.13.4, a passage that would be a good candidate for the scientist's 'electric current' kind of metaphor (prospective technicality, not yet established): φασὶ δὲ...ὅσα...ἔχει τῶν ἀνθῶν ὥσπερ ἠλακάτην τινὰ πεφυκυῖαν ἐκ μέσου ταῦτ' εἶναι γόνιμα, 'they say that those flowers with a kind of distaff growing in the middle are fruitful' – although the φασί may actually imply the normality of ἠλακάτη thus. But as with τις (above, pp. 52, 55), the versatility and deviousness† of ὥσπερ and its lack of any clear-cut categories of use preclude it as an indicator of metaphor – especially insofar as it can qualify *for some other reason* expressions that are, coincidentally, cliché or 'dead metaphor' (cf. D.3.7 above). But for my purposes, the whole question is almost academic: it is very rare for any dubious usage of practical concern to me to recur in an 'apology' formula.

APPENDIX VII

Privative and limiting epithets as a criterion for the presence of live metaphor (*above, p. 56, n.18*)

Arist.*Rh.*1408a.7ff., discussing 'epithets derived from privations', notes that εὐδοκιμεῖ...τοῦτο ἐν ταῖς μεταφοραῖς λεγόμενον ταῖς ἀνάλογον οἷον τὸ φάναι τὴν σάλπιγγα εἶναι μέλος ἄλυρον (cf. also Po.1457b.30ff.). What is in question, then, is what Cope–Sandys call 'privative explanatory epithets' (or equivalent phrases) attached to a metaphor as exemplified by (Twining's example, quoted by Cope–Sandys *ad loc.*)

Isaiah 51.21 Thou drunken, but *not with wine*

and by such Greek examples as

Hes.*Op.*702ff. ...γυναικὸς...
...ἥτ' ἄνδρα καὶ ἴφθιμόν περ ἐόντα
εὔει ἄτερ δαλοῖο

---

* The fact that the Demosthenes passage (like some others) combines ὥσπερ with τις is noteworthy, but no distinctive explanation presents itself.

† Cf. the short list of examples given by Schwyzer 2.668f., which is very sensibly provided with the umbrella heading, '*gleichsam, gewissermassen*, vor ungewöhnlich gebrauchten Ausdrücken u.ä.'

Pi.*O.6.46*f.   ἐθρέψαντο δράκοντες ἀμεμφεῖ
        ἰῷ μελισσᾶν καδόμενοι (i.e. honey)

Thgn.549   ἄγγελος ἄφθογγος (i.e. beacon-fire)

'The same end', notes Twining, 'is often answered by an epithet affirming of the thing expressed some quality of the thing signified' – i.e. by a limiting epithet as

A.*Prom.*1021f. Διὸς. . .πτηνὸς κύων (i.e. eagle)

or, from Keats' *On Melancholy*,

No, no! go not to Lethe, neither twist
Wolf's-bane, tight-rooted, for its *poisonous* wine.

Such instances might seem to belong to a readily recognizable type, and a type, presumably, involving metaphor. If so, the presence of a limiting or negative epithet (etc.) in such a structure might be a reliable indication of the presence of metaphor.

In fact, the same structure can contain other things besides metaphor. Other tropes, for instance (despite Aristotle's ταῖς ἀνάλογον). Thus, the Aristotelian example of τὴν σάλπιγγα. . .μέλος ἄλυρον involves, one might think, *catachresis*. Again, one of Twining's examples is from Dryden's *Song for St Cecilia's Day*,

Jubal struck the *chorded* shell,

where 'shell' is *metonymic* for 'lyre' (the original lyre being a tortoise-shell). Alternatively, the most innocently literal use of words can be so structured, as with

ἔν τ' ἀλύροις κλέοντες ὕμνοις (E.*Alc.*447),

where the hymns are real, unlike the one at A.*Eu.*331f.,

ὕμνος ἐξ Ἐρινύων. . .ἀφόρμικτος

– although no confusion would usually arise in such cases, provided an extended context existed. Much the most serious objection to the indicative value of the structure is the fact that the epithet (etc.) may negate or limit, not metaphor, but cliché or 'dead metaphor'. Thus, the description of heaven as a 'spiritual kingdom', in contradistinction to temporal, earthly, kingdoms, contains no metaphor. 'The kingdom' (of heaven) is cliché, normal idiom, and remains so irrespective of the addition of the limiting epithet. Similarly with Aristophanes' description of his frogs as λιμναῖα κρηνῶν τέκνα (*Ran.*211). The epithet undoubtedly limits the overt sense or use of its noun, in that ordinary (i.e. human) children are not 'marshy'. But in the given sense, τέκνον is cliché, like 'kingdom'. Close parallels are to hand from early lyric (Alc.359 θαλάσσας τέκνον. . .χέλυς), contemporary comedy (Ar.*V.* 1518 = *Trag.Adesp.*69; Pl.Com.173.11), elegy (Ion Eleg.1.11), tragedy (A.*Pe.*618, E.*El.*897, Chaerem.Trag.9 and 10.3) and, for good measure, epic parody (Archestr. 49.3); an unusual distribution (this list is complete), but the spread over the genres and the disproportionately high occurrence in the comedy/parody group in particular and later fifth century verse in general indicate *fin de siècle* poetic cliché. Another good instance: Pi.*P.*4.74 μέσον ὀμφαλὸν εὐδένδροιο. . .ματέρος, i.e. not a human mother, but the earth μήτηρ, which is palpable cliché: quite apart from γῆ being θεῶν μήτηρ at *h.Hom.*30.17, Sol.24.4f., S.*fr.*290 and the common Homeric type exemplified by *Il.*8.47 Ἴδην...μητέρα θηρῶν (so with χθών Hes.*Th.*284), γῆ/γαῖα is the all-embracing μήτηρ at Hes.*Op.*563, Eumel.*fr.*9, Pi.*O.*7.38, A.*Th.*16, E.*Hipp.*601, Pl.*R.*414e, Men.*fr.*287.1.

The point clearly emerges, then, that far from necessarily operating on, and therefore testifying to, a live metaphorical use, the epithet (etc.) can only be presumed to be operative on a *secondary* use of a word, which may be a stock use. As such, it affords no relevant criterion.

APPENDIX VIII

On the history of intentionalism

These additional remarks to §25 make no claim to completeness. A large proportion of all the comments on literature ever made would have some relevance, positive or negative.

1. The stock ancient distinctions between *de industria* and *casu*, *ars* and *natura*, τέχνη and φύσις are not necessarily evaluative (cf. above, p.62, n.9); i.e. the idea of the intended as inherently superior to, or more important than, the unintended is not stressed or not there at all. And unlike e.g. *de industria* or βούλησις or ἐπινοεῖν, τέχνη and *ars* etc. are not strictly intentionalistic expressions; they do not refer specifically to the author's state of mind 'at the time', the particular time of composition. It is symptomatic that in ancient criticism these became catchwords where intentionalistic vocabulary did not. As already noted (above, p. 62, n.9), their importance stems from the didactic function of criticism in antiquity. (N.B. that the *scriptum*/*sententia* kind of contrast was primarily used in legal or other non-literary contexts, as *ad Herenn.*1.19, 2.13; Cic.*Part.Orat.*108; Quintil.7.6.1.)

2. It has always been common enough for *authors* to explain their *own* intentions; Ter.*Eun.*23ff., Spenser's letter to Raleigh, Dante's to Can Grande della Scala, Henry James's prefaces. This is a different matter from *critics'* intentionalism.

3. Where a modern commentator might say 'he *intends* an allusion to...', the typical ancient commentator to Persius (*Prol.*2–3) said: *tangit Ennium qui dicit....* Not 'the poet has...in mind', but τὴν τροπὴν ἔλαβεν ἀπό... (e.g. schol.Ar.*Eq.* 114). So with informal interpretation: 'petimus...quid sit ignotus *huiusce versus* sensus' (Gellius 19.10.12, on an obscure passage in Ennius). The meaning not the intention. On commentaries see further Rutherford 9, 'the notes are few...', and 339f. on the unexpressed subject of the 'metaphrase'. The closest that ancient commentators usually come to any concern with the intention is in the curious schema called *accessus ad auctores* or *materia* or διδασκαλικά or τὰ εἰωθότα κεφά-λαια, the summary list of considerations that prefaces many commentaries of late antiquity and the middle ages. The origin of the list and its contents is obscure, but it has been plausibly traced back to Greek *philosophical* commentaries of the Imperial

period (see Quain). An early Greek exemplar is the commentary of Alexander Aphrodisias on Aristotle, an early Latin one that of Servius on Vergil. The relevance of this to intentionalism is that these lists regularly contain the item *intentio scribentis* (or *agentis*) or, in Greek, σκοπός. Thus Servius: *in exponendis auctoribus haec consideranda sunt: vita, titulus, qualitas, scribentis intentio*. . . . But what does this *intentio* mean, and what does Servius do with it? It emerges that it means 'general object' and that Servius does very little with it. The only comment made in the preface is *intentio Vergilii haec est, Homerum imitari et Augustum laudare a parentibus*, while the body of the commentary hardly displays much more interest in the question (cf. Marrou 25, Bolgar 42). And Servius is not untypical.

4. There are certainly some instances of active intentionalism in antiquity. E.g. Donatus on Ter.*Eun*.3.5.42: *sententia tragica, sed de industria, non errore* (cf. e.g. schol.Ar.*Pax* 381). The *sed*, even without the *errore*, implies evaluation. It apparently matters that it was intended: 'intentional' = 'to some purpose' = 'effective'. Compare the *mot* of Sophocles to Aeschylus (*teste* Chamael.*ap*.Athen. 428f): εἰ καὶ τὰ δέοντα ποιεῖς, ἀλλ' οὖν οὐκ εἰδώς γε ποιεῖς. But it is quite exceptional for ancient *critics* to go this far (for an instance, see Quintil.9.3.2). The critics' intentionalism, such as it is, does not usually go beyond notice of general aspiration: *digna enim fuit illa natura, quae meliora vellet; quod voluit effecit* (Quintil.10.1.131 on Seneca). The strongest expression of intentionalism in antiquity is without question voiced not by a critic, but by a philosopher: Plato. Perhaps in line with the belief that in *philosophical argument* it is essential to know τί ποτ' ἔστιν περὶ οὗ βουλευό-μεθα (*Laches* 185b), the Platonic Socrates shows a remarkable concern for poets' intentions. To begin with, he must have been the one in a million to whom it mattered and who was actually saddened by the fact, evident then as now, that poets are not necessarily reliable interpreters of their own poetry (*Apol*.22, cf. *Lg*. 719). It mattered because, one gathers, Platonism required the poetic intention to be central. Accordingly, we find Platonic espousal of intentionalism on both a theoretical and a practical level. ἑρμηνέα...τοῦ ποιητοῦ τῆς διανοίας is a fine Romantic ideal (albeit of the performer, not the critic), but from the *Ion* (530c). In the *Protagoras* interpretative analyses of Simon.37, notably by Socrates, are conducted in an unmistakable spirit: τοῦτο...οὐχ οὕτως Σιμωνίδης ὑπελάμβανεν ὥσπερ σὺ ὑπολαμβάνεις (341a), ἅ...δοκεῖ διανοεῖσθαι Σ. (341e), οἱ μὲν ταῦτά φασιν τὸν ποιητὴν νοεῖν, οἱ δ' ἕτερα (347e). The poet's meaning rather than the poem's meaning is insistently invoked throughout this part of the dialogue. (Cf. also, on a theoretical level again, *Lg*.668-9, but with the stress seemingly on the 'intention' of the work rather than its author.) That it was Plato who had this orientation is perhaps doubly significant. Not only was he, as philosopher, a rationalist hostile to poetry and concerned to develop a non-poetic method of deliberative enquiry. He was also a philosopher whose system elevated the conceptual above the sensible: reverence for the conception rather than the effect would be natural.

5. One substantial bout of intentionalism in post-classical Latinity is worthy of note, *viz* in medieval theological circles and especially among the scholastics.

Aquinas in particular, in his interpretations of canonical philosophical and theological texts, placed explicit emphasis on the intention (Chenu 129f., 177f.). Typical is: *patet hoc esse contra intentionem Aristotelis, tum quia eodem modo loquendi utitur exemplificando..., tum quia in...expresse ponit...* (quoted by Chenu 129). The popularity of the word *intentio* (in the relevant sense) in early Christian writers (see Blaise *s.v.*) attests the same emphasis; and, one may surely say, this emphasis has much more justification in interpreting holy writ (*vel sim.*) than it has in the interpretation of poetry – and, of course, like most of the other pre-Romantic manifestations of intentionalism, it is not at all literary-critical in origin.

6. Compulsive intentionalism is ultimately incompatible with any plausible literary-critical posture. The only posture it is fully compatible with is that implicit in Herder's proclamation that criticism is to be 'divination of the soul of an author' (1767, see Wellek 1.184). The implication – that the author's soul is more illuminating than the work itself – is pressed to the fullness of utter heresy by Shelley 153: 'the most glorious poetry that has ever been communicated to the world is probably a feeble shadow of the original conception of the poet.' This doctrine goes back, with ironic propriety, to the neo-Platonists, who elevated poets' conceptions to a high status by crediting them with access to the philosopher's 'Ideas' (see Grube 354f. and, for the Platonic influence on Shelley, Abrams 126ff. and 331f.; cf. also Sidney in Gregory Smith 157 and Cic.*Orat*.8ff., in the latter case of visual arts, not literature). Recent attempts to defend intentionalism tend to finish up, more bathetically, in the common *façon de parler* whereby 'intention' is simply redefined as 'meaning'. For instance, F. Cioffi, *Proc.Arist.Soc.* 1963, 85ff., makes various valid criticisms of Wimsatt (see above, p. 63, n.15), but when it comes to arguing his positive alternative – 'the notion of the author's intention is logically tied to the interpretation we give to his work' (p.97) – has only the *façon de parler* to fall back on: 'If we establish the existence of a discrepancy between the interpretation we give to a work of art and that of the author, we haven't shown that the work has a meaning independent of what the author intends, because what the author intends will now be the interpretation given to the work by us and his own statement as to its meaning an aberration.... The work will be considered more conclusive evidence of his intentions than his own statements' (97f.). Cioffi's frankness doesn't make his acrobatics any less absurd.

APPENDIX IX

V–V relations

Relations between one vehicle term and another can be very various, but none of them is to be regarded as interactive. I offer a representative list.

(1) Metaphor as ground term to simile (instead of pivot):

A.*Ag*.1093   εὖρις ἡ ξένη κυνὸς δίκην
Sapph.47   ἔρος δ' ἐτίναξέ μοι
                φρένας, ὡς ἄνεμος...*

On τινάσσειν *vis-à-vis* ἄνεμος, see above, p. 107, n.9.

235

9-2

Yeats, *The Tower*   Decrepit age that has been *tied* to me
                     As *to a dog's tail*
Romeo and Juliet I.5   It seems she *hangs upon the cheek* of night
                     Like *a rich jewel in an Ethiop's ear*
Cymbeline v.5   *Hang* there like *fruit*, my soul,
                     Till the tree die
Macbeth v.2   now does he feel his title
                     Hang loose about him like *a giant's robe*
                     Upon a dwarfish thief *

(2) Metaphor as ground term to simile (instead of support/convergence): †
A.*Ch.*505f.   παῖδες γὰρ ἀνδρὶ κληδόνες σωτήριοι
              θανόντι, φελλοὶ δ' ὣς ἄγουσι δίκτυον‡

Twelfth Night II.4   She never told her love,
              But let concealment, like *a worm i' the bud*,
              Feed on her damask cheek
Wordworth, *Upon*   This city now doth, like *a garment, wear*
Westminster Bridge   The beauty of the morning.

(3) Simile to metaphor:
A.*Eu.*111f.   οἴχεται νεβροῦ δίκην
             καὶ ταῦτα κούφως ἐκ μέσων ἀρκυστάτων
Antony and   his delights
Cleopatra v.2   Were *dolphin*-like; they *showed* his *back above*
              The element they *lived* in.

(4) Metaphor to metaphor ('the same image'): §
A.*Pe.*599ff.   ὅταν κλύδων
             κακῶν ἐπέλθῃ, πάντα δειμαίνειν φίλον,
             ὅταν δ' ὁ δαίμων εὐροῇ . . .
A.*Ag.*841f.   μόνος δ' Ὀδυσσεύς, ὅσπερ οὐχ ἑκὼν ἔπλει,
             ζευχθεὶς ἑτοῖμος ἦν ἐμοὶ σειραφόρος
Eliot, *The Waste*   the last *fingers* of leaf
Land   *Clutch* and sink into the wet bank.
Keats, *On Melancholy* Ay, in the very *temple* of Delight
              Veiled Melancholy has her sovran *shrine*.

(5) Metaphor to metaphor ('different images'):
Semon.7.83f.   τὴν δ' ἐκ μελίσσης· τήν τις εὐτυχεῖ λαβών·

---

     * The presence of 'hang' in structurally identical circumstances in these Shakespearean instances is noteworthy. For another such instance, see the 'hang like icicles' image quoted above, Prolegom.x.

     † Note that this type is not a modern discovery. It is classified as *simile . . . per brevitatem* by the author of *ad Herenn.*4.60 (see McCall 75).

     ‡ On the punctuation of this passage, see Ole Smith 58.

     § Cf. here the Shakespearean passage quoted above, Prolegom.x, where 'frosty' (metaphor) is picked up by 'hang' (metaphor) and 'hang' by 'icicles' (simile).

κείνη γὰρ οἵη μῶμος οὐ προσιҙάνει.*

Macbeth I.7

And pity, like a naked new-born babe,
Striding the blast, or heaven's cherubin, *horsed*
Upon the sightless couriers of the air,
Shall blow the horrid deed in every eye
That tears shall drown the wind. I have no *spur*
To prick the sides of my intent. . . .

(6) More akin to interaction, but still distinct from it, is the use of a word as a bridge between the vehicle of one image and that of another. λαμπρός at A.*Ag.*1180 has already been cited in this connection (above, p. 197) and has been recognized for what it is since Headlam (see Ole Smith 35). Smith 33–7 offers a discussion of such passages in Aeschylus, but unhelpfully puts them side by side with pivotal interactions and also ignores the spectacular instance at *Prom.*881ff. (see below). Headlam–Thomson on *Ag.*1001–4 suggest that the technique is characteristically Aeschylean. It is certainly not *exclusively* Aeschylean: cf. in Pindar ψᾶφον at *O.*10.9 (see Norwood 112) and κέλευθον at *P.*11.39, foreshadowing the πλόου image via evocation of the cliché ὑγρὰ κέλευθα (*Il.*1.312 etc.). But Aeschylus undoubtedly has the most notable examples: alongside *Ag.*1180 one must set *Prom.* 881ff., a passage of considerable complexity (partly recognized by Thomson *ad loc.* and Headlam–Thomson on *Ag.*1001–4).

κραδία δὲ φόβῳ φρένα λακτίζει,
τροχοδινεῖται δ' ὄμμαθ' ἑλίγδην,
ἔξω δὲ δρόμου φέρομαι λύσσης
πνεύματι μάργῳ, γλώσσης ἀκρατής·
θολεροὶ δὲ λόγοι παίουσ' εἰκῇ
στυγνῆς πρὸς κύμασιν ἄτης.

The first image offers us (V_1) a horse and chariot out of control, the details succeeding each other more or less alogically. 881 λακτίζει, the kicking horse: οἱ λακτίζοντες...ἀναβεβαμένοι ἵπποι X.*Eq.Mag.*1.4. 882 τροχο- chariot wheels (*Il.*23.394, Pherecyd.37a Jac.). 882 -δινεῖται, the wheeling of horses: ἵππους... ἐμβριμωμένας δινεῖ A.*Th.*462 (so X.*Eq.*10.2, prob.; δίνευμα X.*Eq.*3.11; δινεύω *Il.*18.543; ὠκυδίνατος Pi.*I.*5.6; ἱπποδινήτος B.5.2). Genuine interaction is involved here – support, the verbal part of the compound being standard in the *T* sense, of 'rolling' eyes: ὄσσε...δινείσθην *Il.*17.680 (so στρεφεδινέω *Il.*16.792, E.*Or.*1459; δῖνος Hp.*VC* 11; δινάω B.17.18; ἐνδινέω Hp.*Epid.*5.99, 7.30; ἀναδινέω Hp.*Mul.* 1.36; σκοτοδινέω Hp.*Steril.*214). 882–3 ἑλίγδην...δρόμου, the chariot on the turn in – or beyond – the course: ἀφραδέως...ἑλίσσεται ἔνθα καὶ ἔνθα, ἵπποι δὲ πλανό- ωνται ἀνὰ δρόμον *Il.*23.320f. (ἑλίσσειν thus again at *Il.*23.309 and 466), ἐκτὸς δρόμου φερόμενον Pl.*Crat.*414b. A second interaction is involved here, *viz* (again) support: ἔξω...φέρομαι is standard in the *T* sense, 'derangement' (for ἔξω, see above, pp.119 and 121; for φέρομαι, *qua T*, e.g. τῇ ἐπιθυμίᾳ...φερόμενοι X.*Mem.* 2.1.4, so A.*Th.*687, Pi.*fr.*10; cf. ἐκφέρεσθαι Th.3.84.1, S.*El.*628). V_2 now appears.

* ἡ μέλιττα πρὸς οὐδὲν προσιҙάνει σαπρόν Arist.*HA* 535a.2 (cf. Campbell on Semon.). The 'metaphor' involved in ἐκ μελίσσης is strictly an item in a creation myth.

The chariot turns surreally into a ship in distress: πνεύματι...θολεροί...παίουσ᾽ ...κύμασιν. A whole set of hitherto unrealized hints now falls into place: Στρυμὼν ...δινηθείς E.*Rh*.353, δίνης ἀργυρέης εἰλιγμένος (of Ocean) Hes.*Th*.791, τὸ... ἑλισσόμενον...κυμάτων Pi.*N*.6.55, ἐν τῷ δινουμένῳ ὕδατι...φέρονται Arist.*Mech*. 858b.4, ἄνεμος ἔξω πλόου ἔβαλεν Pi.*P*.11.39, νᾶα...ἐν ὀρθῷ δρόμῳ Pi.*fr*.1a.5, τὰ ναυάγια...ἐξενεχθέντα ὑπό τε τοῦ ῥοῦ καὶ ἀνέμου Th.1.54.1. (For ἑλίσσεσθαι cf. also Hes.*fr*.70.23, A.*Prom*.138, *Il*.21.11; for ἔξω and/or φέρεσθαι, *Od*.14.314, Hdt.4.110.2, Th.7.53.1, X.*An*.5.7.7, Hanno *Peripl*.1; for δρόμος, Hdt.2.5.2, Scyl.47, Pi.*I*.5.60, A.*Prom*.838, A.*Aj*.889, *Trag.Adesp*.559, which, with A.*Prom*.883 and Pi.*fr*.1a.5, is the complete list, the word in a nautical context being rarer than is sometimes supposed, as by Rose on *Prom*.838.) The 'bridge', then, is ἔξω δὲ δρόμου φέρομαι, exactly applicable to both images, with -δινεῖται and ἐλίγδην providing an additional, rather impressionistic, nexus thereto.

APPENDIX X

Summary of poets' apparent characteristics

'Apparent' is to be stressed. The 'sample' is small for one to be speaking of characteristics. Nevertheless, the various tendencies represented are in general, one would think, fully in line with more widely discernible qualities of the different poets' styles: Pindaric 'delicacy' and so on. As remarked earlier (p. 81), about a third (or less) of the interactions in the corpus are Pindaric, another third (or more) Aeschylean. Inevitably, therefore, it is these two poets whose tendencies will be most evident. I might add that some poets show few instances of interaction or none at all. Thus, Hipponax has only one (cf. above, p. 185) and Corinna none – which is hardly surprising in view of her total avoidance of imagery (see the succinct account by D. L. Page, *Corinna*, London, 1953, 75f.).

1. Pivot to explicit imagery common in Theognis (see above, p. 88 and further instances in §60).

2. Pivot to explicit imagery virtually absent from Pindar (above, pp. 88, 92, 107; see also the instances in §60).

3. Pivot in general not common in Pindar, common in Theognis (p. 89).

4. Noun-glide not conspicuously Pindaric, but characteristically Aeschylean. Pindar favours less concrete types of glide, e.g. the adjectival (pp. 98–102, esp. 101, 120, 187).

5. *V–N* convergence common in both Pindar and Aeschylus; *V–T–N* Aeschylean but not Pindaric (pp. 104f., 108).

6. Convergence to simile involving the ground term is Aeschylean, not Pindaric (p. 105, but cf. a Pindaric instance with comparison, p. 186).

7. Explanatory function of *N* terminology in metaphor characteristic of Pindar, not of Aeschylus (p. 118).

8. The intrusive structure *T* adjective + *V* noun attested only in Pindar (p. 144).

9. Remarkable amount of intrusion in A.*Ag*. (§§48 and 49, esp. p. 148).

10. Pure anticipation most characteristic of Pindar (§52).

11. Among extra-grammatical interactions: most of the instances of link that involve verbal repetition are Aeschylean, but there are no Aeschylean instances among those repetitions *without* any linking force (§54).

12. Retrospective imagery favoured especially by Pindar (§55).

13. Among aural (alliterative) interactions: genitival link particularly Aeschylean, but not so other kinds of simple reinforcing link (§58, cf. pp. 226f.).

14. Most of the best examples of creative (aural) link Aeschylean (§59).

15. Alliteratively enforced pivot to simile comparatively common in Archilochus (§60).

16. Aural interaction in Pindar seems to be confined to link and preparation (see the instances given on pp. 178–91); among other things, there is no trace of any of the marginal 'suggestive' types (see p. 191).

17. Arbitrary Aeschylean combination of aural link and subdued (verb) convergence (p. 198).

18. On Pindaric 'delicacy' and Aeschylean 'vigour': pp. 90f., 97, 100f., 108, 129, 145f., 204f.

19. Interaction categories with a possible 'popular' character or ancestry: alliteratively enforced ground term (usually pivot) to simile and comparison* (pp. 20f., 184, 186, 225); punning convergence (pp. 103f.); T for N intrusion in comparison, i.e. 'more T than V' (pp. 138, 142f.); κ- κακῶν genitival link (pp. 226f.).

APPENDIX XI

ἄωτος *and flowers* (*see above, p. 101*)

The poetic word ἄωτος (or -ον) did not mean *flower*. The only thing that the word could ever have been said to 'mean' is *something to do with cloth/material/wool*, i.e. the Homeric use: λίνοιο...ἄ. *Il*.9.661, οἰὸς ἄ. *Il*.13.599 and 716, *Od*.1.443, ἀώτου...ἐχόμην (the ram's fleece) *Od*.9.434 (cf. A.*Supp*.666 κέρσειεν ἄωτον?). By the time we next meet the word in the early fifth century (Antigenes 1.3 Diehl, Pi.*P*.10.53), it is unmistakably a barely definable γλῶττα and, in retrospect, the need to define the Homeric use with a 'something to do with' indicates that even in early epic the word was on the way to this status. For the classical period, all one can say is: (i) the word was consistently felt to be complimentary and was vaguely used as if it meant *the choicest, the finest* – this being the pretext for the rendering *flower of its kind* (LSJ *s.v.* I). (ii) The classical poets who used it are few and qualitatively unreliable, Bacchylides, Aeschylus, 'Antigenes' and Pindar – especially unreliable, as these poets use it only once each, except for Pindar, who uses it twenty times (*sic*, see Slater *s.v.*). (iii) With such a spread, what one sees is chiefly the *private* poetic associative faculty at work (and mostly Pindar's) and not a public *meaning*. (iv) Even in terms of private association, the evidence in favour of a connection between ἄ. and flowers is slight: (*a*) Antigen.1.3 ῥόδων ἄ.; (*b*) the

---

* Ultimately, one presumes, the very structure of the simile/comparison itself, with its built-in interactive basis, should be included under this heading; cf. above, pp. 16–20 and 88 and note the remarks of Schmid–Stählin 1.424, n.8.

use of the word as object of δρέπειν, Pi.*P*.4.130f. δραπὼν...εὐзοίας ἄωτον, so
N.2.9, cf. *fr*.6b(f) and A.*Supp*.663–6 (where ἄ. is object of κέρσειεν, 'shear', which
prima facie implies hair or fleece, but parallel to ἥβας ἄνθος ἄδρεπτον); (*c*) note also
ἀωτοῦσιν· ἀνθοῦσιν Hsch. For the remaining instances of the word, see B.23.1
and the other Pindaric citations in Slater.

Note finally that there is no visible variation in sense corresponding to the
variation in gender (-ος masc., -ον neut.). The five Homeric instances are, as LSJ
say, indeterminate and may be neuter, as they were evidently taken to be by the
later epic tradition (cf. Oppian's ἄωτα, LSJ *s.fin.*); or may be masculine, in line
with Pindar's practice (ἄωτος *P*.4.188 etc.). This variation doubtless reflects the
same obsolescence of the word and the same private reinterpretation as are more
obviously attested by the 'developments' in the use.

APPENDIX XII

τοῖος γάρ *in Arch. 112*

I have indicated (§46) my idea of the character and distinction of the interaction in
Archilochus' ἔρως ὑπὸ καρδίην ἐλυσθείς. Professor A. E. Raubitschek of Stanford
University has suggested to me the possibility that the τοῖος with which the fragment begins might have been correlative to a οἶος (*vel sim.*). If so, the extant verses
could represent the *Sostück* of a simile whose *Wiestück* referred explicitly to Odysseus under the ram, and in that event we would have the familiar pattern of simile
to metaphor (or *vice versa*). While part of my interpretation would stand, the
stylistic mechanism involved would be radically different and without doubt the
total effect might lose most of its distinctive interest.

The presence of a simile here is not absolutely inconceivable, but, as is easily
demonstrable from epic and lyric parallels, the γάρ following τοῖος makes such a
conjecture extremely implausible. Let me state first that while the following discussion deals primarily with τοῖος, I have included instances of τοιόσδε and τοιοῦτος
where relevant. The usage of these two words implies nothing, in any event, that
would affect my case. The pertinent epic and lyric uses of τοῖος (etc.) can be set
out as follows:

1. τοῖος γάρ is a well-established marker with well-defined characteristics. It
always, naturally, opens sentence or clause. It has no essential connection with
imagery. In its backward reference it does not look back to a correlative, and in its
forward reference it usually precedes a simple relative, if anything. Thus Arch.7.1ff.,
οὔτε τις ἀστῶν...τέρψεται...· τοίους γὰρ κατὰ κῦμα...ἔκλυσεν, and again *Od*.
2.285ff.:

> σοὶ δ' ὁδὸς οὐκέτι δηρὸν ἀπέσσεται, ἣν σὺ μενοινᾷς·
> τοῖος γάρ τοι ἑταῖρος ἐγὼ πατρώιός εἰμι,
> ὅς τοι νῆα θοὴν στελέω...

Similarly *Il*.5.667, 10.145, 13.677, 16.22, 17.164, 21.289, 22.241, 23.16, 23.280,
24.153, 24.182, 24.384; *Od*.1.343, 3.496, 4.206, 4.826, 11.549, 11.556, 13.115, 18.126,

24.62; Sol.3.3; Arch.35 (presumably); Hes.*Sc.*41 (followed by a simile but formally unconnected with it). In effect this τοῖος = 'a great', 'a very notable', 'a special'.* (N.B. that in Alc.119.13, with τοιοῦτος, the combination τοιαύτας γάρ does occur in the context of an image, the so-called 'vine parable', but occurs within the vehicle. The image goes from τὸ κλᾶμμα, the vine twig, and σταφύλαις, the grapes, to τοιαύτας γὰρ ἀπ' ἀμπέλω. There is no question, therefore, of τοιαύτας opening a *Sostück*, and the same goes for the τοῖος γάρ of Hes.*Th.*703, which, as κε, following γάρ, shows, is still part of the *Wiestück*, ὡς εἰ..., of the preceding verse, while the actual correlative to ὡς εἰ is τόσσος in v.705.)

2. When τοῖος is correlative to a preceding οἷος (etc.), when it marks, that is, the movement from simile *Wiestück* to *Sostück*, it is not commonly associated with any connecting particle. *Il.*5.554ff. is typical: οἴω τώ γε λέοντε...τοίω τώ... (warriors). (If a particle does follow this τοῖος, it may well be ἄρα, as at *Il.*2.480ff,: ἠύτε βοῦς...· τοῖον ἄρ' Ἀτρείδην θῆκε Ζεύς....) From (1) and (2) it is clear that τοῖος γάρ and οἷος–τοῖος are unrelated types, and that Archilochus' τοῖος does not, therefore, imply an earlier οἷος. The question now is: could it be anticipatory, correlative to a following οἷος?

3. (i) It is in fact clear that τοῖος–οἷος (etc.) is not a characteristic scheme of an epic simile. What the scheme normally implies is a 'comparison' of this kind (*Od.*7.312): τοῖος ἐὼν οἷός ἐσσι. Similarly Arch.68 (twice): τοῖος ἀνθρώποισι θυμός...ὁκοίην Ζεύς...ἐφ' ἡμέρην ἄγῃ, καὶ φρονεῦσι τοῖ' ὁκοίοισ' ἐγκυρέωσιν ἔργμασιν. Similarly *Il.*5.483f., 7.231, 18.105, 24.375f.; *Od.*1.371, 4.269f., 4.342, 4.421, 9.4, 11.428f., 16.208, 17.133, 17.313f., 17.421, 18.36f., 19.77, 19.314f., 20.89, 21.93f., 21.172f.; cf. (with order reversed) *Od.*2.58ff.

(ii) The similes that are introduced by τοῖος–οἷος (etc.) are few and of these still fewer rank as imagery proper:

*Il.*5.373f.   τίς νύ σε τοιάδ' ἔρεξε...
(= 21.509f.)   μαψιδίως, ὡς εἴ τι κακὸν ῥέζουσαν ἐνωπῇ;
Hes.*Sc.*7f.   τῆς καὶ ἀπὸ κρῆθεν βλεφάρων τ' ἄπο κυανεάων
                  τοῖον ἄηθ' οἷόν τε πολυχρύσου Ἀφροδίτης.
(Cliché: cf. *Il.*19.282; *Od.*17.37, 19.54; Hes.*fr.*30.25, 196.5.)
*h.Merc.*348f.   διέτριβε κέλευθα
                  τοῖα πέλωρ' ὡς εἴ τις ἀραιῇσι δρυσὶ βαίνοι.
*Il.*2.799ff.   ἀλλ' οὔ πω τοιόνδε τοσόνδε τε λαὸν ὄπωπα·
                  λίην γὰρ φύλλοισιν ἐοικότες ἢ ψαμάθοισιν
                  ἔρχονται...

In the last instance the relation is not strictly correlative, and, more important, both in this and the other instances the τοῖος is not τοῖος γάρ.

(iii) There are a few τοῖος–οἷος passages in whch a γάρ does stand in the τοῖος clause; *Od.*1.255ff. εἰ γάρ...τοῖος...τοῖος...οἷος..., where the γάρ is not of the

* Hence the fact that τοῖος was sometimes glossed by ἀγαθός in the ancient commentators: see Pfeiffer on Call.*fr.*627 and Hsch.*s.vv.* τοῖοι and τοῖον.

241

relevant kind; *Il*.1.262f. οὐ γάρ πω τοίους...οἶον... (similarly *Od*.11.499f.), where the γάρ is not relevantly connected with the τοῖος; and *Od*.18.136f. τοῖος γάρ νόος...οἶον ἐπ' ἦμαρ ἄγῃσι πατήρ, where, as with the similar Arch.68 (quoted above), no image is involved. No image is involved, in fact, in any of these four passages.

There is, then, no evidence that τοῖος γάρ–οἶος was ever used as an image structure, any more than οἶος–τοῖος γάρ. The formula τοῖος γάρ has its own significance, unconnected with imagery. It remains possible that an image, explicit or otherwise, involving Odysseus occurred in Archilochus' poem at some point earlier, or indeed later, than τοῖος γάρ, but this is pure speculation; τοῖος γάρ is not evidence for it.

APPENDIX XIII

Conditional metaphor

By 'conditional metaphor' I mean metaphor whose existence is implied by one, and only one, of two possible interpretations, when by the other interpretation no metaphor is in question, but either some other trope (usually metonymy) or no trope at all. The metaphor is, therefore, not inescapably 'there', but conditional on a given interpretation. It is not characteristic of such instances that the alternatives are exclusive (*either/or*); rather that the fact of an alternative is the basic datum (*both/and*). Two English examples:

(i) Keats, *Ode to a Nightingale*:

> That thou, light-wingèd Dryad of the trees,
> In some *melodious* plot
> Of beechen green and shadows numberless
> Singest of summer in full-throated ease.

'Melodious' is, let us say, metonymic – the *bird* being 'melodious', rather than the plot. At the same time, the word contrives to seem to be a 'heightened synonym' of, say, 'harmonious', i.e. a live synaesthetic metaphor.

(ii) Shakespeare, *King Lear* IV.3:

> A *sovereign* shame so elbows him: his own unkindness
> That stripped her from his benediction.

'Sovereign' implies 'shame to do with the sovereignty question' (metonymy) and 'shame that rules him' (metaphor).

From the Greek corpus, likewise:

(iii) Sol.23.13 οἱ δ' ἐφ' ἁρπαγαῖσιν ἦλθον, ἐλπίδ' εἶχον ἀφνεάν. ἀφνεάν: 'hope of riches' (metonymy) and 'rich hope' (metaphor).

(iv) Pi.*O*.13.38f. ποδαρκὴς ἀμέρα: 'day of swift running' (metonymy) and 'fleet-footed day' (metaphor).

(v) B.5.186 εὐδαιμονίας πέταλον: (*a*) 'the olive wreath, source of εὐδαιμονία' (metonymy), (*b*) a metaphor like ὄλβου...ἄνθεα (B.3.92ff., incidentally misprinted ὄλβον in the latest Teubner).

(vi) A.*Ag*.154f. (see above, p. 180) μνάμων μῆνις: (*a*) Clytemnestra, her memory and her anger (metonymy, 'wrath' for 'wrathful woman'), (*b*) personified *Anger* (metaphor). The first interpretation is, as Fraenkel notes, not tenable overall (παλίνορτος in v.154 could hardly be said of Clytemnestra).

In some instances, the alternative to metaphor is re-etymology.

(vii) Thus A.*Supp*.21f.

σὺν τοῖσδ' ἱκετῶν ἐγχειριδίοις
ἐριοστέπτοισι κλάδοισιν.

The suppliants' branches (κλάδοισιν) are their 'daggers' (ἐγχειριδίοις) – their only weapons. At the same time, the word re-etymologizes itself harmlessly into 'in the hands', which their branches are.

(viii) So A.*Ag*.1382 and *Ch*.492: ἀμφίβληστρον, metaphorically 'net', re-etymologically 'something thrown round' (so Fraenkel on *Ag. loc. cit.*).

(ix) So Pi.*N*.8.49, a slight instance, ἐπαοιδαῖς, metaphorically 'spells', re-etymologically the poet's 'songs to' his audience.

(x) In A.*Ag*.1460f. the alternation depends on different derivations: ἦν τότ' ἐν δόμοις / ἔρις ἐρίδματος, ἀνδρὸς οἰζύς. Metaphorically, ἐρίδματος is 'strongly-built' (from δεμ-, as e.g. ἐΰδμητος in ἐΰδμητον περὶ βωμόν *Il*.1.448); non-tropically, 'strongly-subduing' (from δαμ-, as e.g. ἄδμητος, but with active force); cf. Fraenkel *ad loc*. *Qua* δεμ- word, the compound partakes in a remarkable aural chiasmus, δόμοις ἔρις ἐρί-δματος – though it can hardly be said that *qua* δεμ- word, i.e. *qua* metaphor, it is of much interest or force (cf. Denniston–Page *ad loc*.).

APPENDIX XIV

$2N = V_l$

Under the heading of this pseudo-arithmetical equation, I refer to a stylistic feature that might often be characterized as 'matching clichés': a particular kind of co-activation of the connotations of two or more words which is quite distinct from interaction. A conventionally used word – one word – with an appropriate connotation, aligned with the vehicle of a corresponding image, is characteristically felt to be a neutral term. *Two* such separate words in collocation ($2N$) tend, rather, to recreate the image by themselves ($1V$) and so preclude any sense of N–V interaction.

Take Arch.58, on the caprice of the gods:

πολλάκις μὲν ἐκ κακῶν
ἄνδρας ὀρθοῦσιν μελαίνη κειμένους ἐπὶ χθονί,
πολλάκις δ' ἀνατρέπουσι καὶ μάλ' εὖ βεβηκότας
ὑπτίους.

The image is worked out and coherent, but in this context ὀρθοῦν, κεῖσθαι, ἀνα-τρέπειν and εὖ βεβηκέναι are all clichés (*N*).* The only *V* terms, strictly speaking, are

---

* (i) ὀρθώσεις μὲν σεωυτόν, σώσεις δὲ καὶ ἐμέ Hdt.3.122.3. ὀρθοῦν of prosperity, similarly: Alc.76.14 (prob.), Pi.*P*.4.60, *Carm.Conv*.1.2 PMG, A.*Eu*.751, S.*OC* 394, Th.2.60.2. LSJ's treatment of the verb in this and other secondary senses is notably muddled. (ii) κεῖται ἐν ἄλγεσι

μελαίνη ἐπὶ χθονί, a single and relatively light-weight detail, and ὑπτίους, forceful and expressively placed (see above, p. 193 with n.7), but not *effectively* interactive with any or all of the neutral clichés. In effect, by the time κειμένους is reached, the image is known and given: ὀρθοῦσιν and κειμένους, between them, evoke it and the relation between them and μελαίνη ἐπὶ χθονί is not perceptible as an interactive relation between unequals (as between N as V), but only as a relation between V terms – and, at most, V terms of slightly contrasting immediacy. By the time one comes to εὖ βεβηκότας, it is doubtful whether any real N/V contrast is conceivable: even the final ὑπτίους, which stands out rhythmically, hardly stands out terminologically, and its immediacy is only slightly greater.

Parallel instances are not uncommon, e.g.:

(i) Arch.7.5ff., vehicle αἱματόεν δ' ἕλκος, preceded by the coherent clichés ἀνηκέστοισι (ἀνήκεστον κακόν Hes.*Th*.612 – this non-medical sense is in fact the normal one: likewise, Thgn.76, B.*fr*.20D.9, Hdt.1.137.1, Democr.191 etc.; for the medical sense, see e.g. Hp.*Art*.58) and ἐπὶ...ἔθεσαν φάρμακον (Ζεῦ, ἐπὶ Τρώεσσι τίθει κράτος *Il*.1.509, so 23.400 and 406 and – without ἐπί – *Od*.1.321, *Il*.9.637; and φάρμακον κακῶν Carc.7, see above, p. 100 with n.17).

(ii) Thgn.331, vehicle ποσσίν (*sic*), preceded by the clichés μέσσην ὁδὸν ἔρχεο, for which cf. e.g. ἄδικον ὁδὸν ἰόντων Th.3.64.4 (ὁδὸν ἰέναι ethically, likewise, Thgn.382, Hdt.7.12.2, X.*Cyr*.1.6.16, Ar.*Pl*.506) and πάντων μέσ' ἄριστα Thgn.335 (μέσος comparably, e.g. Hdt.7.11.3, Arist.*EN* 1109b.26). If this verse has political reference (see van Groningen *ad loc*.), the specifically political reference of μέσος would be in question (see above, p. 122 with n.1).

(iii) A.*Supp*.91, vehicle ἐπὶ νώτῳ, preceded by clichés πίπτει and ἀσφαλές: πίπτειν is normal in the sense 'turn out' (see above, p. 94 with n.6) and ἀσφαλής, obviously, of certainties in general. The vehicle itself is doubtless taken from wrestling: παλαίων ἔπεσε σκληρῷ χωρίῳ ὕπτιος Hp.*Epid*.5.14 (πίπτω of a fall in wrestling, likewise, B.11.23, Simon.153.2 Diehl). For the concrete – original – sense of ἀσφαλής, 'without tripping' (almost ignored by LSJ), see e.g. ἀσφαλὲς αἰεὶ θρῴσκων *Il*.15.683f., Arch.60.4, Hp.*Vict*.4.90; and for -σφαλ- in specific connection with wrestling, see above, pp. 196f.

Still more common is the collocation of matching clichés (or equivalent) *without* any accompanying V term. Thus e.g. with Pope's injunction to '*goad* the prelate slumbering in his *stall*'. 'Goad' and 'stall' cohere, but the former is a cliché, the latter a punning homonym. Strictly speaking, there is no imagery at all in such cases – which necessarily means that such cases fall well outside the scope of the present study.

θυμός *Od*.21.88, ἀλλ' ὁ μὲν εὖ ἔρδων κεῖμαι Thgn.1317. κεῖσθαι of human misery, similarly: Arch.24.17 West (matching clichés), Thgn.555, A.*Eu*.590, S.*Aj*.323, Ar.*Nub*.126 (matching clichés), Hp.*Int*.14. (iii) ὁ κόλαξ...καὶ φίλους καὶ τὰς πόλεις ἀνατρέπει Diph.24.3. ἀνατρέπειν, 'cause the downfall of', similarly: Alc.141.4, Ar.*Nub*.884, Hdt.1.32.9, Hp.*Art*.68 and the passages listed above, p. 153. (iv) τοῖσιν ἐχθροῖς εὖ βεβηκόσιν S.*El*.979. εὖ βεβηκέναι, 'prosper', similarly: Hdt.7.164.1, Nicom.Com.2 (conj.); βεβηκέναι on its own thus, S.*El*.1095, E.*fr*.1073, Hp.*Loc*. *Hom*.46 (see Littré *ad loc*.).

Bibliography
Texts and Abbreviations

Texts

Except where otherwise indicated, references and citations follow the numeration and text of the following editions:

Sappho and Alcaeus: E. Lobel and D. L. Page, *Poetarum Lesbiorum Fragmenta*, Oxford, 1955.
Pindar's epinicians: B. Snell and H. Maehler, Leipzig, 1971.
Pindar's fragments: B. Snell, ed. 3, Leipzig, 1964.
Bacchylides: B. Snell and H. Maehler, Leipzig, 1970.
The other melic poets: D. L. Page, *Poetae Melici Graeci*, Oxford, 1962.
Theognis: D. Young, Leipzig, 1961.
The other iambic and elegiac poets: E. Diehl, *Anthologia Lyrica Graeca*, ed. 3, Leipzig, vols. 1 (1949) and 3 (1952).*
Aeschylus' plays: G. Murray, ed. 2, Oxford, 1955.†
Aeschylus' fragments: H. J. Mette, *Die Fragmente der Tragödien des Aischylos*, Berlin, 1959.
Hesiod's fragments: R. Merkelbach and M. L. West, *Fragmenta Hesiodea*, Oxford, 1967.
Menander's *Dyscolus:* H. Lloyd-Jones, Oxford, 1960.
Menander's *Scutum* and *Samia:* C. Austin, Berlin, 1969.
Menander's *Sententiae* (Men.*Mon.*): S. Jaekel, Leipzig, 1964.
The other fragments of Menander: A. Koerte and A. Thierfelder, Leipzig, 1955–9.
Anonymous inscriptions are frequently cited from Peek or from Friedländer–Hoffleit (F–H), oracles from Parke–Wormell (P–W) (see the abbreviations below).

For other references and citations I normally follow LSJ.

Abbreviations
The following list contains only those works referred to in abbreviated form in text or notes. Standard commentaries (referred to by the commentator's name) are not included except where confusion might otherwise result.

---

* Instead of Young and the selective Diehl, it would have been convenient to use West's new *Iambi et Elegi Graeci*, but that this long-awaited replacement turned out to be selective itself (e.g. in its total exclusion of epigrams) and also cavalier in its treatment of some authors – notably the so-called *Theognidea* (which œuvre is dismembered, assigned, bracketed etc. with the incaution of old-fashioned analysis of Homer). West, in other words, fails to provide what was chiefly wanted, a straightforward updating of those portions of Bergk's *Poetae Lyrici Graeci* not already superseded; and despite the obvious value of much of his editing, even its more provocative manifestations, I have preferred not to use his edition as the standard.

† D. L. Page's new *Oxford Classical Text* appeared when this book was at an inconveniently advanced stage. Since I had by then committed myself to taking Murray's as the standard text, it seemed simplest to leave it like that except for particular instances (indicated *ad loc.*) where Page's text is definitely preferable.

Kl.P.   Der kleine Pauly, Stuttgart, 1964– .
LSJ   H. G. Liddell and R. Scott, A Greek–English Lexicon, ed. 9, rev. H. S. Jones,
         Oxford, 1925–40. (LSJ, Supplement refers to A Supplement to the above,
         ed. E. A. Barber, Oxford, 1968.)
NED   A New English Dictionary on Historical Principles, corrected and reissued
         as Oxford English Dictionary, Oxford, 1933.
OCD   N. G. L. Hammond and H. H. Scullard, The Oxford Classical Dictionary,
         ed. 2, Oxford, 1970.
RE   Pauly–Wissowa, Real-Encyclopädie der klassischen Altertumswissenschaft,
         Stuttgart, 1894– .

Abrams   M. H. Abrams, The Mirror and the Lamp: Romantic Theory and the Critical
                Tradition, New York, 1953.
Allen AIL   W. S. Allen, 'Ancient Ideas on the Origin and Development of Language',
                Trans. Philol. Soc. 1948, 35ff.
Allen VG   ——, Vox Graeca, Cambridge, 1968.
Allen–Halliday The Homeric Hymns, ed. T. W. Allen and W. R. Halliday (with E. E.
                Sikes), ed. 2, Oxford, 1936.
Bergk PLG   T. Bergk, Poetae Lyrici Graeci, ed. 4, Leipzig, 1882.
Blaise   A. Blaise, Dictionnaire latin–français des auteurs chrétiens (rev. Chirat),
                Strasbourg, 1954.
Bolgar   R. R. Bolgar, The Classical Heritage and its Beneficiaries: from the Carolingian
                Age to the End of the Renaissance, Cambridge, 1954.
Bowra GLP   C. M. Bowra, Greek Lyric Poetry, ed. 2, Oxford, 1961.
Bowra, Pindar   ——, Pindar, Oxford, 1964.
Brink   C. O. Brink, On Reading a Horatian Satire, Sydney, 1965.
Brooke-Rose   C. Brooke-Rose, A Grammar of Metaphor, London, 1958.
Burton   R. W. B. Burton, Pindar's Pythian Odes, Oxford, 1962.
Campbell   D. A. Campbell, Greek Lyric Poetry, London, 1967.
Caplan   Cicero, Ad Herennium, ed. H. Caplan (Loeb), 1954.
Casey   J. Casey, The Language of Criticism, London, 1966.
Chenu   M. D. Chenu, Introduction à l'étude de saint Thomas d'Aquin, Montreal–
                Paris, 1950.
Clemen   W. H. Clemen, The Development of Shakespeare's Imagery, London, 1951.
Danielsson   O. A. Danielsson, 'Erotianea', Eranos 1919, 1ff.
Davison   J. A. Davison, 'Quotations and Allusions in Early Greek Literature',
                Eranos 1955, 125ff.
Defradas   J. E. Defradas, 'Le rôle de l'allitération dans la poésie grecque', Rev.Ét.Anc.
                1958, 36ff.
Denniston GP   J. D. Denniston, The Greek Particles, ed. 2, Oxford, 1959.
Denniston GPS   ——, Greek Prose Style, Oxford, 1952.
Diels–Kranz   H. Diels, Die Fragmente der Vorsokratiker, ed. 6, rev. W. Kranz, Berlin,
                1951–2.
Dieterich   A. Dieterich, Eine Mithrasliturgie, Leipzig, 1903.
Dornseiff   F. Dornseiff, Pindars Stil, Berlin, 1921.
Dover   K. J. Dover, Greek Word Order, Cambridge, 1960.
Dumortier   J. Dumortier, Les images dans la poésie d'Eschyle, Paris, 1935.
Earp   F. R. Earp, The Style of Sophocles, Cambridge, 1944.
Ebeling   H. Ebeling, Lexicon Homericum, Leipzig, 1885.
Empson SCW   W. Empson, The Structure of Complex Words, London, 1951.

BIBLIOGRAPHY: TEXTS AND ABBREVIATIONS

Empson *ST* ——, *Seven Types of Ambiguity*, ed. 2, London, 1947.
Farnell L. R. Farnell, *The Works of Pindar*, vol. II, London, 1932.
G. S. Farnell G. S. Farnell, *Greek Lyric Poetry*, London, 1891.
Fatouros G. Fatouros, *Index Verborum zur frühgriechischen Lyrik*, Heidelberg, 1966.
Fraenkel Ed. Fraenkel, *Aeschylus: Agamemnon*, Oxford, 1962.
Fraenkel *PP* ——, *Plautinisches im Plautus*, Berlin, 1922.
Fränkel *DP* H. Fränkel, *Dichtung und Philosophie des frühen Griechentums*, Munich, 1962.
Fränkel *HG* ——, *Die homerischen Gleichnisse*, Göttingen, 1921.
Friedländer–Hoffleit (or F–H) P. Friedländer and H. B. Hoffleit, *Epigrammata*, Berkeley, 1948.
Frye N. Frye, *Anatomy of Criticism*, Princeton, 1957.
Gautier L. Gautier, *La langue de Xénophon*, Geneva, 1911.
Goethe *Goethe: Sämtliche Werke*, ed. von der Hellen, 40 vols, Stuttgart, 1902–7.
Goheen R. F. Goheen, *The Imagery of Sophocles' Antigone*, Princeton, 1951.
Gow & Page A. S. F. Gow and D. L. Page, *The Greek Anthology: Hellenistic Epigrams*, Cambridge, 1965.
van Groningen B. A. van Groningen, *Théognis: le premier livre*, Amsterdam, 1966.
van Groningen *CLAG* ——, *La composition littéraire archaïque grecque*, ed. 2, Amsterdam, 1960.
Grube G. M. A. Grube, *The Greek and Roman Critics*, Toronto, 1965.
Guiraud P. Guiraud, *La sémantique*, Paris, 1959.
Harvey A. E. Harvey, 'Homeric Epithets in Greek Lyric Poetry', *CQ* 1957, 206ff.
Headlam W. Headlam, 'Metaphor with a note on transference of epithets', *CR* 1902, 434ff.
Headlam *EA* ——, *On Editing Aeschylus*, London, 1891.
Headlam–Thomson = Thomson.
Herescu N. I. Herescu, *La poésie latine: étude des structures phoniques*, Paris, 1960.
Hermann G. Hermann, *Opuscula*, Leipzig, 1827–77.
Hockett C. F. Hockett, *A Course in Modern Linguistics*, New York, 1958.
Hoffmann–Debrunner O. Hoffmann and A. Debrunner, *Geschichte der griechischen Sprache* I, Berlin, 1953.
Housman A. E. Housman, *Juvenalis Saturae*, Cambridge, 1905.
Hulme H. M. Hulme, *Explorations in Shakespeare's Language*, Aberdeen, 1962.
Jaeger W. Jaeger, *Paideia: the Ideals of Greek Culture*, trans. G. Highet, Oxford, 1939–45.
Jebb *AO* R. C. Jebb, *The Attic Orators from Antiphon to Isaeus*, London, 1876.
Johansen *GR* H. F. Johansen, *General Reflection in Tragic Rhesis*, Copenhagen, 1959.
Johansen *SS* ——, 'Some Features of Sentence Structure in Aeschylus' Suppliants', *Class. & Med.* 1954, 1ff.
Johnson *Samuel Johnson: Lives of the English Poets*, ed. G. B. Hill, Oxford, 1905.
Keith A. L. Keith, *Simile and Metaphor in Greek Poetry from Homer to Aeschylus*, Chicago, 1914.
Kirk *SH* G. S. Kirk, *The Songs of Homer*, Cambridge, 1962.
Knights–Cottle L. C. Knights and B. Cottle (edd.), *Metaphor and Symbol*, London, 1960.
Koestler A. Koestler, *The Act of Creation*, London, 1964.
Kranz W. Kranz, *Stasimon*, Berlin, 1933.
Kühner–Gerth R. Kühner, *Ausführliche Grammatik der griechischen Sprache* II, ed. 3, rev. B. Gerth, Hanover, 1898–1904.
Lausberg H. Lausberg, *Handbuch der literarischen Rhetorik*, Munich, 1960.
Leavis *EU* F. R. Leavis, *Education and the University*, new ed., London, 1948.

247

Leavis *IM* F. R. Leavis, 'Imagery and Movement', in *A Selection from Scrutiny*, ed. Leavis, Cambridge, 1968, 1.231ff. (repr. from *Scrutiny* 1945).

Leavis *RV* ——, *Revaluation*, London, 1936.

Lee D. J. N. Lee, *The Similes of the Iliad and the Odyssey Compared*, Melbourne, 1964.

Lesky A. Lesky, *A History of Greek Literature*, ed. 2, trans. C. de Heer and J. A. Willis, London, 1966.

Leumann M. Leumann, *Homerische Wörter*, Basel, 1950.

Leutsch–Schneidewin E. Leutsch and F. G. Schneidewin, *Corpus Paroemiographorum Graecorum*, Göttingen, 1839–51.

Lloyd G. E. R. Lloyd, *Polarity and Analogy*, Cambridge, 1966.

Lloyd-Jones H. Lloyd-Jones, *Appendix* to vol. 2 of *Aeschylus*, ed. H. Weir Smyth (Loeb), 1957, 523ff.

Lobel E. Lobel, 'Ἀλκαίου μέλη, Oxford, 1927.

Lorimer H. L. Lorimer, 'Gold and Ivory in Greek Mythology', in *Greek Poetry and Life* (Essays Presented to Gilbert Murray), Oxford, 1936, 14ff.

McCall M. H. McCall Jr., *Ancient Rhetorical Theories of Simile and Comparison*, Harvard, 1969.

Marrou H. I. Marrou, *Saint Augustin et la fin de la culture antique*, ed. 2, Paris, 1949.

Masson O. Masson, *Les fragments du poète Hipponax*, Paris, 1962.

D. I. Masson D. I. Masson, 'Sound in Poetry', in *Encyclopedia of Poetry and Poetics*, ed. A. Preminger, Princeton, 1965, 784ff.

Miller E. Miller, *Mélanges de littérature grecque*, Paris, 1868.

Nilsson M. P. Nilsson, *Greek Popular Religion*, New York, 1940.

Norwood G. Norwood, *Pindar*, Berkeley, 1945.

Nowottny W. Nowottny, *The Language Poets Use*, London, 1962.

Opelt I. Opelt, 'Alliteration im Griechischen?', *Glotta* 1958, 205ff.

Page *AP* D. L. Page, *Alcman: the Partheneion*, Oxford, 1951.

Page *PMG* ——, *Poetae Melici Graeci* (see *Texts* above).

Page *SA* ——, *Sappho and Alcaeus*, Oxford, 1955.

Parke–Wormell (or P–W) H. W. Parke and D. E. W. Wormell, *The Delphic Oracle*, vol. 2 ('The Oracular Responses'), Oxford, 1956.

Pearson A. C. Pearson, *The Fragments of Sophocles*, Cambridge, 1917.

Peek W. Peek, *Griechische Vers-Inschriften*, Berlin, 1955–.

Pfeiffer R. Pfeiffer, *History of Classical Scholarship*, Oxford, 1968.

Pickard-Cambridge A. W. Pickard-Cambridge, 'The *Niobe* of Aeschylus', in *Greek Poetry and Life* (Essays presented to Gilbert Murray), Oxford, 1936, 106ff.

Pickard-Cambridge–Webster ——, *Dithyramb, Tragedy and Comedy*, ed. 2, rev. T. B. L. Webster, Oxford, 1962.

Porzig W. Porzig, *Aischylos: die attische Tragödie*, Leipzig, 1926.

Powell J. E. Powell, *A Lexicon to Herodotus*, Cambridge, 1938.

Quain E. A. Quain, 'The Medieval *Accessus ad Auctores*', *Traditio* 1945, 215ff.

Quinn K. Quinn, *Latin Explorations*, London, 1963.

Rabe H. Rabe, *Hermogenis Opera*, Leipzig, 1913.

Richards I. A. Richards, *The Philosophy of Rhetoric*, Oxford, 1936.

Ricks C. Ricks, *Milton's Grand Style*, Oxford, 1963.

Roberts W. Rhys Roberts, *Dionysius of Halicarnassus, The Three Literary Letters*, Cambridge, 1901.

Ros J. G. A. Ros, *Die μεταβολή (Variatio) als Stilprinzip des Thukydides*, Paderborn, 1938.

Rumpel   J. Rumpel, *Lexicon Pindaricum*, Leipzig, 1883.
Russell   D. A. Russell, *Longinus, On the Sublime*, Oxford, 1964.
Rutherford   W. G. Rutherford, *A Chapter in the History of Annotation*, London, 1905.
Schenkeveld   D. M. Schenkeveld, *Studies in Demetrius On Style*, Amsterdam, 1964.
Schmid–Stählin W. Schmid and O. Stählin, *Geschichte der griechischen Literatur* I.1–2, Munich, 1929–34.
Schroeder   O. Schroeder, *Pindars Pythien*, Leipzig, 1922.
Schwyzer   E. Schwyzer, *Griechische Grammatik*, Munich, 1939–53.
Shelley   *Shelley's Literary and Philosophical Criticism*, ed. J. Shawcross, Oxford, 1909.
Slater   W. J. Slater, *Lexicon to Pindar*, Berlin, 1969.
Gregory Smith   G. Gregory Smith, *Elizabethan Critical Essays* I, Oxford, 1904.
Ole Smith (or Smith)   Ole Smith, 'Some Observations on the Structure of Imagery in Aeschylus', *Class. & Med.* 1967, 10ff.
Spearing   A. C. Spearing, *Criticism and Medieval Poetry*, London, 1964.
Stanford *AGL* W. B. Stanford, *Ambiguity in Greek Literature*, Oxford, 1939.
Stanford *AS*   ——, *Aeschylus in his Style*, Dublin, 1942.
Stanford *GM*   ——, *Greek Metaphor*, Oxford, 1936.
Stanford *SG*   ——, *The Sound of Greek*, Berkeley, 1967.
Stanford *UT*   ——, *The Ulysses Theme*, Oxford, 1954.
Stern   G. Stern, *Meaning and Change of Meaning*, Göteborg, 1931.
Strömberg   R. Strömberg, *Greek Proverbs*, Göteborg, 1954.
Svartengren   T. H. Svartengren, *Intensifying Similes in English*, Lund, 1918.
Taillardat   J. Taillardat, *Les images d'Aristophane*, Paris, 1965.
Thomson   G. Thomson, *The Oresteia of Aeschylus*, Amsterdam–Prague, 1966.
Tuve   R. Tuve, *Elizabethan and Metaphysical Imagery*, Chicago, 1947.
Ullmann *LS*   S. Ullmann, *Language and Style*, Oxford, 1964.
Ullmann *PS*   ——, *The Principles of Semantics*, ed. 2, Glasgow, 1957.
Ullmann, *Semantics*   ——, *Semantics: An Introduction to the Science of Meaning*, Oxford, 1962.
Volkmann   R. Volkmann, *Die Rhetorik der Griechen und Römer*, ed. 2, Leipzig, 1885.
Waldron   R. A. Waldron, *Sense and Sense Development*, London, 1967.
Webster   T. B. L. Webster, *Greek Art and Literature 700–530 BC*, Otago, 1959.
Wellek   R. Wellek, *A History of Modern Criticism 1750–1950*, London, 1955– .
Wellek–Warren   R. Wellek and A. Warren, *Theory of Literature*, ed. 3, Penguin, 1963.
Westermann   A. Westermann, *Vitarum Scriptores Graeci Minores*, Brunswick, 1845.
Whitman   C. H. Whitman, *Homer and the Heroic Tradition*, Harvard, 1958.
Wilamowitz *SS* U. von Wilamowitz-Moellendorff, *Sappho und Simonides*, Berlin, 1913.
Wilamowitz *TGL*   ——, *Die Textgeschichte der griechischen Lyriker*, Berlin, 1900.
Wilkinson   L. P. Wilkinson, *Golden Latin Artistry*, Cambridge, 1963.
Wimsatt   W. K. Wimsatt Jr., *The Verbal Icon*, Kentucky, 1954.
Wordsworth   *Wordsworth and Coleridge, Lyrical Ballads: The text...and the Prefaces...*, edd. R. L. Brett and A. R. Jones, rev. ed., London, 1965.
Wyld   H. C. Wyld, *A History of Modern Colloquial English*, ed. 3, London, 1936.
Young   D. C. Young, *Three Odes of Pindar*, Leiden, 1968.

INDEXES

References are to pages of this book.

INDEX I: GREEK WORDS

The presence of a word in this list usually implies a lexicographical discussion. * signifies particularly detailed or important discussion of the word in question or of one or more of its uses, where 'important' generally means a notably inadequate treatment in LSJ.

INDEX II: PASSAGES DISCUSSED

N.B. (i) This index includes only passages from the corpus of 'early Greek poetry' (defined on p. 79). Most of the passages listed are interactive and some contain multiple interactions. Those that are not interactive at all are square bracketed. For discussion of passages in, or aspects of, other authors, classical or modern, see the general index.

(ii) It sometimes happens that a single passage is properly discussed in separate places under different numerations. E.g.: A.*Ag*.820 is referred to as such on p. 181, but discussed as part of 'A.*Ag*.818ff.' on pp. 184f. In such cases the passages are listed below under the more (or most) inclusive numeration – in this instance, 818ff.

(iii) The editions used are listed on p. 245.

AESCHYLUS
Ag. (2f.) 184, 186
(5f.) 87, 98, 119, 157
[(13f.) 69]
(32f.) 94
(48ff.) 16–18, 32, 85f., 88,
   91, 146–8
(108ff.) 145f.
[(125) 148]
(132f.) 144, 178f.
(137) 148f.
(154f.) 180, 182, 243
(184ff.) 163, 166f.
(299) 181
(390ff.) 188
[(411) 146]
(479ff.) 158f., 166
(494f.) 172, 178
(524ff.) 200f.
(534ff.) 113
(584) 161
(648ff.) 169, 171
[(653) 226]
(658ff.) 162f., 166
(717) 148
(728) 148
(811ff.) 167
(818ff.) 181, 184f.
(827f.) 106
[(841f.) 236]
(844ff.) 100, 154, 198
(872) 179
(897f.) 181, 187
(966ff.) viif., 24, 140f.

(971f.) 143
(984ff.) 153
(997) 181
(1005) 181
(1005ff.) 139f.
[(1093f.) 18, 128, 235]
(1164ff.) 189
(1178ff.) 197, 199, 237
(1181f.) 181
(1257ff.) 167
(1268) 191
[(1382) 243]
(1395ff.) 160
(1397) 179, 226
(1418) 183
[(1460f.) 243]
(1501ff.) 185
(1504) 102
(1629ff.) 69, 108, 111
(1659f.) 110
Ch. (67) 100
(149f.) 189
(201ff.) 110
(211) 180
(466ff.) 110, 113
[(492) 243]
[(505f.) 236]
(539) 100
(661f.) 100
(775) 136
(863) 120
(915) 166
[(936) 227]
[(946) 227]

(983ff.) 170f.
(1011ff.) 167
(1021ff.) 119
(1033) 109
(1047ff.) 167
Eu. (111f.) 17f., 21, 80, 88,
   129, 236
(131f.) 184, 186
(137) 100
(155ff.) 202f.
(181) 191, 193
(322f.) 120
[(331f.) 232]
(372ff.) 129f.
(387f.) 121f.
(427) 182f.
(466) 181, 183
(516) 179
(765f.) 112
(935ff.) 161
(980ff.) 133
(1001) 180
fr. (223a.8) 226
(237) 179
(273.6f.) 89, 92f., 102,
   162
(273.12f.) 94, 96
[(397) 52]
(419) 181
(461) 190
(530.21) 179
(630) 184–6
(702) 186
Pe.[(49ff.) 65]

255

INDEX III: GENERAL